Get the eBook FREE!

(PDF, ePub, Kindle, and liveBook all included)

We believe that once you buy a book from us, you should be able to read it in any format we have available. To get electronic versions of this book at no additional cost to you, purchase and then register this book at the Manning website.

Go to https://www.manning.com/freebook and follow the instructions to complete your pBook registration.

That's it!
Thanks from Manning!

Spring Security in Action, Second Edition

LAURENȚIU SPILCĂ

MANNING
SHELTER ISLAND

For online information and ordering of this and other Manning books, please visit www.manning.com. The publisher offers discounts on this book when ordered in quantity.

For more information, please contact

Special Sales Department
Manning Publications Co.
20 Baldwin Road
PO Box 761
Shelter Island, NY 11964
Email: orders@manning.com

 Manning Publications Co.
20 Baldwin Road
PO Box 761
Shelter Island, NY 11964

Development editor:	Marina Michaels
Technical editor:	Jean-Francois Morin
Review editor:	Dunja Nikitović
Production editor:	Andy Marinkovich
Copy editor:	Lana Todorovic-Arndt
Proofreader:	Melody Dolab
Technical proofreader:	Jean-Francois Morin
Typesetter:	Tamara Švelić Sabljić
Cover designer:	Marija Tudor

ISBN 9781633437975
Printed in the United States of America

brief contents

contents

foreword

I first got to know Laurențiu Spilcă in 2022, when we virtually collaborated on a Spring-One presentation, and I was happy to finally meet him in person at Devoxx 2023 in Belgium. I was excited when he asked me to write this foreword. I'll start with an excerpt from the book:

> *"Applying a framework incorrectly leads to a less maintainable application. What is worse, sometimes those who fail in using the framework believe that it's the framework's fault."*

This is such an important message! Over the years, I've gotten feedback from the community on several occasions that Spring Security is difficult to understand and has a steep learning curve. Whether or not that is the case, if you dive deep into the framework internals and really gain a profound understanding of the authentication architecture, you will learn how to take advantage of the framework's capabilities, and ultimately, it will become easier to use. This is where the book truly hammers it home and dives deep into Spring Security's authentication architecture, providing clear diagrams accompanied by detailed explanations of each of the main components that collaborate in the authentication-processing flow.

Throughout the book, Laurențiu makes clever use of analogies to help simplify the topic at hand. I really like the analogy used in the authentication architecture section, as he sums it up nicely:

> *"If you know this architecture, you're like a chef who knows their ingredients and can put together any recipe."*

The collaboration diagram used to demonstrate how authentication processing works is excellent. It provides a high-level depiction of the flow and details the primary responsibility of each of the core components as it progresses throughout the book.

The content has a natural flow, starting off with very simple examples and progressing to more advanced examples without overwhelming the reader.

After the book finishes examining the authentication architecture in detail, the next (logical) topic is authorization. This reminds me of a specific question that I repeatedly see in the community: *"What is the difference between authority, role, and permission?"* The book answers this question nicely as it provides very simple real-world examples of an authority, role, and permission, and how these can be associated with a user. It then progresses through general guidelines on how to model authorities in your application based on the functions available and the types of users of the system. Next, it uses these general principles and demonstrates how to define authorization rules in your Spring Security configuration to restrict access control.

Part 4 covers the topics of OAuth 2 and OpenID Connect 1.0. I think it's safe to state that the OAuth 2 and OpenID Connect 1.0 set of specifications is quite overwhelming, making it very difficult for anyone new to grasp their purpose and capabilities. However, this book provides an excellent high-level overview of the core concepts (roles, authorization grant types, access token formats, etc.) defined in the specifications and correlates how these are implemented in Spring Security and Spring Authorization Server. I love the analogy in the book on how the OAuth 2 specification is very similar to accessing an office building, where you need an access card (with limited access) to enter the meeting room in the building. It goes through this real-world use case and refers to the different parts of the OAuth 2 system and the roles that each of them plays.

It then builds a simple example using Spring Authorization Server along with Spring Security's Client and Resource Server support. The examples start off minimally and then demonstrate how to configure clients to perform various grant type flows, for example, authorization code (with PKCE), client credentials, and refresh token. Then it demonstrates common configuration scenarios, for example, configuring opaque tokens and using token introspection and token revocation. Next, it takes it a step further and shows more advanced scenarios with regard to configuring multi-tenancy for resource servers.

To sum it up, this book is a must-read for anyone looking to dive deep into Spring Security's authentication architecture and framework internals, as it will ultimately empower you to take full advantage of the framework's capabilities.

—Joe Grandja, Spring Security Engineer, VMware by Broadcom

The journey through software development is an enthralling dance of building, learning, teaching, and often, unlearning. Ever since I began my journey in 2007, I've found myself gracefully expanding my role from being solely a developer to being a developer and trainer. While both roles have their unique charm, it's the art of imparting knowledge, nurturing curiosity, and witnessing the aha moments of fellow learners that truly lights a fire in me. But let's face it, the realms of development and training are deeply intertwined. To be a torchbearer, illuminating the way for others, one must first have their feet firmly rooted in the constantly evolving terrains of software application.

Over the years, one realization stands out distinctly: while functional aspects of software might be its beating heart, nonfunctional attributes such as security, performance, and maintainability serve as its lifeline. It's simpler to pinpoint a glitch in a function than to navigate the murky waters of security vulnerabilities or performance lags. No wonder many developers, seasoned or not, often hesitate when faced with these nonfunctional intricacies.

Among these, security is not just paramount, but it's imperative. And in the vast realm of security frameworks, Spring Security emerges as a frontrunner, given the widespread adoption and trustworthiness of the Spring ecosystem in the enterprise application domain. Yet, a glaring challenge remains—the steep learning curve associated with Spring Security. The plethora of scattered resources online often feels like puzzle pieces that refuse to fit cohesively, leading even the most tenacious of learners astray.

It was these challenges, coupled with countless consultations witnessing improper or, even worse, vulnerable implementations of Spring Security, that sowed the seeds for the first edition of this book. My vision was clear: provide a guiding star to anyone, be it a Spring novice or aficionado, to master Spring Security.

With the second edition, we delve deep into Spring Security, reflecting on the innovations, changes, and experiences since the first edition. We enhance what was, learn from what wasn't, and introduce what's now essential. It remains my earnest hope that this second edition of *Spring Security in Action* will serve not just as a book, but also as a trusted companion in your journey toward creating secure, robust applications. I envisioned this book as a beacon that ensures that you not only save time but also build with confidence, knowing your applications stand resilient against the ever-evolving threats of the digital realm.

acknowledgments

Creating this book has been a journey I couldn't have embarked upon without the collective wisdom, support, and expertise of numerous exceptional individuals.

First and foremost, a heartfelt thank you to Daniela, my wife and guiding light. Her insights, constant encouragement, and unwavering faith have been instrumental throughout this project.

The entire team at Manning deserves a special mention. Their unwavering commitment and dedication have transformed this manuscript into the invaluable resource it is today. Among them, I'd like to particularly express my appreciation to Marina Micheals and Jean-François Morin. Their professionalism, support, and invaluable advice have significantly enriched this book.

A hearty shoutout to my friend, Ioana Göz, the creative genius behind the illustrations. Her knack for translating my abstract thoughts into delightful visuals has added a unique charm to the pages, providing readers with occasional smiles amid the technical content.

This book has greatly benefited from the meticulous eyes and feedback of numerous reviewers. Their keen observations and constructive feedback have been instrumental in refining its content. A special thanks goes to the dedicated reviewers from Manning, Amarjit Bhandal, Asif Iqbal, Cosimo Damiano Prete, Geoff Williams, Javid Asgarov, Justin Reiser, Luigi Rubino, Manoj Kumar, Marcus Geselle, Michele Adduci, Mikael Byström, Mikhail Malev, Najeeb Arif, Patrick Wanjau, Richard Meinsen, Sachin Handiekar, Simeon Leyzerzon, and Simone Sguazza, and to my trusted circle of friends who lent their expertise.

Lastly, to my colleagues and friends at Endava: your constant encouragement, thoughtful insights, and unwavering belief in my endeavors have been the silent forces driving me forward. I cherish and deeply value your support.

To everyone who has touched this project, in ways big and small, please know that your contributions have been the threads weaving the tapestry of this book. Thank you!

about this book

Security is paramount in software development, and integrating it from the onset is essential. *Spring Security in Action, Second Edition* dives deeply into using Spring Security to infuse application-level security into your projects. Mastery of Spring Security and its correct application is indispensable for every developer. Delving into an application's construction without this knowledge is a risk too great to take.

Who should read this book?

This book targets developers using the Spring Framework for enterprise applications. While I've tailored this book for those new to Spring Security, a foundational understanding of the Spring Framework is necessary, including

- Using the Spring context
- Crafting REST endpoints
- Working with data sources

Chapter 15 delves into security configurations for reactive applications. Hence, a prior understanding of reactive applications and their development using Spring is essential. As we navigate the book, I'll point you to supplementary resources to solidify or introduce necessary topics.

All examples in this book use Java. Given the widespread adoption of Java in the Spring ecosystem, it's assumed readers have a working knowledge of it. However, while some professionals might use languages like Kotlin, the foundation remains similar. The examples can be conveniently adapted to Kotlin if desired.

If you feel you need a refresher on the prerequisites before starting with this book, I warmly recommend *Spring Start Here* (Manning, 2021), another book I wrote.

How this book is organized: A roadmap

I crafted this book to guide you through the vast landscape of Spring Security, from fundamental concepts to more advanced areas. Each part of the book flows naturally into the next, making your journey of learning sequential and immersive. Here's a brief breakdown:

- **Part 1: Say hello to spring security**

  In this part, I introduce you to the modern landscape of security and Spring Security. We'll set the foundation by discussing the pivotal role of security in today's digital age and how Spring Security addresses these challenges.

- **Part 2: Configuring authentication**

  Dive deeply into the core of authentication. I cover essential topics such as user management, password protocols, the crucial role of filters in web application security, and the implementation of authentication.

- **Part 3: Configuring authorization**

  We move from authentication to authorization. Together, we'll explore endpoint-level authorizations, protective measures against threats such as CSRF, and managing CORS, and we'll delve into intricate method-level authorizations and filtering.

- **Part 4: Implementing OAuth 2 and OpenID Connect**

  In this part, I guide you through the world of OAuth 2 and OpenID Connect. You'll learn their significance and set up OAuth 2 servers, resource servers, and clients, thereby fortifying your application security.

- **Part 5: Going reactive**

  Here, I introduce you to the reactive programming paradigm, detailing how to secure reactive applications, so you can ensure your asynchronous operations remain tamper-proof.

- **Part 6: Testing security configurations**

  I emphasize the necessity of pre-deployment testing. We delve into the techniques to ensure your security configurations function precisely as intended.

- **Appendixes**

  Appendixes include resources for official documentation and further reading to supplement your learning and exploration.

While I envisioned this book as a step-by-step journey, those with some prior experience in Spring Security can navigate directly to their areas of interest. However, keep in mind that later chapters may reference concepts from earlier sections. If you're already familiar with Spring Security basics, consider starting with part 3 or part 4 for OAuth 2 and OpenID insights. Those keen on reactive programming can jump to part 5.

No matter where you start, make sure to grasp each concept thoroughly to benefit from the subsequent chapters.

About the code

This book provides over 70 projects, which we'll work on starting with chapter 2 and up to chapter 18. When working on a specific example, I mention the name of the project that implements the example. My recommendation is that you try to write your own example from scratch together with the explanations in the book, and then only use the provided project to compare your solution with my solution. This approach will help you better understand the security configurations you're learning.

Each of the projects is built with Maven, making them easy to import to any IDE. I have used IntelliJ IDEA to write the projects, but you can choose to run them in Eclipse, STS, NetBeans, or any other tool of your choice. The appendix also serves as a refresher on how to create a Spring Boot project.

This book contains many examples of source code, both in numbered listings and in line with normal text. In both cases, source code is formatted in a `fixed-width font like this` to separate it from ordinary text. In many cases, the original source code has been reformatted; we've added line breaks and reworked indentation to accommodate the available page space in the book. In rare cases, even this was not enough, and listings include line-continuation markers (➥). Additionally, comments in the source code have often been removed from the listings when the code is described in the text. Code annotations accompany many of the listings, highlighting important concepts.

You can get executable snippets of code from the liveBook (online) version of this book at https://livebook.manning.com/book/spring-security-in-action-second -edition. The complete code for the examples in the book is available for download from the Manning website at www.manning.com.

liveBook discussion forum

Purchase of *Spring Security in Action, Second Edition* includes free access to liveBook, Manning's online reading platform. Using liveBook's exclusive discussion features, you can attach comments to the book globally or to specific sections or paragraphs. It's a snap to make notes for yourself, ask and answer technical questions, and receive help from the author and other users. To access the forum, go to https://livebook.manning .com/book/spring-security-in-action-second-edition/discussion. You can also learn more about Manning's forums and the rules of conduct at https://livebook.manning .com/discussion.

Manning's commitment to our readers is to provide a venue where a meaningful dialogue between individual readers and between readers and the author can take place. It is not a commitment to any specific amount of participation on the part of the author, whose contribution to the forum remains voluntary (and unpaid). We suggest you try asking the author some challenging questions lest their interest stray! The forum and the archives of previous discussions will be accessible from the publisher's website as long as the book is in print.

about the author

LAURENȚIU SPILCĂ has been a seasoned software developer and trainer since 2007, currently serving as a principal development consultant at Endava. In this role, he spearheads globally recognized projects with installations across the world. Laurențiu's twin passions have consistently been clear: delivering top-tier software and imparting knowledge to fellow developers.

Throughout his career, Laurențiu has ardently believed that it's not just about crafting high-quality software, but also about fostering a culture of shared knowledge and continuous learning. This conviction has led him to design and facilitate courses centered around Java technologies. Over the past decade, he has imparted knowledge to over 3,000 students and has been actively involved in courses at the Mathematics and Informatics Faculty of Bucharest University.

Beyond his contributions in the classroom, Laurențiu is also a recognized author. He has penned three pivotal books in the Java domain: *Spring Security in Action*, *Spring Start Here*, and *Troubleshooting Java*. These publications underscore his commitment to spreading knowledge and facilitating a deeper understanding of Java and its associated technologies.

His commitment to sharing insights extends to global platforms. From the streets of New York and San Francisco to the historic venues of Warsaw, Belgrade, and Berlin, Laurențiu has delivered presentations, tutorials, and workshops that resonate with international audiences.

In his quest to make knowledge widely accessible, Laurenţiu also created a YouTube channel (youtube.com/@laurspilca), dedicated to Java and its adjacent technologies. On this platform, beginners and seasoned developers can examine a wide range of topics, all curated and presented with Laurenţiu's trademark clarity.

Outside of his professional endeavors, Laurenţiu's passions diversify into the realms of travel, music, and the mesmerizing world of scuba diving. Whether navigating the depths of the ocean or the intricacies of code, Laurenţiu's journey is a testament to his spirit of exploration and discovery.

Twitter/X handle: @laurspilca

ABOUT THE TECHNICAL EDITOR

JEAN-FRANÇOIS MORIN is a senior Java developer and architect at Laval University in Quebec City, Canada. He holds a B.Sc. in mathematics, a M.Sc. in computer science, and six Sun/Oracle Java certifications, including Java SE 17 Developer and JAVA EE 6 Enterprise Architect. He is also an experienced Java teacher and a regular Manning collaborator.

about the cover illustration

The figure on the cover of *Spring Security in Action, Second Edition* is captioned "*Homme de Murcie,*" or "Murcie Man," taken from a collection by Jacques Grasset de Saint-Sauveur, published in 1797. Each illustration is finely drawn and colored by hand.

In those days, it was easy to identify where people lived and what their trade or station in life was just by their dress. Manning celebrates the inventiveness and initiative of the computer business with book covers based on the rich diversity of regional culture centuries ago, brought back to life by pictures from collections such as this one.

Part 1

Say hello to Spring Security

Diving into the realm of Spring Security? Let's embark on this journey together! In this initial part of the book, we will set the stage by laying a solid foundation.

Chapter 1 begins by introducing you to the world of Spring Security. As we progress, we'll delve deeper into the essence of software security, attempting to answer pertinent questions such as "What is software security?" and "Why is it of paramount importance?" Moreover, we'll outline the learning trajectory of this book, ensuring you know what to anticipate as you proceed.

Chapter 2 promises to be a hands-on endeavor. We'll kick things off by initiating your very first Spring project. If you've ever wondered about the architecture and class design that drives Spring Security, this chapter will provide a bird's-eye view. But it's not just about understanding the default mechanisms. The book will take things a step further by guiding you through the process of overriding default configurations. This will include deep dives into customizing user details, enhancing authorization at various endpoints, exploring diverse configuration methods, defining your own authentication logic, and efficiently utilizing multiple configuration classes.

By the time you conclude this part, not only will you have a solid grasp of the theoretical underpinnings of Spring Security, but you'll also have a functional app secured with it. It's a combination of understanding the "why" and mastering the "how"—all in a short span of time.

Security today

Developers have become increasingly aware of the need for secure software, and they have been taking responsibility for security from the beginning of software development. Generally, as developers, we begin by learning that the purpose of an application is to solve business problems. This purpose refers to something where data could be processed somehow, persisted, and eventually displayed to the user as specified by requirements. This overview of software development, which is somehow imposed from the early stages of learning these techniques, has the unfortunate disadvantage of hiding practices that are also part of the process. While the

3

application works correctly from the user's perspective, and it eventually does what the user expects in terms of functionality, there are many aspects hidden in the final result.

Nonfunctional software qualities such as performance, scalability, availability, and security, as well as others, can have an effect over time, from the short to the long term. If not taken into consideration early on, these qualities can dramatically affect the profitability of the application owners (figure 1.1). Moreover, the neglect of these considerations can also trigger failures in other systems (for example, by the unwilling participation in a distributed denial of service [DDoS] attack). The hidden aspects of nonfunctional requirements (the fact that it's much more challenging to see if something's missing or incomplete) make these even more dangerous.

Figure 1.1   Users typically focus on what a system should do—its functional aspects. Occasionally, they may consider system performance, a nonfunctional attribute, but it's rare for them to pay attention to security measures. Requirements that don't pertain directly to functionality often go unnoticed compared to those that do.

There are multiple nonfunctional aspects to consider when working on a software system. In practice, all of these are important and need to be treated responsibly in the process of software development. This book focuses on one of these: security. You'll learn how to protect your application, step by step, using Spring Security.

This chapter will show you the big picture of security-related concepts. Throughout the book, we will work on practical examples, and where appropriate, I'll refer back to the description I give in this chapter. Where applicable, I'll also provide you with more details. Here and there, you'll find references to other materials (books, articles, and documentation) on specific subjects useful for further reading.

1.1 Discovering Spring Security

This section discusses the relationship between Spring Security and Spring. First, it is important to understand the link between the two before starting to use them. If we check the official website (https://spring.io/projects/spring-security), we can see that Spring Security is described as a powerful and highly customizable framework for authentication and access control. I would simply say it is a framework that greatly simplifies applying (or baking in) security for Spring applications.

Spring Security is the primary choice for implementing application-level security in Spring applications. Generally, its purpose is to offer you a highly customizable way of implementing authentication, authorization, and protection against common attacks. Spring Security is open source software released under the Apache 2.0 license. You can access its source code on GitHub at http://mng.bz/vPmJ. I highly recommend that you contribute to the project as well.

> **NOTE** You can use Spring Security for both standard web servlets and reactive applications, as well as non-web apps. In this book, we'll use Spring Security with the latest Java long-term supported, Spring, and Spring Boot versions (Java 21, Spring 6, and Spring Boot 3). However, all the book's examples also work with Java 17, the previous long-term supported version.

I can guess that if you opened this book, then you work on Spring applications, and you are interested in securing those. Spring Security is most likely the best choice for you. It's the de facto solution for implementing application-level security for Spring applications. Spring Security, however, doesn't automatically secure your application. It's not some kind of magic panacea that guarantees a vulnerability-free app. Developers need to understand how to configure and customize Spring Security around the needs of their applications. How to do this depends on many factors, from the functional requirements to the architecture.

Technically, applying security with Spring Security in Spring applications is simple. You've already implemented Spring applications, so you know that the framework's philosophy starts with the management of the Spring context. You define beans in the Spring context to allow the framework to manage these based on the configurations you specify.

You use annotations to tell Spring what to do: expose endpoints, wrap methods in transactions, intercept methods in aspects, and so on. The same is true with Spring Security configurations, which is where Spring Security comes into play. You want to use annotations, beans, and in general, a Spring-fashioned configuration style comfortably when defining your application-level security. In a Spring application, the behavior that you need to protect is defined by methods.

To think about application-level security, you can consider your home and the way you allow access to it. Do you place the key under the entrance rug? Do you even have a key for your front door? The same concept applies to applications, and Spring Security helps you develop this functionality. It's a puzzle that offers plenty of choices for building the exact image that describes your system. You can choose to leave your house completely unsecured, or you can decide not to allow everyone to enter your home.

The way you configure security can be straightforward like hiding your key under the rug, or it can be more complicated like choosing a variety of alarm systems, video cameras, and locks. In your applications, you have the same options, but as in real life, the more complexity you add, the more expensive it gets. In an application, this cost refers to the way security affects maintainability and performance.

But how do you use Spring Security with Spring applications? Generally, at the application level, one of the most frequently encountered use cases is when you're deciding whether someone is allowed to perform an action or use some piece of data. Based on configurations, you write Spring Security components that intercept the requests and that ensure whoever makes the requests has permission to access protected resources. The developer configures components to do precisely what's desired. If you mount an alarm system, it's you who should make sure it's set up for the windows as well as for the doors. If you forget to set it up for the windows, it's not the fault of the alarm system that it doesn't trigger when someone forces a window.

Other responsibilities of Spring Security components relate to data storage as well as data transit between different parts of the systems. By intercepting calls to these different parts, the components can act on the data. For example, when data is stored, these components can apply encryption or hashing algorithms. The data encodings keep the data accessible only to privileged entities. In a Spring application, the developer has to add and configure a component to do this part of the job wherever it's needed. Spring Security provides us with a contract through which we know what the framework requires to be implemented, and we write the implementation according to the application design. We can say the same thing about transiting data.

In real-world implementations, you'll find cases in which two communicating components don't trust each other. How can the first know that the second one sent a specific message, and it wasn't sent by someone else? Imagine you have a phone call with somebody to whom you must give private information. How do you make sure that a valid individual with the right to get that data is indeed on the other end, and not somebody else? The same situation is relevant to your application. Spring Security provides components that allow you to solve these problems in several ways, but you must know which part to configure and then set it up in your system. In this way, Spring Security intercepts messages and makes sure to validate communication before the application uses any kind of data sent or received.

Like any framework, one of the primary purposes of Spring is to allow you to write less code to implement the desired functionality. This is also what Spring Security does. It completes Spring as a framework by helping you write less code to perform one of the most critical aspects of an application—security. Spring Security provides predefined functionality to help you avoid writing boilerplate code or repeatedly writing the same logic from app to app. However, it also allows you to configure any of its components, thus providing great flexibility. To briefly recap this discussion:

- You use Spring Security to bake application-level security into your applications in the Spring way. By this, I mean you use annotations, beans, the Spring Expression Language (SpEL), and so on.
- Spring Security is a framework that lets you build application-level security. However, it is up to you, the developer, to understand and use Spring Security properly. Spring Security by itself does not secure an application or sensitive data at rest or in flight.
- This book provides you with the information you need to effectively use Spring Security.

Alternatives to Spring Security

This book is about Spring Security, but as with any solution, I always prefer to have a broad overview. Never forget to learn the alternatives that you have for any option. One of the things I've learned over time is that there's no general right or wrong. The saying "Everything is relative" also applies here!

You won't find a lot of alternatives to Spring Security when it comes to securing a Spring application. One alternative you could consider is Apache Shiro (https://shiro.apache .org). It offers flexibility in configuration and is easy to integrate with Spring and Spring Boot applications. Apache Shiro sometimes makes a good alternative to the Spring Security approach.

If you've already worked with Spring Security, you'll find using Apache Shiro easy and comfortable to learn. It offers its own annotations and design for web applications based on HTTP filters, which greatly simplifies working with web applications. Also, you can secure more than just web applications with Shiro, from smaller command-line and mobile applications to large-scale enterprise applications. And although simple, it's powerful enough to be used for a wide range of things—from authentication and authorization to cryptography and session management.

However, Apache Shiro could be too light for the needs of your application. Spring Security is not just a hammer, but an entire set of tools. It offers a larger scale of possibilities and is designed specifically for Spring applications. Moreover, it benefits from a larger community of active developers, and it is continuously enhanced.

1.2 *What is software security?*

Software systems manage large amounts of data, of which a significant part can be considered sensitive, especially in some parts of the world, for example, given the European General Data Protection Regulations (GDPR) requirements. Any information that you, as a user, consider private is sensitive for your software application. Sensitive data can include harmless information such as a phone number, email address, or identification number, although we generally think more about data that is riskier to lose, like your credit card details. The application should ensure that there's no chance for that information to be accessed, changed, or intercepted. No parties other than the users for whom this data is intended should be able to interact in any way with it. Broadly expressed, this is the meaning of security.

NOTE   GDPR created a lot of buzz globally after its introduction in 2018. It generally represents a set of European laws that refers to data protection and gives people more control over their private data. GDPR applies to the owners of systems that have users in Europe. The owners of such applications risk significant penalties if they don't respect the regulations imposed.

We apply security in layers, with each layer requiring a different approach. Compare these layers to a protected castle (figure 1.2). A hacker needs to bypass several obstacles to obtain the resources managed by the app. The better you secure each layer, the lower the chance that an individual with bad intentions manages to access data or perform unauthorized operations.

Figure 1.2   The Dark Wizard (a hacker) must bypass multiple obstacles (security layers) to steal the Magic Sword (user resources) from the Princess (your application).

Security is a complex subject. In the case of a software system, security doesn't exist only at the application level. For example, for networking, there are problems to be taken into consideration and specific practices to be used, while for storage, it's another discussion altogether. Similarly, there's a different philosophy in terms of deployment and so on. Spring Security is a framework that belongs to application-level security. In this section, you'll get a general picture of this security level and its implications.

Application-level security (figure 1.3) refers to everything that an application should do to protect the environment it executes in, as well as the data it processes and stores. Mind you, this isn't only about the data affected and used by the application. An application might contain vulnerabilities that allow a malicious individual to affect the entire system!

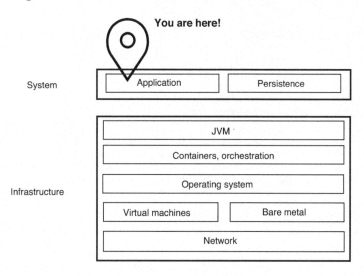

Figure 1.3 We implement security in a hierarchical manner, with each layer building on the foundation of the previous one. This book focuses on explaining how to use Spring Security, a framework that provides application-level security at the very top layer.

To be more explicit, let's discuss some practical cases. We'll consider a situation in which we deploy a system as in figure 1.4. This situation is common for a system designed using a microservices architecture, especially if you deploy it in multiple availability zones in the cloud.

> **NOTE** If you're interested in implementing efficient cloud-oriented Spring apps, I strongly recommend *Cloud Native Spring in Action* by Thomas Vitale (Manning, 2022). In this book, the author focuses on all the needed aspects a professional has to know for implementing well-done Spring apps for cloud deployments.

With such services and microservices architectures, we can encounter various vulnerabilities, so you should exercise caution. As mentioned earlier, security is a cross-cutting concern that we design on multiple layers. When addressing the security concerns of one of the layers, the best practice is to assume as much as possible that the above layer doesn't exist. Think about the analogy with the castle in figure 1.2. If you manage the layer with 30 soldiers, you want to prepare them to be as strong as possible. And you do this despite knowing that before reaching them, someone would need to cross the fiery bridge.

Hacks into VM1 through
a vulnerability of APP 1
deployed there

From here, a hacker
sends messages to other
deployed services.

A hacker can do the same thing for
this service, without the need to get
into the VM of another service, because
the requests between VM 1 and VM 2
are transiting the public network.

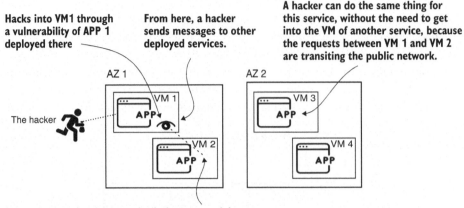

This service does not check the source of the requests.
It believes the requests come from the other service.

Figure 1.4   If a malicious user manages to get access to the virtual machine (VM) and there's no
applied application-level security, a hacker can gain control of the other applications in the system. If
communication occurs between two different availability zones (AZ), a malicious individual will find it
easier to intercept the messages. This vulnerability allows them to steal data or to impersonate users.

With this in mind, let's consider that an individual driven by bad intentions would
be able to log in to the virtual machine (VM) hosting the first application. Let's also
assume that the second application doesn't validate the requests sent by the first application. The attacker can then exploit this vulnerability and control the second application by impersonating the first one.

Also, consider that we deploy the two services to two different locations. Then the
attacker doesn't need to log in to one of the VMs as they can directly act in the middle of
communications between the two applications.

> NOTE   An *availability zone* (AZ in figure 1.4) in terms of cloud deployment is a
> separate data center. This data center is situated far enough geographically (and
> has other dependencies) from other data centers of the same region that, if one
> availability zone fails, the probability that others are failing is minimal. In terms
> of security, an important aspect is that traffic between two different data centers
> generally needs special attention because it often goes across a public network.

I referred earlier to authentication and authorization. These are present in most applications. Through authentication, an application identifies a user (a person or another
application). The purpose of identifying users is to be able to decide afterward what
they should be allowed to do—that's authorization. I provide a lot of details on authentication and authorization, starting with chapter 3 and continuing throughout the
book.

In an application, you often find the need to implement authorization in different
scenarios. Consider another situation: most applications have restrictions regarding
the user accessing certain functionality. Achieving this implies first the need to identify

who creates an access to request a specific feature—that's authentication. We also need to know their privileges to allow the user to use that part of the system. As the system becomes more complex, you'll find different situations that require a specific implementation related to authentication and authorization.

For example, what if you'd like to authorize a particular component of the system against a subset of data or operations on behalf of the user? Let's say the printer needs access to read the user's documents. Should you simply share user credentials with the printer? But that allows the printer more rights than needed! And it also exposes the credentials of the user. Is there a proper way to do this without impersonating the user? These are essential questions and the kind of questions you encounter when developing applications: questions that we not only want to answer, but for which you'll see applications with Spring Security in this book.

Depending on the architecture chosen for the system, you'll find authentication and authorization at the level of the entire system, as well as for any of the components. And as you'll see further along in this book, with Spring Security, you'll sometimes prefer to use authorization even for different tiers of the same component. In chapter 11, we'll talk more about method security, which refers to this aspect. The design gets even more complicated when you have a predefined set of roles and authorities.

I would also like to bring to your attention data storage. Data at rest adds to the responsibility of the application. Your app shouldn't store all its data in a readable format. The application sometimes needs to keep the data either encrypted with a private key or hashed. Secrets such as credentials and private keys can also be considered data at rest. These should be carefully stored, usually in a secrets vault.

> **NOTE** We classify data as "at rest" or "in transition." In this context, *data at rest* refers to data in computer storage or, in other words, persisted data. *Data in transition* applies to all the data that's exchanged from one point to another. Different security measures should, therefore, be enforced, depending on the data type.

Finally, an executing application must manage its internal memory as well. It may sound strange, but data stored in the heap of the application can also present vulnerabilities. Sometimes, the class design allows the app to store sensitive data, such as credentials or private keys, for a long time. In such cases, someone who has the privilege to make a heap dump could find these details and then use them maliciously.

With a short description of these cases, I hope I've managed to provide you with an overview of what we mean by application security, as well as to illustrate the complexity of this subject. Software security is a tangled subject. A person willing to become an expert in this field would need to understand (as well as to apply) and then test solutions for all the layers that collaborate within a system. In this book, however, we'll focus only on presenting all the details of what you specifically need to understand in terms of Spring Security. You'll find out where this framework applies and where it doesn't, how it helps, and why you should use it. Of course, we'll do this with practical examples that you should be able to adapt to your own unique use cases.

1.3   *Why is security important?*

The best way to start thinking about why security is important is from your point of view as a user. Like anyone else, you use applications, and these have access to your data. These can change your data, use it, or expose it. Think about all the apps you use, from your email to your online banking service accounts. How would you evaluate the sensitivity of the data that is managed by all these systems? How about the actions that you can perform using these systems? Similarly to data, some actions are more important than others. You don't care very much about some of those, while others are more significant. Maybe for you, it's not that important if someone can somehow manage to read some of your emails. But I bet you'd care if someone else could empty your bank accounts.

Once you've thought about security from your point of view, try to see a more objective picture. The same data or actions might have another degree of sensitivity to other people. Some people might care a lot more than you if their email is accessed and someone can read their messages. Your application should make sure to protect everything to the desired degree of access. Any leak that allows the use of data and functionalities, as well as the application, to affect other systems is considered a vulnerability, and you need to solve it.

Not considering enough security comes with a price that I'm sure you aren't willing to pay. In general, it's about money. But the cost can differ, and there are multiple ways through which you can lose profitability. It isn't only about losing money from a bank account or using a service without paying for it. These things indeed imply cost. The image of a brand or a company is also valuable, and losing a good image can be expensive—sometimes even more costly than the expenses directly resulting from the exploitation of a vulnerability in the system! The trust that users have in your application is one of its most valuable assets, and it can make the difference between success or failure.

Here are a few fictitious examples. Think about how you would see these as a user. How can these affect the organization responsible for the software?

- A back-office application should manage the internal data of an organization, but somehow, some information leaks out.
- Users of a ride-sharing application observe that money is debited from their accounts on behalf of trips that aren't theirs.
- After an update, users of a mobile banking application are presented with transactions that belong to other users.

In the first situation, the organization using the software, as well as its employees, can be affected. In some instances, the company could be liable and could lose a significant amount of money. In this situation, users don't have the choice to change the application, but the organization can decide to change the provider of their software.

In the second case, users will probably choose to change the service provider. The image of the company developing the application would be dramatically affected. The cost lost in terms of money in this case is much less than the cost in terms of image. Even if payments are returned to the affected users, the application will still lose some customers. This affects profitability and can even lead to bankruptcy. And in the third case, the bank could see dramatic consequences in terms of trust, as well as legal repercussions.

In most of these scenarios, investing in security is safer than what happens if someone exploits a vulnerability in your system. For all the examples, only a small weakness could cause each outcome. For the first example, it could be a broken authentication or a cross-site request forgery (CSRF). For the second and third examples, it could be a lack of method access control. And for all the examples, it could be a combination of vulnerabilities.

Of course, we can go even further from here and discuss the security in defense-related systems. If you consider money important, add human lives to the cost! Can you even imagine what could be the result if a healthcare system was affected? What about systems that control nuclear power? You can reduce any risk by investing early in the security of your application and by allocating enough time for security professionals to develop and test your security mechanisms.

> **NOTE** The lesson learned from those who failed before you is that the cost of an attack is usually higher than the investment cost of avoiding the vulnerability.

In the rest of this book, you'll see examples of ways to apply Spring Security to avoid situations like the ones presented. I guess there will never be enough words written about how important security is. When you have to make a compromise on the security of your system, try to estimate your risks correctly.

1.4 What will you learn in this book?

This book offers a practical approach to learning Spring Security. Throughout the rest of the book, we'll deep dive into Spring Security, proving concepts using simple to more complex examples. To get the most out of this book, you should be comfortable with Java programming, as well as with the basics of the Spring Framework. If you haven't used the Spring Framework or you don't feel comfortable yet using its basics, I recommend you first read *Spring Start Here*, another book I wrote (Manning, 2021). After reading that book, you can enhance your Spring knowledge with *Spring in Action, Sixth Edition*, by Craig Walls (Manning, 2022), as well as *Spring Boot: Up and Running* by Mark Heckler (O'Reilly Media, 2021).

In this book, you'll learn

- The architecture and basic components of Spring Security and how to use it to secure your application
- Authentication and authorization with Spring Security, including the OAuth 2 and OpenID Connect flows, and how these apply to a production-ready application

- How to implement security with Spring Security in different layers of your application
- Different configuration styles and best practices for using them in your project
- Using Spring Security for reactive applications
- Testing your security implementations

To make the learning process smooth for each described concept, we'll work on multiple simple examples.

When we finish, you'll know how to apply Spring Security for the most practical scenarios and understand where to use it and its best practices. I also strongly recommend that you work on all the examples that accompany the explanations.

Summary

- Spring Security is the leading choice for securing Spring applications. It offers a significant number of alternatives that apply to different styles and architectures.
- You should apply security in layers for your system, and for each layer, you need to use different practices.
- Security is a cross-cutting concern that you should consider from the beginning of a software project.
- Usually, the cost of an attack is higher than the cost of investment in avoiding vulnerabilities to begin with.
- Sometimes, the smallest mistakes can cause significant harm. For example, exposing sensitive data through logs or error messages is a common way to introduce vulnerabilities in your application.

Hello, Spring Security

This chapter covers

- Creating your first project with Spring Security
- Designing simple functionalities using the basic components for authentication and authorization
- The underlying concept and how to use it in a given project
- Applying the basic contracts and understanding how they are correlated
- Writing custom implementations for primary responsibilities
- Overriding Spring Boot's default configurations for Spring Security

Spring Boot appeared as an evolutionary stage for application development with the Spring Framework. Replacing the need to write all the configurations, Spring Boot comes with some preconfigured, so you can override only the configurations that don't match your implementations. We also call this approach *convention-over-configuration*. Spring Boot is no longer a new concept, and today, we enjoy writing applications using its third version.

Before Spring Boot, developers used to write dozens of lines of code repeatedly for all the apps they had to create. This situation was less visible in the past when most architectures were developed monolithically. With a monolithic architecture, you only had to write such configurations once at the beginning, and you rarely needed to touch them afterward. With the evolution of service-oriented software architectures, we started to feel the pain of boilerplate code that we had to write when configuring each service. If you find it amusing, you can check out chapter 3 from *Spring in Practice* by Willie Wheeler with Joshua White (Manning, 2013). This chapter describes writing a web application with Spring 3. In this way, you'll understand how many configurations you had to write for one small one-page web application. The chapter is available at http://mng.bz/46la.

For this reason, with the development of recent apps, especially those for microservices, Spring Boot became increasingly popular. Spring Boot provides autoconfiguration for your project and shortens the time required for the setup. We can say it comes with the appropriate philosophy for today's software development.

In this chapter, we'll start with our first application that uses Spring Security. For the apps that you develop with the Spring Framework, Spring Security is an excellent choice for implementing application-level security. We'll use Spring Boot and discuss the defaults configured by convention, with a brief introduction to overriding these defaults. Considering the default configurations provides an excellent introduction to Spring Security, one that also illustrates the concept of authentication.

Once we get started with the first project, we'll discuss various options for authentication in more detail. In chapters 3 through 6, we'll continue with more specific configurations for each of the different responsibilities that you'll see in this first example. You'll also see different ways to apply those configurations, depending on architectural styles. The steps we'll discuss in the current chapter are the following:

1 Create a project with only Spring Security and web dependencies to see how it behaves if no configuration is added. In this way, you'll understand what you should expect from the default configuration for authentication and authorization.

2 Change the project to add functionality for user management by overriding the defaults to define custom users and passwords.

3 After observing that the application authenticates all the endpoints by default, learn that this can be customized as well.

4 Apply different styles for the same configurations to understand best practices.

2.1 *Starting your first project*

Let's create the first project so that we have something as our first example. This project is a small web application exposing a REST endpoint. You'll see how, without doing much, Spring Security secures this endpoint using HTTP Basic authentication. HTTP Basic is a way in which a web app authenticates a user by means of a set of credentials (username and password) that the app gets in the header of the HTTP request.

NOTE With the default configuration, the app has two different authentication mechanisms in place: HTTP Basic and Form Login. However, I decided to take the example step by step and discuss the Form Login in later chapters. But if you try accessing the URL in a browser, you'll find that your app implements a nice form for user authentication and doesn't display an ugly HTTP Basic box for this reason. I don't want you to be confused in case you decide to experiment with a browser, but we'll focus on this in the section on HTTP Basic.

Just by creating the project and adding the correct dependencies, Spring Boot applies default configurations, including a username and a password, when you start the application.

NOTE You have various alternatives to create Spring Boot projects. Some development environments offer the possibility of creating the project directly. For more details, I recommend Mark Heckler's *Spring Boot: Up and Running* (O'Reilly Media, 2021) and *Spring Boot in Practice* (Manning, 2022) by Somnath Musib or even *Spring Start Here* (Manning, 2021), another book I wrote.

The examples in this book refer to the book's companion source code. With each example, I also specify the dependencies that you need to add to your pom.xml file. You can, and I recommend that you do, download the projects provided with the book and the source code available at https://www.manning.com/downloads/2105. The projects will help you if you get stuck with something. You can also use these to validate your final solutions.

NOTE The examples in this book are not dependent on the build tool you choose. You can use either Maven or Gradle. To be consistent, I built all the examples with Maven.

The first project is also the smallest one. It's a simple application exposing a REST endpoint that you can call and then receive a response, as described in figure 2.1. This project is enough for you to learn the first steps when developing an application using Spring Security and Spring Boot. It presents the basics of the Spring Security architecture for authentication and authorization.

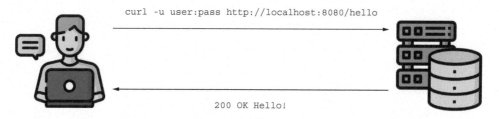

```
curl -u user:pass http://localhost:8080/hello
```

```
200 OK Hello!
```

Figure 2.1 Our initial application employs HTTP Basic for user authentication and authorization when accessing an endpoint. It offers a REST endpoint at a specified route (/hello). Upon a successful request, it issues an HTTP 200 status message along with a response body. This instance illustrates the default authentication and authorization mechanisms set up by Spring Security.

We begin learning Spring Security by creating an empty project and naming it ssia-ch2-ex1. (You'll also find this example with the same name in other projects provided.) The only dependencies you need to write for our first project are `spring-boot-starter-web` and `spring-boot-starter-security`, as shown in listing 2.1. After creating the project, make sure that you add these dependencies to your pom.xml file. The primary purpose of working on this project is to see the behavior of a default-configured application with Spring Security. We also want to understand which components are part of this default configuration, as well as their purpose.

Listing 2.1   Spring Security dependencies for our first web app

```
<dependency>
  <groupId>org.springframework.boot</groupId>
  <artifactId>spring-boot-starter-web</artifactId>
</dependency>
<dependency>
  <groupId>org.springframework.boot</groupId>
  <artifactId>spring-boot-starter-security</artifactId>
</dependency>
```

We could directly start the application now. Spring Boot applies the default configuration of the Spring context for us based on which dependencies we add to the project. However, we won't be able to learn much about security if we don't have at least one endpoint that's secured. Let's create a simple endpoint and call it to see what happens. For this, we add a class to the empty project, and we name this class `HelloController`. To do that, we add the class to a package called `controllers` somewhere in the main namespace of the Spring Boot project.

> **NOTE** Spring Boot scans for components only in the package (and its subpackages) that contains the class annotated with `@SpringBootApplication`. If you annotate classes with any of the stereotype components in Spring outside of the main package, you must explicitly declare the location using the `@Component-Scan` annotation.

In the following listing, the `HelloController` class defines a REST controller and a REST endpoint for our example.

Listing 2.2   The `HelloController` class and a REST endpoint

```
@RestController
public class HelloController {

  @GetMapping("/hello")
  public String hello() {
    return "Hello!";
  }
}
```

The `@RestController` annotation registers the bean in the context and tells Spring that the application uses this instance as a web controller. In addition, the annotation specifies that the application has to set the response body of the HTTP response from the method's return value. The @GetMapping annotation maps the /hello path to the implemented method through a GET request. Once you run the application, besides the other lines in the console, you should see something that looks like

```
Using generated security password: 93a01cf0-794b-4b98-86ef-54860f36f7f3
```

Each time you run the application, it generates a new password and prints this password in the console, as presented in the previous code snippet. You must use this password to call any of the application's endpoints with HTTP Basic authentication. First, let's try to call the endpoint without using the Authorization header:

```
curl http://localhost:8080/hello
```

> **NOTE** In this book, we use cURL to call the endpoints in all the examples. I consider cURL to be the most readable solution. But if you prefer, you can use a tool of your choice. For example, you might want to have a more comfortable graphical interface. In this case, Postman, Insomnia, or Bruno are excellent choices. If the operating system you use does not have any of these tools installed, you probably need to install them yourself.

And the response to the call is

```
{
  "status":401,
  "error":"Unauthorized",
  "message":"Unauthorized",
  "path":"/hello"
}
```

The response status is HTTP 401 Unauthorized. We expected this result, as we didn't use the proper credentials for authentication. By default, Spring Security expects the default username (user) with the provided password (in my case, the one starting with 93a01). Let's try it again but now with the proper credentials:

```
curl -u user:93a01cf0-794b-4b98-86ef-54860f36f7f3 http://localhost:8080/hello
```

The response to the call is

```
Hello!
```

> **NOTE** The HTTP 401 Unauthorized status code is a bit ambiguous. Usually, it's used to represent a failed authentication rather than an authorization. Developers employ it in the design of the application for cases such as missing or incorrect credentials. For a failed authorization, we'd probably use the 403 Forbidden status. Generally, an HTTP 403 means that the server identified the caller of the request, but they don't have the needed privileges for the call that they are trying to make.

Once we send the correct credentials, you can see in the body of the response precisely what the HelloController method we defined earlier returns.

Calling the endpoint with HTTP Basic authentication

With cURL, you can set the HTTP basic username and password with the -u flag. Behind the scenes, cURL encodes the string <username>:<password> in Base64 and sends it as the value of the Authorization header prefixed with the string Basic. And with cURL, it's probably easier for you to use the -u flag. But it's also essential to know what the real request looks like. So let's give it a try and manually create the Authorization header.

In the first step, take the <username>:<password> string and encode it with Base64. When our application sends the call, we need to know how to form the correct value for the Authorization header. You do this using the Base64 tool in a Linux console. You could also find a web page that encodes strings in Base64, like https://www.base64encode .org. This snippet shows the command in a Linux or a Git Bash console (the -n parameter means no trailing new line should be added):

```
echo -n user:93a01cf0-794b-4b98-86ef-54860f36f7f3 | base64
```

Running this command returns the following Base64-encoded string:

```
dXNlcjo5M2EwMWNmMC03OTRiLTRiOTgtODZlZi01NDg2MGYzNmY3ZjM=
```

You can now use the Base64-encoded value as the value of the Authorization header for the call. This call should generate the same result as the one using the -u option:

```
curl -H "Authorization: Basic
dXNlcjo5M2EwMWNmMC03OTRiLTRiOTgtODZlZi01NDg2MGYzNmY3ZjM="
localhost:8080/hello
```

The result of the call is

```
Hello!
```

There are no significant security configurations to discuss with a default project. We mainly use the default configurations to prove that the correct dependencies are in place. It does little for authentication and authorization. This implementation isn't something we want to see in a production-ready application. But the default project is an excellent example that you can use for a start.

With this first example working, at least we know that Spring Security is in place. The next step is to change the configurations so that these apply to our project requirements. First, we'll go deeper with what Spring Boot configures in terms of Spring Security, and then we'll see how we can override the configurations.

2.2   *The big picture of Spring Security class design*

In this section, we discuss the main actors in the overall architecture that take part in the process of authentication and authorization. You need to know this aspect because you'll have to override these preconfigured components to fit the needs of your application. I'll start by describing how Spring Security architecture for authentication and authorization works, and then we'll apply that to the projects in this chapter. It would be too much to discuss all of these at once, so to minimize your learning efforts in this chapter, I'll discuss the high-level picture for each component. You'll learn details about each in the following chapters.

In section 2.1, you saw some logic executing for authentication and authorization. We had a default user, and we got a random password each time we started the application. We were able to use this default user and password to call an endpoint. But where is all this logic implemented? As you probably know already, Spring Boot sets up some components for you, depending on what dependencies you use (i.e., the convention-over-configuration that we discussed at the beginning of this chapter).

Figure 2.2 shows the big picture of the main actors (components) in the Spring Security architecture and the relationships among them. These components have a preconfigured implementation in the first project. In this chapter, I demonstrate what Spring Boot configures in your application in terms of Spring Security. We'll also discuss the relationships among the entities that are part of the authentication flow presented.

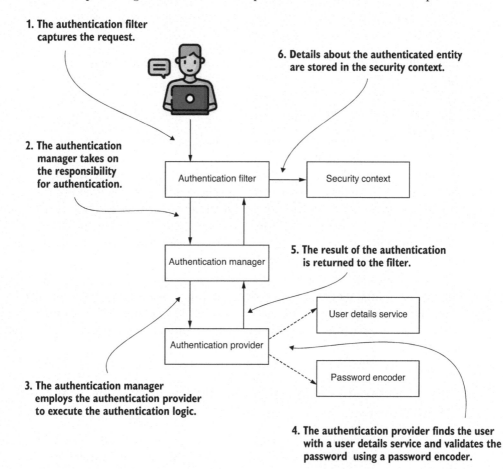

1. The authentication filter captures the request.

6. Details about the authenticated entity are stored in the security context.

2. The authentication manager takes on the responsibility for authentication.

Authentication filter

Security context

Authentication manager

5. The result of the authentication is returned to the filter.

User details service

Authentication provider

Password encoder

3. The authentication manager employs the authentication provider to execute the authentication logic.

4. The authentication provider finds the user with a user details service and validates the password using a password encoder.

Figure 2.2   The core elements involved in Spring Security's authentication process and their interconnections are the focus here. This framework forms the essential structure for executing authentication using Spring Security. Throughout the book, we will frequently reference this architecture while examining various authentication and authorization strategies.

Figure 2.2 shows that

1 The authentication filter delegates the authentication request to the authentication manager, and based on the response, it configures the security context.

2 The authentication manager uses the authentication provider to process authentication.

3 The authentication provider implements the authentication logic.

4 The user details service implements user management responsibility, which the authentication provider uses in the authentication logic.

5 The password encoder implements password management, which the authentication provider uses in the authentication logic.

6 The security context keeps the authentication data after the authentication process. The security context will hold the data until the action ends. Usually, in a thread-per-request app, that means until the app sends a response back to the client.

In the following paragraphs, I'll discuss these autoconfigured beans:

- UserDetailsService
- PasswordEncoder

An object that implements a UserDetailsService interface with Spring Security manages the details about users. Until now, we've used the default implementation provided by Spring Boot. This implementation only registers the default credentials in the internal memory of the application. These default credentials are "user" with a default password that's a universally unique identifier (UUID). The default password is generated randomly when the Spring context is loaded (at the app startup). At this time, the application writes the password to the console where you can see it. Thus, you can use it in the example we just worked on in this chapter.

This default implementation serves only as a proof of concept and allows us to see that the dependency is in place. The implementation stores the credentials in-memory—the application doesn't persist the credentials. This approach is suitable for examples or proof of concepts, but you should avoid it in a production-ready application.

Then we have the PasswordEncoder. The PasswordEncoder does two things:

- Encodes a password (usually using an encryption or a hashing algorithm)
- Verifies if the password matches an existing encoding

Even if it's not as obvious as the UserDetailsService object, the PasswordEncoder is mandatory for the Basic authentication flow. The simplest implementation manages the passwords in plain text and doesn't encode these. We'll discuss in more detail the implementation of this object in chapter 4. For now, you should be aware that a PasswordEncoder exists together with the default UserDetailsService. When we replace the default implementation of the `UserDetailsService`, we must also specify a `PasswordEncoder`.

Spring Boot also chooses an authentication method when configuring the defaults: HTTP Basic access authentication. It's the most straightforward access authentication method. Basic authentication only requires the client to send a username and a password through the HTTP `Authorization` header. In the value of the header, the client attaches the prefix `Basic`, followed by the Base64 encoding of the string that contains the username and password, separated by a colon (:).

> **NOTE** HTTP Basic authentication doesn't offer confidentiality of the credentials. Base64 is only an encoding method for the convenience of the transfer; it's not an encryption or hashing method. While in transit, if intercepted, anyone can see the credentials. Generally, we don't use the HTTP Basic authentication without at least HTTPS for confidentiality. You can read the detailed definition of HTTP Basic in RFC 7617 (https://tools.ietf.org/html/rfc7617).

The `AuthenticationProvider` defines the authentication logic, delegating the user and password management. A default implementation of an `Authentication-Provider` uses the default implementations provided for the `UserDetailsService` and the `PasswordEncoder`. Implicitly, your application secures all the endpoints. Therefore, the only thing that we need to do for our example is to add the endpoint. Also, there's only one user who can access all endpoints, so we can say that there isn't much to do about authorization in this case.

HTTP vs. HTTPS

You might have observed that in the examples presented, I only use HTTP. In practice, however, your applications communicate only over HTTPS. For the examples we discuss in this book, the configurations related to Spring Security aren't different, whether we use HTTP or HTTPS. We won't configure HTTPS for the endpoints in the examples so that you can focus on the examples related to Spring Security. But if you want, you can enable HTTPS for any of the endpoints, as presented in this sidebar.

There are several patterns for configuring HTTPS in a system. In some cases, developers configure HTTPS at the application level; in others, they might use a service mesh, or they could choose to set HTTPS at the infrastructure level. With Spring Boot, you can easily enable HTTPS at the application level, as you'll learn in the next example in this sidebar.

In any of these configuration scenarios, you need a certificate signed by a certification authority (CA). Using this certificate, the client that calls the endpoint knows whether the response comes from the authentication server and that nobody intercepted the communication. You can buy such a certificate if you need it. If you only need to configure HTTPS to test your application, you can generate a self-signed certificate using a tool such as OpenSSL (https://www.openssl.org/). Let's generate our self-signed certificate and then configure it in the project:

```
openssl req -newkey rsa:2048 -x509 -keyout key.pem -out cert.pem -days 365
```

(continued)

After running the `openssl` command in a terminal, you'll be asked for a password and details about your CA. Because it is only a self-signed certificate for a test, you can input any data there; just make sure to remember the password. The command outputs two files: key.pem (the private key) and cert.pem (a public certificate). We'll use these files further to generate our self-signed certificate for enabling HTTPS. In most cases, the certificate is the Public Key Cryptography Standards #12 (PKCS12). Less frequently, we use a Java KeyStore (JKS) format. Let's continue our example with a PKCS12 format (for an excellent discussion on cryptography, I recommend *Real-World Cryptography* by David Wong [Manning, 2020]):

```
openssl pkcs12 -export -in cert.pem -inkey key.pem -out certificate.p12
-name "certificate"
```

The second command we use receives as input the two files generated by the first command and outputs the self-signed certificate.

Note that if you run these commands in a Bash shell on a Windows system, you might need to add `winpty` before it:

```
winpty openssl req -newkey rsa:2048 -x509 -keyout key.pem -out cert.pem
-days 365
winpty openssl pkcs12 -export -in cert.pem -inkey key.pem -out
certificate.p12 -name "certificate"
```

Finally, having the self-signed certificate, you can configure HTTPS for your endpoints. Copy the certificate.p12 file into the resources folder of the Spring Boot project, and add the following lines to your application.properties file:

```
server.ssl.key-store-type=PKCS12
server.ssl.key-store=classpath:certificate.p12
server.ssl.key-store-password=12345
```

The value of the password is the one you specified when running the second command to generate the PKCS12 certificate file.

The password (in my case, `12345`) was requested in the prompt after running the command for generating the certificate. This is why you don't see it in the command. Now let's add a test endpoint to our application and then call it using HTTPS:

```
@RestController
public class HelloController {

  @GetMapping("/hello")
  public String hello() {
    return "Hello!";
  }
}
```

If you use a self-signed certificate, you should configure the tool you use to make the endpoint call so that it skips testing the authenticity of the certificate. If the tool tests the authenticity of the certificate, it won't recognize it as being authentic, and the call won't work. With cURL, you can use the `-k` option to skip testing the authenticity of the certificate:

```
curl -k -u user:93a01cf0-794b-4b98-86ef-54860f36f7f3 https://
localhost:8080/hello
```

The response to the call is

```
Hello!
```

Remember that even if you use HTTPS, the communication between components of your system isn't bulletproof. Many times, I've heard people say, "I'm not encrypting this anymore. I'll use HTTPS!" While helpful in protecting communication, HTTPS is just one of the bricks of the security wall of a system. Always treat the security of your system with responsibility and take care of all the layers involved.

2.3 Overriding default configurations

Now that you know the defaults of your first project, it's time to see how you can replace them. You need to understand the options you have for overriding the default components because this is the way you plug in your custom implementations and apply security as it fits your application. And as you'll learn in this section, the development process is also about how you write configurations to keep your applications highly maintainable. With the projects we'll work on, you'll often find multiple ways to override a configuration. This flexibility can create confusion. I frequently see a mix of different styles of configuring different parts of Spring Security in the same application, which is undesirable. Thus, this flexibility comes with a caution. You need to learn how to choose from these, so this section is also about knowing what your options are.

In some cases, developers choose to use beans in the Spring context for the configuration. In other cases, they override various methods for the same purpose. The speed with which the Spring ecosystem evolved is probably one of the main factors that generated these multiple approaches. Configuring a project with a mix of styles is not desirable, as it makes the code difficult to understand and affects the maintainability of the application. Knowing your options and how to use them is a valuable skill, and it helps you better understand how you should configure application-level security in a project.

In this section, you'll learn how to configure a `UserDetailsService` and a `PasswordEncoder`. These two components usually take part in authentication, and most applications customize them depending on their requirements. While we'll discuss details about customizing them in chapters 3 and 4, it's essential to see how to plug in a custom implementation. The implementations we use in this chapter are all provided by Spring Security.

2.3.1 Customizing user details management

The first component we talked about in this chapter was `UserDetailsService`. As you saw, the application uses this component in the authentication process. In this section, you'll learn to define a custom bean of type `UserDetailsService`. We'll do this to override the default one configured by Spring Boot. As you'll see in more detail in chapter 3, you have the option to create your own implementation or to use a pre-defined one provided by Spring Security. In this chapter, we aren't going to detail the implementations provided by Spring Security or create our own implementation just yet. I'll use an implementation provided by Spring Security, named `InMemoryUser-DetailsManager`. With this example, you'll learn how to plug this kind of object into your architecture.

> **NOTE**   Interfaces in Java define contracts between objects. In the class design of the application, we use interfaces to decouple objects that use one another. To enforce this interface characteristic when discussing those in this book, I mainly refer to them as *contracts*.

To show you how to override this component with an implementation we chose, we'll change what we did in the first example. Doing so allows us to have our own managed credentials for authentication. For this example, we don't implement our class, but we use an implementation provided by Spring Security.

In this example, we use the `InMemoryUserDetailsManager` implementation. Even if it is a bit more than just a `UserDetailsService`, for now, we only refer to it from the perspective of a `UserDetailsService`. This implementation stores credentials in memory, which can then be used by Spring Security to authenticate a request.

> **NOTE**   An `InMemoryUserDetailsManager` implementation isn't meant for production-ready applications, but it's an excellent tool for examples or proofs of concept. In some cases, all you need are users. You don't need to spend the time implementing this part of the functionality. In our case, we use it to understand how to override the default `UserDetailsService` implementation.

We start by defining a configuration class. Generally, we declare configuration classes in a separate package named config. The following listing shows the definition for the configuration class. You can also find the example in the project ssia-ch2-ex2.

> **Listing 2.3   The configuration class for the `UserDetailsService` bean**

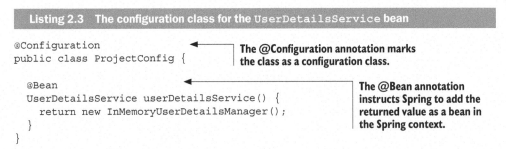

```
@Configuration
public class ProjectConfig {          ◄──────┐  The @Configuration annotation marks
                                             │  the class as a configuration class.

  @Bean                              ◄─────────────────    The @Bean annotation
  UserDetailsService userDetailsService() {                instructs Spring to add the
    return new InMemoryUserDetailsManager();               returned value as a bean in
  }                                                        the Spring context.
}
```

We annotate the class with `@Configuration`. The `@Bean` annotation instructs Spring to add the instance returned by the method to the Spring context. If you execute the code exactly as it is now, you'll no longer see the autogenerated password in the console. The application now uses the instance of type `UserDetailsService` you added to the context instead of the default autoconfigured one. But at the same time, you won't be able to access the endpoint anymore for two reasons:

- You don't have any users.
- You don't have a `PasswordEncoder`.

In figure 2.2, you saw that authentication depends on a `PasswordEncoder` as well. Let's solve these two problems step by step. We need to

1. Create at least one user who has a set of credentials (username and password)
2. Add the user to be managed by our implementation of `UserDetailsService`
3. Define a bean of the type `PasswordEncoder` that our application can use to verify a given password with the one stored and managed by `UserDetailsService`

First, we declare and add a set of credentials that we can use for authentication to the instance of `InMemoryUserDetailsManager`. In chapter 3, we'll discuss more about users and how to manage them. For the moment, let's use a predefined builder to create an object of the type `UserDetails`.

> **NOTE** You'll sometimes see that I use `var` in the code. Java 10 introduced the reserved type name `var`, and you can only use it for local declarations. Although in some cases the way `var` is used in this book could be considered a bad approach from a clean coding perspective, it is done to make the syntax shorter, as well as to hide the variable type. This approach helps you focus on what is relevant for the given example. We'll discuss the types hidden by `var` in later chapters, so you don't have to worry about that type until it's time to analyze it properly.

When building the instance, we must provide the username, the password, and at least one authority. The *authority* is an action allowed for that user, and we can use any string for this. In the next listing, I name the authority `read`, but because we won't use this authority for the moment, this name doesn't really matter.

Listing 2.4 Creating a user with the `User` builder class for `UserDetailsService`

```
@Configuration
public class ProjectConfig {

  @Bean
  UserDetailsService userDetailsService() {
    var user = User.withUsername("john")          Builds the user with a given
                  .password("12345")             username, password, and
                  .authorities("read")           authorities list
                  .build();

    return new InMemoryUserDetailsManager(user);  ◀── Adds the user to be
  }                                                   managed by
}                                                     UserDetailsService
```

NOTE   You'll find the class `User` in the org.springframework.security.core.user-details package. It's the builder implementation we use to create the object to represent the user. Furthermore, as a general rule in this book, if I don't present how to write a class in a code listing, it means Spring Security provides it.

As presented in listing 2.4, we must provide a value for the username, one for the password, and at least one authority. However, this is still not enough to allow us to call the endpoint. We also need to declare a `PasswordEncoder`.

When using the default `UserDetailsService`, a `PasswordEncoder` is also auto-configured. Because we overrode `UserDetailsService`, we also have to declare a `PasswordEncoder`. Trying the example now, you'll see an exception when you call the endpoint. When trying to do the authentication, Spring Security realizes it doesn't know how to manage the password and fails. The exception looks like that in the next code snippet, and you should see it in your application's console. The client gets back an HTTP 401 Unauthorized message and an empty response body:

```
curl -u john:12345 http://localhost:8080/hello
```

The result of the call in the app's console is

```
java.lang.IllegalArgumentException:
There is no PasswordEncoder mapped for the id "null"
    at
org.springframework.security.crypto.
➥password.DelegatingPasswordEncoder$
➥UnmappedIdPasswordEncoder.matches(
➥DelegatingPasswordEncoder.java:289)
➥~[spring-security-crypto-6.0.0.jar:6.0.0]
    at org.springframework.security.crypto.
➥password.DelegatingPasswordEncoder.matches(
➥DelegatingPasswordEncoder.java:237)
➥~[spring-security-crypto-6.0.0.jar:6.0.0]
```

To solve this problem, we can add a `PasswordEncoder` bean in the context, like we did with the `UserDetailsService`. For this bean, we use an existing implementation of `PasswordEncoder`:

```
@Bean
public PasswordEncoder passwordEncoder() {
  return NoOpPasswordEncoder.getInstance();
}
```

NOTE   The `NoOpPasswordEncoder` instance treats passwords as plain text. It doesn't encrypt or hash them. For matching, `NoOpPasswordEncoder` only compares the strings using the underlying `equals(Object o)` method of the `String` class. You shouldn't use this type of `PasswordEncoder` in a production-ready app. `NoOpPasswordEncoder` is a good option for examples where you don't want to focus on the hashing algorithm of the password. Therefore, the developers of the class marked it as `@Deprecated`, and your development environment will show its name with a strikethrough.

You can see the full code of the configuration class in the following listing.

Listing 2.5 The full definition of the configuration class

```
@Configuration
public class ProjectConfig {

  @Bean
  UserDetailsService userDetailsService() {
    var user = User.withUsername("john")
                  .password("12345")
                  .authorities("read")
                  .build();

    return new InMemoryUserDetailsManager(user);
  }

  @Bean
  PasswordEncoder passwordEncoder() {          ◄──────  A new method
    return NoOpPasswordEncoder.getInstance();           annotated with
  }                                                     @Bean to add a
}                                                       PasswordEncoder
                                                        to the context
```

Let's try the endpoint with the new user having the username `john` and the password `12345`:

```
curl -u john:12345 http://localhost:8080/hello
Hello!
```

> **NOTE** Knowing the importance of unit and integration tests, some of you might already wonder why we don't also write tests for our examples. You will actually find the related Spring Security integration tests with all the examples provided in this book. However, to help you focus on the presented topics for each chapter, I have separated the discussion about testing Spring Security integrations and detail this in chapter 18.

2.3.2 Applying authorization at the endpoint level

With new management for the users in place, as described in section 2.3.1, we can now discuss the authentication method and configuration for endpoints. You'll learn plenty of things regarding authorization configuration in chapters 7 through 12. But before diving into details, you must understand the big picture. The best way to achieve this is with our first example. With the default configuration, all the endpoints assume you have a valid user managed by the application. Also, by default, your app uses HTTP Basic authentication, but you can easily override this configuration.

As you'll learn in the next chapters, HTTP Basic authentication doesn't fit into most application architectures. Sometimes, we'd like to change it to match our application. Similarly, not all endpoints of an application need to be secured, and for those that do, we might need to choose different authentication methods and authorization rules. To customize the handling of authentication and authorization, we'll need to define a bean of type `SecurityFilterChain`. For this example, I'll continue writing the code in the project ssia-ch2-ex3.

Listing 2.6   Defining a `SecurityFilterChain` bean

```
@Configuration
public class ProjectConfig {

  @Bean
  SecurityFilterChain configure(HttpSecurity http)
    throws Exception {

    return http.build();
  }

  // Omitted code

}
```

We can then alter the configuration using different methods of the HttpSecurity object, as shown in the next listing.

Listing 2.7   Using the `HttpSecurity` parameter to alter the configuration

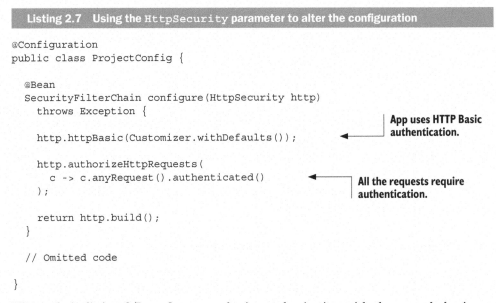

```
@Configuration
public class ProjectConfig {

  @Bean
  SecurityFilterChain configure(HttpSecurity http)
    throws Exception {                                     App uses HTTP Basic
                                                           authentication.
    http.httpBasic(Customizer.withDefaults());

    http.authorizeHttpRequests(
      c -> c.anyRequest().authenticated()                 All the requests require
    );                                                    authentication.

    return http.build();
  }

  // Omitted code

}
```

The code in listing 2.7 configures endpoint authorization with the same behavior as the default one. You can call the endpoint again to see whether it behaves the same as in the previous test from section 2.3.1. With a slight change, you can make all the endpoints accessible without the need for credentials. You'll see how to do this in the following listing.

Listing 2.8   Using `permitAll()` to change the authorization configuration

```
@Configuration
public class ProjectConfig {

  @Bean
```

```
public SecurityFilterChain configure(HttpSecurity http)
  throws Exception {

  http.httpBasic(Customizer.withDefaults());

  http.authorizeHttpRequests(
    c -> c.anyRequest().permitAll()
  );

  return http.build();
}

  // Omitted code
}
```

None of the requests need to be authenticated.

Now we can call the /hello endpoint without the need for credentials. The permitAll() call in the configuration, together with the anyRequest() method, makes all the endpoints accessible without the need for credentials:

```
curl http://localhost:8080/hello
```

The response body of the call is

```
Hello!
```

In this example, we used two configuration methods:

- httpBasic(), which helped us configure the authentication approach. By calling this method, you instructed your app to accept HTTP Basic as an authentication method.
- authorizeHttpRequests(), which helped us configure the authorization rules at the endpoint level. By calling this method, you instructed the app on how to authorize the requests received on specific endpoints.

For both methods, you had to use a Customizer object as a parameter. Customizer is a contract you implement to define the customization for either Spring Security element you configure: the authentication, the authorization, or particular protection mechanisms such as CSRF or CORS (which will be discussed in chapters 9 and 10). The following snippet shows the definition of the Customizer interface. Observe that Customizer is a functional interface (so we can use lambda expressions to implement it), and the withDefaults() method I used in listing 2.8 is, in fact, just a Customizer implementation that does nothing:

```
@FunctionalInterface
public interface Customizer<T> {
  void customize(T t);

  static <T> Customizer<T> withDefaults() {
    return (t) -> {
    };
  }
}
```

In earlier Spring Security versions, you could apply configurations without a `Customizer` object by using a chaining syntax, as shown in the following code snippet. Observe that instead of providing a `Customizer` object to the `authorizeHttpRequests()` method, the configuration just follows the method's call:

```
http.authorizeHttpRequests()
        .anyRequest().authenticated()
```

The reason this approach has been left behind is because a `Customizer` object allows you more flexibility in moving the configuration where needed. Sure, with simple examples, using lambda expressions is comfortable. But in real-world apps, the configurations can grow a lot. In such cases, the ability to move these configurations in separate classes helps you keep the configurations easier to maintain and test.

The purpose of this example is to give you a feeling for how to override default configurations. We'll get into the details about authorization in chapters 7 through 10.

> **NOTE** In earlier versions of Spring Security, a security configuration class needed to extend a class named `WebSecurityConfigurerAdapter`. We don't use this practice anymore. If your app uses an older codebase, or you need to upgrade an older codebase, I recommend you also read the first edition of *Spring Security in Action*.

2.3.3   Configuring in different ways

One of the confusing aspects of creating configurations with Spring Security is having multiple ways to configure the same thing. In this section, you'll learn alternatives for configuring `UserDetailsService` and `PasswordEncoder`. It's essential to know the options you have so that you can recognize these in the examples that you find in this book or other sources like blogs and articles. It's also important that you understand how and when to use these in your application. Further chapters present different examples that extend the information in this section.

Let's take the first project. After we created a default application, we managed to override `UserDetailsService` and `PasswordEncoder` by adding new implementations as beans in the Spring context. Let's find another way of doing the same configurations for `UserDetailsService` and `PasswordEncoder`.

We can directly use the `SecurityFilterChain` bean to set both the `UserDetailsService` and the `PasswordEncoder`, as shown in the following listing. You can find this example in the project ssia-ch2-ex3.

> **Listing 2.9 Setting `UserDetailsService` with the `SecurityFilterChain` bean**

```
@Configuration
public class ProjectConfig {

    @Bean
    public SecurityFilterChain configure(HttpSecurity http)
```

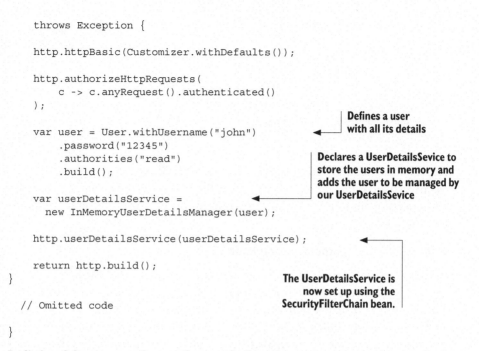

```
        throws Exception {

        http.httpBasic(Customizer.withDefaults());

        http.authorizeHttpRequests(
            c -> c.anyRequest().authenticated()
        );
                                                       Defines a user
        var user = User.withUsername("john")           with all its details
            .password("12345")
            .authorities("read")                    Declares a UserDetailsSevice to
            .build();                               store the users in memory and
                                                    adds the user to be managed by
        var userDetailsService =                    our UserDetailsSevice
          new InMemoryUserDetailsManager(user);

        http.userDetailsService(userDetailsService);

        return http.build();
    }                                               The UserDetailsService is
                                                    now set up using the
    // Omitted code                                 SecurityFilterChain bean.

}
```

In listing 2.9, you can observe that we declare the `UserDetailsService` in the same way as in listing 2.5. The difference is that this is now done locally inside the bean method creating the `SecurityFilterChain`. We also call the `userDetailsService()` method from the `HttpSecurity` to register the `UserDetailsService` instance. The next listing shows the full contents of the configuration class.

Listing 2.10   Full definition of the configuration class

```
@Configuration
public class ProjectConfig {

  @Bean
  SecurityFilterChain configure(HttpSecurity http)
    throws Exception {

    http.httpBasic(Customizer.withDefaults());

    http.authorizeHttpRequests(
        c -> c.anyRequest().authenticated()
    );

    var user = User.withUsername("john")            Creates a new user
        .password("12345")
        .authorities("read")
        .build();
                                                Adds the user to be managed
    var userDetailsService =                    by our UserDetailsService
        new InMemoryUserDetailsManager(user);
```

```
    http.userDetailsService(userDetailsService);        ◄───  Configures
                                                               UserDetailsService
    return http.build();
}

@Bean
PasswordEncoder passwordEncoder() {
    return NoOpPasswordEncoder.getInstance();
}
}
```

Any of these configuration options are correct. The first option, where we add the beans to the context, lets you inject the values in another class where you might potentially need them. But if you don't need that for your case, the second option would be equally good.

2.3.4   *Defining custom authentication logic*

As you've already observed, Spring Security components provide a lot of flexibility, offering many options when adapting them to the architecture of our applications. Up to now, you've learned the purpose of UserDetailsService and Password-Encoder in the Spring Security architecture. You also saw a few ways to configure them. It's time to learn how you can also customize the component that delegates to these, the AuthenticationProvider, as shown in figure 2.3. AuthenticationProvider implements the authentication logic and delegates to the UserDetailsService and PasswordEncoder for user and password management. Thus, we could say that with this section, we go one step deeper into the authentication architecture to learn how to implement custom authentication logic with AuthenticationProvider.

Because this is the first example, I only show you a brief picture so that you better understand the relationship between the components in the architecture. But we'll go into more detail in chapters 3 through 6.

I recommend you consider the responsibilities as designed in the Spring Security architecture. This architecture is loosely coupled with fine-grained responsibilities. That design is one of the things that makes Spring Security flexible and easy to integrate with your applications. Depending on how you make use of its flexibility, you could change the design as well. You must be careful with these approaches as they can complicate your solution. For example, you could choose to override the default AuthenticationProvider in a way in which you no longer needed a UserDetails-Service or PasswordEncoder. With that in mind, listing 2.11 shows how to create a custom authentication provider. You can find this example in the project ssia-ch2-ex4.

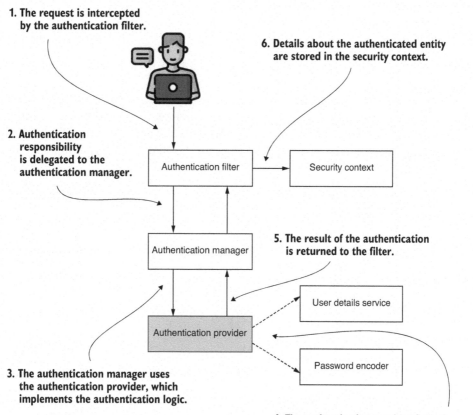

1. The request is intercepted by the authentication filter.

6. Details about the authenticated entity are stored in the security context.

2. Authentication responsibility is delegated to the authentication manager.

5. The result of the authentication is returned to the filter.

3. The authentication manager uses the authentication provider, which implements the authentication logic.

4. The authentication provider finds the user with a user details service and validates the password using a password encoder.

Figure 2.3 The `AuthenticationProvider` implements the authentication logic. It receives the request from the `AuthenticationManager` and delegates finding the user to a `UserDetailsService`, verifying the password to a `PasswordEncoder`.

Listing 2.11 Implementing the `AuthenticationProvider` interface

```
@Component
public class CustomAuthenticationProvider implements AuthenticationProvider {

  @Override
  public Authentication authenticate (Authentication authentication) throws
    AuthenticationException {

    // authentication logic here
  }
```

```
    @Override
    public boolean supports(Class<?> authenticationType) {

        // type of the Authentication implementation here
    }
}
```

The `authenticate(Authentication authentication)` method represents all the logic for authentication, so we'll add an implementation like that in listing 2.12. I'll explain the usage of the `supports()` method in detail in chapter 6. For the moment, I recommend you take its implementation for granted. It's not essential for the current example.

Listing 2.12   Implementing the authentication logic

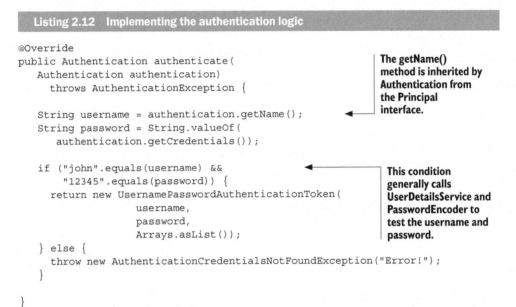

```
@Override
public Authentication authenticate(
    Authentication authentication)
      throws AuthenticationException {

    String username = authentication.getName();
    String password = String.valueOf(
      authentication.getCredentials());

    if ("john".equals(username) &&
        "12345".equals(password)) {
      return new UsernamePasswordAuthenticationToken(
                username,
                password,
                Arrays.asList());
    } else {
      throw new AuthenticationCredentialsNotFoundException("Error!");
    }

}
```

The getName() method is inherited by Authentication from the Principal interface.

This condition generally calls UserDetailsService and PasswordEncoder to test the username and password.

Here the condition of the `if-else` clause is replacing the responsibilities of `User-DetailsService` and `PasswordEncoder`. You are not required to use the two beans, but if you work with users and passwords for authentication, I strongly suggest you separate the logic of their management. Apply it as the Spring Security architecture designed it, even when you override the authentication implementation.

You might find it useful to replace the authentication logic by implementing your own `AuthenticationProvider`. If the default implementation doesn't fit entirely into your application's requirements, you can decide to implement custom authentication logic. The full `AuthenticationProvider` implementation looks like the one in the next listing.

Listing 2.13   The full implementation of the authentication provider

```
@Component
public class CustomAuthenticationProvider
  implements AuthenticationProvider {
```

```
    @Override
    public Authentication authenticate(
       Authentication authentication)
         throws AuthenticationException {

       String username = authentication.getName();
       String password = String.valueOf(authentication.getCredentials());

       if ("john".equals(username) &&
           "12345".equals(password)) {
         return new UsernamePasswordAuthenticationToken(
               username, password, Arrays.asList());
       } else {
         throw new AuthenticationCredentialsNotFoundException("Error!");
       }
    }

    @Override
    public boolean supports(Class<?> authenticationType) {
       return UsernamePasswordAuthenticationToken
                 .class
                 .isAssignableFrom(authenticationType);
    }
}
```

In the configuration class, you can register the AuthenticationProvider using the HttpSecurity authenticationProvider() method shown in the following listing.

Listing 2.14 Registering the new implementation of AuthenticationProvider

```
@Configuration
public class ProjectConfig {

  private final CustomAuthenticationProvider authenticationProvider;

  public ProjectConfig(
    CustomAuthenticationProvider authenticationProvider) {

    this.authenticationProvider = authenticationProvider;
  }

  @Bean
  SecurityFilterChain configure(HttpSecurity http) throws Exception {
    http.httpBasic(Customizer.withDefaults());

    http.authenticationProvider(authenticationProvider);

    http.authorizeHttpRequests(
      c -> c.anyRequest().authenticated()
    );

    return http.build();
  }
}
```

You can now call the endpoint, which is accessible by the only user recognized, as defined by the authentication logic john, with the password 12345:

```
curl -u john:12345 http://localhost:8080/hello
```

The response body is

```
Hello!
```

In chapter 6, you'll learn more about the AuthenticationProvider and how to override its behavior in the authentication process. In the same chapter, we'll also discuss the Authentication interface and its implementations, such as UserPasswordAuthenticationToken.

2.3.5   *Using multiple configuration classes*

In the previously implemented examples, we only used a configuration class. It is, however, good practice to separate the responsibilities even for the configuration classes. We need this separation because the configuration starts to become more complex. In a production-ready application, you probably have more declarations than in our first examples. You also might find it useful to have more than one configuration class to make the project readable.

It's always a good practice to have only one class per responsibility. For this example, we can separate user management configuration from authorization configuration. We do that by defining two configuration classes: UserManagementConfig (defined in the next listing) and WebAuthorizationConfig (defined in listing 2.16). You can find this example in the project ssia-ch2-ex5.

Listing 2.15   Defining the configuration class for user and password management

```
@Configuration
public class UserManagementConfig {

  @Bean
  public UserDetailsService userDetailsService() {
    var userDetailsService = new InMemoryUserDetailsManager();

    var user = User.withUsername("john")
                .password("12345")
                .authorities("read")
                .build();

    userDetailsService.createUser(user);
    return userDetailsService;
  }

  @Bean
  public PasswordEncoder passwordEncoder() {
    return NoOpPasswordEncoder.getInstance();
  }
}
```

In this case, the UserManagementConfig class only contains the two beans responsible for user management: UserDetailsService and PasswordEncoder. The next listing shows this definition.

Listing 2.16 Defining the configuration class for authorization management

```
@Configuration
public class WebAuthorizationConfig {

  @Bean
  SecurityFilterChain configure(HttpSecurity http)
    throws Exception {

    http.httpBasic(Customizer.withDefaults());

    http.authorizeHttpRequests(
        c -> c.anyRequest().authenticated()
    );

    return http.build();
  }
}
```

Here the WebAuthorizationConfig class needs to define a bean of type Security-FilterChain to configure the authentication and authorization rules.

Summary

- Spring Boot provides some default configurations when you add Spring Security to the dependencies of the application.
- You implement the following basic components for authentication and authorization: UserDetailsService, PasswordEncoder, and AuthenticationProvider.
- You can define users with the User class. A user should at least have a username, a password, and an authority. Authorities are actions that you allow a user to do in the context of the application.
- A simple implementation of a UserDetailsService that Spring Security provides is InMemoryUserDetailsManager. You can add users to such an instance of UserDetailsService to manage the user in the application's memory.
- The NoOpPasswordEncoder is an implementation of the PasswordEncoder contract that uses passwords in cleartext. This implementation is good for learning examples and (maybe) proofs of concept, but not for production-ready applications.
- You can use the AuthenticationProvider contract to implement custom authentication logic in the application.
- There are multiple ways to write configurations, but in a single application, you should choose and stick to one approach. This helps to make your code cleaner and easier to understand.

Part 2

Configuring authentication

Authentication stands at the forefront of any secure application, determining who interacts with it. In the second part of this book, we dive right into the heart of this mechanism.

Chapter 3 acquaints you with Spring Security's user management, including the essential `UserDetails` and `GrantedAuthority` contracts, and the nuances of guiding Spring Security on handling users.

Chapter 4 delves into password safety, exploring the `PasswordEncoder` contract, crafting your own, and using Spring Security's Crypto module for encryption and key generation.

Chapter 5 introduces the pivotal role of filters in Spring Security. You'll learn to integrate, order, and employ a variety of filters, enhancing your app's security posture.

Chapter 6 ties everything together. Here you'll discover the essence of the `AuthenticationProvider`, dive deep into custom authentication logic, and familiarize yourself with different login authentication methods, including HTTP Basic and form-based approaches.

By the end of this section, you'll have a robust grasp of the intricate layers and mechanics of authentication in Spring applications.

Managing users

One of my colleagues from the university cooks pretty well. He's not a chef in a fancy restaurant, but he's quite passionate about cooking. One day, when sharing thoughts in a discussion, I asked him about how he manages to remember so many recipes. He told me that's easy. "You don't have to remember the whole recipe, but the way basic ingredients match with each other. It's like some real-world contracts that tell you what you can mix or should not mix. Then for each recipe, you only remember some tricks."

43

This analogy is similar to the way architectures work. With any robust framework, we use contracts to decouple the implementations of the framework from the application built on it. With Java, we use interfaces to define the contracts. A programmer is similar to a chef, knowing how the ingredients work together to choose just the right implementation. The programmer knows the framework's abstractions and uses those to integrate with it.

This chapter is about understanding in detail one of the fundamental roles you encountered in the first example we worked on in chapter 2—the `UserDetails-Service`. Along with the `UserDetailsService`, we'll discuss the following interfaces (contracts):

- `UserDetails`, which describes the user for Spring Security.
- `GrantedAuthority`, which allows us to define actions that the user can execute.
- `UserDetailsManager`, which extends the `UserDetailsService` contract. Beyond the inherited behavior, it also describes actions such as creating a user and modifying or deleting a user's password.

From chapter 2, you already have an idea of the roles the `UserDetailsService` and the `PasswordEncoder` play in the authentication process. But we only discussed how to plug in an instance defined by you instead of using the default one configured by Spring Boot. We have more details to discuss, such as

- The implementations provided by Spring Security and how to use them
- How to define a custom implementation for contracts and when to do so
- Ways to implement interfaces that you find in real-world applications
- Best practices for using these interfaces

The plan is to start with how Spring Security understands the user definition. For this, we'll discuss the `UserDetails` and `GrantedAuthority` contracts. Next, we'll detail the `UserDetailsService` and how `UserDetailsManager` extends this contract. You'll apply implementations for these interfaces (e.g., `InMemoryUserDetailsManager`, `JdbcUserDetailsManager`, and `LdapUserDetailsManager`). When these implementations aren't a good fit for your system, you'll write a custom implementation.

3.1   *Implementing authentication in Spring Security*

In the previous chapter, we got started with Spring Security. In the first example, we discussed how Spring Boot specifies some defaults that define how a new application initially works. You have also learned how to override these defaults using various alternatives that we often find in apps. However, we only considered the surface of these so that you have an idea of what we'll be doing. In this chapter, as well as chapters 4 and 5, we'll discuss these interfaces in more detail, together with different implementations and where you might find them in real-world applications.

Figure 3.1 presents the authentication flow in Spring Security. This architecture is the backbone of the authentication process as implemented by Spring Security. It's important to understand it because you'll rely on it in any Spring Security implementation. You'll observe that we discuss parts of this architecture in almost all the chapters of this book. You'll see it so often that you'll probably learn it by heart, which is good. If you know this architecture, you're like a chef who knows their ingredients and can put together any recipe.

In figure 3.1, the shaded boxes represent the components that we start with: the `UserDetailsService` and `PasswordEncoder`. These two components focus on the part of the flow that I often refer to as "the user management part." In this chapter, the `UserDetailsService` and the `PasswordEncoder` are the components that deal directly with user details and their credentials. We'll discuss the `PasswordEncoder` in detail in chapter 4.

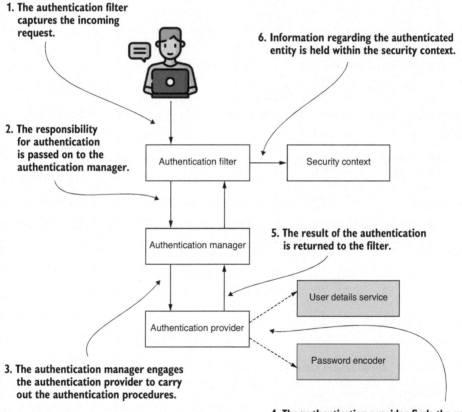

Figure 3.1 Spring Security's authentication flow. The AuthenticationFilter captures the incoming request and passes the task of authentication to the `AuthenticationManager`. The `AuthenticationManager`, in turn, utilizes an authentication provider to carry out the authentication process. For verifying the username and password, the `AuthenticationProvider` relies on a `UserDetailsService` and a `PasswordEncoder`.

As part of user management, we use the `UserDetailsService` and `UserDetails-Manager` interfaces. The `UserDetailsService` is only responsible for retrieving the user by username. This action is the only one needed by the framework to complete authentication. The `UserDetailsManager` adds behavior that refers to adding, modifying, or deleting the user, which is a required functionality in most applications. The separation between the two contracts is an excellent example of the *interface segregation* principle. Separating the interfaces allows for better flexibility because the framework doesn't force you to implement behavior if your app doesn't need it. If the app only needs to authenticate the users, then implementing the `UserDetailsService` contract is enough to cover the desired functionality. To manage the users, `UserDetails-Service` and the `UserDetailsManager` components need a way to represent them.

Spring Security offers the `UserDetails` contract, which you must implement to describe a user in the way the framework understands. As you'll learn in this chapter, in Spring Security, a user has a set of privileges, which are the actions the user is allowed to do. We'll work a lot with these privileges in chapters 7 through 12 when discussing authorization. But for now, Spring Security represents the actions that a user can do with the `GrantedAuthority` interface. We often call these *authorities*, and a user has one or more of them. In figure 3.2, you find a representation of the relationship between the components of the user management part of the authentication flow.

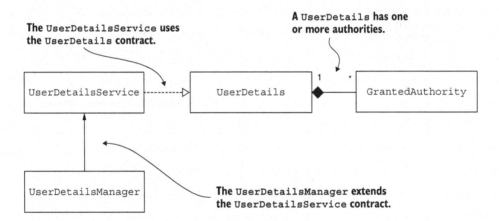

Figure 3.2 **Dependencies between the components involved in user management. The** `UserDetailsService` **retrieves a user's details by searching for the user by name. The user is characterized by the** `UserDetails` **contract. Each user possesses one or more authorities, which are depicted by the** `GrantedAuthority` **interface. For incorporating operations such as create, delete, or modify password for a user, the** `UserDetailsManager` **contract, which expands on the** `UserDetailsService`, **is used to include these functionalities.**

Understanding the links between these objects in the Spring Security architecture and ways to implement them gives you a wide range of options to choose from when working on applications. Any of these options could be the right puzzle piece in the app that you are working on, and you need to make your choice wisely. But to be able to choose, you first need to know what you can choose from.

3.2 Describing the user

In this section, you'll learn how to describe the users of your application so that Spring Security understands them. Learning how to represent users and make the framework aware of them is an essential step in building an authentication flow. Based on the user, the application makes a decision—whether a call to a certain functionality is allowed. To work with users, you first need to understand how to define the prototype of the user in your application. This section describes by example how to establish a blueprint for your users in a Spring Security application.

For Spring Security, a user definition should fulfill the `UserDetails` contract. The `UserDetails` contract represents the user as understood by Spring Security. The class of your application that describes the user must implement this interface, and in this way, the framework understands it.

3.2.1 Describing users with the UserDetails contract

In this section, you'll learn how to implement the `UserDetails` interface to describe the users in your application. We'll discuss the methods declared by the `UserDetails` contract to understand how and why we implement each of them. Let's start first by looking at the interface as presented in the following listing.

> **Listing 3.1 The `UserDetails` interface**

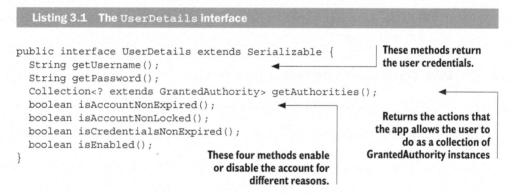

```
public interface UserDetails extends Serializable {
    String getUsername();
    String getPassword();
    Collection<? extends GrantedAuthority> getAuthorities();
    boolean isAccountNonExpired();
    boolean isAccountNonLocked();
    boolean isCredentialsNonExpired();
    boolean isEnabled();
}
```

These methods return the user credentials.

Returns the actions that the app allows the user to do as a collection of GrantedAuthority instances

These four methods enable or disable the account for different reasons.

The `getUsername()` and `getPassword()` methods return, as you'd expect, the username and the password. The app uses these values in the authentication process, and these are the only details related to authentication from this contract. The other five methods all relate to authorizing the user to access the application's resources.

Generally, the app should allow a user to do some actions that are meaningful in the application's context. For example, the user should be able to read, write, or delete data. We say a user has or doesn't have the privilege to perform an action, and an authority represents the privilege a user has. We implement the `getAuthorities()` method to return the group of authorities granted to a user.

> **NOTE** As you'll learn in chapter 6, Spring Security uses authorities to refer either to fine-grained privileges or to roles, which are groups of privileges. To make your reading more effortless, in this book, I refer to the fine-grained privileges as authorities.

Furthermore, as seen in the `UserDetails` contract, a user can

- Let the account expire
- Lock the account
- Let the credentials expire
- Disable the account

Suppose you choose to implement these user restrictions in your application's logic. In that case, you need to implement the methods `isAccountNonExpired()`, `isAccountNonLocked()`, `isCredentialsNonExpired()`, and `isEnabled()`, so that those needing to be enabled return true. Not all applications have accounts that expire or get locked with certain conditions. If you do not need to implement these functionalities in your application, you can simply make these four methods return true.

> **NOTE**   The names of the last four methods in the `UserDetails` interface may sound strange. One could argue that these are not wisely chosen in terms of clean coding and maintainability. For example, the name `isAccountNon-Expired()` looks like a double negation, and at first sight, it might create confusion. But let's analyze all four method names with attention. These are named so that they all return false when the authorization should fail and true otherwise. This is the right approach because the human mind tends to associate the word "false" with negativity and the word "true" with positive scenarios.

3.2.2   *Detailing on the GrantedAuthority contract*

As you observed in the definition of the `UserDetails` interface in section 3.2.1, the actions granted for a user are called authorities. In chapters 7 through 12, we'll write authorization configurations based on these user authorities. Thus, it's essential to know how to define them.

The authorities represent what the user can do in your application. Without them, all users would be equal. While there are simple applications in which the users are equal, in most practical scenarios, an application defines multiple kinds of users. An application might have users who can only read specific information, while others can also modify the data. And you need to make your application differentiate between them, depending on the functional requirements of the application, which are the authorities a user needs. To describe the authorities in Spring Security, you use the `GrantedAuthority` interface.

Before we discuss implementing `UserDetails`, let's understand the `GrantedAuthority` interface. We use this interface in the definition of the user details. It represents a privilege granted to the user. A user must have at least one authority. Here's the implementation of the `GrantedAuthority` definition:

```
public interface GrantedAuthority extends Serializable {
    String getAuthority();
}
```

To create an authority, you only need to find a name for that privilege so you can refer to it later when writing the authorization rules. For example, a user can read the records managed by the application or delete them. You write the authorization rules based on the names you give to these actions.

In this chapter, we'll implement the getAuthority() method to return the authority's name as a String. The GrantedAuthority interface has only one abstract method, and in this book, you'll often find examples in which we use a lambda expression for its implementation. Another possibility is to use the SimpleGrantedAuthority class to create authority instances. The SimpleGrantedAuthority class offers a way to create immutable instances of the type GrantedAuthority. You provide the authority name when building the instance. In the next code snippet, you'll find two examples of implementing a GrantedAuthority. Here we make use of a lambda expression and then use the SimpleGrantedAuthority class:

```
GrantedAuthority g1 = () -> "READ";
GrantedAuthority g2 = new SimpleGrantedAuthority("READ");
```

3.2.3 *Writing a minimal implementation of UserDetails*

In this section, you'll write your first implementation of the UserDetails contract. We start with a basic implementation in which each method returns a static value. Then we change it to a version that you'll more likely find in a practical scenario, one that allows you to have multiple and different instances of users. Now that you know how to implement the UserDetails and GrantedAuthority interfaces, we can write the simplest user definition for an application.

With a class named DummyUser, let's implement a minimal description of a user, as in the following listing. I use this class mainly to demonstrate implementing the methods for the UserDetails contract. Instances of this class always refer to only one user, "bill", who has the password "12345" and an authority named "READ".

Listing 3.2 The DummyUser class

```
public class DummyUser implements UserDetails {

  @Override
  public String getUsername() {
    return "bill";
  }

  @Override
  public String getPassword() {
    return "12345";
  }

  // Omitted code

}
```

The class in listing 3.2 implements the `UserDetails` interface and needs to implement all its methods. You will find here the implementation of `getUsername()` and `getPassword()`. In this example, these methods only return a fixed value for each of the properties.

Next, we add a definition for the list of authorities. The next listing shows the implementation of the `getAuthorities()` method. This method returns a collection with only one implementation of the `GrantedAuthority` interface.

Listing 3.3   Implementation of the `getAuthorities()` method

```
public class DummyUser implements UserDetails {

  // Omitted code

  @Override
  public Collection<? extends GrantedAuthority> getAuthorities() {
    return List.of(() -> "READ");
  }

  // Omitted code

}
```

Finally, you have to add an implementation for the last four methods of the `User-Details` interface. For the `DummyUser` class, these always return true, meaning the user is forever active and usable. You can find the examples in the following listing.

Listing 3.4   Implementation of the last four `UserDetails` interface methods

```
public class DummyUser implements UserDetails {

  // Omitted code

  @Override
  public boolean isAccountNonExpired() {
    return true;
  }

  @Override
  public boolean isAccountNonLocked() {
    return true;
  }

  @Override
  public boolean isCredentialsNonExpired() {
    return true;
  }

  @Override
  public boolean isEnabled() {
    return true;
  }
```

```
// Omitted code
```

}

Of course, this minimal implementation means that all instances of the class represent the same user. It's a good start to understanding the contract, but not something you would do in a real application. For a real application, you should create a class that you can use to generate instances that can represent different users. In this case, your definition would at least have the username and the password as attributes in the class, as shown in the next listing.

> **Listing 3.5   A more practical implementation of the `UserDetails` interface**

```java
public class SimpleUser implements UserDetails {

    private final String username;
    private final String password;

    public SimpleUser(String username, String password) {
        this.username = username;
        this.password = password;
    }

    @Override
    public String getUsername() {
        return this.username;
    }

    @Override
    public String getPassword() {
        return this.password;
    }

    // Omitted code

}
```

3.2.4   *Using a builder to create instances of the UserDetails type*

Some applications are simple and don't need a custom implementation of the User-Details interface. In this section, we take a look at using a builder class provided by Spring Security to create simple user instances. Instead of declaring one more class in your application, you quickly obtain an instance representing your user with the User builder class.

The User class from the org.springframework.security.core.userdetails package is a simple way to build instances of the UserDetails type. Using this class, you can create immutable instances of UserDetails. You need to provide at least a username and a password, and the username shouldn't be an empty string. The following listing demonstrates how to use this builder. Building the user in this way, you don't need to have a custom implementation of the UserDetails contract.

Listing 3.6   Constructing a user with the `User` builder class

```
UserDetails u = User.withUsername("bill")
                    .password("12345")
                    .authorities("read", "write")
                    .accountExpired(false)
                    .disabled(true)
                    .build();
```

With the previous listing as an example, let's dive deeper into the anatomy of the User builder class. The `User.withUsername(String username)` method returns an instance of the builder class `UserBuilder` nested in the `User` class. Another way to create the builder is by starting from another instance of `UserDetails`. In listing 3.7, the first line constructs a `UserBuilder`, starting with the username given as a string. Afterward, we demonstrate how to create a builder beginning with an already existing instance of `UserDetails`.

Listing 3.7   Creating the `User.UserBuilder` instance

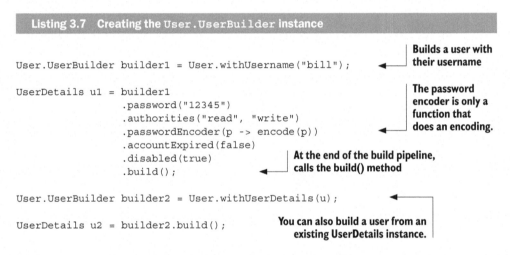

```
User.UserBuilder builder1 = User.withUsername("bill");          ◄─── Builds a user with
                                                                     their username

UserDetails u1 = builder1
                    .password("12345")                          ┌─ The password
                    .authorities("read", "write")               │  encoder is only a
                    .passwordEncoder(p -> encode(p))   ◄────────┘  function that
                    .accountExpired(false)                         does an encoding.
                    .disabled(true)              ┌─ At the end of the build pipeline,
                    .build();            ◄───────┘  calls the build() method

User.UserBuilder builder2 = User.withUserDetails(u);    ◄────────┐

UserDetails u2 = builder2.build();        You can also build a user from an
                                          existing UserDetails instance.
```

You can see with any of the builders defined in listing 3.7 that it is possible to use the builder to obtain a user represented by the `UserDetails` contract. At the end of the build pipeline, you call the `build()` method. It applies the function defined to encode the password if you provide one, constructs the instance of `UserDetails`, and returns it.

> **NOTE**   Note that the password encoder is given here as a `Function<String, String>` and not in the form of the `PasswordEncoder` interface provided by Spring Security. This function's only responsibility is to transform a password in a given encoding. In the next section, we'll discuss in detail the `Password-Encoder` contract from Spring Security that we used in chapter 2. We'll discuss the `PasswordEncoder` contract in more detail in chapter 4.

3.2.5 *Combining multiple responsibilities related to the user*

In the previous section, you learned how to implement the `UserDetails` interface. In real-world scenarios, it's often more complicated. In most cases, you find multiple responsibilities to which a user relates. And if you store users in a database, and then in the application, you would need a class to represent the persistence entity as well. Or if you retrieve users through a web service from another system, then you would probably need a data transfer object to represent the user instances. Assuming the first, a simple but also typical case, let's consider we have a table in an SQL database where we store the users. To make the example shorter, we give each user only one authority. The following listing shows the entity class that maps the table.

Listing 3.8 Defining the JPA `User` entity class

```
@Entity
public class User {

  @Id
  private Long id;
  private String username;
  private String password;
  private String authority;

  // Omitted getters and setters

}
```

If you make the same class also implement the Spring Security contract for user details, the class becomes more complicated. What do you think about how the code looks in the next listing? In my opinion, it is a mess. I would get lost in it.

Listing 3.9 The `User` class has two responsibilities

```
@Entity
public class User implements UserDetails {

  @Id
  private int id;
  private String username;
  private String password;
  private String authority;

  @Override
  public String getUsername() {
    return this.username;
  }

  @Override
  public String getPassword() {
    return this.password;
  }
```

```
public String getAuthority() {
  return this.authority;
}

@Override
public Collection<? extends GrantedAuthority> getAuthorities() {
  return List.of(() -> authority);
}

// Omitted code

}
```

The class contains JPA annotations, getters, and setters, of which both `getUsername()` and `getPassword()` override the methods in the `UserDetails` contract. It has a `getAuthority()` method that returns a `String`, as well as a `getAuthorities()` method that returns a `Collection`. The `getAuthority()` method is just a getter in the class, while `getAuthorities()` implements the method in the `UserDetails` interface. Things get even more complicated when adding relationships to other entities. Again, this code isn't friendly at all!

How can we write this code to be cleaner? The root of the muddy aspect of the previous code example is a mix of two responsibilities. While it's true that you need both in the application, in this case, nobody says that you have to put these into the same class. Let's try to separate those by defining a separate class called `SecurityUser`, which adapts the `User` class. As the next listing shows, the `SecurityUser` class implements the `UserDetails` contract and uses that to plug our user into the Spring Security architecture. The `User` class has only its JPA entity responsibility remaining.

Listing 3.10 Implementing the `User` class only as a JPA entity

```
@Entity
public class User {

  @Id
  private int id;
  private String username;
  private String password;
  private String authority;

  // Omitted getters and setters

}
```

The `User` class in listing 3.10 has only its JPA entity responsibility remaining, and thus, it becomes more readable. If you read this code, you can now focus exclusively on details related to persistence, which are not important from the Spring Security perspective. In the next listing, we implement the `SecurityUser` class to wrap the `User` entity.

Listing 3.11 The `SecurityUser` class implementing the `UserDetails` contract

```java
public class SecurityUser implements UserDetails {

  private final User user;

  public SecurityUser(User user) {
    this.user = user;
  }

  @Override
  public String getUsername() {
    return user.getUsername();
  }

  @Override
  public String getPassword() {
    return user.getPassword();
  }

  @Override
  public Collection<? extends GrantedAuthority> getAuthorities() {
    return List.of(() -> user.getAuthority());
  }

  // Omitted code

}
```

As you can observe, we use the `SecurityUser` class only to map the user details in the system to the `UserDetails` contract understood by Spring Security. To mark the fact that the `SecurityUser` makes no sense without a `User` entity, we make the field final. You have to provide the user through the constructor. The `SecurityUser` class adapts the `User` entity class and adds the needed code related to the Spring Security contract without mixing the code into a JPA entity, thereby implementing multiple different tasks.

> **NOTE** You can find different approaches to separate the two responsibilities. I don't want to say that the approach I present in this section is the best or the only one. Usually, the way you choose to implement the class design varies a lot from one case to another. But the main idea is the same: avoid mixing responsibilities and try to write your code to be as decoupled as possible to increase the maintainability of your app.

3.3   *Instructing Spring Security on how to manage users*

In the previous section, you implemented the UserDetails contract to describe users so that Spring Security understands them. But how does Spring Security manage users? Where are they taken from when comparing credentials, and how do you add new users or change existing ones? In chapter 2, you learned that the framework defines a specific component to which the authentication process delegates user management: the UserDetailsService instance. We even defined a UserDetailsService to override the default implementation provided by Spring Boot.

In this section, we experiment with various ways of implementing the UserDetails-Service class. You'll understand how user management works by implementing the responsibility described by the UserDetailsService contract in our example. After that, you'll find out how the UserDetailsManager interface adds more behavior to the contract defined by the UserDetailsService. At the end of this section, we'll use the provided implementations of the UserDetailsManager interface offered by Spring Security. We'll write an example project where we'll use one of the best-known implementations provided by Spring Security, the JdbcUserDetailsManager class. After learning this, you'll know how to tell Spring Security where to find users, which is essential in the authentication flow.

3.3.1   *Understanding the UserDetailsService contract*

In this section, you'll learn about the UserDetailsService interface definition. Before understanding how and why to implement it, you must first understand the contract. It is time to go into more detail on UserDetailsService and how to work with implementations of this component. The UserDetailsService interface contains only one method, as follows:

```
public interface UserDetailsService {

  UserDetails loadUserByUsername(String username)
      throws UsernameNotFoundException;
}
```

The authentication implementation calls the loadUserByUsername(String username) method to obtain the details of a user with a given username (figure 3.3). The username is, of course, considered unique. The user returned by this method is an implementation of the UserDetails contract. If the username doesn't exist, the method throws a UsernameNotFoundException.

> **NOTE**   The UsernameNotFoundException is a RuntimeException. The throws clause in the UserDetailsService interface is only for documentation purposes. The UsernameNotFoundException inherits directly from the type AuthenticationException, which is the parent of all the exceptions related to the process of authentication. AuthenticationException further inherits the RuntimeException class.

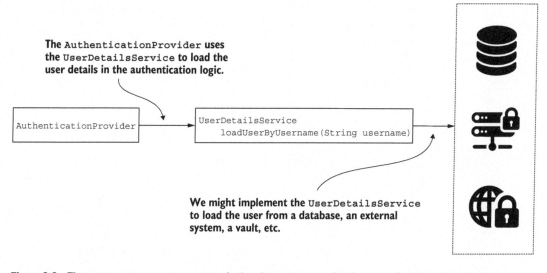

The **AuthenticationProvider uses the UserDetailsService to load the user details in the authentication logic.**

We might implement the **UserDetailsService to load the user from a database, an external system, a vault, etc.**

Figure 3.3 The AuthenticationProvider **is the element responsible for executing the authentication process and utilizes the** UserDetailsService **to gather user details. It invokes the** loadUserByUsername(String username) **method to locate the user based on their username.**

3.3.2 Implementing the UserDetailsService contract

In this section, we work on a practical example to demonstrate the implementation of the UserDetailsService. Your application manages details about credentials and other user aspects. It could be that these are stored in a database or handled by another system that you access through a web service or by other means (figure 3.3). Regardless of how this happens in your system, the only thing Spring Security needs from you is an implementation to retrieve the user by username.

In the next example, we write a UserDetailsService that has an in-memory list of users. In chapter 2, you used a provided implementation that does the same thing, the InMemoryUserDetailsManager. Because you are already familiar with how this implementation works, I have chosen a similar functionality, but this time to implement on our own. We provide a list of users when we create an instance of our UserDetails-Service class. You can find this example in the project ssia-ch3-ex1. In the package named model, we define the UserDetails as presented by the following listing.

> **Listing 3.12   The implementation of the UserDetails interface**

The User class is immutable. You give the values for the three attributes when you build the instance, and these values cannot be changed afterward.

```
public class User implements UserDetails {

    private final String username;
    private final String password;
```

> To make the example simple, a
> user has only one authority.

```
private final String authority;

public User(String username, String password, String authority) {
  this.username = username;
  this.password = password;
  this.authority = authority;
}

@Override
public Collection<? extends GrantedAuthority> getAuthorities() {
  return List.of(() -> authority);
}
```

> Returns a list
> containing only the
> GrantedAuthority
> object with the name
> provided when you
> built the instance

```
@Override
public String getPassword() {
  return password;
}

@Override
public String getUsername() {
  return username;
}

@Override
public boolean isAccountNonExpired() {
  return true;
}
```

> The account does not
> expire or get locked.

```
@Override
public boolean isAccountNonLocked() {
  return true;
}

@Override
public boolean isCredentialsNonExpired() {
  return true;
}

@Override
public boolean isEnabled() {
  return true;
}
}
```

In the package named services, we create a class called `InMemoryUserDetails-Service`. The following listing shows how we implement this class.

Listing 3.13   The implementation of the `UserDetailsService` interface

```
public class InMemoryUserDetailsService implements UserDetailsService {

  private final List<UserDetails> users;
```

> UserDetailsService
> manages the list of
> users in-memory.

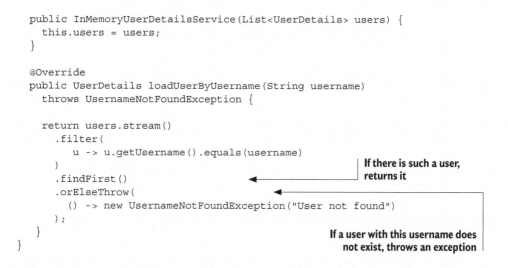

```
public InMemoryUserDetailsService(List<UserDetails> users) {
  this.users = users;
}

@Override
public UserDetails loadUserByUsername(String username)
  throws UsernameNotFoundException {

  return users.stream()
    .filter(
      u -> u.getUsername().equals(username)
    )
    .findFirst()                              If there is such a user,
    .orElseThrow(                             returns it
      () -> new UsernameNotFoundException("User not found")
    );
}                                             If a user with this username does
}                                             not exist, throws an exception
```

The `loadUserByUsername(String username)` method searches the list of users
for the given username and returns the desired `UserDetails` instance. If there is no
instance with that username, it throws a `UsernameNotFoundException`. We can now
use this implementation as our `UserDetailsService`. The next listing shows how we
add it as a bean in the configuration class and register one user within it.

Listing 3.14 `UserDetailsService` **registered as a bean in the configuration class**

```
@Configuration
public class ProjectConfig {

  @Bean
  public UserDetailsService userDetailsService() {
    UserDetails u = new User("john", "12345", "read");
    List<UserDetails> users = List.of(u);
    return new InMemoryUserDetailsService(users);
  }

  @Bean
  public PasswordEncoder passwordEncoder() {
    return NoOpPasswordEncoder.getInstance();
  }
}
```

Finally, we create a simple endpoint and test the implementation. The following listing
defines the endpoint.

Listing 3.15 **The definition of the endpoint used for testing the implementation**

```
@RestController
public class HelloController {

  @GetMapping("/hello")
```

```
  public String hello() {
    return "Hello!";
  }
}
```

When calling the endpoint using cURL, we observe that for user `john` with password `12345`, we get back an HTTP 200 OK. If we use something else, the application returns 401 Unauthorized:

```
curl -u john:12345 http://localhost:8080/hello
```

The response body is

```
Hello!
```

3.3.3 *Implementing the UserDetailsManager contract*

In this section, we discuss using and implementing the `UserDetailsManager` interface. This interface extends and adds more methods to the `UserDetailsService` contract. Spring Security needs the `UserDetailsService` contract to do the authentication. But generally, in applications, there is also a need for managing users. Most of the time, an app should be able to add new users or delete existing ones. In this case, we implement a more particular interface defined by Spring Security, `UserDetailsManager`. It extends `UserDetailsService` and adds more operations that we need to implement:

```
public interface UserDetailsManager extends UserDetailsService {
    void createUser(UserDetails user);
    void updateUser(UserDetails user);
    void deleteUser(String username);
    void changePassword(String oldPassword, String newPassword);
    boolean userExists(String username);
}
```

The `InMemoryUserDetailsManager` object that we used in chapter 2 is actually a `UserDetailsManager`. At that time, we only considered its `UserDetailsService` characteristics. Project ssia-ch3-ex2 accompanies the example in this section.

USING A JDBCUSERDETAILSMANAGER FOR USER MANAGEMENT

Besides the `InMemoryUserDetailsManager`, we often use another `UserDetailManager` implementation, `JdbcUserDetailsManager`. The `JdbcUserDetailsManager` class manages users in an SQL database. It connects to the database directly through JDBC. This way, the `JdbcUserDetailsManager` is independent of any other framework or specification related to database connectivity.

To understand how the `JdbcUserDetailsManager` works, it's best if you put it into action with an example. In the following example, you implement an application that manages the users in a MySQL database using the `JdbcUserDetailsManager`. Figure 3.4 provides an overview of the place the `JdbcUserDetailsManager` implementation takes in the authentication flow.

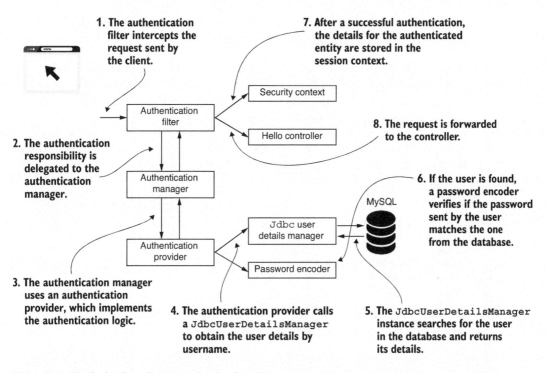

1. The authentication filter intercepts the request sent by the client.

7. After a successful authentication, the details for the authenticated entity are stored in the session context.

2. The authentication responsibility is delegated to the authentication manager.

8. The request is forwarded to the controller.

6. If the user is found, a password encoder verifies if the password sent by the user matches the one from the database.

3. The authentication manager uses an authentication provider, which implements the authentication logic.

4. The authentication provider calls a `JdbcUserDetailsManager` to obtain the user details by username.

5. The `JdbcUserDetailsManager` instance searches for the user in the database and returns its details.

Figure 3.4   The Spring Security authentication flow. Here we use a `JdbcUserDetailsManager` as our `UserDetailsService` component. The `JdbcUserDetailsManager` uses a database to manage users.

You'll start working on our demo application that uses the `JdbcUserDetailsManager` by creating a database and two tables. In our case, we name the database `spring`, and we name one of the tables `users` and the other `authorities`. These names are the default table names known by the `JdbcUserDetailsManager`. As you'll learn at the end of this section, the `JdbcUserDetailsManager` implementation is flexible and lets you override these default names if you want to do so. The purpose of the users table is to keep user records. The `JdbcUserDetailsManager` implementation expects three columns in the `users` table—a username, a password, and enabled—which you can use to deactivate the user.

You can choose to create the database and its structure yourself by using either the command-line tool for your database management system (DBMS) or a client application. For example, for MySQL, you can choose to use MySQL Workbench to do this. But the easiest thing to do would be to let Spring Boot itself run the scripts for you. To do this, just add two more files to your project in the resources folder: schema.sql and data.sql. In the schema.sql file, you add the queries related to the database structure, such as creating, altering, or dropping tables. In the data.sql file, you add the queries that work with the data inside the tables, such as INSERT, UPDATE, or DELETE. Spring Boot automatically runs these files for you when you start the application. A simpler solution for building examples that need databases is using an H2 in-memory database. This way, you don't need to install a separate DBMS solution.

> **NOTE** If you prefer, you could go with H2 as well (as I do in the ssia-ch3-ex2 project) when developing the applications presented in this book. But in most cases, I chose to implement the examples with an external DBMS to make it clear that it's an external component of the system and avoid confusion in this way.

You use the code in the next listing to create the `users` table with a MySQL server. You can add this script to the schema.sql file in your Spring Boot project.

Listing 3.16   The SQL query for creating the `users` table

```
CREATE TABLE IF NOT EXISTS `spring`.`users` (
  `id` INT NOT NULL AUTO_INCREMENT,
  `username` VARCHAR(45) NOT NULL,
  `password` VARCHAR(45) NOT NULL,
  `enabled` INT NOT NULL,
  PRIMARY KEY (`id`));
```

The `authorities` table stores authorities per user. Each record stores a username and an authority granted for the user with that username.

Listing 3.17   The SQL query for creating the `authorities` table

```
CREATE TABLE IF NOT EXISTS `spring`.`authorities` (
  `id` INT NOT NULL AUTO_INCREMENT,
  `username` VARCHAR(45) NOT NULL,
  `authority` VARCHAR(45) NOT NULL,
  PRIMARY KEY (`id`));
```

> **NOTE** For simplicity and to allow you focus on the Spring Security configurations we discuss, in the examples provided with this book, I skip the definitions of indexes or foreign keys.

To make sure you have a user for testing, insert a record in each of the tables. You can add these queries in the data.sql file in the resources folder of the Spring Boot project:

```
INSERT INTO `spring`.`authorities`
(username, authority)
VALUES
('john', 'write');

INSERT INTO `spring`.`users`
(username, password, enabled)
VALUES
('john', '12345', '1');
```

For your project, you need to add at least the dependencies stated in the following listing. Check your pom.xml file to make sure you added these dependencies.

Listing 3.18 Dependencies needed to develop the example project

```
<dependency>
  <groupId>org.springframework.boot</groupId>
  <artifactId>spring-boot-starter-security</artifactId>
</dependency>
<dependency>
  <groupId>org.springframework.boot</groupId>
  <artifactId>spring-boot-starter-web</artifactId>
</dependency>
<dependency>
  <groupId>org.springframework.boot</groupId>
  <artifactId>spring-boot-starter-jdbc</artifactId>
</dependency>
<dependency>
  <groupId>com.h2database</groupId>
  <artifactId>h2</artifactId>
</dependency>
```

NOTE In your examples, you can use any SQL database technology as long as you add the correct JDBC driver to the dependencies.

Remember, you need to add the JDBC driver according to the database technology you use. For example, if you'd use MySQL, you need to add the MySQL driver dependency as presented in the next snippet:

```
<dependency>
  <groupId>mysql</groupId>
  <artifactId>mysql-connector-java</artifactId>
  <scope>runtime</scope>
</dependency>
```

You can configure a data source in the application.properties file of the project or as a separate bean. If you choose to use the application.properties file, you need to add the following lines to that file:

```
spring.datasource.url=jdbc:h2:mem:ssia
spring.datasource.username=sa
spring.datasource.password=
spring.sql.init.mode=always
```

In the configuration class of the project, you define the `UserDetailsService` and the `PasswordEncoder`. The `JdbcUserDetailsManager` needs the `DataSource` to connect to the database. The data source can be autowired through a parameter of the method (as presented in the next listing) or through an attribute of the class.

Listing 3.19 Registering the `JdbcUserDetailsManager` in the configuration class

```
@Configuration
public class ProjectConfig {

  @Bean
  public UserDetailsService userDetailsService(DataSource dataSource) {
```

```
    return new JdbcUserDetailsManager(dataSource);
  }

  @Bean
  public PasswordEncoder passwordEncoder() {
    return NoOpPasswordEncoder.getInstance();
  }
}
```

To access any endpoint of the application, you now need to use HTTP Basic authentication with one of the users stored in the database. To prove this, we create a new endpoint, as shown in the following listing, and then call it with cURL.

Listing 3.20   The test endpoint to check the implementation

```
@RestController
public class HelloController {

  @GetMapping("/hello")
  public String hello() {
    return "Hello!";
  }
}
```

In the next code snippet, you find the result when calling the endpoint with the correct username and password:

```
curl -u john:12345 http://localhost:8080/hello
```

The response to the call is

```
Hello!
```

The JdbcUserDetailsManager also allows you to configure the queries used. In the previous example, we made sure we used the exact names for the tables and columns, as the JdbcUserDetailsManager implementation expects those. But it could be that these names are not the best choice for your application. The next listing shows how to override the queries for the JdbcUserDetailsManager.

Listing 3.21   Changing JdbcUserDetailsManager's queries to find the user

```
@Bean
public UserDetailsService userDetailsService(DataSource dataSource) {
  String usersByUsernameQuery =
      "select username, password, enabled from users where username = ?";
  String authsByUserQuery =
      "select username, authority from spring.authorities where username = ?";

  var userDetailsManager = new JdbcUserDetailsManager(dataSource);
  userDetailsManager.setUsersByUsernameQuery(usersByUsernameQuery);
  userDetailsManager.setAuthoritiesByUsernameQuery(authsByUserQuery);
  return userDetailsManager;
}
```

In the same way, we can change all the queries used by the `JdbcUserDetailsManager` implementation.

EXERCISE Write a similar application for which you name the tables and the columns differently in the database. Override the queries for the `JdbcUser-DetailsManager` implementation (e.g., the authentication works with a new table structure). The project ssia-ch3-ex2 features a possible solution.

USING AN LDAPUSERDETAILSMANAGER FOR USER MANAGEMENT

Spring Security also offers an implementation of `UserDetailsManager` for LDAP. Even if it is less popular than the `JdbcUserDetailsManager`, you can count on it if you need to integrate with an LDAP system for user management. In the project ssia-ch3-ex3, you can find a simple demonstration of using the `LdapUserDetailsManager`. Because I can't use a real LDAP server for this demonstration, I have set up an embedded one in my Spring Boot application. To set up the embedded LDAP server, I defined a simple LDAP Data Interchange Format (LDIF) file. The following listing shows the contents of my LDIF file.

Listing 3.22 The definition of the LDIF file

```
dn: dc=springframework,dc=org          ◄──── Defines the base entity
objectclass: top
objectclass: domain
objectclass: extensibleObject
dc: springframework

dn: ou=groups,dc=springframework,dc=org          ◄──── Defines a group entity
objectclass: top
objectclass: organizationalUnit
ou: groups

dn: uid=john,ou=groups,dc=springframework,dc=org          ◄──── Defines a user
objectclass: top
objectclass: person
objectclass: organizationalPerson
objectclass: inetOrgPerson
cn: John
sn: John
uid: john
userPassword: 12345
```

In the LDIF file, I add only one user for which we need to test the app's behavior at the end of this example. We can add the LDIF file directly to the resources folder. This way, it's automatically in the `classpath`, so we can easily refer to it later. I named the LDIF file server.ldif. To work with LDAP and to allow Spring Boot to start an embedded LDAP server, you need to add pom.xml to the dependencies:

```
<dependency>
  <groupId>org.springframework.security</groupId>
  <artifactId>spring-security-ldap</artifactId>
```

```
</dependency>
<dependency>
  <groupId>com.unboundid</groupId>
  <artifactId>unboundid-ldapsdk</artifactId>
</dependency>
```

In the application.properties file, you also need to add the configurations for the embedded LDAP server, as presented in the following code snippet. The values the app needs to boot the embedded LDAP server include the location of the LDIF file, a port for the LDAP server, and the base domain component (DN) label values:

```
spring.ldap.embedded.ldif=classpath:server.ldif
spring.ldap.embedded.base-dn=dc=springframework,dc=org
spring.ldap.embedded.port=33389
```

Once you have an LDAP server for authentication, you can configure your application to use it. The next listing shows how to configure the `LdapUserDetailsManager` to enable your app to authenticate users through the LDAP server.

Listing 3.23   The definition of the `LdapUserDetailsManager` in the configuration file

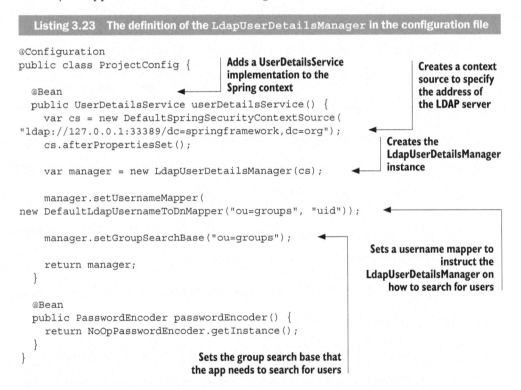

```
@Configuration
public class ProjectConfig {                    Adds a UserDetailsService
                                                implementation to the
  @Bean                                         Spring context
  public UserDetailsService userDetailsService() {
    var cs = new DefaultSpringSecurityContextSource(
"ldap://127.0.0.1:33389/dc=springframework,dc=org");
    cs.afterPropertiesSet();

    var manager = new LdapUserDetailsManager(cs);

    manager.setUsernameMapper(
new DefaultLdapUsernameToDnMapper("ou=groups", "uid"));

    manager.setGroupSearchBase("ou=groups");

    return manager;
  }

  @Bean
  public PasswordEncoder passwordEncoder() {
    return NoOpPasswordEncoder.getInstance();
  }
}
```

Creates a context source to specify the address of the LDAP server

Creates the LdapUserDetailsManager instance

Sets a username mapper to instruct the LdapUserDetailsManager on how to search for users

Sets the group search base that the app needs to search for users

Let's also create a simple endpoint to test the security configuration. I added a controller class, as presented in the next code snippet:

```
@RestController
public class HelloController {
```

```
@GetMapping("/hello")
public String hello() {
  return "Hello!";
}
}
```

Now start the app, and call the /hello endpoint. You need to authenticate with user john if you want the app to allow you to call the endpoint. The next code snippet shows you the result of calling the endpoint with cURL:

```
curl -u john:12345 http://localhost:8080/hello
```

The response to the call is

```
Hello!
```

Summary

- The UserDetails interface is the contract you use to describe a user in Spring Security.

- The UserDetailsService interface is the contract that Spring Security expects you to implement in the authentication architecture to describe the way the application obtains user details.

- The UserDetailsManager interface extends UserDetailsService and adds the behavior related to creating, changing, or deleting a user.

- Spring Security provides a few implementations of the UserDetailsManager contract. Among these are InMemoryUserDetailsManager, JdbcUserDetails-Manager, and LdapUserDetailsManager.

- The JdbcUserDetailsManager class has the advantage of directly using JDBC and does not lock the application in to other frameworks.

Managing passwords

This chapter covers

- Implementing and working with the `PasswordEncoder`
- Using the tools offered by the Spring Security Crypto module

In chapter 3, we discussed managing users in an application implemented with Spring Security. But what about passwords? They're certainly an essential piece of the authentication flow. In this chapter, you'll learn how to manage passwords and secrets in an application implemented with Spring Security. We'll discuss the `PasswordEncoder` contract and the tools offered by the Spring Security Crypto module (SSCM) for the management of passwords.

4.1 Using password encoders

From chapter 3, you should now have a clear image of what the `UserDetails` interface is, as well as multiple ways to use its implementation. But as you learned in chapter 2, different actors manage user representation during the authentication and authorization processes. You also learned that some of these have defaults, like `UserDetailsService` and `PasswordEncoder`. You now know that you can override the defaults. We continue with a deep understanding of these beans and ways to implement them, so in this section, we will analyze the `PasswordEncoder`. Figure 4.1 reminds you of where the `PasswordEncoder` fits into the authentication process.

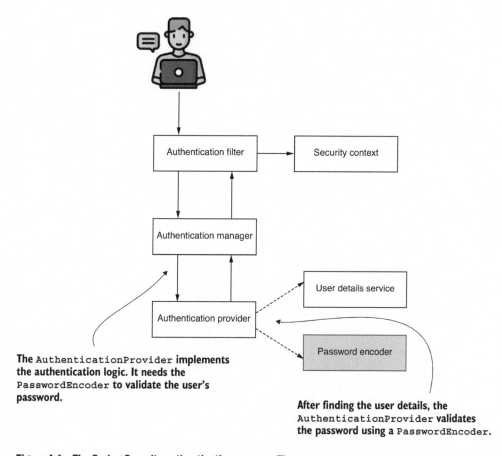

Figure 4.1 The Spring Security authentication process. The AuthenticationProvider **uses the** PasswordEncoder **to validate the user's password in the authentication process.**

Because in general, a system doesn't manage passwords in plain text, these usually undergo a sort of transformation that makes it more challenging to read and steal them. For this responsibility, Spring Security defines a separate contract. To explain it simply in this section, I provide plenty of code examples related to the Password-Encoder implementation. We'll start with understanding the contract, and then we'll write our implementation in a project. Then, in section 4.1.3, I'll provide you with a list of the most well-known and widely used implementations of PasswordEncoder provided by Spring Security.

4.1.1 *The PasswordEncoder contract*

In this section, we discuss the definition of the PasswordEncoder contract. You implement this contract to tell Spring Security how to validate a user's password. In the authentication process, the PasswordEncoder decides whether a password is valid. Every system stores passwords encoded in some way. You preferably store them hashed so that there's no chance someone can read them. The PasswordEncoder can also encode passwords. The methods `encode()` and `matches()`, which the contract declares, are actually the definition of its responsibility. Both are parts of the same contract because these are strongly interlinked. The way the application encodes a password is related to the way the password is validated. Let's first review the contents of the `PasswordEncoder` interface:

```
public interface PasswordEncoder {

  String encode(CharSequence rawPassword);
  boolean matches(CharSequence rawPassword, String encodedPassword);

  default boolean upgradeEncoding(String encodedPassword) {
    return false;
  }
}
```

The interface defines two abstract methods and one with a default implementation. The abstract `encode()` and `matches()` methods are also the ones that you most often hear about when dealing with a `PasswordEncoder` implementation.

The purpose of the `encode(CharSequence rawPassword)` method is to return a transformation of a provided string. In terms of Spring Security functionality, it's used to provide encryption or a hash for a given password. You can use the `matches(Char-Sequence rawPassword, String encodedPassword)` method afterward to check whether an encoded string matches a raw password. You use the `matches()` method in the authentication process to test a provided password against a set of known credentials. The third method, called `upgradeEncoding(CharSequence encodedPassword)`, defaults to false in the contract. If you override it to return true, then the encoded password is encoded again for better security.

In some cases, encoding the encoded password can make it more challenging to obtain the cleartext password from the result. In general, this is a kind of obscurity that I personally don't like. But the framework offers this possibility if you think it applies to your case.

4.1.2   *Implementing your PasswordEncoder*

As you observed, the two methods `matches()` and `encode()` have a strong relationship. If you override them, they should always correspond in terms of functionality: a string returned by the `encode()` method should always be verifiable with the `matches()` method of the same `PasswordEncoder`. In this section, you'll implement the `PasswordEncoder` contract and define the two abstract methods declared by the interface. Knowing how to implement the `PasswordEncoder`, you can choose how the application manages passwords for the authentication process. The most straightforward implementation is a password encoder that considers passwords in plain text: that is, it doesn't do any encoding on the password.

Managing passwords in cleartext is what the instance of `NoOpPasswordEncoder` is precisely. We used this class in our first example in chapter 2. If you were to write your own, it would look something like the following listing.

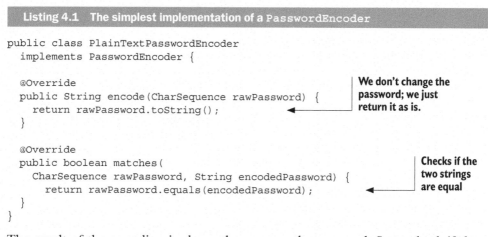

Listing 4.1 The simplest implementation of a PasswordEncoder

```
public class PlainTextPasswordEncoder
  implements PasswordEncoder {

  @Override
  public String encode(CharSequence rawPassword) {        We don't change the
    return rawPassword.toString();                        password; we just
  }                                                        return it as is.

  @Override
  public boolean matches(                                 Checks if the
    CharSequence rawPassword, String encodedPassword) {   two strings
      return rawPassword.equals(encodedPassword);         are equal
  }
}
```

The result of the encoding is always the same as the password. So to check if these match, you only need to compare the strings with `equals()`. A simple implementation of `PasswordEncoder` that uses the hashing algorithm SHA-512 looks like the next listing.

Listing 4.2 Implementing a PasswordEncoder that uses SHA-512

```
public class Sha512PasswordEncoder
  implements PasswordEncoder {

  @Override
  public String encode(CharSequence rawPassword) {
    return hashWithSHA512(rawPassword.toString());
  }

  @Override
  public boolean matches(
    CharSequence rawPassword, String encodedPassword) {
    String hashedPassword = encode(rawPassword);
    return encodedPassword.equals(hashedPassword);
  }

  // Omitted code

}
```

In listing 4.2, we use a method to hash the string value provided with SHA-512. I omit the implementation of this method in listing 4.2, but you can find it in listing 4.3. We call this method from the `encode()` method, which now returns the hash value for its input. To validate a hash against an input, the `matches()` method hashes the raw password in its input and compares it for equality with the hash against which it does the validation.

Listing 4.3   The implementation of the method to hash the input with SHA-512

```
private String hashWithSHA512(String input) {
  StringBuilder result = new StringBuilder();
  try {
    MessageDigest md = MessageDigest.getInstance("SHA-512");
    byte [] digested = md.digest(input.getBytes());
    for (int i = 0; i < digested.length; i++) {
      result.append(Integer.toHexString(0xFF & digested[i]));
    }
  } catch (NoSuchAlgorithmException e) {
    throw new RuntimeException("Bad algorithm");
  }
  return result.toString();
}
```

You'll learn better options to do this in the next section, so don't bother too much with this code for now.

4.1.3   *Choosing from the provided PasswordEncoder implementations*

While knowing how to implement your `PasswordEncoder` is powerful, you must also be aware that Spring Security already provides you with some advantageous implementations. If one of these matches your application, you don't need to rewrite it. In this section, we discuss the `PasswordEncoder` implementation options that Spring Security provides. These are

- `NoOpPasswordEncoder`—Doesn't encode the password but keeps it in cleartext. We use this implementation only for examples. Because it doesn't hash the password, *you should never use it in a real-world scenario.*
- `StandardPasswordEncoder`—Uses SHA-256 to hash the password. This implementation is now deprecated, and *you shouldn't use it for your new implementations.* It's deprecated because it uses a hashing algorithm that we don't consider strong enough anymore, but you might still find this implementation used in existing applications. Preferably, if you find it in existing apps, you should change it with some other, more powerful password encoder.
- `Pbkdf2PasswordEncoder`—Uses the password-based key derivation function 2 (PBKDF2).
- `BCryptPasswordEncoder`—Uses a bcrypt strong hashing function to encode the password.
- `SCryptPasswordEncoder`—Uses a scrypt hashing function to encode the password.

For more about hashing and these algorithms, you can find a good discussion in chapter 2 of *Real-World Cryptography* by David Wong (Manning, 2021) at http://mng.bz/QRJw.

Let's take a look at some examples of how to create instances of these types of `PasswordEncoder` implementations. The `NoOpPasswordEncoder` doesn't encode the password. It has an implementation similar to the `PlainTextPasswordEncoder` from our example in listing 4.1. For this reason, we only use this password encoder with theoretical examples. Also, the `NoOpPasswordEncoder` class is designed as a singleton. You can't call its constructor directly from outside the class, but you can use the `NoOpPasswordEncoder.getInstance()` method to obtain the instance of the class like this:

```
PasswordEncoder p = NoOpPasswordEncoder.getInstance();
```

The `StandardPasswordEncoder` implementation provided by Spring Security uses SHA-256 to hash the password. For the `StandardPasswordEncoder`, you can provide a secret used in the hashing process. You set the value of this secret by the constructor's parameter. If you choose to call the no-arguments constructor, the implementation uses the empty string as a value for the key. However, the `StandardPasswordEncoder` is deprecated now, and I don't recommend that you use it with your new implementations. You could find older applications or legacy code that still uses it, so you should be aware of it. The next code snippet shows how to create instances of this password encoder:

```
PasswordEncoder p = new StandardPasswordEncoder();
PasswordEncoder p = new StandardPasswordEncoder("secret");
```

Another option offered by Spring Security is the `Pbkdf2PasswordEncoder` implementation that uses the PBKDF2 for password encoding. To create instances of the `Pbkdf2PasswordEncoder`, you have the following option:

```
PasswordEncoder p =
    new Pbkdf2PasswordEncoder("secret", 16, 310000, Pbkdf2PasswordEncoder.
SecretKeyFactoryAlgorithm.PBKDF2WithHmacSHA256);
```

The PBKDF2 is a pretty easy, slow-hashing function that performs an HMAC as many times as specified by an iterations argument. The first three parameters received by the last call are the value of a key used for the encoding process, the number of iterations used to encode the password, and the size of the hash. The second and third parameters can influence the strength of the result. The fourth parameter gives the hash width. You can choose the following options:

- PBKDF2WithHmacSHA1
- PBKDF2WithHmacSHA256
- PBKDF2WithHmacSHA512

It is possible to choose more or fewer iterations, as well as the length of the result. The longer the hash, the more powerful the password (the same is true for the hash width). However, be aware that performance is affected by these values: the more iterations, the more resources your application consumes. You should make a wise compromise between the resources consumed for generating the hash and the needed strength of the encoding.

> **NOTE**   In this book, I refer to several cryptography concepts that you might like to know more about. For relevant information on HMACs and other cryptography details, I recommend *Real-World Cryptography* by David Wong (Manning, 2021). Chapter 3 of that book provides detailed information about HMAC. You can find the book at http://mng.bz/XqJG.

Another excellent option offered by Spring Security is the `BCryptPasswordEncoder`, which uses a bcrypt strong hashing function to encode the password. You can instantiate the `BCryptPasswordEncoder` by calling the no-arguments constructor. However, you also have the option to specify a strength coefficient representing the log rounds (logarithmic rounds) used in the encoding process. Moreover, you can also alter the `SecureRandom` instance used for encoding:

```
PasswordEncoder p = new BCryptPasswordEncoder();
PasswordEncoder p = new BCryptPasswordEncoder(4);

SecureRandom s = SecureRandom.getInstanceStrong();
PasswordEncoder p = new BCryptPasswordEncoder(4, s);
```

The log rounds value that you provide affects the number of iterations the hashing operation uses. The number of iterations used is $2^{log\ rounds}$. For the iteration number computation, the value for the log rounds can only be between 4 and 31. You can specify this by calling one of the second or third overloaded constructors, as shown in the previous code snippet.

The last option I present to you is the `SCryptPasswordEncoder` (figure 4.2). This password encoder uses a scrypt hashing function. For the `ScryptPasswordEncoder`, you have the option to create its instances as presented in figure 4.2.

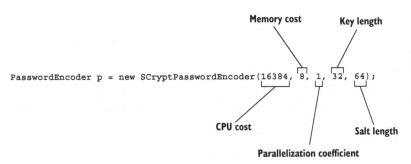

Figure 4.2   The `SCryptPasswordEncoder` constructor takes five parameters and allows you to configure CPU cost, memory cost, key length, and salt length.

4.1.4   *Multiple encoding strategies with DelegatingPasswordEncoder*

In this section, we discuss the cases in which an authentication flow must apply various implementations for matching the passwords. You'll also learn how to apply a useful tool that acts as a `PasswordEncoder` in your application. Instead of having its own implementation, this tool delegates to other objects that implement the `Password-Encoder` interface.

In some applications, you might find it useful to have various password encoders and choose from these depending on some specific configuration. A common scenario in which I find the `DelegatingPasswordEncoder` in production applications is when the encoding algorithm is changed, starting with a particular version of the application. Imagine somebody finds a vulnerability in the currently used algorithm, and you want to change it for newly registered users, but you do not want to change it for existing credentials. You end up having multiple kinds of hashes. How do you manage this situation? While it isn't the only approach for this scenario, a good choice is to use a `DelegatingPasswordEncoder` object.

The `DelegatingPasswordEncoder` is an implementation of the `PasswordEncoder` interface that, instead of implementing its encoding algorithm, delegates to another instance of an implementation of the same contract. The hash starts with a prefix naming the algorithm used to define that hash. The `DelegatingPasswordEncoder` delegates to the correct implementation of the `PasswordEncoder` based on the prefix of the password.

It sounds complicated, but with an example, you can see that it is pretty easy. Figure 4.3 presents the relationship among the `PasswordEncoder` instances. The `DelegatingPasswordEncoder` has a list of `PasswordEncoder` implementations to which it delegates. The `DelegatingPasswordEncoder` stores each of the instances in a map. The `NoOpPasswordEncoder` is assigned to the key noop, while the `BCrypt-PasswordEncoder` implementation is assigned the key bcrypt. When the password has the prefix {noop}, the `DelegatingPasswordEncoder` delegates the operation to the `NoOpPasswordEncoder` implementation. If the prefix is {bcrypt}, then the action is delegated to the `BCryptPasswordEncoder` implementation, as presented in figure 4.4.

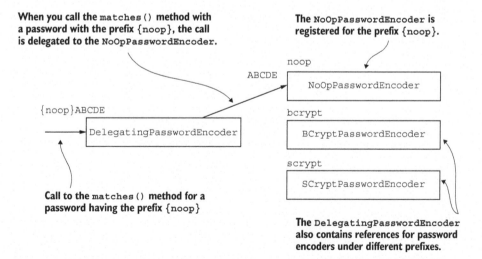

Figure 4.3 In this scenario, the `DelegatingPasswordEncoder` enlists a `NoOpPasswordEncoder` to handle passwords prefixed with {noop}, a `BCryptPasswordEncoder` for those beginning with {bcrypt}, and an `SCryptPasswordEncoder` for passwords starting with {scrypt}. When a password is accompanied by the {noop} prefix, the `DelegatingPasswordEncoder` directs the task to the `NoOpPasswordEncoder` version.

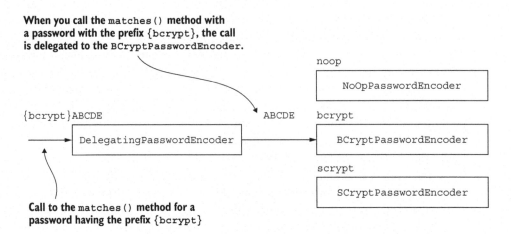

When you call the `matches()` **method with
a password with the prefix** {bcrypt}, **the call
is delegated to the** `BCryptPasswordEncoder`.

noop

NoOpPasswordEncoder

{bcrypt}ABCDE   ABCDE   bcrypt

DelegatingPasswordEncoder   BCryptPasswordEncoder

scrypt

SCryptPasswordEncoder

Call to the `matches()` **method for a
password having the prefix** {bcrypt}

Figure 4.4   Here the `DelegatingPasswordEncoder` **assigns the task of handling** {noop}-
prefixed passwords to the `NoOpPasswordEncoder`, {bcrypt}**-prefixed passwords to the**
`BCryptPasswordEncoder`, **and** {scrypt}**-prefixed passwords to the** `SCryptPasswordEncoder`. **If a
password carries the** {bcrypt} **prefix, the** `DelegatingPasswordEncoder` **routes the process to the**
`BCryptPasswordEncoder`'**s mechanism.**

Next, let's find out how to define a `DelegatingPasswordEncoder`. You start by creating a collection of instances of your desired `PasswordEncoder` implementations, and you put these together in a `DelegatingPasswordEncoder`, as in the following listing.

Listing 4.4   Creating an instance of `DelegatingPasswordEncoder`

```
@Configuration
public class ProjectConfig {

  // Omitted code

  @Bean
  public PasswordEncoder passwordEncoder() {
    Map<String, PasswordEncoder> encoders = new HashMap<>();

    encoders.put("noop", NoOpPasswordEncoder.getInstance());
    encoders.put("bcrypt", new BCryptPasswordEncoder());
    encoders.put("scrypt", new SCryptPasswordEncoder());

    return new DelegatingPasswordEncoder("bcrypt", encoders);
  }
}
```

The `DelegatingPasswordEncoder` is just a tool that acts as a `PasswordEncoder`, so you can use it when you have to choose from a collection of implementations. In listing 4.4, the declared instance of `DelegatingPasswordEncoder` contains references to a `NoOpPasswordEncoder`, a `BCryptPasswordEncoder`, and an `SCryptPasswordEncoder`, and delegates the default to the `BCryptPasswordEncoder` implementation. Based on the prefix of the hash, the `DelegatingPasswordEncoder` uses the right

PasswordEncoder implementation to match the password. This prefix has the key that identifies the password encoder to be used from the map of encoders. If there is no prefix, the DelegatingPasswordEncoder uses the default encoder. The default PasswordEncoder is the one given as the first parameter when constructing the DelegatingPasswordEncoder instance. For the code in listing 4.4, the default PasswordEncoder is bcrypt.

> **NOTE** The curly braces are part of the hash prefix, and those should surround the name of the key. For example, if the provided hash is {noop}12345, the DelegatingPasswordEncoder delegates to the NoOpPasswordEncoder that we registered for the prefix noop. Again, remember that the curly braces are mandatory in the prefix.

If the hash looks like the next code snippet, the password encoder is the one we assign to the prefix {bcrypt}, which is the BCryptPasswordEncoder. This is also the one to which the application will delegate if there is no prefix at all because we defined it as the default implementation:

```
{bcrypt}$2a$10$xn3LI/AjqicFYZFruSwve.681477XaVNaUQbr1gioaWPn4t1KsnmG
```

For convenience, Spring Security offers a way to create a DelegatingPasswordEncoder that has a map to all the standard provided implementations of PasswordEncoder. The PasswordEncoderFactories class provides a createDelegatingPassword-Encoder() static method that returns an implementation of DelegatingPassword-Encoder with a full set of PasswordEncoder mappings and bcrypt as a default encoder:

```
PasswordEncoder passwordEncoder =
PasswordEncoderFactories.createDelegatingPasswordEncoder();
```

Encoding vs. encrypting vs. hashing

In the previous sections, I often used the terms encoding, encrypting, and hashing. I want to briefly clarify these terms and the way they are used throughout the book.

Encoding refers to any transformation of a given input. For example, if we have a function x that reverses a string, function x -> y applied to ABCD produces DCBA.

Encryption is a particular type of encoding in which, to obtain the output, we provide both the input value and a key. The key makes it possible to choose afterward who should be able to reverse the function (obtain the input from the output). The simplest form of representing encryption as a function is

```
(x, k) -> y
```

where x is the input, k is the key, and y is the result of the encryption. This way, an individual who knows the key can use a known function to obtain the input from the output (y, k) -> x. We call this *reverse function decryption*. If the key used for encryption is the same as the one used for decryption, we usually call it a *symmetric* key.

(continued)

If we have two different keys for encryption ((x, k_1) -> y) and decryption ((y, k_2) -> x), then we say that the encryption is done with *asymmetric* keys. Then (k_1, k_2) is called a *key pair*. The key used for encryption, k_1, is also referred to as the *public* key, while k_2 is known as the *private* key. This way, only the owner of the private key can decrypt the data.

Hashing is a particular type of encoding, except the function is only one way. That is, from an output y of the hashing function, you cannot get back the input x. However, there should always be a way to check if an output y corresponds to an input x so we can understand the hashing as a pair of functions for encoding and matching. If hashing is x -> y, then we should also have a matching function (x,y) -> `boolean`.

Sometimes, the hashing function could also use a random value added to the input: (x, k) -> y. We refer to this value as the *salt*. The salt makes the function stronger, enforcing the difficulty of applying a reverse function to obtain the input from the result.

To summarize the contracts we have discussed and applied up to now in this book, table 4.1 briefly describes each of the components.

Table 4.1   The interfaces that represent the main contracts for authentication flow in Spring Security

Contract	Description
`UserDetails`	Represents the user as seen by Spring Security.
`GrantedAuthority`	Defines an action within the purpose of the application that is allowable to the user (for example, read, write, delete, etc.).
`UserDetailsService`	Represents the object used to retrieve user details by username.
`UserDetailsManager`	A more particular contract for `UserDetailsService`. Besides retrieving the user by username, it can also be used to mutate a collection of users or a specific user.
`PasswordEncoder`	Specifies how the password is encrypted or hashed and how to check whether a given encoded string matches a plaintext password.

4.2   Taking advantage of the Spring Security Crypto module

In this section, we discuss the Spring Security Crypto module (SSCM), which is the part of Spring Security that deals with cryptography. Using encryption and decryption functions and generating keys isn't offered out of the box with the Java language, which constrains developers when adding dependencies that provide a more accessible approach to these features.

To make our lives easier, Spring Security also provides its own solution, which enables you to reduce the dependencies of your projects by eliminating the need to use a separate library. The password encoders are also part of the SSCM, even if we have treated them separately in previous sections. In this section, we discuss what other options the SSCM offers that are related to cryptography. You'll see examples of how to use two essential features from the SSCM:

- *Key generators*—Objects used to generate keys for hashing and encryption algorithms
- *Encryptors*—Objects used to encrypt and decrypt data

4.2.1 *Using key generators*

In this section, we discuss key generators. A *key generator* is an object used to generate a specific kind of key, generally required for an encryption or hashing algorithm. The implementations of key generators that Spring Security offers are great utility tools. You'll prefer to use these implementations rather than adding another dependency to your application, and this is why I recommend that you become familiar with them. Let's see some code examples of how to create and apply the key generators.

Two interfaces represent the two main types of key generators: BytesKeyGenerator and StringKeyGenerator. We can build them directly by making use of the factory class KeyGenerators. You can use a string key generator, represented by the StringKey-Generator contract, to obtain a key as a string. Usually, we use this key as a salt value for a hashing or encryption algorithm. You can find the definition of the StringKey-Generator contract in this code snippet:

```
public interface StringKeyGenerator {

    String generateKey();

}
```

The generator has only a generateKey() method that returns a string representing the key value. The next code snippet presents an example of how to obtain a StringKeyGenerator instance and how to use it to get a salt value:

```
StringKeyGenerator keyGenerator = KeyGenerators.string();
String salt = keyGenerator.generateKey();
```

The generator creates an 8-byte key, and it encodes that as a hexadecimal string. The method returns the result of these operations as a string. The second interface describing a key generator is the BytesKeyGenerator, which is defined as follows:

```
public interface BytesKeyGenerator {

  int getKeyLength();
  byte[] generateKey();

}
```

In addition to the `generateKey()` method that returns the key as a `byte[]`, the interface defines another method that returns the key length in number of bytes. A default `BytesKeyGenerator` generates keys of 8-byte length:

```
BytesKeyGenerator keyGenerator = KeyGenerators.secureRandom();
byte [] key = keyGenerator.generateKey();
int keyLength = keyGenerator.getKeyLength();
```

In the previous code snippet, the key generator generates keys of 8-byte length. If you want to specify a different key length, you can do this when obtaining the key generator instance by providing the desired value to the `KeyGenerators.secureRandom()` method:

```
BytesKeyGenerator keyGenerator = KeyGenerators.secureRandom(16);
```

The keys generated by the `BytesKeyGenerator` created with the `KeyGenerators` `.secureRandom()` method are unique for each call of the `generateKey()` method. In some cases, we prefer an implementation that returns the same key value for each call of the same key generator. In this case, we can create a `BytesKeyGenerator` with the `KeyGenerators.shared(int length)` method. In this code snippet, `key1` and `key2` have the same value:

```
BytesKeyGenerator keyGenerator = KeyGenerators.shared(16);
byte [] key1 = keyGenerator.generateKey();
byte [] key2 = keyGenerator.generateKey();
```

4.2.2 *Encrypting and decrypting secrets using encryptors*

In this section, we apply the implementations of encryptors that Spring Security offers with code examples. An *encryptor* is an object that implements an encryption algorithm. When talking about security, encryption and decryption are common operations, so expect to need these in your application.

We often need to encrypt data either when sending it between components of the system or when persisting it. The operations provided by an encryptor are encryption and decryption. There are two types of encryptors defined by the SSCM: `BytesEncryptor` and `TextEncryptor`. While they have similar responsibilities, they treat different data types. `TextEncryptor` manages data as a string. Its methods receive strings as inputs and return strings as outputs, as you can see from the definition of its interface:

```
public interface TextEncryptor {

    String encrypt(String text);
    String decrypt(String encryptedText);

}
```

The `BytesEncryptor` is more generic. You provide its input data as a byte array:

```
public interface BytesEncryptor {

    byte[] encrypt(byte[] byteArray);
    byte[] decrypt(byte[] encryptedByteArray);

}
```

Let's find out what options we have to build and use an encryptor. The factory class `Encryptors` offers us multiple possibilities. For `BytesEncryptor`, we could use the `Encryptors.standard()` or the `Encryptors.stronger()` methods like this:

```
String salt = KeyGenerators.string().generateKey();
String password = "secret";
String valueToEncrypt = "HELLO";

BytesEncryptor e = Encryptors.standard(password, salt);
byte [] encrypted = e.encrypt(valueToEncrypt.getBytes());
byte [] decrypted = e.decrypt(encrypted);
```

Behind the scenes, the standard byte encryptor uses 256-byte AES encryption to encrypt input. To build a stronger instance of the byte encryptor, you can call the `Encryptors.stronger()` method:

```
BytesEncryptor e = Encryptors.stronger(password, salt);
```

The difference is small and happens behind the scenes, where the AES encryption on 256-bit uses Galois/Counter Mode (GCM) as the mode of operation. The standard mode uses cipher block chaining (CBC), which is considered a weaker method.

TextEncryptors come in three main types. You create these three types by calling the `Encryptors.text()` or `Encryptors.delux()`. Besides these methods to create encryptors, there is also a method that returns a dummy `TextEncryptor`, which doesn't encrypt the value. You can use the dummy `TextEncryptor` for demo examples or cases in which you want to test the performance of your application without spending time on encryption. The method that returns this no-op encryptor is `Encryptors.noOpText()`. In the following code snippet, you'll find an example of using a `TextEncryptor`. Even if it is a call to an encryptor, in the example, encrypted and valueToEncrypt are the same:

```
String valueToEncrypt = "HELLO";
TextEncryptor e = Encryptors.noOpText();
String encrypted = e.encrypt(valueToEncrypt);
```

The `Encryptors.text()` encryptor uses the `Encryptors.standard()` method to manage the encryption operation, while the `Encryptors.delux()` method uses an `Encryptors.stronger()` instance like this:

```
String salt = KeyGenerators.string().generateKey();
String password = "secret";
String valueToEncrypt = "HELLO";

TextEncryptor e = Encryptors.text(password, salt);      ◄─┐ Creates a
String encrypted = e.encrypt(valueToEncrypt);              │ TextEncryptor
String decrypted = e.decrypt(encrypted);                   │ object that uses a
                                                           │ salt and a
                                                           │ password
```

Summary

- The `PasswordEncoder` has one of the most critical responsibilities in authentication logic—dealing with passwords.
- Spring Security offers several alternatives in terms of hashing algorithms, which makes the implementation only a matter of choice.
- Spring Security Crypto module (SSCM) offers various alternatives for the implementations of key generators and encryptors.
- Key generators are utility objects that help you generate keys used with cryptographic algorithms.
- Encryptors are utility objects that help you apply data encryption and decryption.

5

A web app's security begins with filters

This chapter covers

- Working with the filter chain
- Defining custom filters
- Using Spring Security classes that implement the
  `Filter` interface

In Spring Security, HTTP filters delegate different responsibilities to an HTTP request. Furthermore, they generally manage each responsibility that must be applied to the request. The filters thus form a chain of responsibilities. A filter receives a request, executes its logic, and eventually delegates the request to the next filter in the chain (figure 5.1).

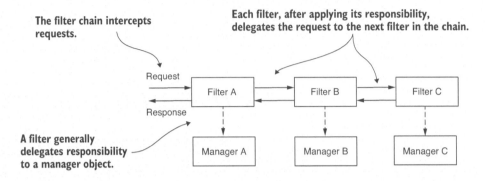

The filter chain intercepts requests.

Each filter, after applying its responsibility, delegates the request to the next filter in the chain.

A filter generally delegates responsibility to a manager object.

Figure 5.1   The request is passed to the filter chain. Every filter engages a manager to execute particular logic upon the request and then passes it down the line to the subsequent filter in the chain.

Let's take an analogy as an example. When you go to the airport, from entering the terminal to boarding the aircraft, you go through multiple filters (figure 5.2). You first present your ticket, then your passport is verified, and afterward, you go through security. At the airport gate, more filters might be applied. For example, in some cases, right before boarding, your passport and visa are verified again. This is an excellent analogy to the filter chain in Spring Security. In the same way, you customize filters in a filter chain with Spring Security. Spring Security provides filter implementations that you add to the filter chain through customization, but you can also define custom filters.

Figure 5.2   At the airport, you proceed through a series of checkpoints before finally boarding your plane. Similarly, Spring Security implements a sequence of filters that process the HTTP requests the application receives.

This chapter will discuss how to use Spring Security to customize filters that are part of the authentication and authorization architecture in a web app. For example, you might want to augment authentication by adding one more step for the user, such as checking their email address or using a one-time password. You can also add functionality referring to auditing authentication events. You'll find various scenarios where applications use auditing authentication, from debugging purposes to identifying a user's behavior. Today's technology and machine learning algorithms can improve applications, for example, by learning the user's behavior and knowing if somebody hacked their account or impersonated the user.

Knowing how to customize the HTTP filter chain of responsibilities is a valuable skill. In practice, applications come with various requirements where default configurations no longer work. You'll need to add or replace existing components of the chain. With the default implementation, you use the HTTP Basic authentication method, which allows you to rely on a username and password. However, in practical scenarios, there are plenty of situations in which you'll need more. Maybe you'll need to implement a different strategy for authentication, notify an external system about an authorization event, or log a successful or failed authentication that's used later in tracing and auditing (figure 5.3). Whatever your scenario is, Spring Security offers you the flexibility of modeling the filter chain precisely as you need it.

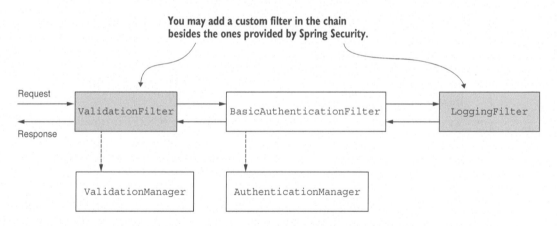

Figure 5.3 You have the option to personalize the filter chain by inserting new filters preceding, following, or in place of current ones. By doing this, you can tailor not only the authentication process but also the complete treatment of requests and responses.

5.1   *Implementing filters in the Spring Security architecture*

This section discusses the way filters and the filter chain work in Spring Security architecture. You need this general overview first to understand the implementation examples we'll work on in the sections that follow. In chapters 2 and 3, we learned that the authentication filter intercepts the request and delegates authentication responsibility further to the authorization manager. If we want to execute certain logic before authentication, we do this by inserting a filter before the authentication filter.

The filters in Spring Security architecture are typical HTTP filters. We can create filters by implementing the `Filter` interface from the jakarta.servlet package. As for any other HTTP filter, you need to override the `doFilter()` method to implement its logic. This method receives the `ServletRequest`, `ServletResponse`, and `FilterChain` as parameters:

- `ServletRequest`—Represents the HTTP request. We use the `ServletRequest` object to retrieve details about the request.
- `ServletResponse`—Represents the HTTP response. We use the `ServletResponse` object to alter the response before sending it back to the client or further along the filter chain.
- `FilterChain`—Represents the chain of filters. We use the `FilterChain` object to forward the request to the next filter in the chain.

> **NOTE** Starting with Spring Boot 3, Jakarta EE replaces the old Java EE specification. Due to this change, you'll observe that some packages changed their prefix from "javax" to "jakarta." For example, types such as `Filter`, `ServletRequest`, and `ServletResponse` were previously in the javax.servlet package, but you now find them in the jakarta.servlet package.

The *filter chain* represents a collection of filters with a defined order in which they act. Spring Security provides some filter implementations and their order for us. The following are among the provided filters:

- `BasicAuthenticationFilter` takes care of HTTP Basic authentication, if present.
- `CsrfFilter` takes care of cross-site request forgery (CSRF) protection, which we'll discuss in chapter 9.
- `CorsFilter` takes care of cross-origin resource sharing (CORS) authorization rules, which we'll also discuss in chapter 10.

You don't need to know all the filters, as you probably won't touch these directly from your code, but you do need to understand how the filter chain works and be aware of a few implementations. In this book, I only explain the filters that are essential to the various topics we discuss.

It is important to understand that an application doesn't necessarily have instances of all these filters in the chain. The chain is longer or shorter, depending on how you configure the application. For example, in chapters 2 and 3, you learned that you need to call the `httpBasic()` method of the `HttpSecurity` class if you want to use the HTTP Basic authentication method. What happens is that if you call the `httpBasic()` method, an instance of `BasicAuthenticationFilter` is added to the chain. Similarly, depending on the configurations you write, the definition of the filter chain will be affected.

You add a new filter to the chain relative to another one (figure 5.4). Or you can add a filter either before, after, or at the position of a known filter. Each position is, in fact, an index (a number), and you might find it also referred to as "the order."

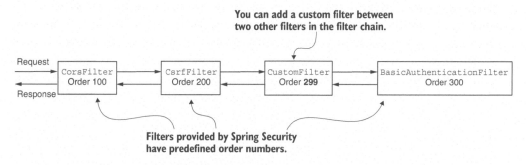

Figure 5.4   Each filter has an order number, which determines the order in which filters are applied to a request. You can add custom filters along with the filters provided by Spring Security.

If you want to learn more about the filters Spring Security provides and their configuration order, you can take a look in enum `SecurityWebFiltersOrder`, available at http://mng.bz/yZEG.

You can add two or more filters in the same position (figure 5.5). In section 5.4, we'll encounter a common case in which this might occur, one that usually creates confusion among developers.

> **NOTE**   If multiple filters have the same position, the order in which they are called is not defined.

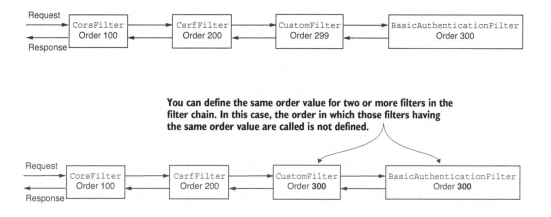

Figure 5.5   You might have multiple filters with the same order value in the chain. In this case, Spring Security doesn't guarantee the order in which they are called.

5.2   *Adding a filter before an existing one in the chain*

This section discusses applying custom HTTP filters before an existing one in the filter chain. You might encounter scenarios in which this is useful. To approach this problem in a practical way, we'll work on a project as an example, and you'll learn to easily implement a custom filter and apply it before an existing one in the filter chain. You can then adapt this example to any similar requirement you might find in a production application.

For our first custom filter implementation, let's consider a trivial scenario. We want to ensure that every request has a header called `Request-Id` (see project ssia-ch5-ex1). We assume that our application uses this header for tracking requests and that this header is mandatory. Simultaneously, we want to validate these assumptions before the application performs authentication. The authentication process might involve querying the database or other resource-consuming actions that we don't want the application to execute if the request format isn't valid. How do we do this? To solve the current requirement only takes two steps, and in the end, the filter chain looks like the one in figure 5.6:

1   *Implement the filter.* Create a `RequestValidationFilter` class that checks that the needed header exists in the request.

2   *Add the filter to the filter chain.* Do this in the configuration class, using the `SecurityFilterChain` bean.

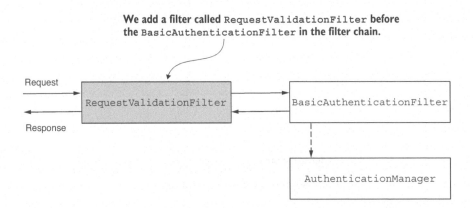

Figure 5.6   For our example, we add a `RequestValidationFilter`, which acts before the authentication filter. The `RequestValidationFilter` ensures that authentication doesn't happen if the validation of the request fails. In our case, the request must have a mandatory header named `Request-Id`.

To accomplish step 1—implementing the filter—we define a custom filter. The next listing shows the implementation.

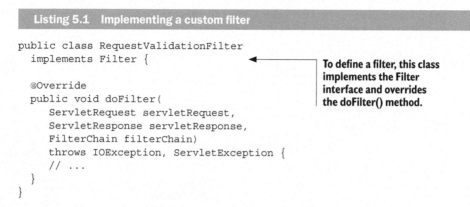

```
public class RequestValidationFilter
  implements Filter {                          ◄───    To define a filter, this class
                                                        implements the Filter
  @Override                                             interface and overrides
  public void doFilter(                                 the doFilter() method.
    ServletRequest servletRequest,
    ServletResponse servletResponse,
    FilterChain filterChain)
    throws IOException, ServletException {
    // ...
  }
}
```

Inside the doFilter() method, we write the logic of the filter. In our example, we check whether the Request-Id header exists. If it does, we forward the request to the next filter in the chain by calling the doFilter() method. If the header doesn't exist, we set an HTTP status 400 Bad Request on the response without forwarding it to the next filter in the chain (figure 5.7). Listing 5.2 presents the logic.

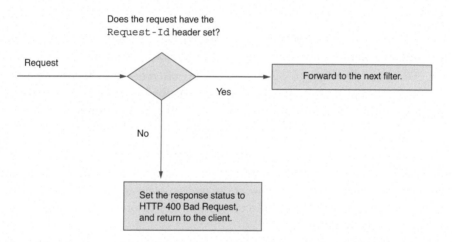

Figure 5.7   The custom filter we add before authentication checks whether the Request-Id header exists. If the header exists upon the request, the application forwards the request to be authenticated. If the header doesn't exist, the application sets the HTTP status 400 Bad Request and returns to the client.

Listing 5.2   Implementing the logic in the doFilter() method

```
@Override
public void doFilter(
  ServletRequest request,
  ServletResponse response,
  FilterChain filterChain)
    throws IOException,
          ServletException {
```

```
var httpRequest = (HttpServletRequest) request;
var httpResponse = (HttpServletResponse) response;

String requestId = httpRequest.getHeader("Request-Id");

if (requestId == null || requestId.isBlank()) {
    httpResponse.setStatus(HttpServletResponse.SC_BAD_REQUEST);
    return;
}

filterChain.doFilter(request, response);

}
```

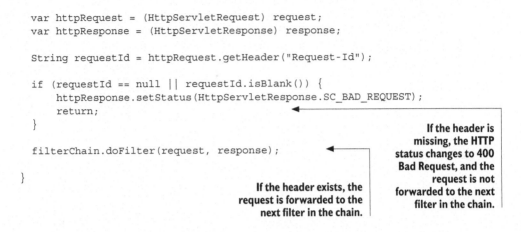

If the header exists, the request is forwarded to the next filter in the chain.

If the header is missing, the HTTP status changes to 400 Bad Request, and the request is not forwarded to the next filter in the chain.

To implement step 2, applying the filter within the configuration class, we use the `addFilterBefore()` method of the `HttpSecurity` object because we want the application to execute this custom filter before authentication. This method receives two parameters:

- *An instance of the custom filter we want to add to the chain*—In our example, this is an instance of the `RequestValidationFilter` class presented in listing 5.1.
- *The type of filter before which we add the new instance*—For this example, because the requirement is to execute the filter logic before authentication, we need to add our custom filter instance before the authentication filter. The class `Basic-AuthenticationFilter` defines the default type of the authentication filter.

Until now, we have referred to the filter dealing with authentication generally as the *authentication* filter. You'll find out in the next chapters that Spring Security also configures other filters. In chapter 9, we'll discuss cross-site request forgery (CSRF) protection, and in chapter 10, we'll discuss cross-origin resource sharing (CORS). Both capabilities also rely on filters.

The next listing shows how to add the custom filter before the authentication filter in the configuration class. To make the example simpler, we use the `permitAll()` method to allow all unauthenticated requests.

> **Listing 5.3   Configuring the custom filter before authentication**

```
@Configuration
public class ProjectConfig {                    Adds an instance of the custom filter before
                                                the authentication filter in the filter chain
    @Bean
    public SecurityFilterChain securityFilterChain(HttpSecurity http)
        throws Exception {

        http.addFilterBefore(
            new RequestValidationFilter(), BasicAuthenticationFilter.class)
```

```
    .authorizeRequests(c -> c.anyRequest().permitAll());


    return http.build();
  }
}
```

We also need a controller class and an endpoint to test the functionality. The next listing defines the controller class.

> **Listing 5.4 The controller class**

```
@RestController
public class HelloController {

  @GetMapping("/hello")
  public String hello() {
    return "Hello!";
  }
}
```

You can now run and test the application. Calling the endpoint without the header generates a response with HTTP status 400 Bad Request. If you add the header to the request, the response status becomes HTTP 200 OK, and you'll also see the response body, Hello! To call the endpoint without the Request-Id header, we use this cURL command:

```
curl -v http://localhost:8080/hello
```

This call generates the following (truncated) response:

```
...
< HTTP/1.1 400
...
```

To call the endpoint and provide the Request-Id header, we use this cURL command:

```
curl -H "Request-Id:12345" http://localhost:8080/hello
```

This call generates the following response body:

```
Hello!
```

5.3 *Adding a filter after an existing one in the chain*

This section illustrates how to add a filter after an existing one in the filter chain. This approach is used when you want to execute some logic after something already existing in the filter chain. Let's assume that you must execute some logic after the authentication process. Examples of this could be notifying a different system after certain authentication events or simply for logging and tracing purposes (figure 5.8). Like in section 5.1, we implement an example to show how to do this. You can adapt it to your needs for a real-world scenario.

For our example, we log all successful authentication events by adding a filter after the authentication filter (figure 5.8). We consider that what bypasses the authentication filter represents a successfully authenticated event, and we want to log it. Continuing the example from section 5.1, we also log the request ID received through the HTTP header.

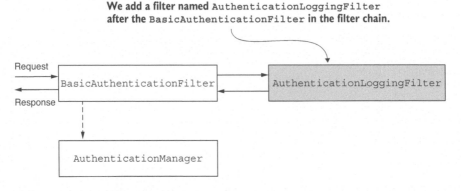

We add a filter named `AuthenticationLoggingFilter` **after the** `BasicAuthenticationFilter` **in the filter chain.**

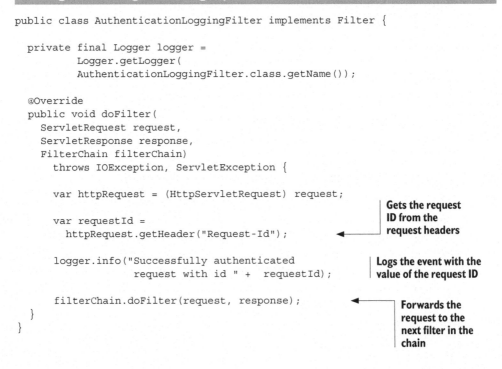

Figure 5.8 We add the `AuthenticationLoggingFilter` **after the** `BasicAuthenticationFilter` **to log the requests that the application authenticates.**

The following listing presents the definition of a filter that logs requests that pass the authentication filter.

Listing 5.5   Defining a filter to log requests

```
public class AuthenticationLoggingFilter implements Filter {

    private final Logger logger =
            Logger.getLogger(
            AuthenticationLoggingFilter.class.getName());

    @Override
    public void doFilter(
      ServletRequest request,
      ServletResponse response,
      FilterChain filterChain)
        throws IOException, ServletException {

      var httpRequest = (HttpServletRequest) request;

      var requestId =
        httpRequest.getHeader("Request-Id");

      logger.info("Successfully authenticated
                  request with id " + requestId);

      filterChain.doFilter(request, response);
    }
}
```

Gets the request ID from the request headers

Logs the event with the value of the request ID

Forwards the request to the next filter in the chain

To add the custom filter in the chain after the authentication filter, you call the add-
FilterAfter() method of HttpSecurity. The next listing shows the implementation.

> **Listing 5.6 Adding a custom filter after an existing one in the filter chain**

```
@Configuration
public class ProjectConfig {

  @Bean
  public SecurityFilterChain securityFilterChain(HttpSecurity http)
    throws Exception {

    http.addFilterBefore(
          new RequestValidationFilter(),
          BasicAuthenticationFilter.class)
       .addFilterAfter(
          new AuthenticationLoggingFilter(),
          BasicAuthenticationFilter.class)
       .authorizeRequests(c -> c.anyRequest().permitAll());


    return http.build();
  }
}
```

Adds an instance of
AuthenticationLoggingFilter
to the filter chain after the
authentication filter

After running the application and calling the endpoint, we observe that for every successful call to the endpoint, the application prints a log line in the console. For the call

```
curl -H "Request-Id:12345" http://localhost:8080/hello
```

the response body is

```
Hello!
```

In the console, you can see a line similar to

```
INFO 5876 --- [nio-8080-exec-2]
[CA]c.l.s.f.AuthenticationLoggingFilter:
[CA]Successfully authenticated request with id 12345
```

5.4   Adding a filter at the location of another in the chain

This section discusses adding a filter at the location of another one in the filter chain.
This approach can especially be used when providing a different implementation for a
responsibility that is already assumed by one of the filters known by Spring Security. A
typical scenario is authentication.

Let's assume that instead of the HTTP Basic authentication flow, you want to implement something different. Instead of using a username and a password as input credentials based on which the application authenticates the user, you need to apply another
approach. Some examples of scenarios that you could encounter are

- Identification based on a static header value for authentication
- Using a symmetric key to sign the request for authentication
- Using a one-time password (OTP) in the authentication process

In our first scenario (identification based on a static key for authentication), the client sends a string to the app in the header of the HTTP request, which is always the same. The application stores these values somewhere, most likely in a database or a secrets vault. Based on this static value, the application identifies the client.

This approach (figure 5.9) offers weak security related to authentication, but architects and developers often choose it in calls between backend applications for its simplicity. The implementations also execute fast because these don't need to do complex calculations, like in the case of applying a cryptographic signature. This way, static keys used for authentication represent a compromise where developers rely more on the infrastructure level in terms of security and also don't leave the endpoints wholly unprotected.

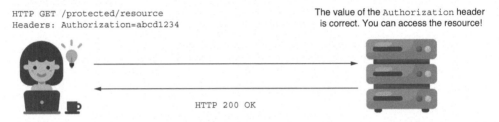

```
HTTP GET /protected/resource                        The value of the Authorization header
Headers: Authorization=abcd1234                     is correct. You can access the resource!



                                    HTTP 200 OK
```

Figure 5.9   The request contains a header with the value of the static key. If this value matches the one known by the application, it accepts the request.

In our second scenario, using symmetric keys to sign and validate requests, both client and server know the value of a key (client and server share the key). The client uses this key to sign a part of the request (for example, to sign the value of specific headers), and the server checks whether the signature is valid using the same key (figure 5.10). The server can store individual keys for each client in a database or a secrets vault. Similarly, you can use a pair of asymmetric keys.

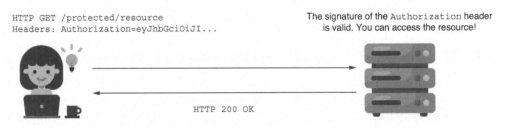

```
HTTP GET /protected/resource                        The signature of the Authorization header
Headers: Authorization=eyJhbGciOiJI...              is valid. You can access the resource!



                                    HTTP 200 OK
```

Figure 5.10   The Authorization header holds a value encrypted with a key shared between the client and server (or encrypted with a private key for which the server possesses the corresponding public key). If the application verifies the signature is valid, it permits the request to proceed.

Finally, for our third scenario, using an OTP in the authentication process, the user receives the OTP via a message or by using an authentication provider app such as Google Authenticator (figure 5.11).

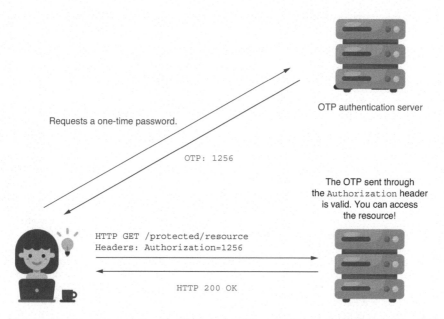

Figure 5.11 **For resource entry, the client must utilize a one-time password (OTP). This OTP is acquired from an external authentication server. Typically, applications employ this method for login processes that necessitate multi-factor authentication.**

Let's implement an example to demonstrate how to apply a custom filter. To keep the case relevant but straightforward, we focus on configuration and consider a simple logic for authentication. In our scenario, we have the value of a static key, which is the same for all requests. To be authenticated, the user must add the correct value of the static key in the `Authorization` header, as presented in figure 5.12. You can find the code for this example in the project ssia-ch5-ex2.

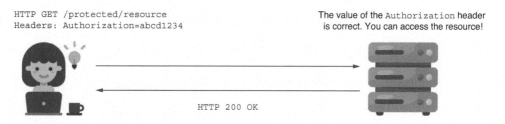

Figure 5.12 **The client adds a static key in the `Authorization` header of the HTTP request. The server checks whether it knows the key before authorizing the requests.**

We start with implementing the filter class, named `StaticKeyAuthentication-Filter`. This class reads the value of the static key from the properties file and verifies whether the value of the `Authorization` header is equal to it. If the values are the same, the filter forwards the request to the next component in the filter chain. If not, the filter sets the value 401 Unauthorized to the HTTP status of the response without forwarding the request in the filter chain. The following listing defines the `StaticKeyAuthenticationFilter` class.

Listing 5.7   The definition of the `StaticKeyAuthenticationFilter` class

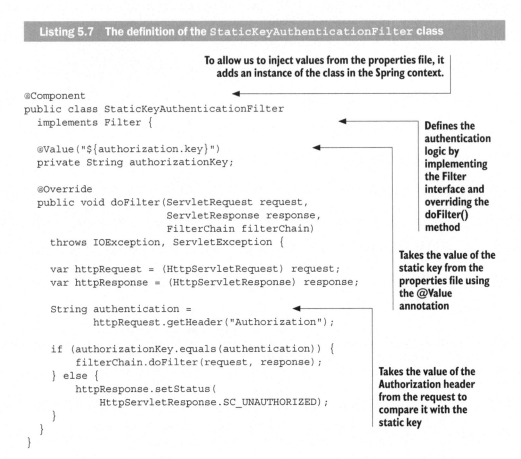

To allow us to inject values from the properties file, it adds an instance of the class in the Spring context.

```
@Component
public class StaticKeyAuthenticationFilter
  implements Filter {

  @Value("${authorization.key}")
  private String authorizationKey;

  @Override
  public void doFilter(ServletRequest request,
                       ServletResponse response,
                       FilterChain filterChain)
    throws IOException, ServletException {

    var httpRequest = (HttpServletRequest) request;
    var httpResponse = (HttpServletResponse) response;

    String authentication =
          httpRequest.getHeader("Authorization");

    if (authorizationKey.equals(authentication)) {
        filterChain.doFilter(request, response);
    } else {
        httpResponse.setStatus(
            HttpServletResponse.SC_UNAUTHORIZED);
    }
  }
}
```

Defines the authentication logic by implementing the Filter interface and overriding the doFilter() method

Takes the value of the static key from the properties file using the @Value annotation

Takes the value of the Authorization header from the request to compare it with the static key

Once we define the filter, we add it to the filter chain at the position of the class `Basic-AuthenticationFilter` by using the `addFilterAt()` method (figure 5.13).

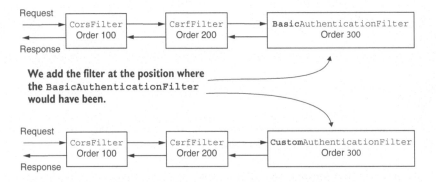

We add the filter at the position where the `BasicAuthenticationFilter` would have been.

Figure 5.13   We add our custom authentication filter at the location where the class `BasicAuthenticationFilter` would have been if we were using HTTP Basic as an authentication method. This means our custom filter has the same ordering value.

But remember what we discussed in section 5.1. When adding a filter at a specific position, Spring Security does not assume it is the only filter at that position. You might add more filters at the same location in the chain. In this case, Spring Security doesn't guarantee the order in which these will act. I repeat this because I've seen many people confused by how it works. Some developers think that when you apply a filter at a position of a known one, it will be replaced. This is not the case! We must make sure we do not add filters that we don't need.

> **NOTE** I advise you not to add multiple filters at the same position in the chain. When you add more filters to the same location, the order in which they are used is not defined. It makes sense to have a definite order in which filters are called. Having a known order makes your application easier to understand and maintain.

In listing 5.8, you can find the definition of the configuration class that adds the filter. Observe that we don't call the `httpBasic()` method from the `HttpSecurity` class here because we don't want the `BasicAuthenticationFilter` instance to be added to the filter chain.

Listing 5.8 Adding the filter in the configuration class

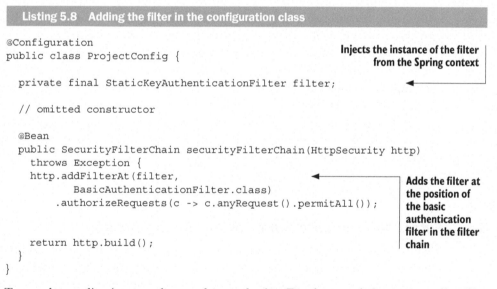

```
@Configuration
public class ProjectConfig {

    private final StaticKeyAuthenticationFilter filter;

    // omitted constructor

    @Bean
    public SecurityFilterChain securityFilterChain(HttpSecurity http)
      throws Exception {
      http.addFilterAt(filter,
            BasicAuthenticationFilter.class)
          .authorizeRequests(c -> c.anyRequest().permitAll());

      return http.build();
    }
}
```

Injects the instance of the filter from the Spring context

Adds the filter at the position of the basic authentication filter in the filter chain

To test the application, we also need an endpoint. For that, we define a controller, like in listing 5.4. You should add a value for the static key on the server in the application .properties file, as shown in

```
authorization.key=SD9cICjlle
```

> **NOTE** Storing passwords, keys, or any other data not meant to be seen by everybody in the properties file is never a good idea for a production application. In our examples, we use this approach for simplicity and to let you focus on the Spring Security configurations we make. But in real-world scenarios, make sure to use a secrets vault to store such kinds of details.

We can now test the application. It is expected that the app will allow requests having the correct value for the `Authorization` header and reject others, returning an HTTP 401 Unauthorized status on the response. The code snippets that follow present the `curl` calls used to test the application. If you use the same value set on the server side for the `Authorization` header, the call is successful, and you'll see the response body, `Hello!` The call

```
curl -H "Authorization:SD9cICjl1e" http://localhost:8080/hello
```

returns this response body:

```
Hello!
```

With the following call, if the `Authorization` header is missing or is incorrect, the response status is HTTP 401 Unauthorized:

```
curl -v http://localhost:8080/hello
```

The response status is

```
...
< HTTP/1.1 401
...
```

In this case, because we don't configure a `UserDetailsService`, Spring Boot configures one automatically, as you learned in chapter 2. But in our scenario, you don't need a `UserDetailsService` at all because the concept of the user doesn't exist. We only validate that the user requesting to call an endpoint on the server knows a given value. Application scenarios are not usually this simple, and they often require a `UserDetailsService`. However, if you anticipate or have a case where this component is not needed, you can disable autoconfiguration. To disable the configuration of the default `UserDetailsService`, you can use the `exclude` attribute of the `@SpringBootApplication` annotation on the main class:

```
@SpringBootApplication(exclude =
  {UserDetailsServiceAutoConfiguration.class })
```

5.5   *Filter implementations provided by Spring Security*

This section discusses classes provided by Spring Security that implement the `Filter` interface. In the examples, we define the filter by implementing this interface directly.

Spring Security offers a few abstract classes that implement the `Filter` interface and for which you can extend your filter definitions. These classes also add functionality your implementations could benefit from when you extend them. For example, you could extend the `GenericFilterBean` class, which allows you to use initialization parameters that you would define in a web.xml descriptor file where applicable. A more useful class that extends the `GenericFilterBean` is `OncePerRequestFilter`. When adding a filter to the chain, the framework doesn't guarantee it will be called only once per request. `OncePerRequestFilter`, as the name suggests, implements logic to make sure that the filter's `doFilter()` method is executed only one time per request.

If you need such functionality in your application, use the classes that Spring provides. However, if you don't need them, I'd always recommend going as simple as possible with your implementations. Too often, I've seen developers extending the GenericFilterBean class instead of implementing the Filter interface in functionalities that don't require the custom logic added by the GenericFilterBean class. When asked why, it seems they don't know. They probably copied the implementation as they found it in examples on the web.

To make it crystal clear how to use such a class, let's write an example. The logging functionality we implemented in section 5.3 is a great candidate for using OncePer-RequestFilter. We want to avoid logging the same requests multiple times. Spring Security doesn't guarantee the filter won't be called more than once, so we have to take care of this ourselves. The easiest way is to implement the filter using the OncePer-RequestFilter class. I wrote this in a separate project called ssia-ch5-ex3.

In listing 5.9, you'll find the change I made for the AuthenticationLogging-Filter class. Instead of implementing the Filter interface directly, as was the case in the example in section 5.3, it now extends the OncePerRequestFilter class. The method we override here is doFilterInternal(). You can find this code in project ssia-ch5-ex3.

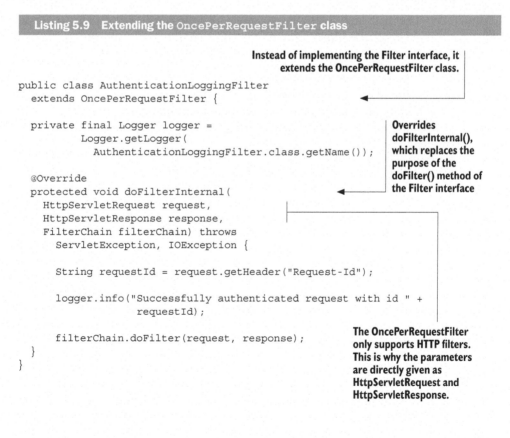

Listing 5.9 Extending the `OncePerRequestFilter` **class**

> Instead of implementing the Filter interface, it
> extends the OncePerRequestFilter class.

```
public class AuthenticationLoggingFilter
  extends OncePerRequestFilter {

  private final Logger logger =
        Logger.getLogger(
          AuthenticationLoggingFilter.class.getName());

  @Override
  protected void doFilterInternal(
    HttpServletRequest request,
    HttpServletResponse response,
    FilterChain filterChain) throws
      ServletException, IOException {

    String requestId = request.getHeader("Request-Id");

    logger.info("Successfully authenticated request with id " +
                requestId);

    filterChain.doFilter(request, response);
  }
}
```

> Overrides
> doFilterInternal(),
> which replaces the
> purpose of the
> doFilter() method of
> the Filter interface

> The OncePerRequestFilter
> only supports HTTP filters.
> This is why the parameters
> are directly given as
> HttpServletRequest and
> HttpServletResponse.

A few short observations about the `OncePerRequestFilter` class that you might find useful:

- *It supports only HTTP requests, but that's actually what we always use.* The advantage is that it casts the types, and we directly receive the requests as `HttpServlet-Request` and `HttpServletResponse`. Remember, with the `Filter` interface, we had to cast the request and the response.
- *You can implement logic to decide whether the filter is applied.* Even if you added the filter to the chain, you might decide it doesn't apply to certain requests. You set this by overriding the `shouldNotFilter(HttpServletRequest)` method. By default, the filter applies to all requests.
- *By default, a* `OncePerRequestFilter` *doesn't apply to asynchronous requests or error dispatch requests.* You can change this behavior by overriding the methods `should-NotFilterAsyncDispatch()` and `shouldNotFilterErrorDispatch()`.

If you find any of these characteristics of the `OncePerRequestFilter` useful in your implementation, I recommend using this class to define your filters.

Summary

- The first layer of the web application architecture, which intercepts HTTP requests, is a filter chain. As for other components in Spring Security architecture, you can customize them to match your requirements.
- You can customize the filter chain by adding new filters before, after, or at the position of an existing filter.
- You can have multiple filters at the same position of an existing filter. In this case, the order in which the filters are executed is not defined.
- Changing the filter chain helps you customize authentication and authorization to match the requirements of your application.

Implementing
authentications
6

This chapter covers

- Implementing authentication logic using a
  custom `AuthenticationProvider`
- Using the HTTP Basic and form-based login
  authentication methods
- Understanding and managing the `Security-`
  `Context` component

Chapters 3 and 4 covered a few of the components acting in the authentication flow. We discussed `UserDetails` and how to define the prototype to describe a user in Spring Security. Next, we used `UserDetails` in examples that showed how the `UserDetailsService` and `UserDetailsManager` contracts work and how to implement them. We discussed and used the leading implementations of these interfaces in examples as well. Finally, you learned how a `PasswordEncoder` manages passwords and how to use one, as well as the Spring Security crypto module (SSCM) with its encryptors and key generators.

The `AuthenticationProvider` layer, however, is responsible for the logic of authentication. The `AuthenticationProvider` is where you find the conditions and instructions that decide whether to authenticate a request. The component that delegates this responsibility to the `AuthenticationProvider` is the

`AuthenticationManager`, which receives the request from the HTTP filter layer, and it was discussed in chapter 5. In this chapter, we'll look at the authentication process, which has only two possible results:

- *The entity making the request is not authenticated.* The user is not recognized, and the application rejects the request without delegating to the authorization process. Usually, the response status sent back to the client in this case is HTTP 401 Unauthorized.
- *The entity making the request is authenticated.* The details about the requester are stored so that the application can use them for authorization. As you'll find out in this chapter, `SecurityContext` is responsible for the details regarding the current authenticated request.

To remind you of the actors and the links between them, figure 6.1 shows the diagram that we already saw in chapter 2.

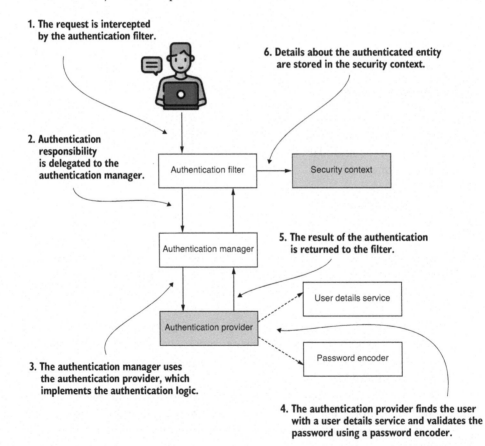

1. The request is intercepted by the authentication filter.

6. Details about the authenticated entity are stored in the security context.

2. Authentication responsibility is delegated to the authentication manager.

Authentication filter

Security context

Authentication manager

5. The result of the authentication is returned to the filter.

User details service

Authentication provider

Password encoder

3. The authentication manager uses the authentication provider, which implements the authentication logic.

4. The authentication provider finds the user with a user details service and validates the password using a password encoder.

Figure 6.1   The authentication flow in Spring Security. This process outlines the method by which the application recognizes the individual submitting a request. The elements that are the focus of this chapter are highlighted. In this context, the `AuthenticationProvider` is responsible for carrying out the authentication procedure, and the `SecurityContext` retains the information regarding the request that has been authenticated.

This chapter covers the remaining parts of the authentication flow (the shaded boxes in figure 6.1). Then, in chapters 7 and 8, you'll learn how authorization works, which is the process that follows authentication in the HTTP request. First, we need to discuss how to implement the `AuthenticationProvider` interface. You need to know how Spring Security understands a request in the authentication process.

   To show a clear description of how to represent an authentication request, we'll start with the `Authentication` interface. Once we discuss it, we can go further and observe what happens with the details of a request after successful authentication. Then we can discuss the `SecurityContext` interface and the way Spring Security manages it. Near the end of the chapter, you'll learn how to customize the HTTP Basic authentication method. We'll also discuss another option for authentication that can be used in our applications—the form-based login.

6.1 Understanding the AuthenticationProvider

In enterprise applications, you might find yourself in a situation in which the default implementation of authentication based on username and password does not apply. In addition, when it comes to authentication, your application may require the implementation of several scenarios (figure 6.2). For example, you might want the user to be able to prove who they are by using a code received in an SMS message or displayed by a specific application. Or you might need to implement authentication scenarios where the user has to provide a certain kind of key stored in a file. You might even need to use a representation of the user's fingerprint to implement the authentication logic. A framework's purpose is to be flexible enough to allow you to implement any of these scenarios.

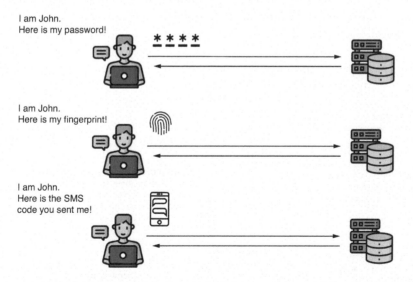

Figure 6.2   An application may require various methods of authentication implementation. Although a username and password suffice for most situations, there are instances where the process of authenticating a user may be more complex.

A framework usually provides a set of the most used implementations, but of course, it cannot cover all the possible options. In terms of Spring Security, you can use the `AuthenticationProvider` contract to define any custom authentication logic. In this section, you'll learn to represent the authentication event by implementing the `Authentication` interface and then create your custom authentication logic with an `AuthenticationProvider`. To achieve our goal

- In section 6.1.1, we analyze how Spring Security represents the authentication event.
- In section 6.1.2, we discuss the `AuthenticationProvider` contract, which is responsible for the authentication logic.
- In section 6.1.3, you'll write custom authentication logic by implementing the `AuthenticationProvider` contract in an example.

6.1.1 *Representing the request during authentication*

This section discusses how Spring Security understands a request during the authentication process. It is important to touch on this before diving into implementing custom authentication logic. As you'll learn in section 6.1.2, to implement a custom `AuthenticationProvider`, you first need to understand how to describe the authentication event. Here, we'll take a look at the contract representing authentication and discuss the methods you need to know.

`Authentication` is one of the essential interfaces involved in the process with the same name. The `Authentication` interface represents the authentication request event and holds the details of the entity that requests access to the application. You can use the information related to the authentication request event during and after the authentication process. The user requesting access to the application is called a *principal*. If you've ever used Java Security in any app, you probably know that an interface named `Principal` represents the same concept. The `Authentication` interface of Spring Security extends this contract (figure 6.3).

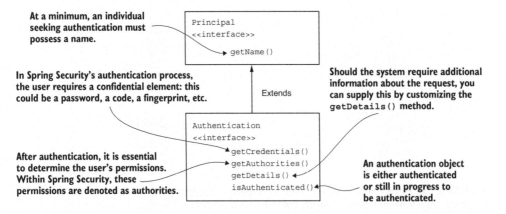

Figure 6.3 The `Authentication` agreement extends the `Principal` agreement. It introduces additional stipulations, such as the necessity for a password or the option to provide further specifics regarding the authentication request. Certain aspects, such as the array of authorities, are specific to Spring Security.

The `Authentication` contract in Spring Security not only represents a principal, but it also adds information on whether the authentication process finishes, as well as a collection of authorities. The fact that this contract was designed to extend the `Principal` contract from Java Security is a plus in terms of compatibility with implementations of other frameworks and applications. This flexibility allows for more facile migrations to Spring Security from applications that implement authentication in another fashion.

Let's find out more about the design of the `Authentication` interface in the following listing.

> **Listing 6.1 The `Authentication` interface as declared in Spring Security**

```
public interface Authentication extends Principal, Serializable {

    Collection<? extends GrantedAuthority> getAuthorities();
    Object getCredentials();
    Object getDetails();
    Object getPrincipal();
    boolean isAuthenticated();
    void setAuthenticated(boolean isAuthenticated)
        throws IllegalArgumentException;
}
```

For the moment, the only methods of this contract that you need to learn are these:

- `isAuthenticated()`—Returns true if the authentication process ends or false if the authentication process is still in progress
- `getCredentials()`—Returns a password or any secret used in the authentication process
- `getAuthorities()`—Returns a collection of granted authorities for the authenticated request

We'll discuss the other methods for the `Authentication` contract in later chapters, where appropriate for the implementations considered.

6.1.2 Implementing custom authentication logic

This section deals with implementing custom authentication logic. We analyze the Spring Security contract related to this responsibility to understand its definition. With these details, you can implement custom authentication logic with a code example in section 6.1.3.

The `AuthenticationProvider` in Spring Security takes care of the authentication logic. The default implementation of the `AuthenticationProvider` interface delegates the responsibility of finding the system's user to a `UserDetailsService`. It uses the `PasswordEncoder` as well for password management in the authentication process. The following listing gives the definition of the `AuthenticationProvider`, which you need to define a custom authentication provider for your application.

Listing 6.2 The `AuthenticationProvider` interface

```
public interface AuthenticationProvider {

  Authentication authenticate(Authentication authentication)
    throws AuthenticationException;

  boolean supports(Class<?> authentication);
}
```

The `AuthenticationProvider` responsibility is strongly coupled with the `Authentication` contract. The `authenticate()` method receives an `Authentication` object as a parameter and returns an `Authentication` object. We implement the `authenticate()` method to define the authentication logic. Here, we quickly summarize the way you should implement the `authenticate()` method:

- The method should throw an `AuthenticationException` if the authentication fails.
- If the method receives an authentication object not supported by your implementation of `AuthenticationProvider`, then the method should return null. This way, we have the possibility of using multiple `Authentication` types separated at the HTTP-filter level.
- The method should return an `Authentication` instance representing a fully authenticated object. For this instance, the `isAuthenticated()` method returns true, and it contains all the necessary details about the authenticated entity. Usually, the application also removes sensitive data, such as a password from this instance. After a successful authentication, the password is no longer required, and keeping these details can potentially expose them to unwanted eyes.

The second method in the `AuthenticationProvider` interface is `supports (Class<?> authentication)`. You can implement this method to return true if the current `AuthenticationProvider` supports the type provided as an `Authentication` object. Observe that even if this method returns true for an object, there is still a chance that the `authenticate()` method will reject the request by returning null. Spring Security is designed to be more flexible, allowing users to implement an `AuthenticationProvider` that can reject an authentication request based on its details, and not only based on its type.

An analogy of how the authentication manager and authentication provider work together to validate or invalidate an authentication request is having a more complex lock for your door. You can open this lock either by using a card or an old-fashioned physical key (figure 6.4). The lock itself is the authentication manager that decides whether to open the door. To make that decision, it delegates to the two authentication providers: one that knows how to validate the card or the other that knows how to verify the physical key. If you present a card to open the door, the authentication provider that works only with physical keys complains that it is not familiar with this kind of authentication. However, the other provider supports this kind of authentication and verifies whether the card is valid for the door. This is the purpose of the `supports()` methods.

In addition to testing the authentication type, Spring Security adds one more layer for flexibility. The door's lock can recognize multiple kinds of cards. In this case, when you present a card, one of the authentication providers could say, "I understand this as being a card. But it isn't the type of card I can validate!" This happens when `supports()` returns true but `authenticate()` returns null.

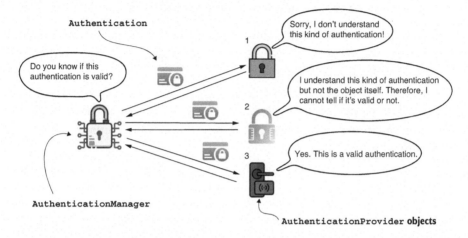

Figure 6.4 The `AuthenticationManager` delegates to one of the available authentication providers. The `AuthenticationProvider` might not support the provided authentication type. However, if it does support the object type, it might not know how to authenticate that specific object. The authentication is evaluated, and an `AuthenticationProvider` that can say whether or not the request is correct responds to the `AuthenticationManager`.

Figure 6.5 shows the alternative scenario where one of the `AuthenticationProvider` objects recognizes the `Authentication` but decides it's not valid. In this case, the result will be an `AuthenticationException` that ends up as a 401 Unauthorized HTTP status in the HTTP response in a web app.

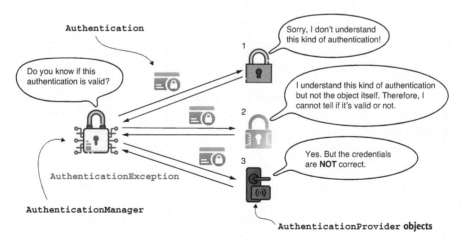

Figure 6.5 If none of the `AuthenticationProvider` objects recognize the `Authentication` or any of them rejects it, the result is an `AuthenticationException`.

6.1.3   *Applying custom authentication logic*

In this section, we implement custom authentication logic. You can find this example in the project ssia-ch6-ex1. With this example, you apply what you've learned about the `Authentication` and `AuthenticationProvider` interfaces in sections 6.1.1 and 6.1.2. In listings 6.3 and 6.4, we build an example of how to implement a custom `AuthenticationProvider`. These steps, also presented in figure 6.5, are as follows:

1 Declare a class that implements the `AuthenticationProvider` contract.
2 Decide which kinds of `Authentication` objects are supported by the new `AuthenticationProvider`.
3 Implement the `supports(Class<?> c)` method to specify which type of authentication is supported by the `AuthenticationProvider` that we define.
4 Implement the `authenticate(Authentication a)` method to implement the authentication logic.
5 Register an instance of the new `AuthenticationProvider` implementation with Spring Security.

> **Listing 6.3   Overriding the `supports()` method of the `AuthenticationProvider`**

```
@Component
public class CustomAuthenticationProvider
  implements AuthenticationProvider {

  // Omitted code

  @Override
  public boolean supports(Class<?> authenticationType) {
    return authenticationType
           .equals(UsernamePasswordAuthenticationToken.class);
  }
}
```

In listing 6.3, we define a new class that implements the `AuthenticationProvider` interface. We mark the class with `@Component` to have an instance of its type in the context managed by Spring. Then we must decide what kind of `Authentication` interface implementation this `AuthenticationProvider` supports. That depends on what type we expect to be provided as a parameter to the `authenticate()` method. If we don't customize anything at the authentication filter level (as discussed in chapter 5), then the class `UsernamePasswordAuthenticationToken` defines the type. This class is an implementation of the `Authentication` interface and represents a standard authentication request with username and password.

With this definition, we made the `AuthenticationProvider` support a specific kind of key. Once we have specified the scope of our `AuthenticationProvider`, we implement the authentication logic by overriding the `authenticate()` method, as shown in following listing.

Listing 6.4 Implementing the authentication logic

```
@Component
public class CustomAuthenticationProvider
  implements AuthenticationProvider {

  private final UserDetailsService userDetailsService;
  private final PasswordEncoder passwordEncoder;

  // Omitted constructor

  @Override
  public Authentication authenticate(Authentication authentication) {
    String username = authentication.getName();
    String password = authentication.getCredentials().toString();

    UserDetails u = userDetailsService.loadUserByUsername(username);

    if (passwordEncoder.matches(password, u.getPassword())) {
      return new UsernamePasswordAuthenticationToken(
            username,
            password,
            u.getAuthorities());                          ◀──  If the password
    } else {                                                   matches, it returns
      throw new BadCredentialsException                        an implementation
              ("Something went wrong!");     ◀──               of the Authentication
    }                                                          contract with the
  }                                                            necessary details.
          If the password doesn't match, it throws an
  // Omitted code   exception of type AuthenticationException.
}                   BadCredentialsException inherits from
                    AuthenticationException.
```

The logic in listing 6.4 is simple, and figure 6.6 provides a visual presentation of this logic. We use the `UserDetailsService` implementation to get the `UserDetails`. If the user doesn't exist, the `loadUserByUsername()` method should throw an `AuthenticationException`. In this case, the authentication process stops, and the HTTP filter sets the response status to HTTP 401 Unauthorized. If the username does exist, we can further check the user's password with the `matches()` method of the `PasswordEncoder` from the context. If the password does not match, then again, an `AuthenticationException` should be thrown. If the password is correct, the `AuthenticationProvider` returns an instance of `Authentication` marked as "authenticated," which contains the request details.

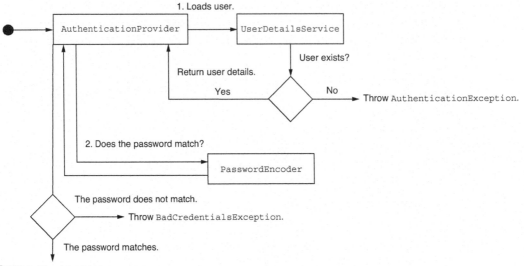

1. Loads user.

AuthenticationProvider → UserDetailsService

User exists?

Return user details.

Yes   No

Throw AuthenticationException.

2. Does the password match?

PasswordEncoder

The password does not match.

→ Throw BadCredentialsException.

The password matches.

Return Authentication.

Figure 6.6 The `AuthenticationProvider` **enacts a tailored authentication procedure. It confirms the authentication request by retrieving user details through a specific** `UserDetailsService` **implementation, and it validates the password using a** `PasswordEncoder` **if the password is correct. If the user is not found or the password is inaccurate, the** `AuthenticationProvider` **will raise an** `AuthenticationException`.

To plug in the new implementation of the `AuthenticationProvider`, we define a `SecurityFilterChain` bean. This is demonstrated in the following listing.

Listing 6.5 Registering the `AuthenticationProvider` **in the configuration class**

```
@Configuration
public class ProjectConfig {

  private final AuthenticationProvider authenticationProvider;

  // Omitted constructor

  @Bean
  public SecurityFilterChain securityFilterChain(HttpSecurity http)
    throws Exception {

    http.httpBasic(Customizer.withDefaults());

    http.authenticationProvider(authenticationProvider);

    http.authorizeHttpRequests(c -> c.anyRequest().authenticated());

    return http.build();
  }

  // Omitted code
}
```

NOTE In listing 6.5, the dependency injection is employed with a field declared using the `AuthenticationProvider` interface. Spring recognizes the `AuthenticationProvider` as an interface (which is an abstraction). However, Spring knows that it needs to find an instance of an implementation in its context for that specific interface. In our case, the implementation is the instance of `CustomAuthenticationProvider`, which is the only one of this type that we declared and added to the Spring context using the `@Component` annotation. For a refresher on dependency injection, I recommend *Spring Start Here* (Manning, 2021), another book I wrote.

That's it! You successfully customized the implementation of the `Authentication-Provider`. You can now customize the authentication logic for your application where you need it.

How to fail in application design

Applying a framework incorrectly leads to a less maintainable application. What is worse, sometimes those who fail in using the framework believe that it's the framework's fault. Let me tell you a story.

One winter, the head of development in a company I worked with as a consultant called me to help them with the implementation of a new feature. They needed to apply a custom authentication method in a component of their system developed with Spring in its early days. Unfortunately, when implementing the application's class design, the developers didn't rely properly on Spring Security's backbone architecture.

They only used the filter chain, reimplementing entire features from Spring Security as custom code.

Developers observed that with time, customizations became increasingly difficult. However, nobody took action to redesign the component properly and use the contracts as intended in Spring Security. Much of the difficulty came from not knowing Spring's capabilities. One of the lead developers said, "It's only the fault of this Spring Security! This framework is hard to apply, and it's difficult to use it with any customization." I was a bit shocked at his observation. I know that Spring Security is sometimes difficult to understand and that the framework is known for not having a soft learning curve. But I've never experienced a situation in which I couldn't find a way to design an easy-to-customize class with Spring Security!

We investigated the problem together, and I realized the application developers used perhaps only 10% of what Spring Security has to offer. Then I presented a two-day workshop on Spring Security, focusing on what we could do for the specific system component they had to change and how to do it.

Everything ended with the decision to completely rewrite a lot of custom code to rely on Spring Security correctly and thus make the application easier to extend to meet their concerns for security implementations. We also discovered some other problems unrelated to Spring Security, but that's another story.

(continued)

Here are a few lessons for you to take from this story:

- A framework, and especially the one widely used in applications, is written by many smart individuals, and it's hard to believe that it can be implemented badly. Always analyze your application before concluding that any problem may be the framework's fault.
- When deciding to use a framework, make sure you understand, at least, its basics.
- Be mindful of the resources you use to learn about the framework. Sometimes, articles you find on the web show how to do quick workarounds and not necessarily how to correctly implement a class design.
- Use multiple sources in your research. To clarify your misunderstandings, write a proof of concept when unsure how to use something.
- If you decide to use a framework, use it as much as possible for its intended purpose. For example, say you use Spring Security, and you observe that for security implementations, you tend to write more custom code instead of relying on what the framework offers. You should question why this happens.

When we rely on functionalities implemented by a framework, we enjoy several benefits. We know they are tested, and there are fewer changes that include vulnerabilities. Likewise, a good framework relies on abstractions, which help you create maintainable applications. Remember that when you write your own implementations, you're more susceptible to including vulnerabilities.

6.2 *Using the SecurityContext*

This section discusses the security context. We analyze how it works, how to access data, and how the application manages it in different thread-related scenarios. Once you finish this section, you'll know how to configure the security context for various situations. This way, you can use the details about the authenticated user stored by the security context in configuring authorization in chapters 7 and 8.

It is likely that you will need details about the authenticated entity following the authentication process. You might, for example, need to refer to the username or the authorities of the currently authenticated user. Is this information still accessible after the authentication process finishes? Once the AuthenticationManager completes the authentication process successfully, it stores the Authentication instance for the rest of the request (see figure 6.7). The instance storing the Authentication object is called the *security context*.

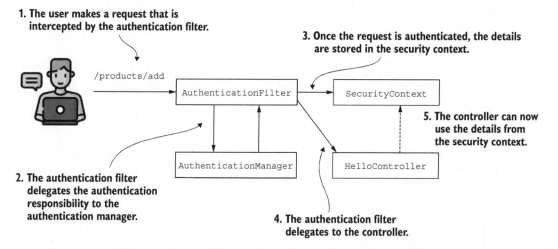

1. The user makes a request that is intercepted by the authentication filter.

3. Once the request is authenticated, the details are stored in the security context.

2. The authentication filter delegates the authentication responsibility to the authentication manager.

4. The authentication filter delegates to the controller.

5. The controller can now use the details from the security context.

Figure 6.7   After successful authentication, the authentication filter stores the details of the authenticated entity in the security context. From there, the controller implementing the action mapped to the request can access these details when needed.

The security context of Spring Security is described by the `SecurityContext` interface and defined in the following listing.

Listing 6.6   The `SecurityContext` interface

```
public interface SecurityContext extends Serializable {

    Authentication getAuthentication();
    void setAuthentication(Authentication authentication);
}
```

As you can tell from the contract definition, the primary responsibility of the Security-Context is to store the Authentication object. But how is the SecurityContext itself managed? Spring Security offers three strategies to manage the SecurityContext with an object in the role of a manager. It's named the SecurityContextHolder:

- MODE_THREADLOCAL—Allows each thread to store its own details in the security context. In a thread-per-request web application, this is a common approach, as each request has an individual thread.
- MODE_INHERITABLETHREADLOCAL—Similar to MODE_THREADLOCAL, but it also instructs Spring Security to copy the security context to the next thread in case of an asynchronous method. This way, we can say that the new thread running the @Async method inherits the security context. The @Async annotation is used with methods to instruct Spring to call the annotated method on a separate thread.
- MODE_GLOBAL—Makes all the threads of the application see the same security context instance.

In addition to these three strategies for managing the security context provided by Spring Security, this section also illustrates what happens when you define your own threads that are not known by Spring. As you will learn, for these cases, you need to explicitly copy the details from the security context to the new thread. Spring Security cannot automatically manage objects that are not in Spring's context, but it offers some great utility classes.

6.2.1   Using a holding strategy for the security context

The first strategy for managing the security context is the MODE_THREADLOCAL strategy, and it is also the default for managing the security context used by Spring Security. With this strategy, Spring Security uses ThreadLocal to manage the context. Thread-Local is an implementation provided by the JDK. This implementation works as a collection of data but ensures that each thread of the application can only see the data stored in its dedicated part of the collection. This way, each request has access to its security context. No thread will have access to another's ThreadLocal. That means that in a web application, each request can see only its own security context. We could say that this is also what you generally want to have for a backend web application.

Figure 6.8 offers an overview of this functionality. Each request (A, B, and C) has its own allocated thread (T1, T2, and T3), so each request only sees the details stored in its own security context. However, this also means that if a new thread is created (for example, when an asynchronous method is called), the new thread will have its own security context as well. The details from the parent thread (the original thread of the request) are not copied to the security context of the new thread.

> **NOTE** Here we discuss a traditional servlet application where each request is tied to a thread. This architecture only applies to the traditional servlet application where each request has its own thread assigned. It does not apply to reactive applications. We'll discuss the security for reactive approaches in detail in chapter 17.

Being the default strategy for managing the security context, this process does not need to be explicitly configured. Just ask for the security context from the holder using the static getContext() method wherever you need it after the end of the authentication process. In listing 6.7, you find an example of obtaining the security context in one of the application endpoints. From the security context, you can further get the Authentication object, which stores the details about the authenticated entity. You can find the examples discussed in this section as part of the project ssia-ch6-ex2.

After authentication, request A will have the details about the authenticated entity in security context A.

The new thread has its own security context A', but the details from the original thread of the request weren't copied.

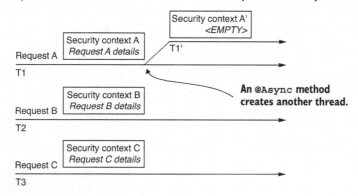

Each request has its own thread and access to one security context.

Figure 6.8 Each request has its own thread represented by an arrow. Each thread has access only to its own security context details. When a new thread is created (for example, by an @Async method), the details from the parent thread aren't copied.

Listing 6.7 Obtaining the `SecurityContext` from the `SecurityContextHolder`

```
@GetMapping("/hello")
public String hello() {
  SecurityContext context = SecurityContextHolder.getContext();
  Authentication a = context.getAuthentication();

  return "Hello, " + a.getName() + "!";
}
```

Obtaining the authentication from the context is even more comfortable at the endpoint level, as Spring knows to inject it directly into the method parameters. You don't need to refer every time to the `SecurityContextHolder` class explicitly. This approach, as presented in the following listing, is better.

Listing 6.8 Spring injects `Authentication` value in the parameter of the method

```
@GetMapping("/hello")
public String hello(Authentication a) {
  return "Hello, " + a.getName() + "!";
}
```
Spring Boot injects the current Authentication in the method parameter.

When calling the endpoint with a correct user, the response body contains the username. For example:

```
curl -u user:99ff79e3-8ca0-401c-a396-0a8625ab3bad http://localhost:8080/hello
Hello, user!
```

6.2.2   *Using a holding strategy for asynchronous calls*

It is easy to stick with the default strategy for managing the security context. In a lot of cases, it is the only thing you need. MODE_THREADLOCAL offers the ability to isolate the security context for each thread, and it makes the security context more natural to understand and manage. However, there are also cases in which this does not apply.

The situation gets more complicated if we have to deal with multiple threads per request. Look at what happens if you make the endpoint asynchronous. The thread that executes the method is no longer the same thread that serves the request. Think about an endpoint like the one presented in the next listing.

> **Listing 6.9   An @Async method served by a different thread**

```
                                              Being @Async, the method is
                                              executed on a separate thread.
@GetMapping("/bye")
@Async
public void goodbye() {
   SecurityContext context = SecurityContextHolder.getContext();
   String username = context.getAuthentication().getName();

   // do something with the username
}
```

To enable the functionality of the @Async annotation, I have also created a configuration class and annotated it with @EnableAsync:

```
@Configuration
@EnableAsync
public class ProjectConfig {

}
```

> **NOTE**   Sometimes in articles or forums, the configuration annotations are placed over the main class. For example, you might find that certain examples use the @EnableAsync annotation directly over the main class. This approach is technically correct because we annotate the main class of a Spring Boot application with the @SpringBootApplication annotation, which includes the @Configuration characteristic. However, in a real-world application, we prefer to keep the responsibilities apart, and we never use the main class as a configuration class. To make things as clear as possible for the examples in this book, I prefer to keep these annotations over the @Configuration class, similar to how you'll find them in practical scenarios.

If you try the code as it is now, it will throw a NullPointerException on the line that gets the name from the authentication, which is

```
String username = context.getAuthentication().getName()
```

This is because the method now executes on another thread that does not inherit the security context. For this reason, the `Authorization` object is null and, in the context of the presented code, causing a `NullPointerException`. In this case, you could solve the problem by using the `MODE_INHERITABLETHREADLOCAL` strategy. This can be set either by calling the `SecurityContextHolder.setStrategyName()` method or by using the system property `spring.security.strategy`. By setting this strategy, the framework knows to copy the details of the original thread of the request to the newly created thread of the asynchronous method (figure 6.9).

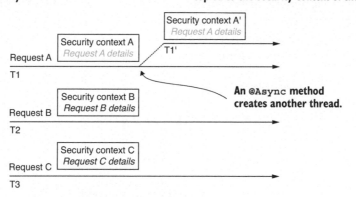

After authentication, request A will have the details about the authenticated entity in security context A.

The new thread has its own security context A', and the details from the original thread are copied to the security context of the new thread.

Each request has its own thread and access to one security context.

Figure 6.9 When using the `MODE_INHERITABLETHREADLOCAL`, the framework copies the security context details from the original thread of the request to the security context of the new thread.

The next listing presents a way to set the security context management strategy by calling the `setStrategyName()` method.

Listing 6.10 Using `InitializingBean` to set `SecurityContextHolder` mode

```
@Configuration
@EnableAsync
public class ProjectConfig {

  @Bean
  public InitializingBean initializingBean() {
    return () -> SecurityContextHolder.setStrategyName(
      SecurityContextHolder.MODE_INHERITABLETHREADLOCAL);
  }
}
```

After calling the endpoint, you will observe that the security context is propagated correctly to the next thread by Spring. Additionally, `Authentication` is not null anymore.

> **NOTE**   This works only when the framework creates the thread itself (for exam-
> ple, in the case of an `@Async` method). If your code creates the thread, you will
> run into the same problem even with the `MODE_INHERITABLETHREADLOCAL` strat-
> egy. This happens because in this case, the framework does not know about the
> thread that your code creates. We'll discuss how to solve the problems of these
> cases in sections 6.2.4 and 6.2.5.

6.2.3   *Using a holding strategy for standalone applications*

If what you need is a security context shared by all the application threads, change the
strategy to `MODE_GLOBAL` (figure 6.10). You would not use this strategy for a web server
as it doesn't fit the general picture of the application. A backend web application manages independently the requests it receives, so it really makes more sense to have the
security context separated per request instead of one context for all of them. Still, this
can be a good use for a standalone application.

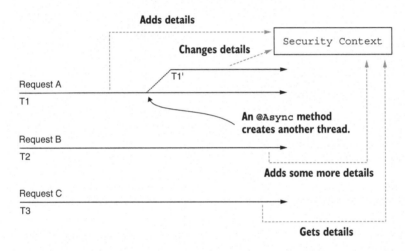

Figure 6.10   With `MODE_GLOBAL` used as the security context management strategy, all the threads
access the same security context. This implies that these all have access to the same data and
can change that information. Because of this, race conditions can occur, and you must take care of
synchronization.

As the following code snippet shows, you can change the strategy like we did with
`MODE_INHERITABLETHREADLOCAL`. You can use the method `SecurityContextHolder`
`.setStrategyName()` or the system property `spring.security.strategy`:

```
@Bean
public InitializingBean initializingBean() {
    return () -> SecurityContextHolder.setStrategyName(
        SecurityContextHolder.MODE_GLOBAL);
}
```

Also, be aware that the `SecurityContext` is not thread safe. So with this strategy in
which all the threads of the application can access the `SecurityContext` object, you
need to take care of concurrent access.

6.2.4 *Forwarding the security context with DelegatingSecurityContextRunnable*

You have learned that you can manage the security context with three modes provided by Spring Security: MODE_THREADLOCAL, MODE_INHERITEDTHREADLOCAL, and MODE_GLOBAL. By default, the framework only makes sure to provide a security context for the request thread, and this security context is only accessible to that thread. However, the framework doesn't take care of newly created threads (for example, in case of an asynchronous method). Furthermore, you learned that for this situation, you must explicitly set a different mode for the management of the security context. But we still have a singularity: What happens when your code starts new threads without the framework knowing about them? Sometimes we name these *self-managed* threads because it is we who manage them, not the framework. In this section, we apply some utility tools provided by Spring Security that help you propagate the security context to newly created threads.

No specific strategy of the SecurityContextHolder offers you a solution to self-managed threads. In this case, you need to take care of the security context propagation. One solution for this is to use the DelegatingSecurityContextRunnable to decorate the tasks you want to execute on a separate thread. The DelegatingSecurityContextRunnable extends Runnable. You can use it following the execution of the task when there is no value expected. If you have a return value, then you can use the Callable<T> alternative, which is DelegatingSecurityContextCallable<T>. Both classes represent tasks executed asynchronously, as any other Runnable or Callable. Moreover, these make sure to copy the current security context for the thread that executes the task. As figure 6.11 shows, these objects decorate the original tasks and copy the security context to the new threads.

The DelegatingSecurityContextCallable **decorates
the** Callable **task that will be executed on a separate thread.**

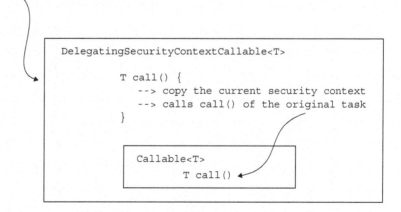

Figure 6.11 DelegatingSecurityContextCallable **is designed as a decorator of the** Callable **object. When building such an object, you provide the callable task that the application executes asynchronously.** DelegatingSecurityContextCallable **copies the details from the security context to the new thread and then executes the task.**

The next listing presents the use of `DelegatingSecurityContextCallable`. Let's start by defining a simple endpoint method that declares a `Callable` object. The `Callable` task returns the username from the current security context.

Listing 6.11   Defining a `Callable` object and executing it as a task on a separate thread

```
@GetMapping("/ciao")
public String ciao() throws Exception {
  Callable<String> task = () -> {
      SecurityContext context = SecurityContextHolder.getContext();
      return context.getAuthentication().getName();
  };

  // Omitted code

}
```

We continue the example by submitting the task to an `ExecutorService`. The response of the execution is retrieved and returned as a response body by the endpoint.

Listing 6.12   Defining an `ExecutorService` and submitting the task

```
@GetMapping("/ciao")
public String ciao() throws Exception {
  Callable<String> task = () -> {
      SecurityContext context = SecurityContextHolder.getContext();
      return context.getAuthentication().getName();
  };

  ExecutorService e = Executors.newCachedThreadPool();
  try {
     return "Ciao, " + e.submit(task).get() + "!";
  } finally {
     e.shutdown();
  }
}
```

If you run the application as is, you get nothing more than a `NullPointerException`. Inside the newly created thread to run the callable task, the authentication does not exist anymore, and the security context is empty. To solve this problem, we decorate the task with `DelegatingSecurityContextCallable`, which provides the current context to the new thread, as shown in the following listing.

Listing 6.13   Running the task decorated by `DelegatingSecurityContextCallable`

```
@GetMapping("/ciao")
public String ciao() throws Exception {
  Callable<String> task = () -> {
    SecurityContext context = SecurityContextHolder.getContext();
    return context.getAuthentication().getName();
  };

  ExecutorService e = Executors.newCachedThreadPool();
  try {
```

```
        var contextTask = new DelegatingSecurityContextCallable<>(task);
        return "Ciao, " + e.submit(contextTask).get() + "!";
    } finally {
        e.shutdown();
    }
}
```

Calling the endpoint now, you can observe that Spring propagated the security context to the thread in which the tasks execute:

```
curl -u user:2eb3f2e8-debd-420c-9680-48159b2ff905 http://localhost:8080/ciao
```

The response body for this call is

```
Ciao, user!
```

6.2.5 *Forwarding the security context with DelegatingSecurityContextExecutorService*

When dealing with threads that our code starts without letting the framework know about them, we must manage propagation of the details from the security context to the next thread. In section 6.2.4, you applied a technique to copy the details from the security context by making use of the task itself. Spring Security provides some great utility classes such as `DelegatingSecurityContextRunnable` and `DelegatingSecurity-ContextCallable`. These classes decorate the tasks you execute asynchronously and also take the responsibility for copying the details from the security context so that your implementation can access those from the newly created thread. However, we have a second option to deal with the security context propagation to a new thread, and this is to manage propagation from the thread pool instead of from the task itself. In this section, you'll learn how to apply this technique by using more great utility classes provided by Spring Security.

An alternative to decorating tasks is to use a particular type of `Executor`. In the next example, you can observe that the task remains a simple `Callable<T>`, but the thread still manages the security context. The propagation of the security context happens because an implementation called `DelegatingSecurityContextExecutorService` decorates the `ExecutorService`. The `DelegatingSecurityContextExecutor-Service` also takes care of the security context propagation, as presented in figure 6.12.

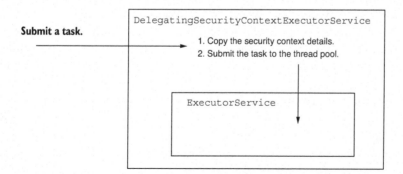

Figure 6.12 `DelegatingSecurityContextExecutorService` **decorates an** `ExecutorService` **and propagates the security context details to the next thread before submitting the task.**

The code in the following listing shows how to use a DelegatingSecurityContext-
ExecutorService to decorate an ExecutorService so that when you submit the task,
it takes care of propagating the details of the security context.

```
@GetMapping("/hola")
public String hola() throws Exception {
  Callable<String> task = () -> {
    SecurityContext context = SecurityContextHolder.getContext();
    return context.getAuthentication().getName();
  };

  ExecutorService e = Executors.newCachedThreadPool();
  e = new DelegatingSecurityContextExecutorService(e);
  try {
    return "Hola, " + e.submit(task).get() + "!";
  } finally {
    e.shutdown();
  }
}
```

Call the endpoint to test that the DelegatingSecurityContextExecutorService
correctly delegated the security context:

```
curl -u user:5a5124cc-060d-40b1-8aad-753d3da28dca http://localhost:8080/hola
```

The response body for this call is

```
Hola, user!
```

> **NOTE** Of the classes that are related to concurrency support for the security con-
> text, you should keep in mind the ones presented in table 6.1.

Spring offers various implementations of the utility classes that can be used in your
application to manage the security context when creating your own threads. In section 6.2.4, you implemented DelegatingSecurityContextCallable. In this section,
we use DelegatingSecurityContextExecutorService. If you need to implement
security context propagation for a scheduled task, then you will be happy to hear that
Spring Security also offers you a decorator named DelegatingSecurityContext-
ScheduledExecutorService. This mechanism is similar to the Delegating-
SecurityContextExecutorService presented in this section, with the difference
that it decorates a ScheduledExecutorService, allowing you to work with scheduled
tasks.

   Additionally, for more flexibility, Spring Security offers you a more abstract version
of a decorator called DelegatingSecurityContextExecutor. This class directly decorates an Executor, which is the most abstract contract of this hierarchy of thread pools.
You can choose it for the design of your application when you want to be able to replace
the implementation of the thread pool with any of the choices the language provides.

Table 6.1   Objects responsible for delegating the security context to a separate thread

Class	Description
`DelegatingSecurityContextExecutor`	Implements the `Executor` interface and is designed to decorate an `Executor` object with the capability of forwarding the security context to the threads created by its pool.
`DelegatingSecurityContextExecutorService`	Implements the `ExecutorService` interface and is designed to decorate an `ExecutorService` object with the capability of forwarding the security context to the threads created by its pool.
`DelegatingSecurityContextScheduledExecutorService`	Implements the `ScheduledExecutorService` interface and is designed to decorate a `ScheduledExecutorService` object with the capability of forwarding the security context to the threads created by its pool.
`DelegatingSecurityContextRunnable`	Implements the `Runnable` interface and represents a task that is executed on a different thread without returning a response. Above a normal `Runnable`, it can also propagate a security context to use on the new thread.
`DelegatingSecurityContextCallable`	Implements the `Callable` interface and represents a task that is executed on a different thread and that will eventually return a response. Above a normal `Callable`, it can also propagate a security context to use on the new thread.

6.3   *Understanding HTTP Basic and form-based login authentications*

Up to now, we've only used HTTP Basic as the authentication method, but throughout this book, you'll learn that there are other possibilities as well. The HTTP Basic authentication method is simple, which makes it an excellent choice for examples and demonstration purposes or proof of concept. But for the same reason, it might not fit all the real-world scenarios that you'll need to implement.

In this section, you'll learn more configurations related to HTTP Basic. In addition, we'll talk about a new authentication method called `formLogin`. In the rest of this book, we'll discuss other authentication methods, which match different kinds of architectures well. We'll compare them so that you can understand the best practices, as well as the anti-patterns for authentication.

6.3.1   *Using and configuring HTTP Basic*

You are aware that HTTP Basic is the default authentication method, and we have seen the way it works in various examples in chapter 3. In this section, we add more details regarding the configuration of this authentication method.

For theoretical scenarios, the defaults that the HTTP Basic authentication comes with are great. However, in a more complex application, you might find the need to customize some of these settings. For example, you might want to implement a specific logic for the case in which the authentication process fails. You might even need to set some values on the response sent back to the client in this case. Let's consider these cases with practical examples to understand how you can implement this. I want to point out again how you can set this method explicitly, as shown in the following listing. You can find this example in the project ssia-ch6-ex3.

Listing 6.15   Setting the HTTP Basic authentication method

```
@Configuration
public class ProjectConfig {

  @Bean
  public SecurityFilterChain configure(HttpSecurity http)
    throws Exception {

    http.httpBasic(Customizer.withDefaults());

    return http.build();
  }
}
```

You can call the `httpBasic()` method of the `HttpSecurity` instance with a parameter of `Customizer` type. This parameter allows you to set up some configurations related to the authentication method, for example, the realm name, as shown in listing 6.16. You can think about the realm as a protection space that uses a specific authentication method. For a complete description, refer to RFC 2617 at https://tools.ietf.org/html/rfc2617.

Listing 6.16   Configuring the realm name for the response of failed authentications

```
@Bean
public SecurityFilterChain configure(HttpSecurity http)
  throws Exception {

  http.httpBasic(c -> {
    c.realmName("OTHER");
    c.authenticationEntryPoint(new CustomEntryPoint());
  });

  http.authorizeHttpRequests(c -> c.anyRequest().authenticated());

  return http.build();
}
```

Listing 6.16 presents an example of changing the realm name. The lambda expression used is, in fact, an object of type `Customizer<HttpBasicConfigurer<Http-Security>>`. The parameter of type `HttpBasicConfigurer<HttpSecurity>` allows us to call the `realmName()` method to rename the realm. You can use cURL with the `-v` flag to get a wordy HTTP response in which the realm name is indeed changed. However, note that you'll find the `WWW-Authenticate` header in the response only when the HTTP response status is 401 Unauthorized and not when the HTTP response status is 200 OK. Here's the call to cURL:

```
curl -v http://localhost:8080/hello
```

The response of the call is

```
/
...
< WWW-Authenticate: Basic realm="OTHER"
...
```

In addition, by using a `Customizer`, we can customize the response for a failed authentication. You need to do this if the client of your system expects something specific in the response in the case of a failed authentication. You might need to add or remove one or more headers. Or you can have some logic that filters the body to make sure that the application doesn't expose any sensitive data to the client.

> **NOTE** Always exercise caution about the data that you expose outside of the system. One of the most common mistakes (which is also part of the OWASP top ten vulnerabilities; see https://owasp.org/www-project-top-ten/) is exposing sensitive data. Working with the details that the application sends to the client for a failed authentication is always a point of risk for revealing confidential information.

To customize the response for a failed authentication, we can implement an `AuthenticationEntryPoint`. Its `commence()` method receives the `HttpServletRequest`, the `HttpServletResponse`, and the `AuthenticationException` that cause the authentication to fail. Listing 6.17 demonstrates a way to implement the `AuthenticationEntryPoint`, which adds a header to the response and sets the HTTP status to 401 Unauthorized.

> **NOTE** It's a little bit ambiguous that the name of the `AuthenticationEntryPoint` interface doesn't reflect its usage on authentication failure. In the Spring Security architecture, this is used directly by a component called `Exception-TranslationManager`, which handles any `AccessDeniedException` and `AuthenticationException` thrown within the filter chain. You can view the `ExceptionTranslationManager` as a bridge between Java exceptions and HTTP responses.

Listing 6.17 Implementing an `AuthenticationEntryPoint`

```
public class CustomEntryPoint
  implements AuthenticationEntryPoint {

  @Override
  public void commence(
    HttpServletRequest httpServletRequest,
    HttpServletResponse httpServletResponse,
    AuthenticationException e)
      throws IOException, ServletException {

      httpServletResponse
        .addHeader("message", "Luke, I am your father!");
      httpServletResponse
        .sendError(HttpStatus.UNAUTHORIZED.value());

    }
}
```

You can then register the `CustomEntryPoint` with the HTTP Basic method in the configuration class. The following listing presents the configuration class for the custom entry point.

Listing 6.18 Setting the custom `AuthenticationEntryPoint`

```
@Bean
public SecurityFilterChain configure(HttpSecurity http)
  throws Exception {

  http.httpBasic(c -> {
    c.realmName("OTHER");
    c.authenticationEntryPoint(new CustomEntryPoint());
  });


  http.authorizeHttpRequests().anyRequest().authenticated();

  return http.build();
}
```

If you now make a call to an endpoint so that the authentication fails, you should find the newly added header in the response:

```
curl -v http://localhost:8080/hello
```

The response of the call is

```
...
< HTTP/1.1 401
< Set-Cookie: JSESSIONID=459BAFA7E0E6246A463AD19B07569C7B; Path=/; HttpOnly
< message: Luke, I am your father!
...
```

6.3.2 Implementing authentication with form-based login

When developing a web application, you would probably like to present a user-friendly login form where the users can input their credentials. Furthermore, you might like your authenticated users to be able to surf through the web pages after they logged in and to be able to log out. For a small web application, you can take advantage of the form-based login method. In this section, you learn to apply and configure this authentication method for your application. To achieve this, we write a small web application that uses form-based login. Figure 6.13 describes the flow we'll implement. The examples in this section are part of the project ssia-ch6-ex4.

> **NOTE** I link this method to a small web application because this way, we use a server-side session for managing the security context. For larger applications requiring horizontal scalability, using a server-side session for managing the security context is undesirable. We'll discuss these aspects in more detail in chapters 12 through 15 when dealing with OAuth 2.

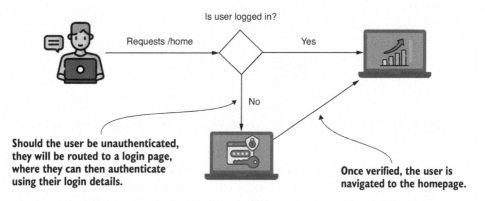

Figure 6.13 Using form-based login. A user who has not yet been authenticated is sent to a form to log in with their credentials. After the application has verified their identity, they are directed to the application's main page.

To change the authentication method to form-based login, using the `HttpSecurity` object of the `SecurityFilterChain` bean instead of `httpBasic()`, call the `form-Login()` method of the `HttpSecurity` parameter. The following listing presents this change.

Listing 6.19 Changing the authentication method to a form-based login

```
@Configuration
public class ProjectConfig {

  @Bean
  public SecurityFilterChain securityFilterChain(HttpSecurity http)
```

```
    throws Exception {

    http.formLogin(Customizer.withDefaults());

    http.authorizeHttpRequests(c -> c.anyRequest().authenticated());

    return http.build();
  }
}
```

Even with this minimal configuration, Spring Security has already configured a login form, as well as a log-out page for your project. Starting the application and accessing it with the browser should redirect you to a login page (figure 6.14).

Figure 6.14   **The default login page auto-configured by Spring Security when using the** `formLogin()` **method**

You can log in using the default provided credentials as long as you do not register your `UserDetailsService`. These are, as we learned in chapter 2, username `user` and a UUID password that is printed in the console when the application starts. Because there is no other page defined, you are redirected to a default error page after a successful login. The application relies on the same architecture for authentication that we encountered in previous examples. So, as shown in figure 6.14, you need to implement a controller for the application homepage. The difference is that instead of having a simple JSON-formatted response, we want the endpoint to return HTML that can be interpreted by the browser as our web page. Because of this, we choose to stick to the Spring MVC flow and have the view rendered from a file after the execution of the action defined in the controller. Figure 6.15 presents the Spring MVC flow for rendering the homepage of the application.

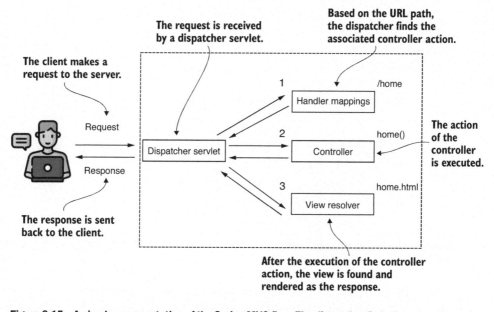

The request is received by a dispatcher servlet.

Based on the URL path, the dispatcher finds the associated controller action.

The client makes a request to the server.

The action of the controller is executed.

The response is sent back to the client.

After the execution of the controller action, the view is found and rendered as the response.

Figure 6.15 A simple representation of the Spring MVC flow. The dispatcher finds the controller action associated with the given path (/home in this case). After executing the controller action, the view is rendered, and the response is sent back to the client.

To add a simple page to the application, you first must create an HTML file in the resources/static folder of the project. I call this file home.html. Inside it, type some text that you will be able to find afterward in the browser. You can just add a heading (for example, `<h1>Welcome</h1>`). After creating the HTML page, a controller needs to define the mapping from the path to the view. The following listing presents the definition of the action method for the home.html page in the controller class.

Listing 6.20 Defining the action method of the controller for the home.html page

```
@Controller
public class HelloController {

  @GetMapping("/home")
  public String home() {
    return "home.html";
  }
}
```

Keep in mind that it is not a `@RestController` but a simple `@Controller`. Because of this, Spring does not send the value returned by the method in the HTTP response. Instead, it finds and renders the view with the name home.html.

Trying to access the /home path now, you are first asked if you want to log in. After a successful login, you are redirected to the homepage, where the welcome message appears. You can now access the /logout path, and this should redirect you to a log-out page (figure 6.16).

Figure 6.16   The log-out page configured by Spring Security for the form-based login authentication method

After attempting to access a path without being logged in, the user is automatically redirected to the login page. After a successful login, the application redirects the user back to the path they tried to originally access. If that path does not exist, the application displays a default error page. The `formLogin()` method returns an object of type `FormLoginConfigurer<HttpSecurity>`, which allows us to work on customizations. For example, you can do this by calling the `defaultSuccessUrl()` method, as shown in the following listing.

Listing 6.21   Setting a default success URL for the login form

```
@Bean
public SecurityFilterChain securityFilterChain(HttpSecurity http)
  throws Exception {

  http.formLogin(c -> c.defaultSuccessUrl("/home", true));

  http.authorizeHttpRequests(c -> c.anyRequest().authenticated());

  return http.build();
}
```

If you need to go even more into depth with this, using the `AuthenticationSuccess-Handler` and `AuthenticationFailureHandler` objects offers a more detailed customization approach. These interfaces let you implement an object through which you can apply the logic executed for authentication. If you want to customize the logic for successful authentication, you can define an `AuthenticationSuccessHandler`. The `onAuthenticationSuccess()` method receives the servlet request, servlet response, and the `Authentication` object as parameters. In the next listing, you'll find an example of implementing the `onAuthenticationSuccess()` method to make different redirects depending on the granted authorities of the logged-in user.

Listing 6.22 Implementing an `AuthenticationSuccessHandler`

```
@Component
public class CustomAuthenticationSuccessHandler
  implements AuthenticationSuccessHandler {

  @Override
  public void onAuthenticationSuccess(
    HttpServletRequest httpServletRequest,
    HttpServletResponse httpServletResponse,
    Authentication authentication)
      throws IOException {

    var authorities = authentication.getAuthorities();

    var auth =
            authorities.stream()
              .filter(a -> a.getAuthority().equals("read"))
              .findFirst();

    if (auth.isPresent()) {
      httpServletResponse
        .sendRedirect("/home");
    } else {
      httpServletResponse
        .sendRedirect("/error");
    }
  }
}
```

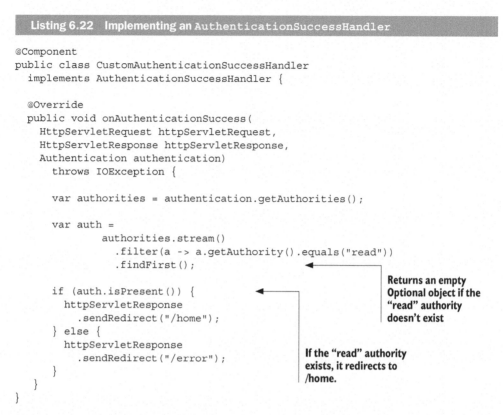

Returns an empty Optional object if the "read" authority doesn't exist

If the "read" authority exists, it redirects to /home.

There are situations in practical scenarios when a client expects a certain format of the response in case of failed authentication. They may expect a different HTTP status code than 401 Unauthorized or additional information in the body of the response. The most typical case I have found in applications involves sending a *request identifier*. This request identifier has a unique value used to trace back the request among multiple systems, and the application can send it in the body of the response in case of failed authentication. Another situation is when you want to sanitize the response to make sure that the application doesn't expose sensitive data outside of the system. You might want to define custom logic for failed authentication simply by logging the event for further investigation.

If you would like to customize the logic that the application executes when authentication fails, you can do this similarly with an `AuthenticationFailureHandler` implementation. For example, if you want to add a specific header for any failed authentication, you could do something like what is shown in listing 6.23. You could, of course, implement any logic here as well. For the `AuthenticationFailure-Handler`, `onAuthenticationFailure()` receives the request, response, and the `Authentication` object.

Listing 6.23   Implementing an `AuthenticationFailureHandler`

```
@Component
public class CustomAuthenticationFailureHandler
  implements AuthenticationFailureHandler {

  @Override
  public void onAuthenticationFailure(
    HttpServletRequest httpServletRequest,
    HttpServletResponse httpServletResponse,
    AuthenticationException e)   {

    try {

      httpServletResponse.setHeader("failed",
        LocalDateTime.now().toString());
      httpServletResponse.sendRedirect("/error");

    } catch (IOException ex) {
      throw new RuntimeException(ex);
    }
  }
}
```

To use the two objects, you need to register them in the `securityFilterChain()` method on the `FormLoginConfigurer` object returned by the `formLogin()` method. The following listing shows how to do this.

Listing 6.24   Registering the handler objects in the configuration class

```
@Configuration
public class ProjectConfig {

  private final CustomAuthenticationSuccessHandler
authenticationSuccessHandler;
  private final CustomAuthenticationFailureHandler
authenticationFailureHandler;

// Omitted constructor

@Bean
public UserDetailsService uds() {
  var uds = new InMemoryUserDetailsManager();

  uds.createUser(
    User.withDefaultPasswordEncoder()
        .username("john")
        .password("12345")
        .authorities("read")
        .build()
  );

  uds.createUser(
    User.withDefaultPasswordEncoder()
        .username("bill")
        .password("12345")
```

```
        .authorities("write")
        .build()
    );

    return uds;
}

@Bean
public SecurityFilterChain configure(HttpSecurity http)
  throws Exception {

  http.formLogin(c ->
    c.successHandler(authenticationSuccessHandler)
     .failureHandler(authenticationFailureHandler)
  );

  http.authorizeHttpRequests(c -> c.anyRequest().authenticated());

  return http.build();
  }
}
```

For now, if you try to access the /home path using HTTP Basic with the proper user-name and password, you are returned a response with the status HTTP 302 Found. This is how the application tells you that it is trying to do a redirect. Even if you have provided the right username and password, it won't consider these and will instead try to send you to the login form as requested by the `formLogin` method. You can, how-ever, change the configuration to support both the HTTP Basic and the form-based login methods, like in the following listing.

Listing 6.25 Using form-based login and HTTP Basic together

```
@Bean
public SecurityFilterChain securityFilterChain(HttpSecurity http)
  throws Exception {

  http.formLogin(c ->
    c.successHandler(authenticationSuccessHandler)
     .failureHandler(authenticationFailureHandler)
  );

  http.httpBasic(Customizer.withDefaults());

  http.authorizeHttpRequests(c -> c.anyRequest().authenticated());

  return http.build();
}
```

Accessing the /home path now works with both the form-based login and HTTP Basic authentication methods:

```
curl -u user:cdd430f6-8ebc-49a6-9769-b0f3ce571d19 http://localhost:8080/home
```

The response of the call is

```
<h1>Welcome</h1>
```

Summary

- The `AuthenticationProvider` is the component that allows you to implement custom authentication logic.

- When you implement custom authentication logic, it's a good practice to keep the responsibilities decoupled. For user management, the `Authentication-Provider` delegates to a `UserDetailsService`, and for the responsibility of password validation, the `AuthenticationProvider` delegates to a `PasswordEncoder`.

- The `SecurityContext` keeps details about the authenticated entity after successful authentication.

- You can use three strategies to manage the security context: `MODE_THREADLOCAL`, `MODE_INHERITABLETHREADLOCAL`, and `MODE_GLOBAL`. Access from different threads to the security context details works differently, depending on the mode you choose.

- Remember that when using the shared-thread local mode, it's only applied for threads managed by Spring. The framework won't copy the security context for the threads that are not governed by it.

- Spring Security offers you great utility classes to manage the threads created by your code, about which the framework is now aware. To manage the `Security-Context` for the threads you create, you can use
  - `DelegatingSecurityContextRunnable`
  - `DelegatingSecurityContextCallable`
  - `DelegatingSecurityContextExecutor`

- Spring Security autoconfigures a form for login and an option to log out with the form-based login authentication method, `formLogin()`. It is straightforward to use when developing small web applications.

- The `formLogin` authentication method is highly customizable. Moreover, you can use this type of authentication together with the HTTP Basic method.

Part 3

Configuring authorization

Once an application determines your identity, the crucial phase of deciding your permissions ensues: authorization. Implementing it correctly is pivotal, as missteps can compromise user privacy and data integrity. In this part of the book, I'll walk you through the intricate layers of authorization and safeguarding against common vulnerabilities.

Chapter 7 offers a deep dive into the realm of access restrictions, focusing on user authorities and roles, and providing insights on how to apply these restrictions universally.

Chapter 8 continues the journey, presenting advanced methods, such as `requestMatchers()`, to select and enforce authorization restrictions. It also introduces the use of regular expressions for more granular control.

Chapter 9 addresses the pressing concern of cross-site request forgery (CSRF). By understanding its mechanism in Spring Security, you'll be empowered to apply and customize CSRF protection effectively.

Chapter 10 introduces the concept of cross-origin resource sharing (CORS), illuminating how it operates and guiding you through applying CORS policies through annotations and `CorsConfigurer`.

Chapter 11 ventures into method security, ensuring individual functions within your application uphold strict authorization principles. This includes both pre- and postauthorization rules and advanced permissions settings for methods.

Chapter 12 rounds off with filtering techniques at the method level, covering aspects from pre- to postfiltering, and integrating them within Spring Data repositories.

By the end of this part, you'll have garnered the expertise to meticulously design and implement comprehensive authorization strategies, ensuring your application remains both functional and fortified.

Configuring endpoint-level authorization: Restricting access

This chapter covers

- Defining authorities and roles
- Applying authorization rules on endpoints

Some years ago, I was skiing in the beautiful Carpathian Mountains when I witnessed a funny scene. About 10, maybe 15 people were queuing up to get into the cabin to go to the top of the ski slope. A well-known pop artist showed up, accompanied by two bodyguards. He confidently strode up, expecting to skip the queue because he was famous. Reaching the head of the line, he got a surprise. "Ticket, please!" said the person managing the boarding, who then had to explain, "Well, you first need a ticket, and second, there is no priority line for this boarding, sorry. The queue ends there." He pointed to the end of the queue. Often in life, it doesn't matter who you are. We can say the same about software applications. It doesn't matter who you are when trying to access a specific functionality or data!

Up to now, we've only discussed authentication, which is, as you learned, the process in which the application identifies the caller of a resource. In previous examples, we didn't implement any rules to decide whether to approve a request. We only cared if the system knew the user or not. In most applications, it doesn't happen that all the users identified by the system can access every resource in it. In this chapter, we'll discuss authorization. *Authorization* is the process during which the system decides whether an identified client has permission to access the requested resource (figure 7.1).

**Figure 7.1
Authorization
is the process
during which
the application
decides whether
an authenticated
entity is allowed to
access a resource.
Authorization always
happens after
authentication.**

In Spring Security, once the application ends the authentication flow, it delegates the request to an authorization filter. The filter allows or rejects the request based on the configured authorization rules (figure 7.2).

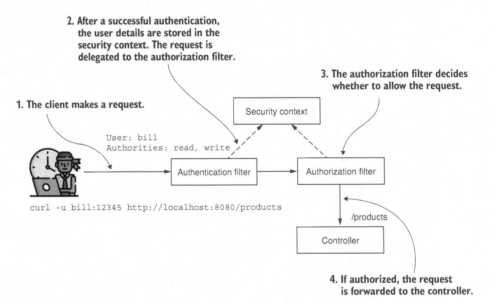

Figure 7.2   Upon the client's request initiation, the authentication filter verifies the user's identity. Following successful verification, the authentication filter places the user's details into the security context and passes the request on to the authorization filter. This filter then assesses whether the request should be allowed. It makes this determination using the user information provided in the security context.

To cover all the essential details on authorization, in this chapter, we will

- Gain an understanding of what an authority is and apply access rules on all end-points based on a user's authorities
- Learn how to group authorities in roles and how to apply authorization rules based on a user's roles

In chapter 8, we'll continue with selecting endpoints to which we'll apply the authorization rules. For now, let's look at authorities and roles and how these can restrict access to our applications.

7.1 *Restricting access based on authorities and roles*

In this section, you will learn about the concepts of authorization and roles. You use these to secure all the endpoints of your application. It is necessary to understand these concepts before you can apply them in real-world scenarios, where different users have different permissions. Based on the privileges users have, they can only execute a specific action. The application provides privileges as authorities and roles.

In chapter 3, you implemented the `GrantedAuthority` interface. This contract was introduced when we discussed another essential component: the `UserDetails` interface. We didn't work with `GrantedAuthority` then because, as you'll learn in this chapter, this interface is mainly related to the authorization process. We can now return to `Granted-Authority` to examine its purpose. Figure 7.3 presents the relationship between the `UserDetails` contract and the `GrantedAuthority` interface. Once we finish discussing this contract, you'll learn how to use these rules individually or for specific requests.

The `UserDetailsService` retrieves the user details during the authentication process.

A user has one or more authorities.

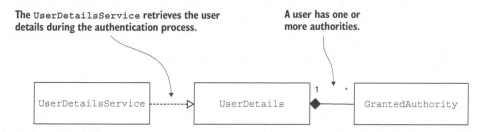

Figure 7.3 A user possesses one or more authorities (permissible actions). Throughout the authentication phase, the `UserDetailsService` retrieves comprehensive details about the user, encompassing their authorities. Following a successful authentication, the application employs these authorities, as depicted by the `GrantedAuthority` interface, to carry out authorization.

Listing 7.1 shows the definition of the `GrantedAuthority` contract. An *authority* is an action that a user can perform with a system resource. An authority has a name that the `getAuthority()` behavior of the object returns as a `String`. We use the name of the authority when defining the custom authorization rule. Often, an authorization rule can look like this: "Jane is allowed to *delete* the product records," or "John is allowed to *read* the document records." In these cases, *delete* and *read* are the granted authorities. The application allows the users Jane and John to perform these actions, which often have names such as read, write, or delete.

Listing 7.1 The `GrantedAuthority` contract

```
public interface GrantedAuthority extends Serializable {
  String getAuthority();
}
```

The `UserDetails`, which is the contract describing the user in Spring Security, has a collection of `GrantedAuthority` instances, as presented in figure 7.3. You can allow a user one or more privileges. The `getAuthorities()` method returns the collection of `GrantedAuthority` instances. In listing 7.2, you can review this method in the `UserDetails` contract. We implement this method so that it returns all the authorities granted for the user. After the authentication ends, the authorities become part of the details about the user that logged in, which the application can use to grant permissions.

Listing 7.2 The `getAuthorities()` method from the `UserDetails` contract

```
public interface UserDetails extends Serializable {
  Collection<? extends GrantedAuthority> getAuthorities();

  // Omitted code
}
```

7.1.1 *Restricting access for all endpoints based on user authorities*

This section discusses how to limit access to endpoints for specific users. Up to now in our examples, any authenticated user could call any endpoint of the application. Now you'll learn to customize this access. In the apps you find in production, you can call some of the endpoints of the application, even if you are unauthenticated, while for others, you need special privileges (figure 7.4). We'll write several examples so that you learn various ways in which you can apply these restrictions with Spring Security.

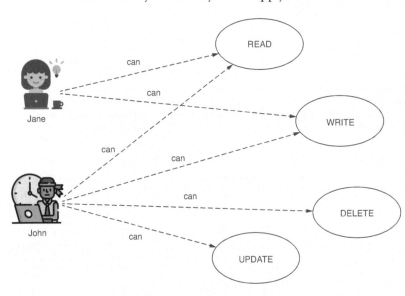

Figure 7.4 **Authorities define the permissible operations users can execute within the application. These operations inform the creation of authorization protocols, restricting certain requests to endpoints to users with designated authorities. For instance, Jane is limited to reading and writing at the endpoint, whereas John has the capacity to read, write, delete, and modify at that endpoint.**

Now that you can recall the `UserDetails` and `GrantedAuthority` contracts and the relationship between them, it is time to write a small app that applies an authorization rule. With this example, you learn a few alternatives to configure access to endpoints based on the user's authorities. We start a new project that I named ssia-ch7-ex1. I show you three ways in which you can configure access as mentioned using these methods:

- `hasAuthority()`—Receives as parameters only one authority for which the application configures the restrictions. Only users having that authority can call the endpoint.

- `hasAnyAuthority()`—Can receive more than one authority for which the application configures the restrictions. I remember this method as "has any of the given authorities." The user must have at least one of the specified authorities to make a request.

  I recommend using this method or the `hasAuthority()` method for their simplicity, depending on the number of privileges you assign. These are simple to read in configurations and make your code easier to understand.

- `access()`—Offers unlimited possibilities for configuring access because the application builds the authorization rules based on a custom object named `AuthorizationManager` that you implement. You can provide any implementation for the `AuthorizationManager` contract, depending on your case. Spring Security provides a few implementations as well. The most common implementation is the `WebExpressionAuthorizationManager`, which helps you apply authorization rules based on Spring Expression Language (SpEL). But using the `access()` method can make the authorization rules more difficult to read and understand. For this reason, I recommend it as the lesser solution and only if you cannot apply the `hasAnyAuthority()` or `hasAuthority()` methods.

The only dependencies needed in your pom.xml file are `spring-boot-starter-web` and `spring-boot-starter-security`. These dependencies are enough to approach all three solutions previously enumerated. You can find this example in the project ssia-ch7-ex1:

```
<dependency>
  <groupId>org.springframework.boot</groupId>
  <artifactId>spring-boot-starter-security</artifactId>
</dependency>
<dependency>
  <groupId>org.springframework.boot</groupId>
  <artifactId>spring-boot-starter-web</artifactId>
</dependency>
```

We also add an endpoint in the application to test our authorization configuration:

```
@RestController
public class HelloController {

  @GetMapping("/hello")
  public String hello() {
```

```
    return "Hello!";
  }
}
```

In a configuration class, we declare an `InMemoryUserDetailsManager` as our `User-DetailsService` and add two users, John and Jane, to be managed. Each user has a different authority. You can see how to do this in the following listing.

Listing 7.3   Declaring the `UserDetailsService` and assigning users

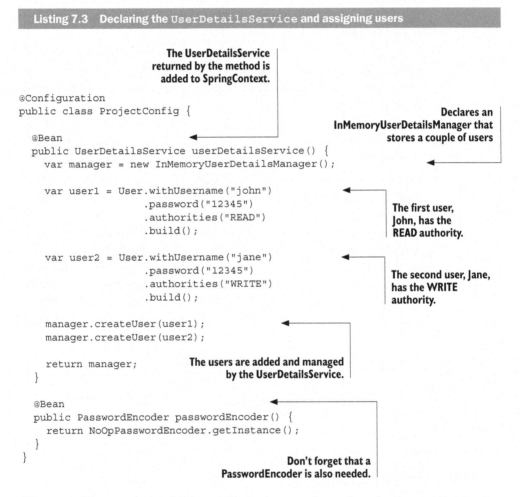

**The UserDetailsService
returned by the method is
added to SpringContext.**

```
@Configuration
public class ProjectConfig {

  @Bean
  public UserDetailsService userDetailsService() {
    var manager = new InMemoryUserDetailsManager();

    var user1 = User.withUsername("john")
                    .password("12345")
                    .authorities("READ")
                    .build();

    var user2 = User.withUsername("jane")
                    .password("12345")
                    .authorities("WRITE")
                    .build();

    manager.createUser(user1);
    manager.createUser(user2);

    return manager;
  }

  @Bean
  public PasswordEncoder passwordEncoder() {
    return NoOpPasswordEncoder.getInstance();
  }
}
```

**Declares an
InMemoryUserDetailsManager that
stores a couple of users**

**The first user,
John, has the
READ authority.**

**The second user, Jane,
has the WRITE
authority.**

**The users are added and managed
by the UserDetailsService.**

**Don't forget that a
PasswordEncoder is also needed.**

The next thing we do is add the authorization configuration. In chapter 2, when we worked on the first example, you saw how we could make all the endpoints accessible for everyone. To do that, we created a `SecurityFilterChain` bean in the app's context, similar to what is presented in the next listing.

Listing 7.4   Making all the endpoints accessible for everyone without authentication

```
@Configuration
public class ProjectConfig {

  // Omitted code

  @Bean
  public SecurityFilterChain securityFilterChain(HttpSecurity http)
    throws Exception {

    http.httpBasic(Customizer.withDefaults());

    http.authorizeHttpRequests(
        c -> c.anyRequest().permitAll()
    );                                         ◄──── Permits access for all
                                                     the requests
    return http.build();
  }
}
```

The authorizeHttpRequests() method lets us continue with specifying authorization rules on endpoints. The anyRequest() method indicates that the rule applies to all the requests, regardless of the URL or HTTP method used. The permitAll() method allows access to all matched requests, authenticated or not.

Let's say we want to make sure that only users having WRITE authority can access all endpoints. For our example, this means only Jane. We can achieve our goal and restrict access this time based on a user's authorities. Take a look at the code in the following listing.

Listing 7.5   Restricting access to only users having WRITE authority

```
@Configuration
public class ProjectConfig {

  // Omitted code

  @Bean
  public SecurityFilterChain securityFilterChain(HttpSecurity http)
    throws Exception {

    http.httpBasic(Customizer.withDefaults());

    http.authorizeHttpRequests(
        c -> c.anyRequest()
          .hasAuthority("WRITE")
    );                               ◄──── Specifies the condition
                                           in which the user has
    return http.build();                   access to endpoints
  }
}
```

You can see that the permitAll() method was replaced with the hasAuthority() method. You provide the name of the authority allowed to the user as a parameter of the hasAuthority() method. The application needs to authenticate the request first, and then, based on the user's authorities, the app decides whether to allow the call.

We can now start to test the application by calling the endpoint with each of the two users. When we call the endpoint with user Jane, the HTTP response status is 200 OK, and we see the response body "Hello!" When we call it with user John, the HTTP response status is 403 Forbidden, and we get an empty response body back. For example, calling this endpoint with user Jane

```
curl -u jane:12345 http://localhost:8080/hello
```

we get this response:

```
Hello!
```

Calling the endpoint with user John

```
curl -u john:12345 http://localhost:8080/hello
```

we get this response:

```
{
  "status":403,
  "error":"Forbidden",
  "message":"Forbidden",
  "path":"/hello"
}
```

Similarly, we can use the hasAnyAuthority() method. This method has the parameter varargs; this way, it can receive multiple authority names. The application permits the request if the user has at least one of the authorities provided as a parameter to the method. You can replace hasAuthority() in the previous listing with hasAny-Authority("WRITE"), in which case, the application works precisely in the same way. If, however, you replace hasAuthority() with hasAnyAuthority("WRITE", "READ"), then requests from users having either authority are accepted. For our case, the application allows the requests from both John and Jane. The following listing shows how to apply the hasAnyAuthority() method.

Listing 7.6   Applying the hasAnyAuthority() method

```
@Configuration
public class ProjectConfig {

  // Omitted code

  @Bean
  public SecurityFilterChain securityFilterChain(HttpSecurity http)
    throws Exception {

    http.httpBasic(Customizer.withDefaults());

    http.authorizeHttpRequests(
```

```
        c -> c.anyRequest()
            .hasAnyAuthority("WRITE", "READ");
    );

    return http.build();
    }
}
```

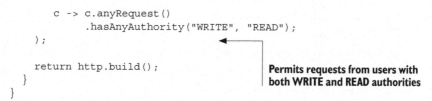

**Permits requests from users with
both WRITE and READ authorities**

You can successfully call the endpoint now with any of our two users. Here's the call for John:

```
curl -u john:12345 http://localhost:8080/hello
```

The response body is

```
Hello!
```

And the call for Jane is

```
curl -u jane:12345 http://localhost:8080/hello
```

The response body is

```
Hello!
```

To specify access based on user authorities, the third way you find in practice is the `access()` method. The `access()` method is more general, however. It receives as a parameter an `AuthorizationManager` implementation. You can provide any implementation for this object that can apply any kind of logic that defines the authorization rules. This method is powerful, and it doesn't refer only to authorities. However, this method also makes the code more difficult to read and understand. For this reason, I recommend it as the last option, and only if you can't apply one of the `hasAuthority()` or `hasAnyAuthority()` methods presented earlier in this section.

To make this method easier to understand, I first present it as an alternative to specifying authorities with the `hasAuthority()` and `hasAnyAuthority()` methods. In this example, you'll use an `AuthorizationManager` implementation where you must provide a SpEL expression as a parameter. The authorization rule we defined becomes more challenging to read, and this is why I don't recommend this approach for simple rules. However, the `access()` method has the advantage of allowing you to customize rules through the `AuthorizationManager` implementation you provide as a parameter. And this is really powerful! As with SpEL expressions, you can basically define any condition.

> **NOTE** In most situations, the required restrictions can be implemented with the `hasAuthority()` and `hasAnyAuthority()` methods, and I recommend that you use these. Use the `access()` method only if the other two options do not fit and you want to implement more generic authorization rules.

We start with a simple example to match the same requirement as in the previous cases. If you only have to test whether the user has specific authorities, the expression you need to use with the `access()` method can be one of the following:

- `hasAuthority('WRITE')`—Stipulates that the user needs the `WRITE` authority to call the endpoint.
- `hasAnyAuthority('READ', 'WRITE')`—Specifies that the user needs one of either the `READ` or `WRITE` authorities. With this expression, you can enumerate all the authorities for which you want to allow access.

Observe that these expressions have the same name as the methods presented earlier in this section. The following listing demonstrates how to use the `access()` method.

Listing 7.7   Using the `access()` method to configure access to the endpoints

```
@Configuration
public class ProjectConfig {

  // Omitted code

  @Bean
  public SecurityFilterChain securityFilterChain(HttpSecurity http)
    throws Exception {

    http.httpBasic(Customizer.withDefaults());

    http.authorizeHttpRequests(
      c -> c.anyRequest()
              .access("hasAuthority('WRITE')")
    );

    return http.build();               Authorizes requests from users
  }                                    with the WRITE authority
}
```

The example presented in listing 7.7 proves how the `access()` method complicates the syntax if you use it for straightforward requirements. In such a case, you should instead use the `hasAuthority()` or the `hasAnyAuthority()` method directly. But the `access()` method is not all evil. As stated earlier, it offers flexibility. You'll find situations in real-world scenarios in which you could use it to write more complex expressions, based on which the application grants access. You wouldn't be able to implement these scenarios without the `access()` method.

In listing 7.8, you can find the `access()` method applied with an expression that's not easy to write otherwise. Precisely, the configuration presented in listing 7.8 defines two users, John and Jane, who have different authorities. The user John has only read authority, while Jane has read, write, and delete authorities. The endpoint should be accessible to those users who have read authority, but not to those that have delete authority.

NOTE   In Spring apps, you find various styles and conventions for naming authorities. Some developers use all caps, while other use all lowercase letters. In my opinion, all these choices are OK as long as you keep them consistent in your app. In this book, I use different styles in the examples so that you can observe more approaches that you might encounter in real-world scenarios.

It is a hypothetical example, of course, but it's simple enough to be easy to understand and complex enough to prove why the `access()` method is more powerful. To implement this with the `access()` method, you can use an `AuthorizationManager` implementation that takes a SpEL expression. The SpEL expression must reflect the requirement. For example:

```
"hasAuthority('read') and !hasAuthority('delete')"
```

The next listing illustrates how to apply the `access()` method with a more complex expression. You can find this example in the project named ssia-ch7-ex2 .

Listing 7.8 Applying the `access()` method with a more complex expression

```java
@Configuration
public class ProjectConfig {

  @Bean
  public UserDetailsService userDetailsService() {
    var manager = new InMemoryUserDetailsManager();

    var user1 = User.withUsername("john")
            .password("12345")
            .authorities("read")
            .build();

    var user2 = User.withUsername("jane")
            .password("12345")
            .authorities("read", "write", "delete")
            .build();

    manager.createUser(user1);
    manager.createUser(user2);

    return manager;
  }

  @Bean
  public PasswordEncoder passwordEncoder() {
    return NoOpPasswordEncoder.getInstance();
  }

  @Bean
  public SecurityFilterChain securityFilterChain(HttpSecurity http)
    throws Exception {

    http.httpBasic(Customizer.withDefaults());

    String expression =
            """hasAuthority('read') and          ⟵  States that the user must
            !hasAuthority('delete')                  have the authority read but
            """;                                      not the authority delete

    http.authorizeHttpRequests(
      c -> c.anyRequest()
```

```
                    .access(new WebExpressionAuthorizationManager(expression));

        );


        return http.build();
    }
}
```

Let's test our application now by calling the /hello endpoint for user John:

```
curl -u john:12345 http://localhost:8080/hello
```

The body of the response is

```
Hello!
```

And when calling the endpoint with user Jane

```
curl -u jane:12345 http://localhost:8080/hello
```

the body of the response is

```
{
    "status":403,
    "error":"Forbidden",
    "message":"Forbidden",
    "path":"/hello"
}
```

The user John has only read authority and can call the endpoint successfully. However, Jane also has delete authority and is not authorized to call the endpoint. The HTTP status for the call by Jane is 403 Forbidden.

With these examples, you can see how to set constraints regarding the authorities that a user requires to have to access some specified endpoints. Of course, we haven't discussed selecting yet, which requests to be secured based on the path or the HTTP method. We have instead applied the rules for all requests regardless of the endpoint exposed by the application. Once we finish executing the same configuration for user roles, we'll discuss how to select the endpoints to which you apply the authorization configurations.

7.1.2 *Restricting access for all endpoints based on user roles*

In this section, we discuss restricting access to endpoints based on roles. Roles are another way to refer to what a user can do (figure 7.5). You also find these in real-world applications, so this is why it is important to understand roles and the difference between roles and authorities. In this section, we apply several examples using roles so that you'll know all the practical scenarios in which the application uses roles and how to write configurations for these cases.

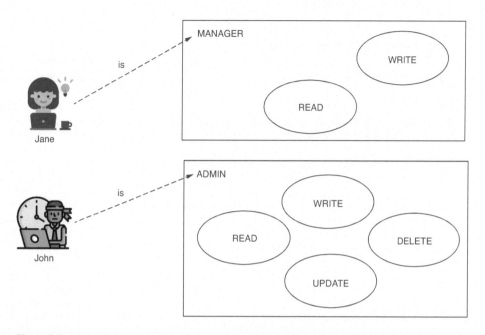

Figure 7.5 Roles are coarse grained. Each user with a specific role can only do the actions granted by that role. When applying this philosophy in authorization, a request is allowed based on the purpose of the user in the system. Only users who have a specific role can call a certain endpoint.

Spring Security understands authorities as fine-grained privileges on which we apply restrictions. Roles are like badges for users. These give a user privileges for a group of actions. Some applications always provide the same groups of authorities to specific users. Imagine that in your application a user can either only have read authority or have all (read, write, and delete) authorities. In this case, it might be more comfortable to think that those users who can only read have a role named READER, while the others have the role ADMIN. Having the ADMIN role means that the application grants you read, write, update, and delete privileges. You could potentially have more roles. For example, if at some point the requests specify that you also need a user who is only allowed to read and write, you can create a third role named MANAGER for your application.

> **NOTE** When using an approach with roles in the application, you won't have to define authorities anymore. The authorities exist, in this case as a concept, and can appear in the implementation requirements. But in the application, you only have to define a role to cover one or more such actions a user is privileged to do.

The names that you give to roles are like the names for authorities—it's your own choice. We could say that roles are coarse grained when compared with authorities. Behind the scenes, anyway, roles are represented using the same contract in Spring

Security, `GrantedAuthority`. When defining a role, its name should start with the `ROLE_` prefix. At the implementation level, this prefix specifies the difference between a role and an authority. You'll find the example we work on in this section in the project ssia-ch7-ex3. In the next listing, let's take a look at the change I made to the previous example.

Listing 7.9   Setting roles for users

```
@Configuration
public class ProjectConfig {

  @Bean
  public UserDetailsService userDetailsService() {
    var manager = new InMemoryUserDetailsManager();

    var user1 = User.withUsername("john")
                    .password("12345")
                    .authorities("ROLE_ADMIN")          Having the ROLE_
                    .build();                           prefix,
                                                        GrantedAuthority
    var user2 = User.withUsername("jane")               now represents a
                    .password("12345")                  role.
                    .authorities("ROLE_MANAGER")
                    .build();

    manager.createUser(user1);
    manager.createUser(user2);

    return manager;
  }

  // Omitted code

}
```

To set constraints for user roles, you can use one of the following methods:

- `hasRole()`—Receives as a parameter the role name for which the application authorizes the request.
- `hasAnyRole()`—Receives as parameters the role names for which the application approves the request.
- `access()`—Uses an `AuthorizationManager` to specify the role or roles for which the application authorizes requests. In terms of roles, you could use `hasRole()` or `hasAnyRole()` as SpEL expressions together with the `WebExpression-AuthorizationManager` implementation.

As you observe, the names are similar to the methods presented in section 7.1.1. We use these in the same way, but to apply configurations for roles instead of authorities. My recommendations are also similar: use the `hasRole()` or `hasAnyRole()` methods as your first option, and fall back to using `access()` only when the previous two don't apply. The next listing shows what the `securityFilterChain()` method looks like now.

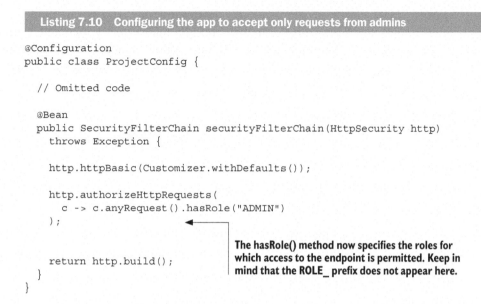

```
@Configuration
public class ProjectConfig {

  // Omitted code

  @Bean
  public SecurityFilterChain securityFilterChain(HttpSecurity http)
    throws Exception {

    http.httpBasic(Customizer.withDefaults());

    http.authorizeHttpRequests(
      c -> c.anyRequest().hasRole("ADMIN")
    );

    return http.build();
  }
}
```

Listing 7.10   Configuring the app to accept only requests from admins

The hasRole() method now specifies the roles for which access to the endpoint is permitted. Keep in mind that the ROLE_ prefix does not appear here.

NOTE   A critical thing to observe is that we use the ROLE_ prefix only to declare the role. But when we use the role, we do it only by its name.

When testing the application, you should observe that user John can access the endpoint, while Jane receives an HTTP 403 Forbidden. To call the endpoint with user John, use

```
curl -u john:12345 http://localhost:8080/hello
```

The response body is

```
Hello!
```

And to call the endpoint with user Jane, use

```
curl -u jane:12345 http://localhost:8080/hello
```

The response body is

```
{
  "status":403,
  "error":"Forbidden",
  "message":"Forbidden",
  "path":"/hello"
}
```

When building users with the User builder class, like we did in the example for this section, you specify the role by using the roles() method. This method creates the GrantedAuthority object and automatically adds the ROLE_ prefix to the names you provide.

NOTE   Make sure the parameter you provide for the `roles()` method does not include the `ROLE_` prefix. If that prefix is inadvertently included in the `role()` parameter, the method throws an exception. In short, when using the `authorities()` method, include the `ROLE_` prefix. When using the `roles()` method, do not include the `ROLE_` prefix.

In listing 7.11, you can see the correct way to use the `roles()` method instead of the `authorities()` method when you design access based on roles. You can also compare this listing with listing 7.9 to observe the difference between using authorities and roles.

Listing 7.11   Setting up roles with the `roles()` method

```
@Configuration
public class ProjectConfig {

  @Bean
  public UserDetailsService userDetailsService() {
    var manager = new InMemoryUserDetailsManager();

    var user1 = User.withUsername("john")
                    .password("12345")
                    .roles("ADMIN")          ◀─┐  The roles() method
                    .build();                   │  specifies the user's
                                                │  roles.
    var user2 = User.withUsername("jane")
                    .password("12345")
                    .roles("MANAGER")
                    .build();

    manager.createUser(user1);
    manager.createUser(user2);

    return manager;
  }

  // Omitted code
}
```

More on the access() method

In sections 7.1.1 and 7.1.2, you learned to use the `access()` method to apply authorization rules referring to authorities and roles. In general, in an application, the authorization restrictions are related to authorities and roles. However, it's important to remember that the `access()` method is generic, and it only depends on what implementation of the `AuthorizationManager` contract you provide as a parameter. Moreover, in our example, we only used the `WebExpressionAuthorizationManager` implementation that applies the authorization restrictions based on a SpEL expression. With the examples I present, I focus on teaching you how to apply it for authorities and roles, but in practice, `WebExpressionAuthorizationManager` receives any SpEL expression. It doesn't need to be related to authorities and roles.

A straightforward example would be configuring access to the endpoint to be allowed only after 12:00 pm. To solve something like this, you can use the following SpEL expression:

```
T(java.time.LocalTime).now().isAfter(T(java.time.LocalTime).of(12, 0))
```

For more about SpEL expressions, see the Spring Framework documentation:

http://mng.bz/M9J7

We could say that with the `access()` method, you can basically implement any kind of rule. The possibilities are endless. Just don't forget that in applications, we always strive to keep syntax as simple as possible. Complicate your configurations only when you don't have any other choice. You'll find this example applied in the project ssia-ch7-ex4.

7.1.3   *Restricting access to all endpoints*

In this section, we discuss restricting access to all requests. You learned in section 5.2 that by using the `permitAll()` method, you can permit access for all requests. You also learned that you can apply access rules based on authorities and roles. But what you can also do is deny all requests. The `denyAll()` method is just the opposite of the `permitAll()` method. In the next listing, you can see how to use the `denyAll()` method.

Listing 7.12   **Using the `denyAll()` method to restrict access to endpoints**

```
@Configuration
public class ProjectConfig {

  // Omitted code

  @Bean
  public SecurityFilterChain securityFilterChain(HttpSecurity http)
    throws Exception {

    http.httpBasic(Customizer.withDefaults());

    http.authorizeHttpRequests(
      c -> c.anyRequest().denyAll()
    );                              ◄──┐  Uses denyAll() to
                                       │  restrict access for
    return http.basic();               │  everyone
  }
}
```

Where could you use such a restriction? You won't find it used as much as the other methods, but there are cases in which requirements make it necessary. Let me show you a couple of cases to clarify this point.

Let's assume that you have an endpoint receiving an email address as a path variable. You want to allow requests that have the value of the variable addresses ending in .com. You don't want the application to accept any other format for the email address. (You'll learn in the next chapter how to apply restrictions for a group of requests based on the path and HTTP method and even for path variables.) For this requirement, you use a regular expression to group requests that match your rule and then use the denyAll() method to instruct your application to deny all these requests (figure 7.6).

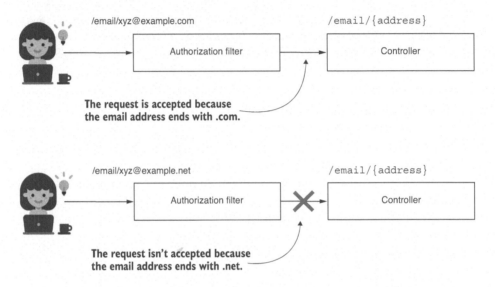

Figure 7.6   When the user calls the endpoint with a value of the parameter ending in .com, the application accepts the request. When the user calls the endpoint and provides an email address ending in .net, the application rejects the call. To achieve such behavior, you can use the denyAll() method for all endpoints for which the value of the parameter doesn't end with .com.

You can also imagine an application designed like in figure 7.7. A few services implement the use cases of the application, which are accessible by calling endpoints available at different paths. But to call an endpoint, the client requests another service that we can call a gateway. In this architecture, there are two separate services of this type. In figure 7.7, I called these Gateway A and Gateway B. The client requests Gateway A if they want to access the /products path. But for the /articles path, the client has to request Gateway B. Each of the gateway services is designed to deny all requests to other paths that these do not serve. This simplified scenario can help you easily understand the denyAll() method. In a production application, you could find similar cases in more complex architectures.

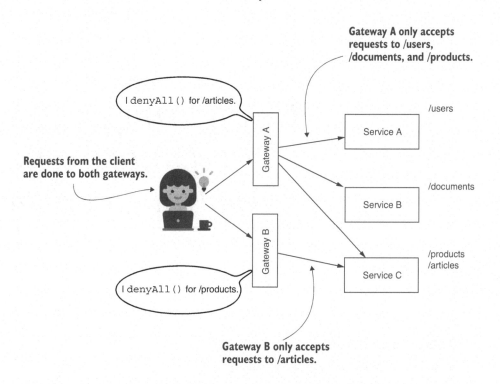

Figure 7.7 Access is done through Gateways A and B. Each of the gateways delivers only requests for specific paths and denies all others.

Applications in production face various architectural requirements, which could look strange sometimes. A framework must allow the needed flexibility for any situation you might encounter. For this reason, the denyAll() method is as important as all the other options you learned in his chapter.

Summary

- Authorization is the process during which the application decides whether an authenticated request is permitted. Authorization always happens after authentication.
- You configure how the application authorizes requests based on the authorities and roles of an authenticated user.
- In your application, you can also specify that certain requests are possible for unauthenticated users.
- You can configure your app to reject any request, using the denyAll() method, or permit any requests, using the permitAll() method.

Configuring endpoint-level authorization: Applying restrictions

This chapter covers

- Selecting requests to apply restrictions using matcher methods
- Learning best-case scenarios for each matcher method

In chapter 7, you learned how to configure access based on authorities and roles. But we only applied the configurations for all endpoints. In this chapter, you'll learn how to apply authorization constraints to a specific group of requests. In production applications, it's less probable that you'll apply the same rules for all requests. You have endpoints that can be called only by specific users, while other endpoints might be accessible to everyone. Depending on the business requirements, each application has its own custom authorization configuration. Let's discuss the options available to refer to different requests when we write access configurations.

Even though we didn't pay attention to it, the first matcher method you used was the `anyRequest()` method. And because it was used in previous chapters, you know now that it refers to all requests, regardless of the path or HTTP method. It is the way to say "any request" or, sometimes, "any other request."

First, let's talk about selecting requests by path; then we can also add the HTTP method to the scenario. To choose the requests to which we apply authorization configuration, we use the `requestMatchers()` method.

8.1 Using the requestMatchers() method to select endpoints

In this section, you will learn how to use the `requestMatchers()` method in general so that in sections 8.2 through 8.4, we can continue describing various approaches to selecting HTTP requests for which you need to apply authorization restrictions. By the end of this chapter, you'll be able to apply the `requestMatchers()` method in any authorization configurations you might need to write for your application's requirements. Let's start with a straightforward example.

We create an application that exposes two endpoints: /hello and /ciao. We want to make sure that only users having the ADMIN role can call the /hello endpoint. Similarly, we want to make sure that only users having the MANAGER role can call the /ciao endpoint. You can find this example in the project ssia-ch8-ex1. The following listing defines the controller class.

Listing 8.1 The definition of the controller class

```
@RestController
public class HelloController {

  @GetMapping("/hello")
  public String hello() {
    return "Hello!";
  }

  @GetMapping("/ciao")
  public String ciao() {
    return "Ciao!";
  }
}
```

In the configuration class, we declare an `InMemoryUserDetailsManager` as our `UserDetailsService` instance and add two users with different roles. The user John has the ADMIN role, while Jane has the MANAGER role. To specify that only users having the ADMIN role can call the endpoint /hello when authorizing requests, we use the `requestMatchers()` method. The next listing presents the definition of the configuration class.

Listing 8.2 The definition of the configuration class

```
@Configuration
public class ProjectConfig {

  @Bean
  public UserDetailsService userDetailsService() {
    var manager = new InMemoryUserDetailsManager();

    var user1 = User.withUsername("john")
            .password("12345")
            .roles("ADMIN")
            .build();
```

```
        var user2 = User.withUsername("jane")
                .password("12345")
                .roles("MANAGER")
                .build();

    manager.createUser(user1);
    manager.createUser(user2);

    return manager;
}

@Bean
public PasswordEncoder passwordEncoder() {
  return NoOpPasswordEncoder.getInstance();
}

@Bean
public SecurityFilterChain securityFilterChain(HttpSecurity http)
  throws Exception {

  http.httpBasic(Customizer.withDefaults());

  http.authorizeHttpRequests(
    c -> c.requestMatchers("/hello").hasRole("ADMIN")
          .requestMatchers("/ciao").hasRole("MANAGER")

  );

  return http.build();
}

}
```

> Only calls the path /hello if the user has the ADMIN role

> Only calls the path /ciao if the user has the MANAGER role

You can run and test this application. When you call the endpoint /hello with user John, you get a successful response. But if you call the same endpoint with user Jane, the response status returns an HTTP 403 Forbidden. Similarly, for the endpoint /ciao, you can only use Jane to get a successful result. For user John, the response status returns an HTTP 403 Forbidden. You can see the example calls using cURL in the code snippets that follow. To call the endpoint /hello for user John, use

```
curl -u john:12345 http://localhost:8080/hello
```

The response body is

```
Hello!
```

To call the endpoint /hello for user Jane, use

```
curl -u jane:12345 http://localhost:8080/hello
```

The response body is

```
{
  "status":403,
  "error":"Forbidden",
```

```
    "message":"Forbidden",
    "path":"/hello"
}
```

To call the endpoint /ciao for user Jane, use

```
curl -u jane:12345 http://localhost:8080/ciao
```

The response body is

```
Ciao!
```

To call the endpoint /ciao for user John, use

```
curl -u john:12345 http://localhost:8080/ciao
```

The response body is

```
{
    "status":403,
    "error":"Forbidden",
    "message":"Forbidden",
    "path":"/ciao"
}
```

If you now add any other endpoint to your application, it is accessible by default to anyone, even unauthenticated users. Let's assume you add a new endpoint /hola as presented in the next listing.

Listing 8.3   Adding a new endpoint for path /hola to the application

```
@RestController
public class HelloController {

  // Omitted code

  @GetMapping("/hola")
  public String hola() {
    return "Hola!";
  }
}
```

When you access this new endpoint, you see that it is accessible with or without having a valid user. The code snippets that follow display this behavior. To call the endpoint /hola without authenticating, use

```
curl http://localhost:8080/hola
```

The response body is

```
Hola!
```

To call the endpoint /hola for user John, use

```
curl -u john:12345 http://localhost:8080/hola
```

The response body is

```
Hola!
```

You can make this behavior more visible if you like by using the `permitAll()` method. You do this by using the `anyRequest()` matcher method at the end of the configuration chain for the request authorization, as presented in listing 8.4.

> **NOTE**   It is good practice to make all your rules explicit. Listing 8.4 clearly and unambiguously indicates the intention to permit requests to endpoints for everyone, except for the endpoints /hello and /ciao.

Listing 8.4   Marking additional requests explicitly as accessible without authentication

```
@Configuration
public class ProjectConfig {

  // Omitted code

  @Bean
  public SecurityFilterChain securityFilterChain(HttpSecurity http)
    throws Exception {

    http.httpBasic(Customizer.withDefaults());

    http.authorizeHttpRequests(
        c -> c.requestMatchers("/hello").hasRole("ADMIN")
          .requestMatchers("/ciao").hasRole("MANAGER")
          .anyRequest().permitAll()                         ◄——┐  The permitAll() method
                                                               │  states that all other
    );                                                         │  requests are allowed
                                                               │  without authentication.
    return http.build();
  }
}
```

> **NOTE**   When you use matchers to refer to requests, the order of the rules should be from particular to general. This is why the `anyRequest()` method cannot be called before a more specific `requestMatchers()` method.

Unauthenticated vs. failed authentication

If you have designed an endpoint to be accessible to anyone, you can call it without providing a username and a password for authentication. In this case, Spring Security won't do the authentication. If you, however, provide a username and a password, Spring Security evaluates them in the authentication process. If they are wrong (not known by the system), authentication fails, and the response status will be 401 Unauthorized. To be more precise, if you call the /hola endpoint for the configuration presented in listing 8.4, the app returns the body `Hola!` as expected, and the response status is 200 OK. For example:

```
curl http://localhost:8080/hola
```

The response body is

```
Hola!
```

However, if you call the endpoint with invalid credentials, the status of the response is 401 Unauthorized. In the next call, I use an invalid password:

```
curl -u bill:abcde http://localhost:8080/hola
```

The response body is

```
{
    "status":401,
    "error":"Unauthorized",
    "message":"Unauthorized",
    "path":"/hola"
}
```

This behavior might look strange, but it makes sense, as the framework evaluates any username and password if you provide them in the request. As you learned in chapter 7, the application always does authentication before authorization, as this figure shows.

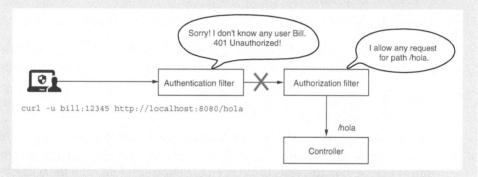

The authorization filter allows any request to the /hola path. However, because the application first executes the authentication logic, the request is never forwarded to the authorization filter. Instead, the authentication filter replies with an HTTP 401 Unauthorized.

In conclusion, any situation in which authentication fails will generate a response with the status 401 Unauthorized, and the application won't forward the call to the endpoint. The `permitAll()` method refers to authorization configuration only, and if authentication fails, the call will not be allowed further.

You could decide, of course, to make all the other endpoints accessible only for authenticated users. To do this, you would change the `permitAll()` method with `authenticated()` as presented in the following listing. Similarly, you could even deny all other requests by using the `denyAll()` method.

Listing 8.5 Making other requests accessible for all authenticated users

```
@Configuration
public class ProjectConfig {

  // Omitted code

  @Bean
  public SecurityFilterChain securityFilterChain(HttpSecurity http)
    throws Exception {

    http.httpBasic(Customizer.withDefaults());

    http.authorizeHttpRequests(
      c -> c.requestMatchers("/hello").hasRole("ADMIN")
         .requestMatchers("/ciao").hasRole("MANAGER")
         .anyRequest().authenticated()

    );

    return http.build();
  }
}
```

All other requests are accessible only by authenticated users.

You've become familiar with using matcher methods to refer to requests for which you want to configure authorization restrictions. Now we must go into more depth with the syntaxes you can use.

In most practical scenarios, multiple endpoints can have the same authorization rules, so you don't have to set them up endpoint by endpoint. Furthermore, you sometimes need to specify the HTTP method, not just the path, like we've done until now.

Other times, you only need to configure rules for an endpoint when its path is called with HTTP GET. In this case, you'd need to define different rules for HTTP POST and HTTP DELETE. In the next section, we take each type of matcher method and discuss these aspects in detail.

8.2   *Selecting requests to apply authorization restrictions*

In this section, we deep dive into configuring request matchers. Using the `request-Matchers()` method is a common approach to refer to requests for applying authorization configuration. Thus, I expect you to have many opportunities to use this method to refer to requests in the applications you develop.

This matcher uses the standard ANT syntax (table 8.1) for referring to paths. The syntax is the same as the one you use when writing endpoint mappings with annotations such as `@RequestMapping`, `@GetMapping`, `@PostMapping`, and so forth. The two methods you can use to declare MVC matchers are

- `requestMatchers(HttpMethod method, String... patterns)`—Lets you specify both the HTTP method to which the restrictions apply and the paths. This method is useful if you want to apply different restrictions for different HTTP methods for the same path.

- `requestMatchers(String... patterns)`—Simpler and easier to use if you only need to apply authorization restrictions based on paths. The restrictions can automatically apply to any HTTP method used with the path.

In this section, we approach multiple ways of using `requestMatchers()` methods. To demonstrate this, we start by writing an application that exposes multiple endpoints.

For the first time, we write endpoints that can be called with other HTTP methods besides GET. You might have observed that until now, I've avoided using other HTTP methods. The reason for this is that Spring Security by default applies protection against cross-site request forgery (CSRF). In chapter 9, we'll discuss how Spring Security mitigates this vulnerability by using CSRF tokens. But to make things simpler for the current example and to be able to call all endpoints, including those exposed with POST, PUT, or DELETE, we need to disable CSRF protection in our `securityFilter-Chain()` method:

```
http.csrf(
  c -> c.disable()
);
```

> **NOTE** We disable CSRF protection now only to allow you to focus for the moment on the discussed topic: matcher methods. But don't rush to consider this a good approach. In chapter 9, we'll talk in detail about the CSRF protection provided by Spring Security.

We start by defining four endpoints to use in our tests:

- /a using the HTTP method GET
- /a using the HTTP method POST
- /a/b using the HTTP method GET
- /a/b/c using the HTTP method GET

With these endpoints, we can consider different scenarios for authorization configuration. The next listing provides the definitions of these endpoints. You can find this example in the project ssia-ch8-ex2.

Listing 8.6 Definition of the four endpoints for which we configure authorization

```
@RestController
public class TestController {

  @PostMapping("/a")
  public String postEndpointA() {
    return "Works!";
  }

  @GetMapping("/a")
  public String getEndpointA() {
    return "Works!";
  }
```

```
@GetMapping("/a/b")
public String getEnpointB() {
  return "Works!";
}

@GetMapping("/a/b/c")
public String getEnpointC() {
  return "Works!";
}
}
```

We also need a couple of users with different roles. To keep things simple, we continue using an InMemoryUserDetailsManager. In the next listing, you can see the definition of the UserDetailsService in the configuration class.

Listing 8.7 The definition of the UserDetailsService

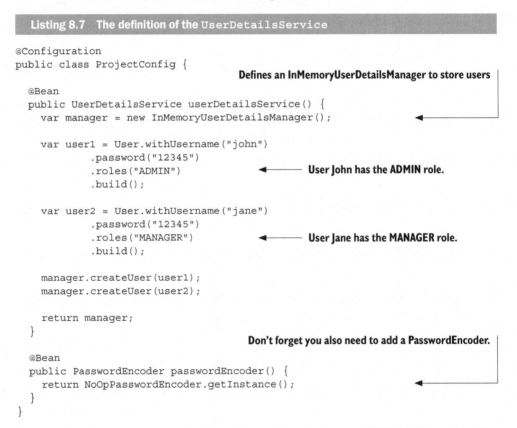

```
@Configuration
public class ProjectConfig {
                                        Defines an InMemoryUserDetailsManager to store users
  @Bean
  public UserDetailsService userDetailsService() {
    var manager = new InMemoryUserDetailsManager();

    var user1 = User.withUsername("john")
            .password("12345")
            .roles("ADMIN")                       User John has the ADMIN role.
            .build();

    var user2 = User.withUsername("jane")
            .password("12345")
            .roles("MANAGER")                     User Jane has the MANAGER role.
            .build();

    manager.createUser(user1);
    manager.createUser(user2);

    return manager;
  }
                                        Don't forget you also need to add a PasswordEncoder.
  @Bean
  public PasswordEncoder passwordEncoder() {
    return NoOpPasswordEncoder.getInstance();
  }
}
```

Let's start with the first scenario. For requests done using an HTTP GET method for the /a path, the application needs to authenticate the user. For the same path, requests using an HTTP POST method don't require authentication. The application denies all other requests. The following listing shows the configurations that you need to write to achieve this setup.

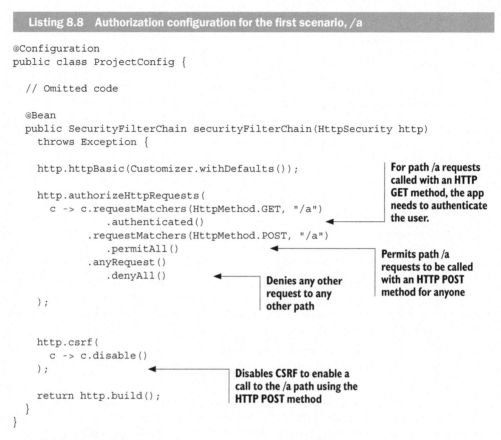

Listing 8.8 Authorization configuration for the first scenario, /a

```
@Configuration
public class ProjectConfig {

  // Omitted code

  @Bean
  public SecurityFilterChain securityFilterChain(HttpSecurity http)
    throws Exception {

    http.httpBasic(Customizer.withDefaults());

    http.authorizeHttpRequests(
      c -> c.requestMatchers(HttpMethod.GET, "/a")
              .authenticated()
            .requestMatchers(HttpMethod.POST, "/a")
              .permitAll()
            .anyRequest()
              .denyAll()
    );

    http.csrf(
      c -> c.disable()
    );

    return http.build();
  }
}
```

For path /a requests called with an HTTP GET method, the app needs to authenticate the user.

Permits path /a requests to be called with an HTTP POST method for anyone

Denies any other request to any other path

Disables CSRF to enable a call to the /a path using the HTTP POST method

In the code snippets that follow, we analyze the results of the calls to the endpoints for the configuration presented in listing 8.8. For the call to path /a using the HTTP method POST without authenticating, use this cURL command:

```
curl -XPOST http://localhost:8080/a
```

The response body is

```
Works!
```

When calling path /a using HTTP GET without authenticating, use

```
curl -XGET http://localhost:8080/a
```

The response is

```
{
  "status":401,
  "error":"Unauthorized",
  "message":"Unauthorized",
  "path":"/a"
}
```

If you want to change the response to a successful one, you need to authenticate with a valid user. For the following call

```
curl -u john:12345 -XGET http://localhost:8080/a
```

the response body is

```
Works!
```

However, user John isn't allowed to call path /a/b, so authenticating with his credentials for this call generates a 403 Forbidden:

```
curl -u john:12345 -XGET http://localhost:8080/a/b
```

The response is

```
{
  "status":403,
  "error":"Forbidden",
  "message":"Forbidden",
  "path":"/a/b"
}
```

With this example, you now know how to differentiate requests based on the HTTP method. But what if multiple paths have the same authorization rules? Of course, we can enumerate all the paths for which we apply authorization rules; however, if we have too many paths, this makes reading code uncomfortable. In addition, we might know from the beginning that a group of paths with the same prefix always has the same authorization rules. We want to make sure that adding a new path to the same group doesn't also change the authorization configuration. To manage these cases, we use *path expressions*. Let's prove these in an example.

For the current project, we want to ensure that the same rules apply for all requests for paths starting with /a/b. These paths in our case are /a/b and /a/b/c. To achieve this, we use the ** operator. You can find this example in the project ssia-ch8-ex3.

Listing 8.9   Changes in the configuration class for multiple paths

```
@Configuration
public class ProjectConfig {

  // Omitted code

  @Bean
  public void configure(HttpSecurity http)
    throws Exception {

    http.httpBasic(Customizer.withDefaults());

    http.authorizeHttpRequests(
      c -> c.requestMatchers( "/a/b/**").authenticated()
          .anyRequest().permitAll();

    );

    http.csrf(
```

The /a/b/** expression refers to all paths prefixed with /a/b.

```
      c -> c.disable()
   );

   return http.build();
  }
}
```

With the configuration given in listing 8.9, you can call path /a without being authenticated, but for all paths prefixed with /a/b, the application needs to authenticate the user. The following code snippets present the results of calling the /a, /a/b, and /a/b/c endpoints. First, to call the /a path without authenticating, use

```
curl http://localhost:8080/a
```

The response body is

```
Works!
```

To call the /a/b path without authenticating, use

```
curl http://localhost:8080/a/b
```

The response is

```
{
  "status":401,
  "error":"Unauthorized",
  "message":"Unauthorized",
  "path":"/a/b"
}
```

To call the /a/b/c path without authenticating, use

```
curl http://localhost:8080/a/b/c
```

The response is

```
{
  "status":401,
  "error":"Unauthorized",
  "message":"Unauthorized",
  "path":"/a/b/c"
}
```

As presented in the previous examples, the ** operator refers to any number of pathnames. You can use it as we have done in the last example so that you can match requests with paths having a known prefix. You can also use it in the middle of a path to refer to any number of pathnames or to refer to paths ending in a specific pattern, like /a/**/c. Therefore, /a/**/c would not only match /a/b/c but also /a/b/d/c and a/b/c/d/e/c and so on. If you only want to match one pathname, then you can use a single *. For example, a/*/c would match a/b/c and a/d/c but not a/b/d/c.

Because you generally use path variables, these can be useful to apply authorization rules for such requests. You can even apply rules referring to the path variable value. Do you remember the discussion from section 8.1 about the denyAll() method and restricting all requests?

Let's turn now to a more suitable example of what you have learned in this section. We have an endpoint with a path variable, and we want to deny all requests that use a value for the path variable that has anything else other than digits. You can find this example in the project ssia-ch8-ex4. The following listing presents the controller.

Listing 8.10   The definition of an endpoint with a path variable in a controller class

```
@RestController
public class ProductController {

  @GetMapping("/product/{code}")
  public String productCode(@PathVariable String code) {
    return code;
  }
}
```

The next listing shows how to configure authorization so that only calls that have a value containing only digits are always permitted, while all other calls are denied.

Listing 8.11   Configuring the authorization to permit only specific digits

```
@Configuration
public class ProjectConfig {

  @Bean
  public SecurityFilterChain securityFilterChain(HttpSecurity http)
    throws Exception {

    http.httpBasic(Customizer.withDefaults());

    http.authorizeHttpRequests(
      c -> c.requestMatchers("/product/{code:^[0-9]*$}")     ◄─────┐
        .permitAll()
      .anyRequest()
        .denyAll()                              The regex refers to
                                               strings of any length,
    );                                         containing any digit.


    return http.build();
  }
}
```

NOTE   When using parameter expressions with a regex, make sure to not have a space between the name of the parameter, the colon (:), and the regex, as displayed in the listing.

Running this example, you can see the result as presented in the following code snippets. The application only accepts the call when the path variable value has digits only. To call the endpoint using the value `1234a`, use

```
curl http://localhost:8080/product/1234a
```

The response is

```
{
  "status":401,
  "error":"Unauthorized",
  "message":"Unauthorized",
  "path":"/product/1234a"
}
```

To call the endpoint with the value `12345`, use

```
curl http://localhost:8080/product/12345
```

The response is

```
12345
```

We extensively discussed and included plenty of examples of how to refer to requests using the `requestMatchers()` method. Table 8.1 is a refresher for the path expressions used in this section. You can refer to it later when you want to recall any of them.

Table 8.1 Common expressions used for path matching with MVC matchers

Expression	Description
`/a`	Only path /a.
`/a/*`	The * operator replaces one pathname. In this case, it matches /a/b or /a/c, but not /a/b/c.
`/a/**`	The ** operator replaces multiple pathnames. In this case, /a, /a/b, and /a/b/c are a match for this expression.
`/a/{param}`	This expression applies to the path /a with a given path parameter.
`/a/{param:regex}`	This expression applies to the path /a with a given path parameter only when the value of the parameter matches the given regular expression.

8.3 *Using regular expressions with request matchers*

This section discusses regular expression (regex). You should already know what regular expressions are, but you don't need to be an expert on the subject. Any of the books recommended at https://www.regular-expressions.info/books.html are excellent resources from which you can learn about the subject in more depth. For writing regex, I also often use online generators such as https://regexr.com/ (figure 8.1).

Figure 8.1   Letting your cat play on the keyboard is not the best solution for generating regular expressions (regex). To learn how to generate regexes, you can use an online generator such as https://regexr.com/.

Sections 8.2 and 8.3 showed that in most cases, it is possible use path expression syntaxes to refer to requests to which you apply authorization configurations. In some cases, however, you might have more particular requirements, and you cannot solve those with path expressions. An example of such a requirement could be, "Deny all requests when paths contain specific symbols or characters." For these scenarios, you need to use a more powerful expression like a regex.

You can use regexes to represent any format of a string, so they offer limitless possibilities for this matter. However, they have the disadvantage of being difficult to read, even when applied to simple scenarios. For this reason, you might prefer to use path expressions and fall back to regexes only when you have no other options. To implement a regex request matcher, you can use the `requestMatchers()` method with a `RegexRequestMatcher` implementation as parameter.

To show how regex matchers work, let's put them into action by building an application that provides video content to its users. The application that presents the video gets its content by calling the endpoint /video/{country}/{language}. For the sake of the example, the application receives the country and language in two path variables from where the user makes the request. We consider that any authenticated user can see the video content if the request comes from the United States, Canada, or the United Kingdom, or if they use English.

You can find this example implemented in the project ssia-ch8-ex5. The endpoint we need to secure has two path variables, as shown in the following listing. This makes the requirement complicated to implement with request matchers.

Listing 8.12   The definition of the endpoint for the controller class

```
@RestController
public class VideoController {

  @GetMapping("/video/{country}/{language}")
  public String video(@PathVariable String country,
                      @PathVariable String language) {
    return "Video allowed for " + country + " " + language;
  }
}
```

For a condition on a single path variable, we can write a regex directly in the path expression. We referred to such an example in section 8.2, but I didn't go into detail at that time because we weren't discussing regexes.

Let's assume you have the endpoint /email/{email}. You want to apply a rule using a matcher only to the requests that send an address ending in .com as a value of the email parameter. In that case, you write a request matcher as presented by the next code snippet. You can find the complete example in the project ssia-ch8-ex6:

```
http.authorizeHttpRequests(
    c -> c.requestMatchers("/email/{email:.*(?:.+@.+\\.com)}" ).permitAll()
        .anyRequest().denyAll();

);
```

If you test such a restriction, you can see that the application only accepts emails ending in .com. For example, to call the endpoint to jane@example.com, you can use

```
curl http://localhost:8080/email/jane@example.com
```

The response body is

```
Allowed for email jane@example.com
```

And to call the endpoint to jane@example.net, you use

```
curl http://localhost:8080/email/jane@example.net
```

The response body is

```
{
  "status":401,
  "error":"Unauthorized",
  "message":"Unauthorized",
  "path":/email/jane@example.net
}
```

It is fairly easy and makes it even clearer why we encounter regex matchers less frequently. However, as I said earlier, requirements are sometimes complex. You'll find it handier to use regex matchers when you find something like the following:

- Specific configurations for all paths containing phone numbers or email addresses

- Specific configurations for all paths having a certain format, including what is sent through all the path variables

Back to our regex matchers example (ssia-ch8-ex6): when you need to write a more complex rule, eventually referring to more path patterns and multiple path variable values, it's easier to write a regex matcher. Listing 8.13 presents the definition for the configuration class that uses a regex matcher to solve the requirement given for the /video/{country}/{language} path. We also add two users with different authorities to test the implementation.

Listing 8.13 The configuration class using a regex matcher

```
@Configuration
public class ProjectConfig {

  @Bean
  public UserDetailsService userDetailsService() {
    var uds = new InMemoryUserDetailsManager();

    var u1 = User.withUsername("john")
                 .password("12345")
                 .authorities("read")
                 .build();

    var u2 = User.withUsername("jane")
                 .password("12345")
                 .authorities("read", "premium")
                 .build();

    uds.createUser(u1);
    uds.createUser(u2);

    return uds;
  }

  @Bean
  public PasswordEncoder passwordEncoder() {
    return NoOpPasswordEncoder.getInstance();
  }

  @Bean
  public SecurityFilterChain securityFilterChain(HttpSecurity http)
    throws Exception {

    http.httpBasic(Customizer.withDefaults());

    http.authorizeHttpRequests(

        c -> c.regexMatchers(".*/(us|uk|ca)+/(en|fr).*")
                .authenticated()
              .anyRequest()
```

We use a regex to match the paths for which the user only needs to be authenticated.

```
            .hasAuthority("premium");

    );

  }
}
```

**Configures the other paths
for which the user needs to
have premium access**

Running and testing the endpoints confirm that the application applied the authorization configurations correctly. The user John can call the endpoint with the country code US and language en, but he can't call the endpoint for the country code FR and language fr due to the restrictions we configured. Calling the /video endpoint and authenticating user John for the US region and the English language looks like this:

```
curl -u john:12345 http://localhost:8080/video/us/en
```

The response body is

```
Video allowed for us en
```

Calling the /video endpoint and authenticating user John for the FR region and the French language looks like this:

```
curl -u john:12345 http://localhost:8080/video/fr/fr
```

The response body is

```
{
  "status":403,
  "error":"Forbidden",
  "message":"Forbidden",
  "path":"/video/fr/fr"
}
```

Having premium authority, user Jane makes both calls with success. For the first call

```
curl -u jane:12345 http://localhost:8080/video/us/en
```

the response body is

```
Video allowed for us en
```

For the second call

```
curl -u jane:12345 http://localhost:8080/video/fr/fr
```

the response body is

```
Video allowed for fr fr
```

Regexes are powerful tools. You can use them to refer to paths for any given requirement. However, because regexes are hard to read and can become quite long, they should remain your last choice. Use them only if path expressions don't offer you a solution to your problem.

In this section, I used the simplest example I could imagine so that the needed regex would be short. But in more complex scenarios, the regex can become much longer. Of course, you'll find experts who say any regex is easy to read. For example, a regex used to match an email address might look like the one in the next code snippet. Can you easily read and understand it?

```
(?:[a-z0-9!#$%&'*+/=?^_`{|}~-]+(?:\.[a-z0-9!#$%&'*+/=?^_`{|}~-
]+)*|"(?:[\x01-\x08\x0b\x0c\x0e-\x1f\x21\x23-\x5b\x5d-\x7f]|\\[\x01-
\x09\x0b\x0c\x0e-\x7f])*")@(?:(?:[a-z0-9](?:[a-z0-9-]*[a-z0-9])?\.)+[a-z0
-9](?:[a-z0-9-]*[a-z0-9])?|\[(?:(?:25[0-5]|2[0-4][0-9]|[01]?[0-9][0
-9]?)\.){3}(?:25[0-5]|2[0-4][0-9]|[01]?[0-9][0-9]?|[a-z0-9-]*[a-z0
-9]:(?:[\x01-\x08\x0b\x0c\x0e-\x1f\x21-\x5a\x53-\x7f]|\\[\x01-
\x09\x0b\x0c\x0e-\x7f])+)\])
```

Summary

- In real-world scenarios, different authorization rules are applied for different requests.
- The requests for which authorization rules are configured are specified based on the path and HTTP method. To do this, you use the `requestMatchers()` method.
- When requirements are too complex to be solved with path expressions, you can implement them using more powerful regexes.

Configuring CSRF
protection

This chapter covers

- Understanding CSRF attacks
- Implementing CSRF protection
- Customizing CSRF protection

You have learned about the filter chain and its purpose in the Spring Security architecture. We worked on several examples in chapter 5, where we customized the filter chain. But Spring Security also adds its own filters to the chain. This chapter discusses the filter that configures CSRF (cross-site request forgery) protection. You'll learn to customize the filters to make a perfect fit for your scenarios.

You have probably observed that in most of the examples up to now, we only implemented our endpoints with HTTP GET. Moreover, when we needed to configure HTTP POST, we also had to add a supplementary instruction to the configuration to disable CSRF protection. The reason why you can't call an endpoint with HTTP POST directly is because of CSRF protection, which is enabled by default in Spring Security.

We'll now discuss CSRF protection and when to use it in your applications. CSRF is a widespread type of attack, and vulnerable applications can force users to execute unwanted actions on a web application following authentication. You don't want the applications you develop to be CSRF vulnerable and allow attackers to trick your users into executing unwanted actions.

Because it's essential to understand how to mitigate these vulnerabilities, we start by reviewing what CSRF is and how it works. We then discuss the CSRF token mechanism that Spring Security uses to mitigate CSRF vulnerabilities. We continue with obtaining a token and using it to call an endpoint with the HTTP POST method. We prove this using a small application with REST endpoints. Once you learn how Spring Security implements its CSRF token mechanism, we discuss how to use it in real-world application scenarios. Finally, you'll learn possible customizations of the CSRF token mechanism in Spring Security.

9.1   *How CSRF protection works in Spring Security*

This section discusses how Spring Security implements CSRF protection. It is essential to understand first the underlying mechanism of CSRF protection. I encounter many situations in which misunderstanding the way CSRF protection works leads to its misuse, either because it is disabled in scenarios where it should be enabled or the other way around. Like any other feature in a framework, you must use it correctly to bring value to your applications.

For example, consider this scenario (figure 9.1): you are at work, using a web tool to store and manage your files. With this tool, in a web interface, you can add new files, add new versions for your records, and even delete them. You receive an email asking you to open a page for a specific reason (for example, a promotion at your favorite store). You open the page, but the page is blank, or it redirects you to a known website (the online shop of your favorite store). You go back to your work finding that all your files are gone!

What happened? You were logged into your work application so you could manage your files. When you add, change, or delete a file, the web page you interact with calls some endpoints from the server to execute these operations. When you opened the foreign page by clicking the unknown link in the email, that page called your app's backend and executed actions on your behalf (i.e., it deleted your files).

It could do that because you logged in previously, so the server trusted that the actions came from you. You might think that someone couldn't trick you so easily into clicking a link from a foreign email or message, but trust me, this happens to many people. Most web app users aren't aware of security risks. So it's wiser if you, who know all the tricks, protect your users and build secure apps rather than rely on your apps' users to protect themselves.

CSRF attacks assume that a user is logged into a web application. The attacker tricks users into opening a page containing scripts that execute actions in the same application the user was working on. Because the user has already logged in (as we've assumed from the beginning), the forgery code can now impersonate the user and do actions on their behalf.

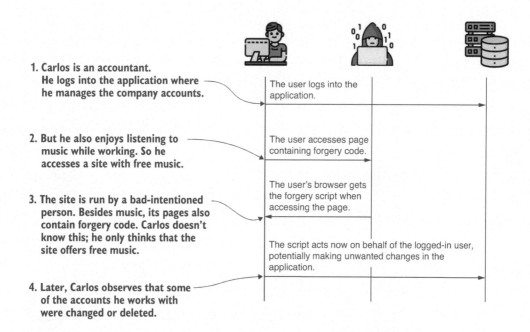

1. **Carlos is an accountant. He logs into the application where he manages the company accounts.**

   The user logs into the application.

2. **But he also enjoys listening to music while working. So he accesses a site with free music.**

   The user accesses page containing forgery code.

3. **The site is run by a bad-intentioned person. Besides music, its pages also contain forgery code. Carlos doesn't know this; he only thinks that the site offers free music.**

   The user's browser gets the forgery script when accessing the page.

   The script acts now on behalf of the logged-in user, potentially making unwanted changes in the application.

4. **Later, Carlos observes that some of the accounts he works with were changed or deleted.**

Figure 9.1   After the user logs into their account, they access a page containing forgery code. This code impersonates the user and can execute unwanted actions on behalf of the user.

How do we protect our users from such scenarios? CSRF protection aims to ensure that only the frontend of web applications can perform mutating operations (by convention, HTTP methods other than GET, HEAD, TRACE, or OPTIONS). Then a foreign page, like the one in our example, can't act on behalf of the user.

How can we achieve this? What you know for sure is that before being able to do any action that could change data, a user must send a request using HTTP GET to see the web page at least once. When this happens, the application generates a unique token. The application now accepts only requests for mutating operations (POST, PUT, DELETE, etc.) that contain this unique value in the header.

The application considers that knowing the token's value is proof that it is the app itself making the mutating request and not another system. Any page containing mutating calls, such as POST, PUT, DELETE, and so on, should receive through the CSRF token the response, and the page must use this token when making mutating calls.

The starting point of CSRF protection is a filter in the filter chain called Csrf-Filter. The CsrfFilter intercepts requests and allows all those that use these HTTP methods: GET, HEAD, TRACE, and OPTIONS. For all other requests, the filter expects to receive a header containing a token. If this header does not exist or contains an incorrect token value, the application rejects the request and sets the response status to HTTP 403 Forbidden.

What is this token, and where does it come from? These tokens are nothing more than string values. You must add the token in the request's header when you use any method other than GET, HEAD, TRACE, or OPTIONS. If you don't do this, the application doesn't accept the request, as presented in figure 9.2.

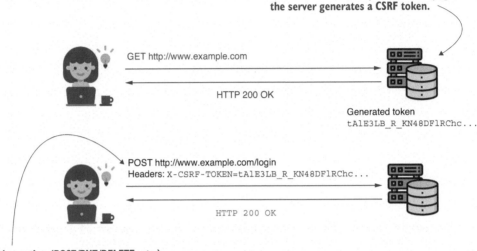

When the user first opens the web page, the server generates a CSRF token.

GET http://www.example.com

HTTP 200 OK

Generated token
tA1E3LB_R_KN48DF1RChc...

POST http://www.example.com/login
Headers: X-CSRF-TOKEN=tA1E3LB_R_KN48DF1RChc...

HTTP 200 OK

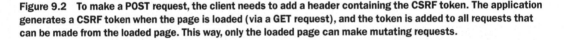

Any mutating action (POST/PUT/DELETE, etc.)
should now have the CSRF token in its HTTP headers.

Figure 9.2   To make a POST request, the client needs to add a header containing the CSRF token. The application generates a CSRF token when the page is loaded (via a GET request), and the token is added to all requests that can be made from the loaded page. This way, only the loaded page can make mutating requests.

The CsrfFilter (figure 9.3) uses a component named CsrfTokenRepository to manage the CSRF token values that generate new tokens, store tokens, and eventually invalidate these. By default, the CsrfTokenRepository stores the token on the HTTP session and generates the tokens as random string values. In most cases, this is enough, but as you'll learn in section 9.3, you can use your own implementation of CsrfTokenRepository if the default one doesn't apply to the requirements you need to implement.

In this section, I explained how CSRF protection works in Spring Security with plenty of text and figures. But I want to enforce your understanding with a small code example as well. You'll find this code as part of the project named ssia-ch9-ex1. Let's create an application that exposes two endpoints. We can call one of these with HTTP GET and the other with HTTP POST.

As you know by now, you are not able to call endpoints with POST directly without disabling CSRF protection. In this example, you learn how to call the POST endpoint without disabling CSRF protection. You need to obtain the CSRF token so that you can use it in the header of the call, which you do with HTTP POST.

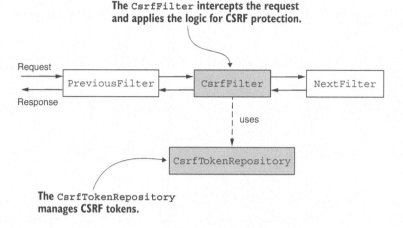

The `CsrfFilter` intercepts the request and applies the logic for CSRF protection.

The `CsrfTokenRepository` manages CSRF tokens.

Figure 9.3 The `CsrfFilter` is one of the filters in the filter chain. It receives the request and eventually forwards it to the next filter in the chain. To manage CSRF tokens, `CsrfFilter` uses a `CsrfTokenRepository`.

As you learn from this example, the `CsrfFilter` adds the generated CSRF token to the attribute of the HTTP request named _csrf (figure 9.4). If we know this, we know that after the `CsrfFilter`, we can find this attribute and take the token value from it. For this small application, we choose to add a custom filter after the `CsrfFilter`, as you learned in chapter 5. You use this custom filter to print the CSRF token in the console of the application that the app generates when we call the endpoint using HTTP GET. We can then copy the token value from the console and use it to make the mutating call with HTTP POST. In listing 9.1, you can find the definition of the controller class with the two endpoints that we use for a test.

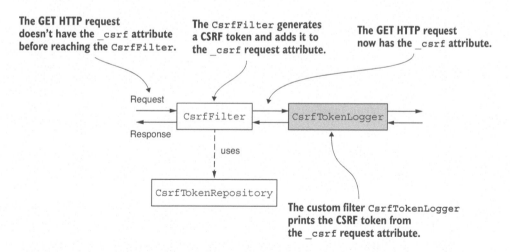

The GET HTTP request doesn't have the _csrf attribute before reaching the `CsrfFilter`.

The `CsrfFilter` generates a CSRF token and adds it to the _csrf request attribute.

The GET HTTP request now has the _csrf attribute.

The custom filter `CsrfTokenLogger` prints the CSRF token from the _csrf request attribute.

Figure 9.4 Inserting the `CsrfTokenLogger` (highlighted) following the `CsrfFilter` allows it to retrieve the token's value from the request's _csrf attribute, which is where the `CsrfFilter` deposits it. The `CsrfTokenLogger` outputs the CSRF token onto the application's console, from where it can be retrieved for use in making an HTTP POST request to an endpoint.

Listing 9.1   The controller class with two endpoints

```
@RestController
public class HelloController {

  @GetMapping("/hello")
  public String getHello() {
    return "Get Hello!";
  }

  @PostMapping("/hello")
  public String postHello() {
    return "Post Hello!";
  }
}
```

Listing 9.2 defines the custom filter we use to print the value of the CSRF token in the console. I named the custom filter `CsrfTokenLogger`. When called, the filter obtains the value of the CSRF token from the _csrf request attribute and prints it in the console. The name of the request attribute, _csrf, is where the `CsrfFilter` sets the value of the generated CSRF token as an instance of the class `CsrfToken`. This instance of `CsrfToken` contains the string value of the CSRF token. You can obtain it by calling the `getToken()` method.

Listing 9.2   The definition of the custom filter class

```
public class CsrfTokenLogger implements Filter {

  private Logger logger =
        Logger.getLogger(CsrfTokenLogger.class.getName());

  @Override
  public void doFilter(
    ServletRequest request,
    ServletResponse response,
    FilterChain filterChain)
      throws IOException, ServletException {

      CsrfToken o =
       (CsrfToken) request.getAttribute("_csrf");      ◄──── Takes the value of
                                                             the token from the
                                                             _csrf request
                                                             attribute and
                                                             prints it in the
      logger.info("CSRF token " + token.getToken());        console

      filterChain.doFilter(request, response);
  }
}
```

In the configuration class, we add the custom filter. The next listing presents the configuration class. Observe that I don't disable CSRF protection in the listing.

Listing 9.3   Adding the custom filter in the configuration class

```
@Configuration
public class ProjectConfig {

  @Bean
  public SecurityFilterChain configure(HttpSecurity http)
    throws Exception {

    http.addFilterAfter(
            new CsrfTokenLogger(), CsrfFilter.class)
        .authorizeHttpRequests(
            c -> c.anyRequest().permitAll()
        );


    return http.build();
  }
}
```

We can now test the endpoints. We begin by calling the endpoint with HTTP GET. Because the default implementation of the `CsrfTokenRepository` interface uses the HTTP session to store the token value on the server side, we also need to remember the session ID. For this reason, I add the -v flag to the call so that I can see more details from the response, including the session ID. Calling the endpoint

```
curl -v http://localhost:8080/hello
```

returns this (truncated) response:

```
...
< Set-Cookie: JSESSIONID=21ADA55E10D70BA81C338FFBB06B0206;
...
Get Hello!
```

Following the request in the application console, you can find a log line that contains the CSRF token:

```
INFO 21412 --- [nio-8080-exec-1] c.l.ssia.filters.CsrfTokenLogger : CSRF
token tAlE3LB_R_KN48DFlRChc…
```

> **NOTE** You might ask yourself how clients get the CSRF token. They can neither guess it nor read it in the server logs. I designed this example so that it's easier for you to understand how CSRF protection implementation works. As you'll find in section 9.2, the backend application has the responsibility to add the value of the CSRF token in the HTTP response to be used by the client.

If you call the endpoint using the HTTP POST method without providing the CSRF token, the response status is 403 Forbidden, as this command line shows:

```
curl -XPOST http://localhost:8080/hello
```

The response body is

```
{
    "status":403,
    "error":"Forbidden",
    "message":"Forbidden",
    "path":"/hello"
}
```

But if you provide the correct value for the CSRF token, the call is successful. You also need to specify the session ID (JSESSIONID) because the default implementation of CsrfTokenRepository stores the value of the CSRF token on the session:

```
curl -X POST    http://localhost:8080/hello
-H 'Cookie: JSESSIONID=21ADA55E10D70BA81C338FFBB06B0206'
-H 'X-CSRF-TOKEN: tAlE3LB_R_KN48DFlRChc…'
```

The response body is

```
Post Hello!
```

9.2   *Using CSRF protection in practical scenarios*

In this section, we discuss applying CSRF protection in practical situations. Now that you know how CSRF protection works in Spring Security, you need to know where you should use it in the real world. Which kinds of applications need to use CSRF protection?

You use CSRF protection for web apps running in a browser, where you should expect that mutating operations can be done by the browser that loads the displayed content of the app. The most basic example I can provide here is a simple web application developed on the standard Spring MVC flow. We already made such an application when discussing form login in chapter 6, and that web app actually used CSRF protection. Did you notice that the login operation in that application used HTTP POST? Then why didn't we need to do anything explicitly about CSRF in that case? The reason why we didn't observe this was because we didn't develop any mutating operation there.

For the default form login, Spring Security correctly applies CSRF protection for us. The framework takes care of adding the CSRF token to the login request. Let's now develop a similar application to look more closely at how CSRF protection works. As figure 9.5 shows, in this section we

- Build an example of a web application with the login form
- Look at how the default implementation of the login uses CSRF tokens
- Implement an HTTP POST call from the main page

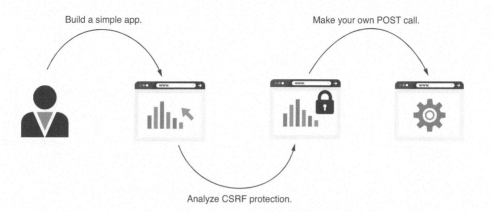

Build a simple app.

Make your own POST call.

Analyze CSRF protection.

Figure 9.5   The plan. In this section, we start by building and analyzing a simple app to understand how Spring Security applies CSRF protection, and then we write our own POST call.

In this example application, you'll notice that the HTTP POST call won't work until we correctly use the CSRF tokens, and here, you'll learn how to apply the CSRF tokens in a form on such a web page. To implement this application, we start by creating a new Spring Boot project. You can find this example in the project ssia-ch9-ex2. The next code snippet presents the needed dependencies:

```
<dependency>
    <groupId>org.springframework.boot</groupId>
    <artifactId>spring-boot-starter-security</artifactId>
</dependency>
<dependency>
    <groupId>org.springframework.boot</groupId>
    <artifactId>spring-boot-starter-thymeleaf</artifactId>
</dependency>
<dependency>
    <groupId>org.springframework.boot</groupId>
    <artifactId>spring-boot-starter-web</artifactId>
</dependency>
```

Next, of course, we need to configure the form login and at least one user. The following listing presents the configuration class, which defines the `UserDetailsService`, adds a user, and configures the `formLogin` method.

Listing 9.4   The definition of the configuration class

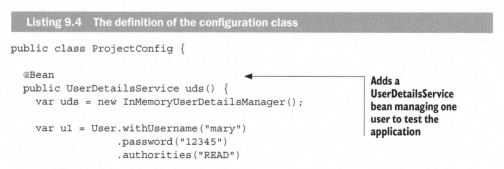

```
public class ProjectConfig {

  @Bean
  public UserDetailsService uds() {
    var uds = new InMemoryUserDetailsManager();

    var u1 = User.withUsername("mary")
              .password("12345")
              .authorities("READ")
```

Adds a UserDetailsService bean managing one user to test the application

```
                  .build();

      uds.createUser(u1);

      return uds;                    Adds a
  }                                  PasswordEncoder

                                                        Creates a bean of type
  @Bean                                                 SecurityFilterChain to set the
  public PasswordEncoder passwordEncoder() {            form login authentication
    return NoOpPasswordEncoder.getInstance();           method and specifies that only
  }                                                     authenticated users can access
                                                        any of the endpoints
  @Bean
  public SecurityFilterChain securityFilterChain(HttpSecurity http)
    throws Exception {

    http.formLogin(
      c -> c.defaultSuccessUrl("/main", true)
    );


    http.authorizeHttpRequests(
      c -> c.anyRequest().authenticated()
    );


    return http.build();
  }
}
```

We add a controller class for the main page in a package named controllers and in a
main.html file in the resources/templates folder of the Maven project. The main.html
file can remain empty for the moment because on the first execution of the application, we only focus on how the login page uses the CSRF tokens. The following listing
presents the MainController class, which serves the main page.

Listing 9.5   The definition of the MainController class

```
@Controller
public class MainController {

  @GetMapping("/main")
  public String main() {
    return "main.html";
  }
}
```

After running the application, you can access the default login page. If you inspect
the form using the inspect element function of your browser, you can observe that the
default implementation of the login form sends the CSRF token. This is why your login
works with CSRF protection enabled even if it uses an HTTP POST request! Figure 9.6
shows how the login form sends the CSRF token through hidden input.

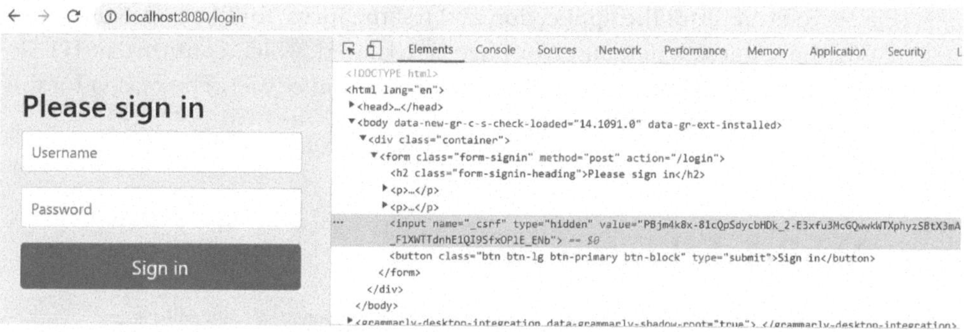

Figure 9.6 The default form login uses a hidden input to send the CSRF token in the request. This is why the login request that uses an HTTP POST method works with CSRF protection enabled.

But what about developing our own endpoints that use POST, PUT, or DELETE as HTTP methods? For these, we must take care of sending the value of the CSRF token if CSRF protectionW is enabled. To test this, let's add an endpoint using HTTP POST to our application. We call this endpoint from the main page, and we create a second controller for this, called `ProductController`. Within this controller, we define an endpoint, /product/add, that uses HTTP POST. Next, we use a form on the main page to call this endpoint. The following listing defines the `ProductController` class.

Listing 9.6 The definition of the `ProductController` class

```
@Controller
@RequestMapping("/product")
public class ProductController {

  private Logger logger =
    Logger.getLogger(ProductController.class.getName());

  @PostMapping("/add")
  public String add(@RequestParam String name) {
    logger.info("Adding product " + name);
    return "main.html";
  }
}
```

The endpoint receives a request parameter and prints it in the application console. The following listing shows the definition of the form defined in the main.html file.

Listing 9.7 The definition of the form in the main.html page

```
<form action="/product/add" method="post">
  <span>Name:</span>
  <span><input type="text" name="name" /></span>
  <span><button type="submit">Add</button></span>
</form>
```

Now you can rerun the application and test the form. You'll observe that when submitting the request, a default error page is displayed, which confirms an HTTP 403 Forbidden status on the response from the server (figure 9.7). The reason for this status is the absence of the CSRF token.

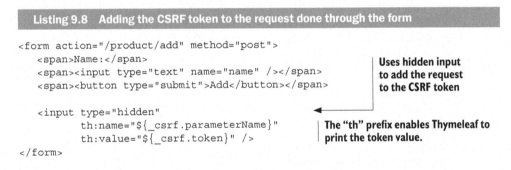

Figure 9.7   If the CSRF token is not included, the server will reject any requests made using the HTTP POST method. The user will be rerouted to a standard error page that displays a status of HTTP 403 Forbidden in the response.

To solve this problem and make the server allow the request, we need to add the CSRF token to the request done through the form. An easy way to do this is to use a hidden input component, as you saw in the default form login. This can be implemented as presented in the following listing.

Listing 9.8   Adding the CSRF token to the request done through the form

```
<form action="/product/add" method="post">
   <span>Name:</span>
   <span><input type="text" name="name" /></span>        Uses hidden input
   <span><button type="submit">Add</button></span>       to add the request
                                                          to the CSRF token

   <input type="hidden"
          th:name="${_csrf.parameterName}"               The "th" prefix enables Thymeleaf to
          th:value="${_csrf.token}" />                    print the token value.
</form>
```

NOTE   In the example, we use Thymeleaf because it provides a straightforward way to obtain the request attribute value in the view. In our case, we need to print the CSRF token. Remember that the `CsrfFilter` adds the value of the token in the _csrf attribute of the request. It's not mandatory to do this with Thymeleaf. You can use any alternative of your choice to print the token value to the response.

After rerunning the application, you can test the form again. This time, the server accepts the request, and the application prints the log line in the console, proving that the execution is successful. Furthermore, if you inspect the form, you can find the hidden input with the value of the CSRF token (figure 9.8).

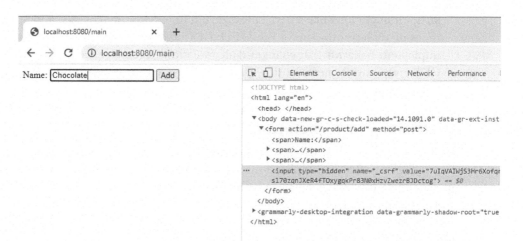

Figure 9.8　The form defined on the main page now sends the value for the CSRF token in the request. This way, the server allows the request and executes the controller action. In the source code for the page, you can now find the hidden input used by the form to send the CSRF token in the request.

After submitting the form, you should find in the application console a line similar to this one:

```
INFO 20892 --- [nio-8080-exec-7] c.l.s.controllers.ProductController   :
Adding product Chocolate
```

Of course, for any action or asynchronous JavaScript request your page uses to call a mutating action, you need to send a valid CSRF token. This is the most common way used by an application to make sure the request doesn't come from a third party. A third-party request could try to impersonate the user to execute actions on their behalf.

CSRF tokens work well in an architecture where the same server is responsible for both the frontend and the backend, mainly for its simplicity. But CSRF tokens don't work well when the client is independent of the backend solution it consumes. This scenario happens when you have a mobile application as a client or a web frontend developed independently. A web client developed with a framework such as Angular, ReactJS, or Vue.js is ubiquitous in web application architectures, and this is why you need to know how to implement the security approach for these cases as well. We'll discuss these kinds of designs in part 4 of this book.

In chapters 13 through 16, you'll learn to implement the OAuth 2 specification, which has excellent advantages in decoupling the component. This makes the authentication from the resources for which the application authorizes the client.

NOTE It might look like a trivial mistake, but in my experience, I see it too many times in applications—never use HTTP GET with mutating operations! Do not implement behavior that changes data and allows it to be called with an HTTP GET endpoint. Remember that calls to HTTP GET endpoints don't require a CSRF token.

9.3   *Customizing CSRF protection*

In this section, you learn how to customize the CSRF protection solution offered by Spring Security. Because applications have various requirements, any implementation provided by a framework needs to be flexible enough to be easily adapted to different scenarios. The CSRF protection mechanism in Spring Security is no exception. In this section, the examples let you apply the most frequently encountered needs in the customization of the CSRF protection mechanism. These are

- Configuring paths for which CSRF applies
- Managing CSRF tokens

We use CSRF protection only when the page that consumes resources produced by the server is itself generated by the same server. It can be a web application where the consumed endpoints are exposed by a different origin, as we discussed in section 9.2, or a mobile application. In the case of mobile applications, you can use the OAuth 2 flow, which we'll discuss in chapters 13 through 16.

By default, CSRF protection applies to any path for endpoints called with HTTP methods other than GET, HEAD, TRACE, or OPTIONS. You already know from chapter 5 how to completely disable CSRF protection. But what if you want to disable it only for some of your application paths? You can do this configuration quickly with a `Customizer` object, similar to the way we customized HTTP Basic for form-login methods in chapter 6.

Here, we create a new project and add only the web and security dependencies, as presented in the next code snippet. You can find this example in the project ssia-ch9-ex3. Here are the dependencies:

```
<dependency>
  <groupId>org.springframework.boot</groupId>
  <artifactId>spring-boot-starter-security</artifactId>
</dependency>
<dependency>
  <groupId>org.springframework.boot</groupId>
  <artifactId>spring-boot-starter-web</artifactId>
</dependency>
```

In this application, we add two endpoints called with HTTP POST, but we want to exclude one of these from using CSRF protection (figure 9.9). Listing 9.9 defines the controller class for this, which I name `HelloController`.

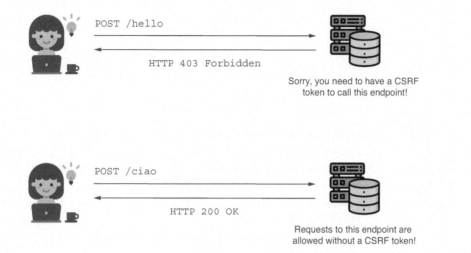

Figure 9.9 **The application requires a CSRF token for the /hello endpoint called with HTTP POST but allows HTTP POST requests to the /ciao endpoint without a CSRF token.**

Listing 9.9 The definition of the `HelloController` class

```
@RestController
public class HelloController {

  @PostMapping("/hello")
  public String postHello() {
    return "Post Hello!";
  }

  @PostMapping("/ciao")
  public String postCiao() {
    return "Post Ciao";
  }
}
```

The /hello path remains under CSRF protection. You can't call the endpoint without a valid CSRF token.

The /ciao path can be called without a CSRF token.

To make customizations on CSRF protection, you can use the csrf() method of the HttpSecurity object in the securityFilterChain() method with a Customizer object. The next listing presents this approach.

Listing 9.10 A `Customizer` object for the configuration of CSRF protection

```
@Configuration
public class ProjectConfig {

  @Bean
  public SecurityFilterChain securityFilterChain(HttpSecurity http)
    throws Exception {

    http.csrf(c -> {
      c.ignoringRequestMatchers("/ciao");
```

The parameter of the lambda expression is a CsrfConfigurer. By calling its methods, you can configure CSRF protection in various ways.

```
    });

    http.authorizeHttpRequests(
        c -> c.anyRequest().permitAll()
    );

    return http.build();
}
```

Calling the `ignoringRequestMatchers(String paths)` method, you can specify the path expressions representing the paths that you want to exclude from the CSRF protection mechanism. A more general approach is to use a `RequestMatcher`. Using this allows you to apply the exclusion rules with regular path expressions as well as with regexes (regular expressions). When using the `ignoringRequestMatchers()` method of the `CsrfCustomizer` object, you can provide any `RequestMatcher` as a parameter. The next code snippet shows how to use the `ignoringRequestMatchers()` method with an `MvcRequestMatcher` instead of using `ignoringRequestMatchers()` with a path given as a `String` value:

```
HandlerMappingIntrospector i = new HandlerMappingIntrospector();
MvcRequestMatcher r = new MvcRequestMatcher(i, "/ciao");
c.ignoringRequestMatchers(r);
```

Or you can similarly use a regex matcher:

```
String pattern = ".*[0-9].*";
String httpMethod = HttpMethod.POST.name();
RegexRequestMatcher r = new RegexRequestMatcher(pattern, httpMethod);
c.ignoringRequestMatchers(r);
```

Another need often found in the requirements of the application is customizing the management of CSRF tokens. As you learned, by default, the application stores CSRF tokens in the HTTP session on the server side. This simple approach is suitable for small applications, but it's not great for applications that serve a large number of requests and that require horizontal scaling. The HTTP session is stateful and reduces the scalability of the application.

Let's suppose you want to change the way the application manages tokens and store them somewhere in a database rather than in the HTTP session. Spring Security offers three contracts that you need to implement to do this:

- `CsrfToken`—Describes the CSRF token itself
- `CsrfTokenRepository`—Describes the object that creates, stores, and loads CSRF tokens
- `CsrfTokenRequestHandler`—Describes the object that manages the way in which the generated CSRF token is set upon the HTTP request

The `CsrfToken` object has three main characteristics that you need to specify when implementing the contract (listing 9.11 defines the `CsrfToken` contract):

- The name of the header in the request that contains the value of the CSRF token (default named X-CSRF-TOKEN)
- The name of the attribute of the request that stores the value of the token (default named _csrf)
- The value of the token

```
public interface CsrfToken extends Serializable {

  String getHeaderName();
  String getParameterName();
  String getToken();
}
```

Generally, you only need the instance of the CsrfToken type to store the three details in the attributes of the instance. For this functionality, Spring Security offers an implementation called DefaultCsrfToken that we also use in our example. Default-CsrfToken implements the CsrfToken contract and creates immutable instances containing the required values: the name of the request attribute and header, and the token itself.

The interface CsrfTokenRepository is the contract that represents the component managing CSRF tokens. To change the way the application manages the tokens, you need to implement the CsrfTokenRepository interface, which allows you to plug your custom implementation into the framework. Let's change the current application we use in this section to add a new implementation for CsrfTokenRepository, which stores the tokens in a database. Figure 9.10 presents the components we implement for this example and the link between them.

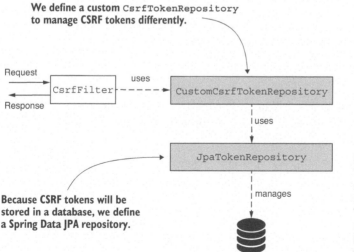

We define a custom CsrfTokenRepository to manage CSRF tokens differently.

Because CSRF tokens will be stored in a database, we define a Spring Data JPA repository.

Figure 9.10
The CsrfToken uses a custom implementation of CsrfTokenRepository. This custom implementation uses a JpaRepository to manage CSRF tokens in a database.

In our example, we use a table in a database to store CSRF tokens. We assume the client has an ID to identify themselves uniquely. The application needs this identifier to obtain the CSRF token and validate it. Generally, this unique ID would be obtained during login and should be different each time the user logs in. This strategy of managing tokens is similar to storing them in memory. In this case, you use a session ID. Thus, the new identifier for this example merely replaces the session ID.

An alternative to this approach would be to use CSRF tokens with a defined lifetime. With such an approach, tokens expire after a time you define. You can store tokens in the database without linking them to a specific user ID. You only need to check if a token provided via an HTTP request exists and is not expired to decide whether you allow that request.

> **EXERCISE** Once you finish with this example where we use an identifier to which we assign the CSRF token, implement the second approach where you use CSRF tokens that expire.

To make our example shorter, we only focus on the implementation of the `Csrf-TokenRepository`, and we need to consider that the client already has a generated identifier. To work with the database, we need to add a couple more dependencies to the pom.xml file:

```
<dependency>
   <groupId>org.springframework.boot</groupId>
   <artifactId>spring-boot-starter-data-jpa</artifactId>
</dependency>
<dependency>
   <groupId>com.mysql</groupId>
   <artifactId>mysql-connector-j</artifactId>
</dependency>
```

In the application.properties file, we need to add the properties for the database connection:

```
spring.datasource.url=jdbc:mysql://localhost/spring
➥?useLegacyDatetimeCode=false&serverTimezone=UTC
spring.datasource.username=root
spring.datasource.password=
spring.sql.init.mode=always
```

To allow the application to create the needed table in the database at the start, you can add the schema.xml file in the resources folder of the project. This file should contain the query for creating the table:

```
CREATE TABLE IF NOT EXISTS `spring`.`token` (
    `id` INT NOT NULL AUTO_INCREMENT,
    `identifier` VARCHAR(45) NULL,
    `token` TEXT NULL,
PRIMARY KEY (`id`));
```

We use Spring Data with a JPA implementation to connect to the database, so we need to define the entity class and the `JpaRepository` class. In a package named entities, we define the JPA entity as presented in the following listing.

Listing 9.12   The definition of the JPA entity class

```
@Entity
public class Token {

  @Id
  @GeneratedValue(strategy = GenerationType.IDENTITY)
  private int id;

  private String identifier;
  private String token;

  // Omitted code

}
```

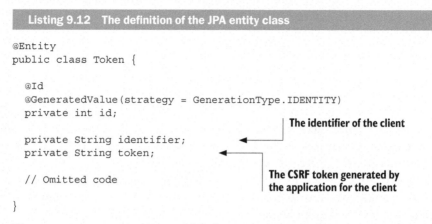

The identifier of the client

The CSRF token generated by the application for the client

The JpaTokenRepository, which is our JpaRepository contract, can be defined as shown in the following listing. The only method you need is findTokenBy-Identifier(), which gets the CSRF token from the database for a specific client.

Listing 9.13   The definition of the JpaTokenRepository interface

```
public interface JpaTokenRepository
  extends JpaRepository<Token, Integer> {

  Optional<Token> findTokenByIdentifier(String identifier);
}
```

With access to the implemented database, we can now start writing the CsrfToken-Repository implementation, which I call CustomCsrfTokenRepository. The next listing defines this class, which overrides the three methods of CsrfTokenRepository.

Listing 9.14   The implementation of the CsrfTokenRepository contract

```
@Component
public class CustomCsrfTokenRepository implements CsrfTokenRepository {

  private final JpaTokenRepository jpaTokenRepository;

  // Omitted constructor

  @Override
  public CsrfToken generateToken(
    HttpServletRequest httpServletRequest) {
    // ...
  }

  @Override
  public void saveToken(
    CsrfToken csrfToken,
    HttpServletRequest httpServletRequest,
    HttpServletResponse httpServletResponse) {
    // ...
  }
```

```
@Override
public CsrfToken loadToken(
  HttpServletRequest httpServletRequest) {
  // ...
  }
}
```

`CustomCsrfTokenRepository` injects an instance of `JpaTokenRepository` from the Spring context to gain access to the database. `CustomCsrfTokenRepository` uses this instance to retrieve or to save the CSRF tokens in the database. The CSRF protection mechanism calls the `generateToken()` method when the application needs to generate a new token. Listing 9.15 illustrates implementation of this method for our exercise. We use the `UUID` class to generate a new random UUID value, and we keep the same names for the request header and attribute, `X-CSRF-TOKEN` and `_csrf`, as in the default implementation offered by Spring Security.

Listing 9.15   The implementation of the `generateToken()` method

```
@Override
public CsrfToken generateToken(HttpServletRequest httpServletRequest) {
  String uuid = UUID.randomUUID().toString();
  return new DefaultCsrfToken("X-CSRF-TOKEN", "_csrf", uuid);
}
```

The `saveToken()` method saves a generated token for a specific client. In the case of the default CSRF protection implementation, the application uses the HTTP session to identify the CSRF token. In our case, we assume that the client has a unique identifier. The client sends the value of its unique ID in the request with the header named `X-IDENTIFIER`. In the method logic, we check whether the value exists in the database. If it does, we update the database with the new value of the token. If not, we create a new record for this ID with the new value of the CSRF token. The following listing presents the implementation of the `saveToken()` method.

Listing 9.16   The implementation of the `saveToken()` method

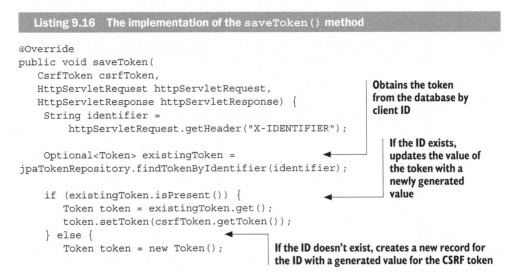

```
@Override
public void saveToken(
  CsrfToken csrfToken,
  HttpServletRequest httpServletRequest,
  HttpServletResponse httpServletResponse) {                Obtains the token
  String identifier =                                        from the database by
    httpServletRequest.getHeader("X-IDENTIFIER");            client ID

  Optional<Token> existingToken =                            If the ID exists,
jpaTokenRepository.findTokenByIdentifier(identifier);        updates the value of
                                                             the token with a
                                                             newly generated
  if (existingToken.isPresent()) {                           value
    Token token = existingToken.get();
    token.setToken(csrfToken.getToken());
  } else {
    Token token = new Token();          If the ID doesn't exist, creates a new record for
                                        the ID with a generated value for the CSRF token
```

```
        token.setToken(csrfToken.getToken());
        token.setIdentifier(identifier);
        jpaTokenRepository.save(token);
    }
}
```

The `loadToken()` method implementation loads the token details (if these exist) or returns null otherwise. The following listing shows this implementation.

Listing 9.17 The implementation of the `loadToken()` method

```
@Override
public CsrfToken loadToken(
  HttpServletRequest httpServletRequest) {

  String identifier = httpServletRequest.getHeader("X-IDENTIFIER");

  Optional<Token> existingToken =
    jpaTokenRepository
      .findTokenByIdentifier(identifier);

  if (existingToken.isPresent()) {
    Token token = existingToken.get();
    return new DefaultCsrfToken(
                "X-CSRF-TOKEN",
                "_csrf",
                token.getToken());
  }

  return null;
}
```

We use a custom implementation of the `CsrfTokenRepository` to declare a bean in the configuration class. We then plug the bean into the CSRF protection mechanism with the `csrfTokenRepository()` method of `CsrfConfigurer`. The next listing defines this configuration class.

Listing 9.18 The configuration class for the custom `CsrfTokenRepository`

```
@Configuration
public class ProjectConfig {

  private final CustomCsrfTokenRepository customTokenRepository;

  // Omitted constructor

  @Bean
  public SecurityFilterChain securityFilterChain(HttpSecurity http)
    throws Exception {

    http.csrf(c -> {
      c.csrfTokenRepository(customTokenRepository);     ⟵─────┐
    });
```

Uses the Customizer<CsrfConfigurer<HttpSecurity>> object to plug the new CsrfTokenRepository implementation into the CSRF protection mechanism

```
http.authorizeHttpRequests(
  c -> c.anyRequest().permitAll()
);

return http.build();
}

}
```

The last piece we need to plug in for everything to work well is a `CsrfTokenRequest-Handler`. Fortunately, we can use an implementation that Spring Security provides—the `CsrfTokenRequestAttributeHandler`. This implementation simply uses the `generateToken()` method of the `CsrfTokenRepository` to generate a new token when an endpoint is called using the HTTP GET method. It then adds the generated `CsrfToken` upon the request as an attribute.

You can customize the simple behavior of the `CsrfTokenRequestAttribute-Handler` object by extending its class. For example, the default implementation Spring Security uses (named `XorCsrfTokenRequestAttributeHandler`) has a more complex behavior. This implementation generates a random value using a `SecureRandom` object and then mixes its byte array with the token generated by the `CsrfTokenRepository` using an XOR logic operation.

However, to avoid adding too much complexity to our example and allow you focus on the configuration part, we will set up a simple `CsrfTokenRequestAttribute-Handler` to handle the management of the CSRF token on the HTTP request object. The next listing shows you how to configure the `CsrfTokenRequestAttribute-Handler` in the configuration class.

> **Listing 9.19   The configuration class for the custom `CsrfTokenRepository`**

```
@Configuration
public class ProjectConfig {

  private final CustomCsrfTokenRepository customTokenRepository;

  // Omitted constructor

  @Bean
  public SecurityFilterChain securityFilterChain(HttpSecurity http)
    throws Exception {

    http.csrf(c -> {
      c.csrfTokenRepository(customTokenRepository);
      c.csrfTokenRequestHandler(
        new CsrfTokenRequestAttributeHandler()
      );
    });

    http.authorizeHttpRequests(
      c -> c.anyRequest().permitAll()
```

Setting the CsrfTokenRequestAttributeHandler object to manage the setup of the CSRF token on the HTTP request

```
    );

    return http.build();
  }

}
```

In the definition of the controller class presented in listing 9.9, we also add an end-point that uses the HTTP GET method. We need this method to obtain the CSRF token when testing our implementation:

```
@GetMapping("/hello")
public String getHello() {
  return "Get Hello!";
}
```

You can now start the application and test the new implementation for managing the token. We call the endpoint using HTTP GET to obtain a value for the CSRF token. When making the call, we must use the client's ID within the X-IDENTIFIER header, as assumed from the requirement. A new value of the CSRF token is generated and stored in the database. Here's the call:

```
curl -H "X-IDENTIFIER:12345" http://localhost:8080/hello
Get Hello!
```

If you search the token table in the database, you find that the application added a new record for the client with identifier 12345. In my case, the generated value for the CSRF token, which I can see in the database, is 2bc652f5-258b-4a26-b456-928e9bad71f8. We use this value to call the /hello endpoint with the HTTP POST method, like the next code snippet presents. Of course, we also must provide the client ID that's used by the application to retrieve the token from the database to compare it with the one we provide in the request:

```
curl -XPOST -H "X-IDENTIFIER:12345" -H "X-CSRF-TOKEN:2bc652f5-258b-4a26-b456-
928e9bad71f8" http://localhost:8080/hello
Post Hello!
```

Figure 9.11 describes the flow.

If we try to call the /hello endpoint with POST without providing the needed headers, we get a response back with the HTTP status 403 Forbidden. To confirm this, call the endpoint with

```
curl -XPOST http://localhost:8080/hello
```

The response body is

```
{
  "status":403,
  "error":"Forbidden",
  "message":"Forbidden",
  "path":"/hello"
}
```

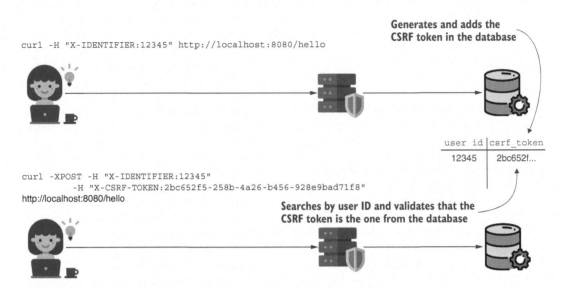

Figure 9.11   First, the GET request generates the CSRF token and stores its value in the database. Any following POST request must send this value. Then the `CsrfFilter` checks whether the value in the request corresponds with the one in the database. Based on this, the request is accepted or rejected.

Summary

- A CSRF is a type of attack where the user is tricked into accessing a page containing a forgery script. This script can impersonate a user logged into an application and execute actions on their behalf.
- CSRF protection is by default enabled in Spring Security.
- The entry point of CSRF protection logic in the Spring Security architecture is an HTTP filter.
- You can customize the capability that offers CSRF protection. Spring Security offers three simple contracts that you can implement and plug in to define custom CSRF protection capabilities:
  - `CsrfToken`—Describes the CSRF token itself
  - `CsrfTokenRepository`—Describes the object that creates, stores, and loads CSRF tokens
  - `CsrfTokenRequestHandler`—Describes the object that manages the way in which the generated CSRF token is set upon the HTTP request

Configuring CORS

This chapter covers

- Defining CORS
- Applying CORS configurations

In this chapter, we discuss cross-origin resource sharing (CORS) and how to apply it with Spring Security. First, what is CORS, and why should you care? The need for CORS stems from web applications. By default, browsers don't allow requests made for any domain other than the one from which the site is loaded. For example, if you access the site from example.com, the browser won't let the site make requests to api.example.com. Figure 10.1 illustrates this concept.

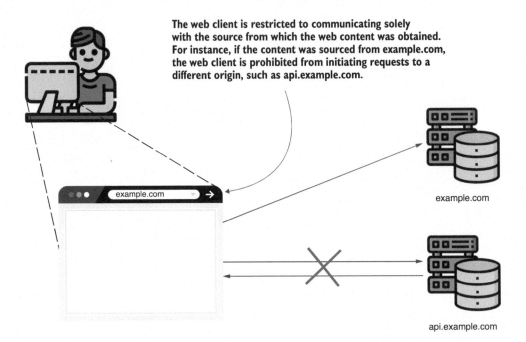

The web client is restricted to communicating solely with the source from which the web content was obtained. For instance, if the content was sourced from example.com, the web client is prohibited from initiating requests to a different origin, such as api.example.com.

example.com

api.example.com

Figure 10.1   Cross-origin resource sharing (CORS). When accessed from example.com, the website cannot make requests to api.example.com because they would be cross-domain requests.

We can briefly say that an app uses the CORS mechanism to relax this strict policy and allow requests made between different origins in some conditions. You need to know this because it's likely you will have to use it for your applications, especially nowadays where the frontend and backend are separate applications. It is common that a frontend application is developed using frameworks such as Angular, ReactJS, or Vue and hosted at a domain such as example.com, but it calls endpoints on the backend hosted at another domain, such as api.example.com.

This chapter provides some examples from which you can learn how to apply CORS policies for your web applications. It also shows how to avoid leaving security breaches in your applications.

10.1   How does CORS work?

This section discusses how CORS applies to web applications. If you are the owner of example.com, and for some reason the developers from example.org decide to call your REST endpoints (api.example.com) from their website, they won't be able to. The same situation can happen if a domain loads your application using an `iframe` (see figure 10.2).

> **NOTE**   An `iframe` is an HTML element used to embed content generated by a web page into another web page (e.g., to integrate the content from example .org inside a page from example.com).

Any situation in which an application makes calls between two different domains is prohibited. Of course, you can encounter situations in which you need to make such calls, and this is when CORS will allow you to specify from which domain your application allows requests and what details can be shared. The CORS mechanism works based on HTTP headers (figure 10.3).

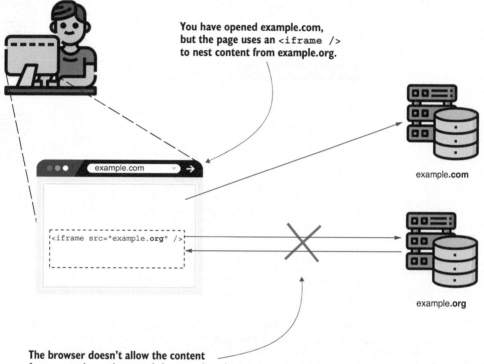

Figure 10.2 Even if the example.org page is loaded in an `iframe` from the example.com domain, the calls from the content loaded in example.org won't load. Furthermore, even if the application makes a request, the browser won't accept the response.

The most important are

- `Access-Control-Allow-Origin`—Specifies the foreign domains (origins) that can access resources on your domain.
- `Access-Control-Allow-Methods`—Lets us refer only to some HTTP methods in situations when we want to allow access to a different domain, but only to specific HTTP methods. For example, you use this if you're going to enable example.com to call some endpoint, but only with HTTP GET.
- `Access-Control-Allow-Headers`—Adds limitations to which headers you can use in a specific request. For example, you don't want the client to be able to send a specific header for a given request.

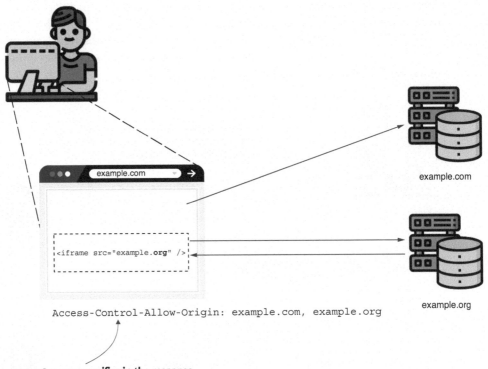

Access-Control-Allow-Origin: example.com, example.org

example.org specifies in the response
header what origins the browser accepts.
The browser accepts and displays the content.

Figure 10.3 Enabling cross-origin requests. The example.org server adds the Access-Control
-Allow-Origin **header to specify the origins of the request for which the browser should accept the
response. If the domain from which the call was made is enumerated in the origins, the browser accepts
the response.**

With Spring Security, by default, none of these headers are added to the response.
So let's start at the beginning: What happens when you make a cross-origin call if you
don't configure CORS in your application? When the application makes the request, it
expects that the response has an Access-Control-Allow-Origin header containing
the origins accepted by the server. If this doesn't happen, as in the case of default Spring
Security behavior, the browser won't accept the response. Let's demonstrate this with
a small web application. We create a new project using the dependencies presented by
the next code snippet (you can find this example in the project ssia-ch10-ex1):

```
<dependency>
    <groupId>org.springframework.boot</groupId>
    <artifactId>spring-boot-starter-security</artifactId>
</dependency>
<dependency>
    <groupId>org.springframework.boot</groupId>
    <artifactId>spring-boot-starter-web</artifactId>
</dependency>
<dependency>
```

```
    <groupId>org.springframework.boot</groupId>
    <artifactId>spring-boot-starter-thymeleaf</artifactId>
</dependency>
```

We define a controller class having an action for the main page and a REST endpoint. Because the class is a normal Spring MVC @Controller class, we also must add the @ResponseBody annotation explicitly to the endpoint. The following listing defines the controller.

Listing 10.1 The definition of the controller class

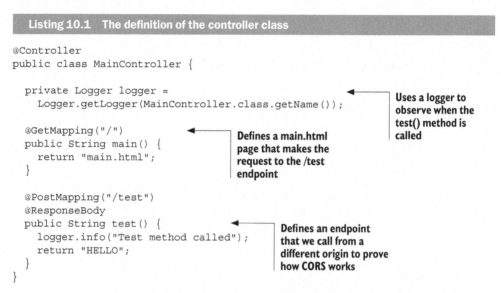

```
@Controller
public class MainController {

  private Logger logger =
    Logger.getLogger(MainController.class.getName());

  @GetMapping("/")
  public String main() {
    return "main.html";
  }

  @PostMapping("/test")
  @ResponseBody
  public String test() {
    logger.info("Test method called");
    return "HELLO";
  }
}
```

Uses a logger to observe when the test() method is called

Defines a main.html page that makes the request to the /test endpoint

Defines an endpoint that we call from a different origin to prove how CORS works

Furthermore, we need to define the configuration class where we disable CSRF protection to make the example simpler and allow you to focus on the CORS mechanism only. Additionally, we allow unauthenticated access to all endpoints. The next listing defines this configuration class.

Listing 10.2 The definition of the configuration class

```
@Configuration
public class ProjectConfig {

  @Bean
  public SecurityFilterChain securityFilterChain(HttpSecurity http)
    throws Exception {

    http.csrf(
      c -> c.disable()
    );

    http.authorizeHttpRequests(
      c -> c.anyRequest().permitAll()
    );


    return http.build();
  }
}
```

Of course, we also need to define the main.html file in the resources/templates folder of the project. The main.html file contains the JavaScript code that calls the /test endpoint. To simulate the cross-origin call, we can access the page in a browser using the domain localhost. From the JavaScript code, we make the call using the IP address 127.0.0.1. Even if localhost and 127.0.0.1 refer to the same host, the browser sees these as different strings and considers them different domains. The next listing defines the main.html page.

Listing 10.3   The main.html page

```
<!DOCTYPE HTML>
<html lang=»en»>
  <head>
    <script>
      const http = new XMLHttpRequest();
      const url='http://127.0.0.1:8080/test';     ◄─────   Calls the endpoint
      http.open("POST", url);                              using 127.0.0.1 as
      http.send();                                         host to simulate the
                                                           cross-origin call
      http.onreadystatechange = (e) => {
        document                        ◄──────   Sets the response
          .getElementById("output")              body to the output
          .innerHTML = http.responseText;        div in the page body
      }
    </script>
  </head>
  <body>
    <div id="output"></div>
  </body>
</html>
```

When starting the application and opening the page in a browser with localhost:8080, we can observe that the page doesn't display anything. We expected to see HELLO on the page because this is what the /test endpoint returns. However, when we check the browser console, what we see is an error printed by the JavaScript call. The error looks like this:

```
Access to XMLHttpRequest at 'http://127.0.0.1:8080/test' from origin
'http://localhost:8080' has been blocked by CORS policy: No 'Access-
Control-Allow-Origin' header is present on the requested resource.
```

The error message tells us that the response wasn't accepted because the Access -Control-Allow-Origin HTTP header doesn't exist. This behavior happens because we didn't configure anything regarding CORS in our Spring Boot application, and by default, it doesn't set any header related to CORS. So the browser's behavior of not displaying the response is correct. I would like you, however, to notice that in the application console, the log proves the method was called. The next code snippet shows what you find in the application console:

```
INFO 25020 --- [nio-8080-exec-2]
➥c.l.s.controllers.MainController :
➥Test method called
```

This aspect is important! I meet many developers who understand CORS as a restriction similar to authorization or CSRF protection. Instead of being a restriction, CORS helps to relax a rigid constraint for cross-domain calls. And even with restrictions applied, in some situations, the endpoint can be called. This behavior doesn't always happen. Sometimes, the browser first makes a call using the HTTP OPTIONS method to test whether the request should be allowed. We call this test request a *preflight* request. If the preflight request fails, the browser won't attempt to honor the original request.

The preflight request and the decision whether to make it are the responsibility of the browser. You don't have to implement this logic. However, it is important to understand it so you won't be surprised to see cross-origin calls to the backend, even if you did not specify any CORS policies for specific domains. This could also happen when you have a client-side app developed with a framework such as Angular or ReactJS. Figure 10.4 presents this request flow. When the browser omits making the preflight request if the HTTP method is GET, POST, or OPTIONS, it only has some basic headers, as described in the official documentation at https://fetch.spec.whatwg.org/#http-cors-protocol.

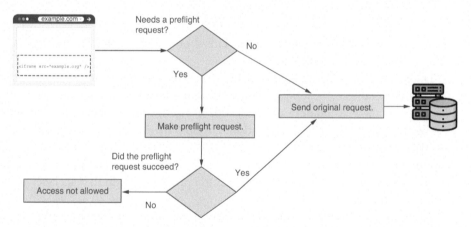

Figure 10.4   For simple requests, the browser sends the original request directly to the server. The browser rejects the response if the server doesn't allow the origin. In some cases, the browser sends a preflight request to test whether the server accepts the origin. If the preflight request succeeds, the browser sends the original request.

In our example, the browser makes the request, but we don't accept the response if the origin is not specified there, as shown in figures 10.1 and 10.2. The CORS mechanism is, in the end, related to the browser and not a way to secure endpoints. The only thing it guarantees is that only origin domains that you allow can make requests from specific pages in the browser.

10.2 Applying CORS policies with the @CrossOrigin annotation

This section discusses how to configure CORS to allow requests from different domains using the @CrossOrigin annotation. You can place the @CrossOrigin annotation directly above the method that defines the endpoint and configure it using the allowed origins and methods. As you learn in this section, the advantage of using the @Cross-Origin annotation is that it makes it easy to configure CORS for each endpoint.

We use the application we created in section 10.1 to demonstrate how @CrossOrigin works. To make the cross-origin call work in the application, the only thing you need to do is to add the @CrossOrigin annotation over the test() method in the controller class. The following listing shows how to use the annotation to make the localhost an allowed origin.

Listing 10.4   Making localhost an allowed origin

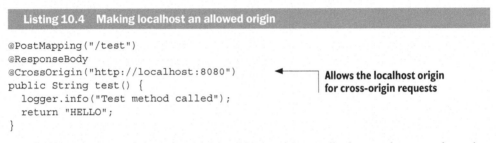

```
@PostMapping("/test")
@ResponseBody
@CrossOrigin("http://localhost:8080")          Allows the localhost origin
public String test() {                          for cross-origin requests
  logger.info("Test method called");
  return "HELLO";
}
```

You can rerun and test the application. This should now display on the page the string returned by the /test endpoint: HELLO.

The value parameter of @CrossOrigin receives an array to let you define multiple origins; for example, @CrossOrigin({"example.com", "example.org"}). You can also set the allowed headers and methods using the allowedHeaders attribute and the methods attribute of the annotation. For both origins and headers, you can use the asterisk (*) to represent all headers or all origins. However, I recommend you exercise caution with this approach. It's always better to filter the origins and headers that you want to allow and never allow any domain to implement code that accesses your applications' resources.

By allowing all origins, you expose the application to cross-site scripting (XSS) requests, which eventually can lead to DDoS attacks. I personally avoid allowing all origins even in test environments. I know that applications sometimes happen to run on wrongly defined infrastructures that use the same data centers for both test and production. It is wiser to treat all layers on which security applies independently, as we discussed in chapter 1, and to avoid assuming that the application doesn't have particular vulnerabilities because the infrastructure doesn't allow it.

The advantage of using @CrossOrigin to specify the rules directly where the endpoints are defined is that it creates good transparency of the rules. The disadvantage is that it might become wordy, forcing you to repeat a lot of code. It also imposes the risk that the developer might forget to add the annotation for newly implemented endpoints. In section 10.3, we discuss applying the CORS configuration centralized within the configuration class.

10.3 *Applying CORS using a CorsConfigurer*

Although using the `@CrossOrigin` annotation is easy, as you learned in section 10.2, you might find it more comfortable in a lot of cases to define CORS configuration in one place. In this section, we change the example we worked on in sections 10.1 and 10.2 to apply CORS configuration in the configuration class using a `Customizer`. The next listing shows the changes we need to make in the configuration class to define the origins we want to allow.

> **Listing 10.5   Defining CORS configurations centralized in the configuration class**

```
@Configuration
public class ProjectConfig {

  @Bean
  public SecurityFilterChain securityFilterChain(HttpSecurity http)
    throws Exception {

    http.cors(c -> {                                      ◄─── Calls cors() to
      CorsConfigurationSource source = request -> {            define the CORS
        CorsConfiguration config = new CorsConfiguration();    configuration.
        config.setAllowedOrigins(                              Within it, we
            List.of("example.com", "example.org"));            create a
        config.setAllowedMethods(                              CorsConfiguration
            List.of("GET", "POST", "PUT", "DELETE"));          object where we
        config.setAllowedHeaders(List.of("*"));                set the allowed
        return config;                                         origins and
      };                                                       methods.
      c.configurationSource(source);
    });

    http.csrf(
      c -> c.disable()
    );

    http.authorizeHttpRequests(
      c -> c.anyRequest().permitAll()
    );


    return http.build();
  }
}
```

The `cors()` method that we call from the `HttpSecurity` object receives as a parameter a `Customizer<CorsConfigurer>` object. For this object, we set a `CorsConfigurationSource`, which returns `CorsConfiguration` for an HTTP request. `CorsConfiguration` is the object that states which are the allowed origins, methods, and headers. If you use this approach, you must at least specify the origins and the methods. If you only specify the origins, your application won't allow the requests. This behavior happens because a `CorsConfiguration` object doesn't define any methods by default.

In this example, to make the explanation straightforward, I provide the implementation for `CorsConfigurationSource` as a lambda expression using the `Security-FilterChain` bean directly. I strongly recommend separating this code in a different class in your applications. In real-world applications, you could have much longer code, so it could become difficult to read if not separated by the configuration class.

Summary

- CORS refers to the situation in which a web application hosted on a specific domain tries to access content from another domain.
- By default, the browser doesn't allow cross-origin requests to happen. CORS configuration thus enables you to allow a part of your resources to be called from a different domain in a web application run in the browser.
- You can configure CORS both for an endpoint using the `@CrossOrigin` annotation or centralized in the configuration class using the `cors()` method of the `HttpSecurity` object.

Implementing authorization at the method level

11

This chapter covers

- Method security in Spring applications
- Preauthorization of methods based on authorities, roles, and permissions
- Postauthorization of methods based on authorities, roles, and permissions

Up to now, we've discussed various ways of configuring authentication. We started with the most straightforward approach, HTTP Basic, in chapter 2, and then I showed you how to set form login in chapter 6. However, in terms of authorization, we only discussed configuration at the endpoint level. Suppose your app is not a web application—can't you use Spring Security for authentication and authorization as well? Spring Security is a good fit for scenarios where your app isn't used via HTTP endpoints. In this chapter, you'll learn how to configure authorization at the method level. We'll use this approach to configure authorization in both web and non-web applications, and we'll call it *method security* (figure 11.1).

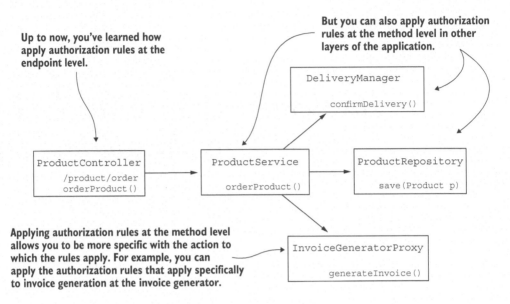

Figure 11.1 Method security allows you to be more granular and apply authorization rules at any specifically chosen level of your application.

For non-web applications, method security allows us to implement authorization rules even if we don't have endpoints. In web applications, this approach gives us the flexibility to apply authorization rules to different app layers, not just at the endpoint level. Let's dive into the chapter and learn how to apply authorization at the method level with method security.

11.1 *Enabling method security*

This section will show how to enable authorization at the method level and the different options that Spring Security offers for applying various authorization rules. This approach provides you with greater flexibility in applying authorization. It's an essential skill that allows you to solve situations in which authorization cannot be configured just at the endpoint level.

By default, method security is disabled, so if you want to use this functionality, you first need to enable it. Furthermore, method security offers multiple approaches for applying authorization. We discuss these approaches and then implement them in examples in the following sections of this chapter and in chapter 12. Briefly, you can do two main things with global method security:

- *Call authorization*—Decides whether someone can call a method according to some implemented privilege rules (preauthorization) or if someone can access what the method returns after the method executes (postauthorization).
- *Filtering*—Decides what a method can receive through its parameters (prefiltering) and what the caller can receive back from the method after the method executes (postfiltering). We'll discuss and implement filtering in chapter 12.

11.1.1 *Understanding call authorization*

One of the approaches for configuring authorization rules used with method security is *call authorization*. The call authorization approach refers to applying authorization rules that decide if a method can be called or that allow the method to be called and then decide if the caller can access the value returned by the method. Often, we need to decide if someone can access a piece of logic depending on either the provided parameters or its result. So let's discuss call authorization and then apply it to some examples.

How does method security work? What's the mechanism behind applying the authorization rules? When we enable method security in our application, we actually enable a Spring aspect. This aspect intercepts the calls to the method for which we apply authorization rules, and based on these authorization rules, it decides whether to forward the call to the intercepted method (figure 11.2).

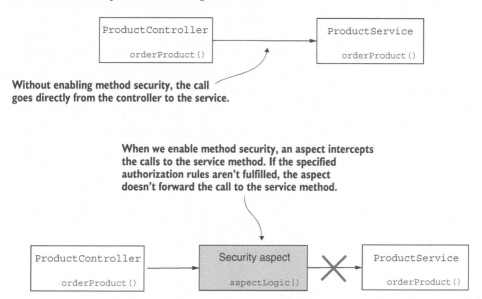

Figure 11.2　When we enable global method security, an aspect intercepts the call to the protected method. If the given authorization rules aren't respected, the aspect doesn't delegate the call to the protected method.

Plenty of implementations in Spring framework rely on aspect-oriented programming (AOP). Method security is just one of the many components in Spring applications relying on aspects. If you need a refresher on aspects and AOP, I recommend you read chapter 6 of *Spring Start Here* (Manning, 2021), another book I wrote. Briefly, we classify the call authorization as

- *Preauthorization*—The framework checks the authorization rules before the method call.

- *Postauthorization*—The framework checks the authorization rules after the method executes.

Let's take both approaches, describe them, and implement them with some examples.

USING PREAUTHORIZATION TO SECURE ACCESS TO METHODS

Say we have a method `findDocumentsByUser(String username)` that returns to the caller documents for a specific user. The caller provides through the method's parameters the user's name for which the method retrieves the documents. Assume you need to ensure that the authenticated user can only obtain their own documents. Can we apply a rule to this method so that only the method calls that receive the username of the authenticated user as a parameter are allowed? Yes! This is something we do with preauthorization.

When we apply authorization rules that completely forbid anyone to call a method in specific situations, we call this *preauthorization* (figure 11.3). This approach implies that the framework verifies the authorization conditions before executing the method. If the caller doesn't have the permissions according to the authorization rules that we define, the framework doesn't delegate the call to the method. Instead, the framework throws an exception named `AccessDeniedException`. This is by far the most frequently used approach to global method security.

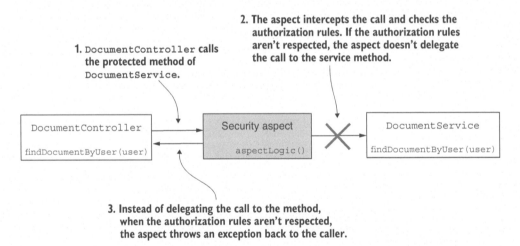

2. The aspect intercepts the call and checks the authorization rules. If the authorization rules aren't respected, the aspect doesn't delegate the call to the service method.

1. `DocumentController` **calls the protected method of** `DocumentService`.

3. Instead of delegating the call to the method, when the authorization rules aren't respected, the aspect throws an exception back to the caller.

Figure 11.3   With preauthorization, the authorization rules are verified before delegating the method call further. The framework won't delegate the call if the authorization rules aren't respected, and instead, it will throw an exception to the method caller.

Usually, we don't want a functionality to be executed at all if some conditions aren't met. You can apply conditions based on the authenticated user, and you can also refer to the values the method received through its parameters.

USING POSTAUTHORIZATION TO SECURE A METHOD CALL

When we apply authorization rules that allow someone to call a method but not necessarily to obtain the result returned, we're using *postauthorization* (figure 11.4). With postauthorization, Spring Security checks the authorization rules after the method executes. You can use this kind of authorization to restrict access to the method return in certain conditions. Because postauthorization happens after method execution, you can apply the authorization rules on the result returned.

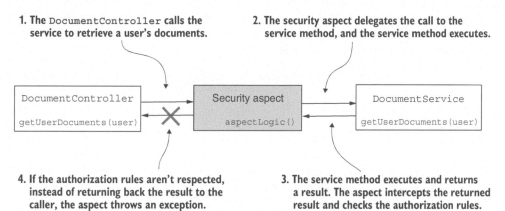

1. The `DocumentController` **calls the service to retrieve a user's documents.**

2. The security aspect delegates the call to the service method, and the service method executes.

4. If the authorization rules aren't respected, instead of returning back the result to the caller, the aspect throws an exception.

3. The service method executes and returns a result. The aspect intercepts the returned result and checks the authorization rules.

Figure 11.4   With postauthorization, the aspect delegates the call to the protected method. After the protected method finishes execution, the aspect checks the authorization rules. If the rules aren't respected, instead of returning the result to the caller, the aspect throws an exception.

Usually, we use postauthorization to apply authorization rules based on what the method returns after execution. But be careful with postauthorization! If the method mutates something during its execution, the change happens regardless of whether authorization is successful.

> **NOTE**   Even with the `@Transactional` annotation, a change isn't rolled back if postauthorization fails. The exception thrown by the postauthorization functionality happens after the transaction manager commits the transaction.

11.1.2 *Enabling method security in your project*

In this section, we'll work on a project to apply the preauthorization and postauthorization features offered by method security. Method security isn't enabled by default in a Spring Security project. To use it, you need to first enable it. However, enabling this functionality is straightforward. You do this by simply using the `@EnableMethod-Security` annotation on the configuration class.

I created a new project for this example, ssia-ch11-ex1. For this project, I wrote a `ProjectConfig` configuration class, as presented in listing 11.1. On the configuration class, we add the `@EnableMethodSecurity` annotation. Method security offers us the following three approaches to define the authorization rules that we discuss in this chapter:

- The pre-/postauthorization annotations (enabled by default)
- The JSR 250 annotation, `@RolesAllowed`
- The `@Secured` annotation

Because in almost all cases, pre-/postauthorization annotations are the only approach used, we discuss it in this chapter. This approach is pre-enabled once you add the `@EnableMethodSecurity` annotation. We present a short overview of the other two options at the end of this chapter.

Listing 11.1   Enabling method security

```
@Configuration
@EnableMethodSecurity
public class ProjectConfig {
}
```

You can use global method security with any authentication approach, from HTTP Basic authentication to OAuth 2 (which you'll learn in the third part of this book). To keep it simple and allow you to focus on new details, we provide method security with HTTP Basic authentication. For this reason, the pom.xml file for the projects in this chapter only needs the web and Spring Security dependencies, as the next code snippet presents:

```
<dependency>
    <groupId>org.springframework.boot</groupId>
    <artifactId>spring-boot-starter-security</artifactId>
</dependency>
<dependency>
    <groupId>org.springframework.boot</groupId>
    <artifactId>spring-boot-starter-web</artifactId>
</dependency>
```

> **NOTE**   In the previous Spring Security versions, we used the `@EnableGlobal-MethodSecurity` annotation, and the pre- and postauthorization weren't enabled by default. If you need to work with method authorization and a previous Spring Security version (older than 6), you may find chapter 16 from the first edition of *Spring Security in Action* useful.

11.2 Applying preauthorization rules

In this section, we implement an preauthorization example. For our example, we continue with the project `ssia-ch11-ex1` started in section 11.1. As discussed in section 11.1, preauthorization implies defining authorization rules that Spring Security applies before calling a specific method. If the rules aren't respected, the framework doesn't call the method.

The application we implement in this section has a simple scenario. It exposes an endpoint, /hello, which returns the string "Hello", followed by a name. To obtain the name, the controller calls a service method (figure 11.5). This method applies a preauthorization rule to verify the user has write authority.

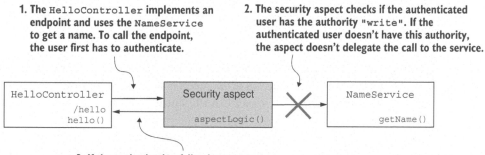

1. The `HelloController` implements an endpoint and uses the `NameService` to get a name. To call the endpoint, the user first has to authenticate.

2. The security aspect checks if the authenticated user has the authority "write". If the authenticated user doesn't have this authority, the aspect doesn't delegate the call to the service.

3. If the authorization fails, the aspect throws an exception back to the controller.

Figure 11.5 To call the `getName()` method of `NameService`, the authenticated user needs to have write authority. If the user doesn't have this authority, the framework won't allow the call and will throw an exception.

I added a `UserDetailsService` and a `PasswordEncoder` to make sure I have some users to authenticate. To validate our solution, we need two users: one with write authority and another without it. We prove that the first user can successfully call the endpoint, while for the second user, the app throws an authorization exception when trying to call the method. The following listing shows the complete definition of the configuration class, which defines the `UserDetailsService` and the `PasswordEncoder`.

Listing 11.2 The configuration class for `UserDetailsService` and `PasswordEncoder`

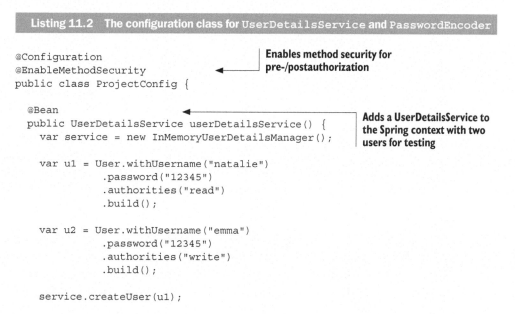

```
@Configuration
@EnableMethodSecurity          Enables method security for
public class ProjectConfig {   pre-/postauthorization

    @Bean                                                       Adds a UserDetailsService to
    public UserDetailsService userDetailsService() {            the Spring context with two
      var service = new InMemoryUserDetailsManager();           users for testing

      var u1 = User.withUsername("natalie")
                 .password("12345")
                 .authorities("read")
                 .build();

      var u2 = User.withUsername("emma")
                 .password("12345")
                 .authorities("write")
                 .build();

      service.createUser(u1);
```

```
    service.createUser(u2);

    return service;
  }

  @Bean
  public PasswordEncoder passwordEncoder() {
    return NoOpPasswordEncoder.getInstance();
  }
}
```

> Adds a PasswordEncoder to the Spring context

To define the authorization rule for this method, we use the `@PreAuthorize` annotation. The `@PreAuthorize` annotation receives as a value a Spring Expression Language (SpEL) expression that describes the authorization rule. In this example, we apply a simple rule.

You can define restrictions for users based on their authorities using the `hasAuthority()` method. You learned about the `hasAuthority()` method in chapter 7, where we discussed applying authorization at the endpoint level. The following listing defines the service class, which provides the value for the name.

Listing 11.3 The service class defining the preauthorization rule on the method

```
@Service
public class NameService {

  @PreAuthorize("hasAuthority('write')")
  public String getName() {
    return "Fantastico";
  }
}
```

> Defines the authorization rule. Only users having write authority can call the method.

We define the controller class in the following listing. It uses `NameService` as a dependency.

Listing 11.4 The controller class implementing the endpoint and using the service

```
@RestController
public class HelloController {

  private final NameService nameService;

  // omitted constructor

  @GetMapping("/hello")
  public String hello() {
    return "Hello, " + nameService.getName();
  }
}
```

> Injects the service from the context

> Calls the method for which we apply the preauthorization rules

You can now start the application and test its behavior. We expect only user Emma to be authorized to call the endpoint because she has written authorization. The next code snippet presents the calls for the endpoint with our two users, Emma and Natalie. To call the /hello endpoint and authenticate with user Emma, use this cURL command:

```
curl -u emma:12345 http://localhost:8080/hello
```

The response body is

```
Hello, Fantastico
```

To call the /hello endpoint and authenticate with user Natalie, use this cURL command:

```
curl -u natalie:12345 http://localhost:8080/hello
```

The response body is

```
{
  "status":403,
  "error":"Forbidden",
  "message":"Forbidden",
  "path":"/hello"
}
```

Similarly, you can use any other expression we discussed in chapter 7 for endpoint authentication. Here's a short recap of them:

- hasAnyAuthority()—Specifies multiple authorities. The user must have at least one of these authorities to call the method.
- hasRole()—Specifies a role a user must have to call the method.
- hasAnyRole()—Specifies multiple roles. The user must have at least one of them to call the method.

Let's extend our example to prove how you can use the values of the method parameters to define the authorization rules (figure 11.6). You find this example in the project named ssia-ch11-ex2.

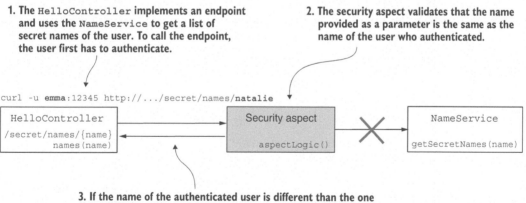

1. The HelloController implements an endpoint and uses the NameService to get a list of secret names of the user. To call the endpoint, the user first has to authenticate.

2. The security aspect validates that the name provided as a parameter is the same as the name of the user who authenticated.

```
curl -u emma:12345 http://.../secret/names/natalie
```

HelloController	Security aspect	NameService
/secret/names/{name}	aspectLogic()	getSecretNames(name)
names(name)		

3. If the name of the authenticated user is different than the one provided as a parameter, the aspect doesn't delegate the call to the service class, and it throws back an exception.

Figure 11.6 When implementing preauthorization, we can use the values of the method parameters in the authorization rules. In our example, only the authenticated user can retrieve information about their secret names.

For this project, I defined the same `ProjectConfig` class as in our first example so that we can continue working with our two users, Emma and Natalie. The endpoint now takes a value through a path variable and calls a service class to obtain the "secret names" for a given username. Of course, in this case, the secret names are just an invention of mine referring to a characteristic of the user, which is something that not everyone can see. I define the controller class as presented in the next listing.

Listing 11.5   The controller class defining an endpoint for testing

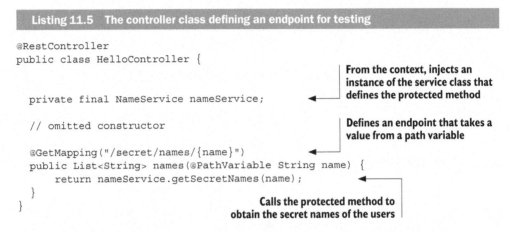

```
@RestController
public class HelloController {

    private final NameService nameService;

    // omitted constructor

    @GetMapping("/secret/names/{name}")
    public List<String> names(@PathVariable String name) {
        return nameService.getSecretNames(name);
    }
}
```

From the context, injects an instance of the service class that defines the protected method

Defines an endpoint that takes a value from a path variable

Calls the protected method to obtain the secret names of the users

Now let's take a look at how to implement the `NameService` class in listing 11.6. The expression we use for authorization now is `#name == authentication.principal.username`. In this expression, we use `#name` to refer to the value of the `getSecretNames()` method parameter called `name`, and we have access directly to the authentication object that we can use to refer to the currently authenticated user. The expression we use indicates that the method can be called only if the authenticated user's username is the same as the value sent through the method's parameter. In other words, a user can only retrieve its own secret names.

Listing 11.6   The `NameService` class defining the protected method

```
@Service
public class NameService {

    private Map<String, List<String>> secretNames =
        Map.of(
            "natalie", List.of("Energico", "Perfecto"),
            "emma", List.of("Fantastico"));

    @PreAuthorize
        ("#name == authentication.principal.username")
    public List<String> getSecretNames(String name) {
        return secretNames.get(name);
    }
}
```

Uses #name to represent the value of the method parameters in the authorization expression

We start the application and test it to prove it works as desired. The next code snippet shows the application behavior when calling the endpoint, providing the value of the path variable equal to the name of the user:

```
curl -u emma:12345 http://localhost:8080/secret/names/emma
```

The response body is

```
["Fantastico"]
```

When authenticating with the user Emma, we try to get Natalie's secret names. The call doesn't work:

```
curl -u emma:12345 http://localhost:8080/secret/names/natalie
```

The response body is

```
{
  "status":403,
  "error":"Forbidden",
  "message":"Forbidden",
  "path":"/secret/names/natalie"
}
```

The user Natalie can, however, obtain her own secret names. The next code snippet proves this:

```
curl -u natalie:12345 http://localhost:8080/secret/names/natalie
```

The response body is

```
["Energico","Perfecto"]
```

> **NOTE** Remember, you can apply method security to any layer of your application. In the examples presented in this chapter, you find the authorization rules applied for methods of the service classes. However, you can apply authorization rules with method security to any part of your application: controllers, repositories, managers, proxies, and so on.

11.3 *Applying postauthorization rules*

Say you want to allow a call to a method, but in certain circumstances, you want to ensure the caller doesn't receive the returned value. When we want to apply an authorization rule that is verified after the call of a method, we use postauthorization. It may sound a little bit awkward at the beginning: Why would someone be able to execute the code but not get the result? Well, it's not about the method itself, but imagine this method retrieves some data from a data source, say, a web service or a database. The conditions you need to add for authorization depend on the received data. So you allow the method to execute, but you validate what it returns, and if it doesn't meet the criteria, you don't let the caller access the return value.

To apply postauthorization rules with Spring Security, we use the `@PostAuthorize` annotation, which is similar to `@PreAuthorize`, discussed in section 11.2. The annotation receives the SpEL as a value, defining an authorization rule. We continue with an example showing how to use the `@PostAuthorize` annotation and define post-authorization rules for a method (figure 11.7).

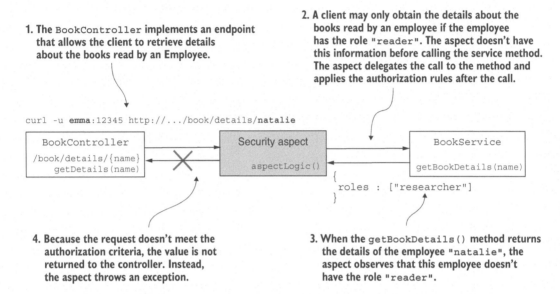

1. The `BookController` implements an endpoint that allows the client to retrieve details about the books read by an Employee.

2. A client may only obtain the details about the books read by an employee if the employee has the role `"reader"`. The aspect doesn't have this information before calling the service method. The aspect delegates the call to the method and applies the authorization rules after the call.

```
curl -u emma:12345 http://.../book/details/natalie
```

BookController
/book/details/{name}
getDetails(name)

Security aspect
aspectLogic()

BookService
getBookDetails(name)

{
roles : ["researcher"]
}

4. Because the request doesn't meet the authorization criteria, the value is not returned to the controller. Instead, the aspect throws an exception.

3. When the `getBookDetails()` method returns the details of the employee `"natalie"`, the aspect observes that this employee doesn't have the role `"reader"`.

Figure 11.7   With postauthorization, we don't protect the method from being called, but we protect the returned value from being exposed if the defined authorization rules aren't respected.

The scenario for our example, for which I created a project named ssia-ch11-ex3, defines an object `Employee`. Our `Employee` has a name, a list of books, and a list of authorities. We associate each `Employee` to a user of the application. To stay consistent with the other examples in this chapter, we define the same users, Emma and Natalie. We want to make sure that the method caller gets the employee details only if the employee has read authority. Because we don't know the authorities associated with the employee record until we retrieve it, we need to apply the authorization rules after the method execution. For this reason, we use the `@PostAuthorize` annotation.

The configuration class is like the one we used in the previous examples. But for your convenience, I repeat it in the next listing.

Listing 11.7   Enabling method security and defining users

```
@Configuration
@EnableMethodSecurity
public class ProjectConfig {

  @Bean
  public UserDetailsService userDetailsService() {
    var service = new InMemoryUserDetailsManager();

    var u1 = User.withUsername(„natalie")
```

```
                    .password("12345")
                    .authorities("read")
                    .build();

        var u2 = User.withUsername("emma")
                    .password("12345")
                    .authorities("write")
                    .build();

        service.createUser(u1);
        service.createUser(u2);

        return service;
    }

    @Bean
    public PasswordEncoder passwordEncoder() {
        return NoOpPasswordEncoder.getInstance();
    }
}
```

We also need to declare a class to represent the `Employee` object with its name, book list, and roles list. The following listing defines the `Employee` class.

Listing 11.8   The definition of the `Employee` class

```
public class Employee {

    private String name;
    private List<String> books;
    private List<String> roles;

    // Omitted constructor, getters, and setters
}
```

We probably get our employee details from a database. To keep our example shorter, I use a `Map` with a couple of records that we consider as our data source. In listing 11.9, you find the definition of the `BookService` class. The `BookService` class also contains the method for which we apply the authorization rules. Observe that the expression we use with the `@PostAuthorize` annotation refers to the value returned by the method `returnObject`. The postauthorization expression can use the value returned by the method, which is available after the method executes.

Listing 11.9   The `BookService` class defining the authorized method

```
@Service
public class BookService {

    private Map<String, Employee> records =
        Map.of("emma",
                new Employee("Emma Thompson",
                    List.of("Karamazov Brothers"),
                    List.of("accountant", "reader")),
```

```
            "natalie",
            new Employee("Natalie Parker",
                List.of("Beautiful Paris"),
                List.of("researcher"))
        );
    @PostAuthorize("returnObject.roles.contains('reader')")
    public Employee getBookDetails(String name) {
        return records.get(name);
    }
}
```

**Defines the expression
for postauthorization**

Let's also write a controller and implement an endpoint to call the method for which we applied the authorization rule. The following listing presents this controller class.

Listing 11.10   The controller class implementing the endpoint

```
@RestController
public class BookController {

    private final BookService bookService;

    // omitted constructor

    @GetMapping("/book/details/{name}")
    public Employee getDetails(@PathVariable String name) {
        return bookService.getBookDetails(name);
    }
}
```

You can now start the application and call the endpoint to observe the app's behavior. In the next code snippets, you find examples of calling the endpoint. Any of the users can access the details of Emma because the returned list of roles contains the string `"reader"`, but no user can obtain the details for Natalie. Calling the endpoint to get the details for Emma and authenticating with user Emma, we implement the following command:

```
curl -u emma:12345 http://localhost:8080/book/details/emma
```

The response body is

```
{
    "name":"Emma Thompson",
    "books":["Karamazov Brothers"],
    "roles":["accountant","reader"]
}
```

Calling the endpoint to get the details for Emma and authenticating with user Natalie, we use

```
curl -u natalie:12345 http://localhost:8080/book/details/emma
```

The response body is

```
{
    "name":"Emma Thompson",
```

```
   "books":["Karamazov Brothers"],
   "roles":["accountant","reader"]
}
```

Calling the endpoint to get the details for Natalie and authenticating with user Emma, we use

```
curl -u emma:12345 http://localhost:8080/book/details/natalie
```

The response body is

```
{
  "status":403,
  "error":"Forbidden",
  "message":"Forbidden",
  "path":"/book/details/natalie"
}
```

Calling the endpoint to get the details for Natalie and authenticating with user Natalie, we use this command:

```
curl -u natalie:12345 http://localhost:8080/book/details/natalie
```

The response body is

```
{
  "status":403,
  "error":"Forbidden",
  "message":"Forbidden",
  "path":"/book/details/natalie"
}
```

NOTE You can use both `@PreAuthorize` and `@PostAuthorize` for the same method if your requirements need to have both preauthorization and postauthorization.

11.4 *Implementing permissions for methods*

Up to now, you learned how to define rules with simple expressions for preauthorization and postauthorization. Now let's assume the authorization logic is more complex, and you cannot write it in one line. It's definitely not comfortable to write huge SpEL expressions. I never recommend using long SpEL expressions in any situation, regardless of whether it's an authorization rule or not. It simply creates hard-to-read code, and this affects the app's maintainability. When you need to implement complex authorization rules instead of writing long SpEL expressions, take the logic out in a separate class. Spring Security provides the concept of *permission*, which makes it easy to write the authorization rules in a separate class so that your application is easier to read and understand.

In this section, we apply authorization rules using permissions in a project. I named this project `ssia-ch11-ex4`. In this scenario, you have an application managing documents. Every document has an owner, which is the user who created the document. To get the details of an existing document, a user either must be an admin or they must be the owner of the document. We implement a permission evaluator to solve this requirement. The following listing defines the `document`, which is only a plain Java object.

Listing 11.11 The `Document` class

```
public class Document {

  private String owner;

  // Omitted constructor, getters, and setters
}
```

To mock the database and make our example shorter for your comfort, I created a repository class that manages a few document instances in a `Map`. This class is presented in the next listing.

Listing 11.12 The `DocumentRepository` class managing a few `Document` instances

```
@Repository
public class DocumentRepository {

  private Map<String, Document> documents =      ◄──── Identifies each document
    Map.of(«abc123», new Document(«natalie»),          by a unique code and
           «qwe123», new Document(«natalie»),          names the owner
           «asd555», new Document(«emma»));

  public Document findDocument(String code) {    ◄──── Obtains a document by
    return documents.get(code);                        using its unique
  }                                                    identification code
}
```

A service class defines a method that uses the repository to obtain a document by its code. The method in the service class is the one for which we apply the authorization rules. The logic of the class is simple. It defines a method that returns the `Document` by its unique code. We annotate this method with `@PostAuthorize` and use a `has-Permission()` SpEL expression. This method allows us to refer to an external authorization expression that we implement further in this example. Meanwhile, observe that the parameters we provide to the `hasPermission()` method are the `returnObject`, which represents the value returned by the method, and the name of the role for which we allow access, which is `'ROLE_admin'`. The definition of this class is presented in the following listing.

Listing 11.13 The `DocumentService` class implementing the protected method

```
@Service
public class DocumentService {

  private final DocumentRepository documentRepository;

  // omitted constructor
```

```
@PostAuthorize
("hasPermission(returnObject, 'ROLE_admin')")
public Document getDocument(String code) {
  return documentRepository.findDocument(code);
  }
}
```

**Uses the hasPermission()
expression to refer to an
authorization expression**

It's our duty to implement the permission logic. And we do this by writing an object that implements the `PermissionEvaluator` contract. The `PermissionEvaluator` contract provides two ways to implement the permission logic:

- *By object and permission*—Used in the current example, it assumes the permission evaluator receives two objects: one that's subject to the authorization rule and one that offers extra details needed for implementing the permission logic.
- *By object ID, object type, and permission*—Assumes the permission evaluator receives an object ID, which it can use to retrieve the needed object. It also receives a type of object, which can be used if the same permission evaluator applies to multiple object types, and it needs an object offering extra details for evaluating the permission.

In the next listing, you find the `PermissionEvaluator` contract with two methods.

Listing 11.14 The `PermissionEvaluator` contract definition

```
public interface PermissionEvaluator {

    boolean hasPermission(
            Authentication a,
            Object subject,
            Object permission);

    boolean hasPermission(
            Authentication a,
            Serializable id,
            String type,
            Object permission);
}
```

For the current example, it's enough to use the first method. We already have the subject, which in our case, is the value returned by the method. We also send the role name `'ROLE_admin'`, which, as defined by the example's scenario, can access any document. Of course, in our example, we could have directly used the name of the role in the permission evaluator class and avoided sending it as a value of the `hasPermission()` object. Here, we only do the former for the sake of the example. In a real-world scenario, which might be more complex, you have multiple methods, and details needed in the authorization process might differ between each of them. For this reason, you have a parameter that you can send the needed details for use in the authorization logic from the method level.

For your awareness and to avoid confusion, I'd also like to mention that you don't have to pass the `Authentication` object. Spring Security automatically provides this parameter value when calling the `hasPermission()` method. The framework knows the value of the authentication instance because it is already in the `SecurityContext`. In the next listing, you find the `DocumentsPermissionEvaluator` class, which in our example implements the `PermissionEvaluator` contract to define the custom authorization rule.

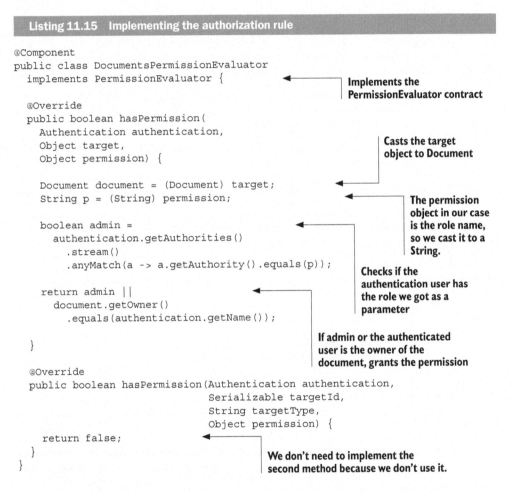

Listing 11.15 Implementing the authorization rule

```
@Component
public class DocumentsPermissionEvaluator
  implements PermissionEvaluator {            ←─────  Implements the
                                                      PermissionEvaluator contract

  @Override
  public boolean hasPermission(
    Authentication authentication,
    Object target,                                    Casts the target
    Object permission) {                              object to Document

    Document document = (Document) target;     ←─
    String p = (String) permission;                   The permission
                                                      object in our case
    boolean admin =                            ←──    is the role name,
      authentication.getAuthorities()                 so we cast it to a
        .stream()                                     String.
        .anyMatch(a -> a.getAuthority().equals(p));
                                                  Checks if the
    return admin ||                            ←─ authentication user has
      document.getOwner()                         the role we got as a
        .equals(authentication.getName());        parameter

                                             If admin or the authenticated
  }                                          user is the owner of the
                                             document, grants the permission
  @Override
  public boolean hasPermission(Authentication authentication,
                               Serializable targetId,
                               String targetType,
                               Object permission) {
    return false;                            ←─
  }                                             We don't need to implement the
}                                               second method because we don't use it.
```

To make Spring Security aware of our new `PermissionEvaluator` implementation, we have to define a `MethodSecurityExpressionHandler` bean in the configuration class. The following listing presents how to define a `MethodSecurityExpression-Handler` to make the custom `PermissionEvaluator` known.

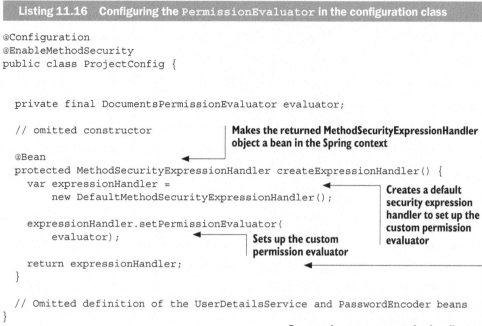

Listing 11.16 Configuring the `PermissionEvaluator` in the configuration class

```
@Configuration
@EnableMethodSecurity
public class ProjectConfig {


    private final DocumentsPermissionEvaluator evaluator;

    // omitted constructor

    @Bean
    protected MethodSecurityExpressionHandler createExpressionHandler() {
        var expressionHandler =
            new DefaultMethodSecurityExpressionHandler();

        expressionHandler.setPermissionEvaluator(
            evaluator);

        return expressionHandler;
    }

    // Omitted definition of the UserDetailsService and PasswordEncoder beans
}
```

Makes the returned MethodSecurityExpressionHandler object a bean in the Spring context

Creates a default security expression handler to set up the custom permission evaluator

Sets up the custom permission evaluator

Returns the custom expression handler to be added to the Spring context

NOTE We use here an implementation for `MethodSecurityExpressionHandler` named `DefaultMethodSecurityExpressionHandler` that Spring Security provides. You could also implement a custom `MethodSecurityExpression-Handler` to define custom SpEL expressions you use to apply the authorization rules. You rarely need to do this in a real-world scenario, and for this reason, we won't implement such a custom object in our examples. I just wanted to make you aware that this is possible.

I separate the definition of the `UserDetailsService` and `PasswordEncoder` to let you focus only on the new code. In listing 11.17, you can find the rest of the configuration class. The only important thing to notice about the users is their roles. User Natalie is an admin and can access any document. User Emma is a manager and can only access her own documents.

Listing 11.17 The full definition of the configuration class

```
@Configuration
@EnableMethodSecurity
public class ProjectConfig {

    private final DocumentsPermissionEvaluator evaluator;

    // Omitted constructor
```

```java
@Override
protected MethodSecurityExpressionHandler createExpressionHandler() {
  var expressionHandler =
      new DefaultMethodSecurityExpressionHandler();

  expressionHandler.setPermissionEvaluator(evaluator);

  return expressionHandler;
}


@Bean
public UserDetailsService userDetailsService() {
  var service = new InMemoryUserDetailsManager();

  var u1 = User.withUsername("natalie")
            .password("12345")
            .roles("admin")
            .build();

   var u2 = User.withUsername("emma")
            .password("12345")
            .roles("manager")
            .build();

  service.createUser(u1);
  service.createUser(u2);

  return service;
}

@Bean
public PasswordEncoder passwordEncoder() {
  return NoOpPasswordEncoder.getInstance();
}
}
```

To test the application, we define an endpoint. The following listing presents this definition.

Listing 11.18 Defining the controller class and implementing an endpoint

```java
@RestController
public class DocumentController {

  private final DocumentService documentService;

  // Omitted constructor

  @GetMapping("/documents/{code}")
  public Document getDetails(@PathVariable String code) {
    return documentService.getDocument(code);
  }
}
```

Let's run the application and call the endpoint to observe its behavior. User Natalie can access the documents regardless of their owner. User Emma can only access the documents she owns. Calling the endpoint for a document that belongs to Natalie and authenticating with the user "natalie", we use this command:

```
curl -u natalie:12345 http://localhost:8080/documents/abc123
```

The response body is

```
{
  "owner":"natalie"
}
```

Calling the endpoint for a document that belongs to Emma and authenticating with the user "natalie", we use

```
curl -u natalie:12345 http://localhost:8080/documents/asd555
```

The response body is

```
{
  "owner":"emma"
}
```

Calling the endpoint for a document that belongs to Emma and authenticating with the user "emma", we use

```
curl -u emma:12345 http://localhost:8080/documents/asd555
```

The response body is

```
{
  "owner":"emma"
}
```

Calling the endpoint for a document that belongs to Natalie and authenticating with the user "emma", we use

```
curl -u emma:12345 http://localhost:8080/documents/abc123
```

The response body is

```
{
  "status":403,
  "error":"Forbidden",
  "message":"Forbidden",
  "path":"/documents/abc123"
}
```

In a similar manner, you can use the second `PermissionEvaluator` method to write your authorization expression. The second method refers to using an identifier and subject type instead of the object itself. For example, say that we want to change the current example to apply the authorization rules before the method is executed, using

@PreAuthorize. In this case, we don't have the returned object yet. But instead of having the object itself, we have the document's code, which is its unique identifier. The next listing shows you how to change the permission evaluator class to implement this scenario. I separated the examples in a project named ssia-ch11-ex5, which you can run individually.

Listing 11.19   Changes in the DocumentsPermissionEvaluator **class**

```
@Component
public class DocumentsPermissionEvaluator
  implements PermissionEvaluator {

  private final DocumentRepository documentRepository;

  // Omitted constructor

  @Override
  public boolean hasPermission(Authentication authentication,
                               Object target,
                               Object permission) {
    return false;                          ◀──────┐  No longer defines the authorization rules
  }                                               │  through the first method

  @Override
  public boolean hasPermission(Authentication authentication,
                               Serializable targetId,
                               String targetType,
                               Object permission) {

    String code = targetId.toString();               ◀──────┐  Instead of
    Document document = documentRepository.findDocument(code);│  having the
                                                             │  object, we
    String p = (String) permission;                          │  have its ID,
                                                             │  and we get the
                                                             │  object using
    boolean admin =                                          │  the ID.
            authentication.getAuthorities()
                .stream()
                .anyMatch(a -> a.getAuthority().equals(p));

      return admin ||                          ◀──────┐
        document.getOwner().equals(                    │  If the user is an admin or the
          authentication.getName());                   │  owner of the document, the user
  }                                                     │  can access the document.
}
```

Of course, we also need to use the proper call to the permission evaluator with the @PreAuthorize annotation. In the following listing, you find the change I made in the DocumentService class to apply the authorization rules with the new method.

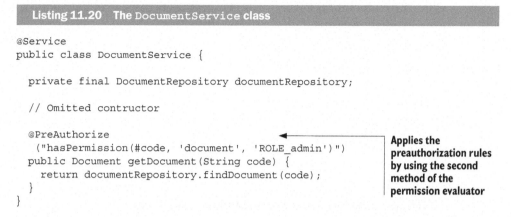

Listing 11.20 The `DocumentService` class

```
@Service
public class DocumentService {

  private final DocumentRepository documentRepository;

  // Omitted contructor

  @PreAuthorize
    ("hasPermission(#code, 'document', 'ROLE_admin')")
  public Document getDocument(String code) {
    return documentRepository.findDocument(code);
  }
}
```

Applies the preauthorization rules by using the second method of the permission evaluator

You can rerun the application and check the behavior of the endpoint. You should see the same result as in the case where we used the first method of the permission evaluator to implement the authorization rules. The user Natalie is an admin and can access details of any document, while the user Emma can only access the documents she owns. Calling the endpoint for a document that belongs to Natalie and authenticating with the user `"natalie"`, we issue

```
curl -u natalie:12345 http://localhost:8080/documents/abc123
```

The response body is

```
{
  "owner":"natalie"
}
```

Calling the endpoint for a document that belongs to Emma and authenticating with the user `"natalie"`, we issue

```
curl -u natalie:12345 http://localhost:8080/documents/asd555
```

The response body is

```
{
  "owner":"emma"
}
```

Calling the endpoint for a document that belongs to Emma and authenticating with the user `"emma"`, we issue

```
curl -u emma:12345 http://localhost:8080/documents/asd555
```

The response body is

```
{
  "owner":"emma"
}
```

Calling the endpoint for a document that belongs to Natalie and authenticating with the user `"emma"`, we issue

```
curl -u emma:12345 http://localhost:8080/documents/abc123
```

The response body is

```
{
  "status":403,
  "error":"Forbidden",
  "message":"Forbidden",
  "path":"/documents/abc123"
}
```

Using the @Secured and @RolesAllowed annotations

Throughout this chapter, we discussed applying authorization rules with global method security. We started by learning that this functionality is disabled by default and that you can enable it using the `@EnableMethodSecurity` annotation over the configuration class. Moreover, when using pre- and postauthorization, you don't need to specify a certain way to apply the authorization rules using an attribute of the `@EnableMethodSecurity` annotation. We used the annotation like this:

```
@EnableMethodSecurity
```

The `@EnableMethodSecurity` annotation offers two attributes that you can use to enable different annotations. You use the `jsr250Enabled` attribute to enable the `@RolesAllowed` annotation and the `securedEnabled` attribute to enable the `@Secured` annotation. Using these two annotations is less powerful than using `@PreAuthorize` and `@PostAuthorize`, and the chances that you'll find them in real-world scenarios are small. Even so, I'd like to make you aware of both, but without spending too much time on the details.

You enable the use of these annotations the same way we did for preauthorization and postauthorization by setting to true the attributes of the `@EnableMethodSecurity`. You enable the attributes that represent the use of one kind of annotation, either `@Secure` or `@RolesAllowed`. You can find an example of how to do this in the next code snippet:

```
@EnableMethodSecurity(
    jsr250Enabled = true,
    securedEnabled = true
)
```

Once you've enabled these attributes, you can use the `@RolesAllowed` or `@Secured` annotations to specify which roles or authorities the logged-in user needs to have to call a certain method. The next code snippet shows you how to use the `@RolesAllowed` annotation to specify that only users having the role ADMIN can call the `getName()` method:

```
@Service
public class NameService {

  @RolesAllowed("ADMIN")
  public String getName() {
     return "Fantastico";
  }
}
```

Similarily, you can use the `@Secured` annotation instead of the `@RolesAllowed` annotation:

```
@Service
public class NameService {
  @Secured("ROLE_ADMIN")
  public String getName() {
     return "Fantastico";
  }
}
```

You can now test your example. The next code snippet shows how to do this:

```
curl -u emma:12345 http://localhost:8080/hello
```

The response body is

```
Hello, Fantastico
```

To call the endpoint and authenticating with the user Natalie, use

```
curl -u natalie:12345 http://localhost:8080/hello
```

The response body is

```
{
  "status":403,
  "error":"Forbidden",
  "message":"Forbidden",
  "path":"/hello"
}
```

You can find a full example using the `@RolesAllowed` and `@Secured` annotations in the project ssia-ch9-ex6.

Summary

- Spring Security allows you to apply authorization rules for any application layer, not only at the endpoint level. To do this, we enable the method security functionality.
- The method security functionality is disabled by default. To enable it, we use the `@EnableMethodSecurity` annotation over the configuration class of your application.

- You can apply authorization rules that the application checks before the call to a method. If these authorization rules aren't followed, the framework doesn't allow the method to execute. When we test the authorization rules before the method call, we use preauthorization.

- To implement preauthorization, we use the `@PreAuthorize` annotation with the value of a SpEL expression that defines the authorization rule.

- If we want to only decide after the method call if the caller can use the returned value and if the execution flow can proceed, we use postauthorization.

- To implement postauthorization, we use the `@PostAuthorize` annotation with the value of a SpEL expression that represents the authorization rule.

- When implementing complex authorization logic, you should separate this logic into another class to make your code easier to read. In Spring Security, a common way to do this is by implementing a `PermissionEvaluator`.

- Spring Security offers compatibility with older specifications such as the `@RolesAllowed` and `@Secured` annotations. You can use these, but they are less powerful than `@PreAuthorize` and `@PostAuthorize`, and the chances that you'll find them used with Spring in a real-world scenario are very low.

Implementing filtering at the method level

This chapter covers

- Using prefiltering to restrict what a method receives as parameter values
- Using postfiltering to restrict what a method returns
- Integrating filtering with Spring Data

In chapter 11, you learned how to apply authorization rules using global method security. We worked on examples using the @PreAuthorize and @PostAuthorize annotations. When you use these annotations, the application either allows the method call, or it completely rejects it. Suppose you don't want to forbid the call to a method, but you want to make sure that the parameters sent to it follow some rules. Or, in another scenario, you want to make sure that after the method is called, the method's caller only receives an authorized part of the returned value. This functionality is called *filtering*, and it is classified into two categories:

- *Prefiltering*—The framework filters the values of the parameters before calling the method.
- *Postfiltering*—The framework filters the returned value after the method call.

Filtering works differently than call authorization (figure 12.1). With filtering, the framework executes the call and doesn't throw an exception if a parameter or returned value doesn't follow an authorization rule you define. Instead, it filters out elements that don't follow the specified conditions.

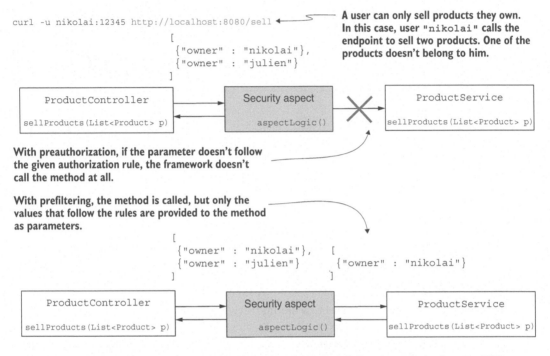

Figure 12.1   The client calls the endpoint providing a value that doesn't follow the authorization rule. With preauthorization, the method isn't called at all, and the caller receives an exception. With prefiltering, the aspect calls the method but only provides the values that follow the given rules.

It's important to mention at the beginning that you can only apply filtering to collections and arrays. You use prefiltering only if the method receives as a parameter an array or a collection of objects. The framework filters this collection or array according to rules you define. The same is valid for postfiltering: you can only apply this approach if the method returns a collection or an array. The framework filters the value the method returns based on rules you specify.

12.1   *Applying prefiltering for method authorization*

This section discusses the mechanism behind prefiltering, and then we implement prefiltering in an example. You can use filtering to instruct the framework to validate values sent via the method parameters when someone calls a method. The framework filters values that don't match the given criteria and calls the method only with values that do match them. This functionality is called *prefiltering* (figure 12.2).

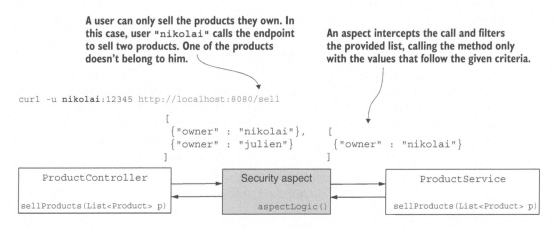

Figure 12.2 With prefiltering, an aspect intercepts the call to the protected method. The aspect filters the values that the caller provides as the parameter and sends to the method only values that follow the defined rules.

You find requirements in real-world examples where prefiltering applies well because it decouples authorization rules from the business logic the method implements. Say you implement a use case where you process only specific details owned by the authenticated user. This use case can be called from multiple places. Still, its responsibility always states that only details of the authenticated user can be processed, regardless of who invokes the use case. Instead of making sure the invoker of the use case applies the authorization rules correctly, you make the case apply its own authorization rules. Of course, you might do this inside the method. But decoupling authorization logic from business logic enhances the maintainability of your code and makes it easier for others to read and understand it.

As in the case of call authorization, which we discussed in chapter 11, Spring Security also implements filtering by using aspects. Aspects intercept specific method calls and can augment them with other instructions. For prefiltering, an aspect intercepts methods annotated with the @PreFilter annotation and filters the values in the collection provided as a parameter according to the criteria you define (figure 12.3).

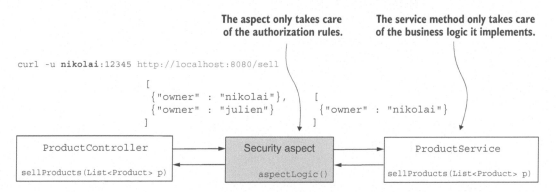

Figure 12.3 With prefiltering, we decouple the authorization responsibility from the business implementation. The aspect provided by Spring Security only takes care of the authorization rules, and the service method only takes care of the business logic of the use case it implements.

Similar to the @PreAuthorize and @PostAuthorize annotations discussed in chapter 11, you set authorization rules as the value of the @PreFilter annotation. In these rules, which you provide as SpEL expressions, you use filterObject to refer to any element inside the collection or array provided as a parameter to the method.

To see prefiltering applied, let's work on a project. I named this project ssia-ch12-ex1. Say you have an application for buying and selling products, and its backend implements the endpoint /sell. The application's frontend calls this endpoint when a user sells a product. But the logged-in user can only sell products they own. Let's implement a simple scenario of a service method called to sell the products received as a parameter. With this example, you learn how to apply the @PreFilter annotation, as this is what we use to make sure that the method only receives products owned by the currently logged-in user.

Once we create the project, we write a configuration class to ensure we have a couple of users to test our implementation. You find the straightforward definition of the configuration class in listing 12.1. The configuration class that I call ProjectConfig only declares a UserDetailsService and a PasswordEncoder, and I annotate it with @EnableMethodSecurity. For the filtering annotation, we still need to use the @EnableMethodSecurity annotation and enable the pre-/postauthorization annotations. The provided UserDetailsService defines the two users we need in our tests: Nikolai and Julien.

> ## Listing 12.1   Configuring users and enabling method security

```
@Configuration
@EnableMethodSecurity
public class ProjectConfig {

  @Bean
  public UserDetailsService userDetailsService() {
    var uds = new InMemoryUserDetailsManager();

    var u1 = User.withUsername("nikolai")
            .password("12345")
            .authorities("read")
            .build();

    var u2 = User.withUsername("julien")
            .password("12345")
            .authorities("write")
            .build();

    uds.createUser(u1);
    uds.createUser(u2);

    return uds;
  }

  @Bean
```

```
  public PasswordEncoder passwordEncoder() {
    return NoOpPasswordEncoder.getInstance();
  }
}
```

I describe the product using the model class presented in the next listing.

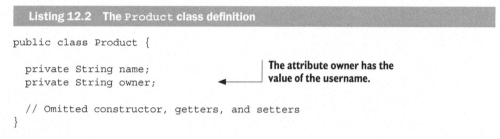

Listing 12.2 The `Product` class definition

```
public class Product {

    private String name;
    private String owner;

    // Omitted constructor, getters, and setters
}
```

The attribute owner has the value of the username.

The `ProductService` class defines the service method we protect with `@PreFilter`. You can find the `ProductService` class in listing 12.3. In that listing, before the `sellProducts()` method, you can observe the use of the `@PreFilter` annotation. The Spring Expression Language (SpEL) used with the annotation is `filterObject .owner == authentication.name`, which allows only values where the `owner` attribute of the `Product` equals the username of the logged-in user. On the left side of the equals operator in the SpEL expression, we use `filterObject`. With `filterObject`, we refer to objects in the list as parameters. Because we have a list of products, the `filterObject` in our case is of type `Product`. For this reason, we can refer to the product's `owner` attribute. On the right side of the equals operator in the expression, we use the `authentication` object. For the `@PreFilter` and `@PostFilter` annotations, we can directly refer to the authentication object, which is available in the `SecurityContext` after authentication (figure 12.4).

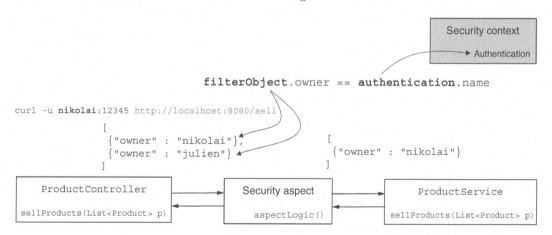

Figure 12.4 When using prefiltering by `filterObject`, we refer to the objects inside the list that the caller provides as a parameter. The authentication object is the one stored after the authentication process in the security context.

The service method returns the list exactly as it receives it. This way, we can test and validate that the framework filtered the list as we expected by checking the list returned in the HTTP response body.

Listing 12.3   Using the `@PreFilter` annotation in the `ProductService` class

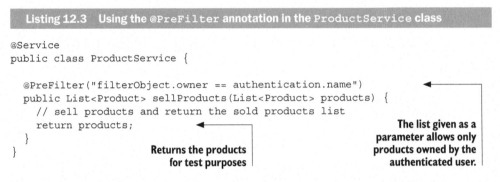

```
@Service
public class ProductService {

  @PreFilter("filterObject.owner == authentication.name")
  public List<Product> sellProducts(List<Product> products) {
    // sell products and return the sold products list
    return products;
  }
}
```

Returns the products for test purposes

The list given as a parameter allows only products owned by the authenticated user.

To make our tests easier, I define an endpoint to call the protected service method. Listing 12.4 defines this endpoint in a controller class called `ProductController`. Here, to make the endpoint call shorter, I create a list and directly provide it as a parameter to the service method. In a real-world scenario, this list should be provided by the client in the request body. You can also observe that I use `@GetMapping` for an operation suggesting a mutation, which is nonstandard. But know that I do this to avoid dealing with CSRF protection in our example, and this allows you to focus on the subject at hand. You learned about CSRF protection in chapter 9.

Listing 12.4   The controller class implementing the endpoint we use for tests

```
@RestController
public class ProductController {

  private final ProductService productService;

  // omitted constructor

  @GetMapping("/sell")
  public List<Product> sellProduct() {
    List<Product> products = new ArrayList<>();

    products.add(new Product("beer", "nikolai"));
    products.add(new Product("candy", "nikolai"));
    products.add(new Product("chocolate", "julien"));

    return productService.sellProducts(products);
  }
}
```

Let's start the application and see what happens when we call the /sell endpoint. Observe the three products from the list we provided as a parameter to the service method. I assign two of the products to user Nikolai and the other one to user Julien. When we call the endpoint and authenticate with user Nikolai, we expect to see in the response only the two products associated with her. When we call the endpoint and authenticate with Julien, in the response, we should only find the one product associated with Julien. In the following code snippet, you find the test calls and their results. To call the endpoint /sell and authenticate with user Nikolai, use this command:

```
curl -u nikolai:12345 http://localhost:8080/sell
```

The response body is

```
[
  {"name":"beer","owner":"nikolai"},
  {"name":"candy","owner":"nikolai"}
]
```

To call the endpoint /sell and authenticate with user Julien, use

```
curl -u julien:12345 http://localhost:8080/sell
```

The response body is

```
[
  {"name":"chocolate","owner":"julien"}
]
```

You need to be careful about the fact that the aspect changes the given collection. In our case, don't expect it to return a new List instance. In fact, it's the same instance from which the aspect removed the elements that didn't match the given criteria. This is important to take into consideration. You must always make sure that the collection instance you provide is not immutable. Providing an immutable collection to be processed results in an exception at execution time because the filtering aspect won't be able to change the collection's contents (figure 12.5).

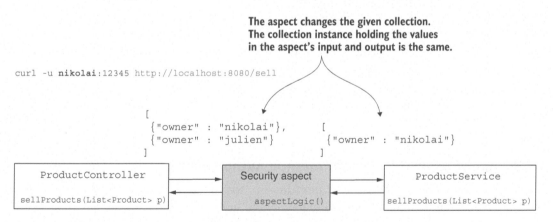

Figure 12.5 The aspect intercepts and changes the collection given as the parameter. You need to provide a mutable instance of a collection so the aspect can change it.

The next listing presents the same project we worked on earlier in this section, but I changed the List definition with an immutable instance as returned by the List .of() method to test what happens in this situation.

Listing 12.5   Using an immutable collection

```
@RestController
public class ProductController {

  private final ProductService productService;

  // omitted constructor

  @GetMapping("/sell")
  public List<Product> sellProduct() {
    List<Product> products = List.of(
            new Product("beer", "nikolai"),
            new Product("candy", "nikolai"),
            new Product("chocolate", "julien"));

    return productService.sellProducts(products);
  }
}
```

List.of() returns an immutable instance of the list.

I separated this example in the project ssia-ch12-ex2 folder so that you can test it your-self as well. Running the application and calling the /sell endpoint results in an HTTP response with status 500 Internal Server Error and an exception in the console log, as presented in the next code snippet:

```
curl -u julien:12345 http://localhost:8080/sell
```

The response body is

```
{
  "status":500,
  "error":"Internal Server Error",
  "path":"/sell"
}
```

In the application console, you can find an exception similar to the one presented in the following code snippet:

```
java.lang.UnsupportedOperationException: null
    at java.base/java.util.ImmutableCollections.uoe(ImmutableCollections.
java:73) ~[na:na]
...
```

12.2   *Applying postfiltering for method authorization*

In this section, we implement postfiltering. Say we have the following scenario. An application that has a frontend implemented in Angular and a Spring-based backend manages some products. Users own products, and they can obtain details only for their products. To get the details of their products, the frontend calls endpoints exposed by the backend (figure 12.6).

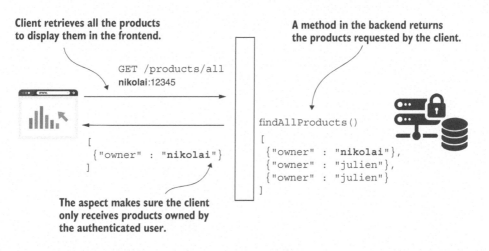

Figure 12.6 Postfiltering scenario. A client calls an endpoint to retrieve data it needs to display in the frontend. A postfiltering implementation ensures that the client only gets data owned by the currently authenticated user.

On the backend in a service class, the developer wrote a method `List<Product>` `findProducts()` that retrieves the product details. The client application displays these details in the frontend. How could the developer make sure that anyone calling this method only receives products they own and not products owned by others? An option to implement this functionality by keeping the authorization rules decoupled from the business rules of the application is called *postfiltering*. This section discusses how postfiltering works and demonstrate its implementation in an application.

Similar to prefiltering, postfiltering also relies on an aspect. This aspect allows a call to a method, but once the method returns, the aspect takes the returned value and makes sure that it follows the rules you define. As in the case of prefiltering, postfiltering changes a collection or an array returned by the method. You provide the criteria that the elements inside the returned collection should follow. The postfilter aspect filters from the returned collection or arrays those elements that don't follow your rules.

To apply postfiltering, you need to use the `@PostFilter` annotation. The `@PostFilter` annotation works similar to all the other pre-/postannotations we used in chapter 11 and in this chapter. You provide the authorization rule as a SpEL expression for the annotation's value, and that rule is the one that the filtering aspect uses, as shown in figure 12.7. Also, similar to prefiltering, postfiltering only works with arrays and collections. Make sure you apply the `@PostFilter` annotation only for methods that have an array or a collection as a return type.

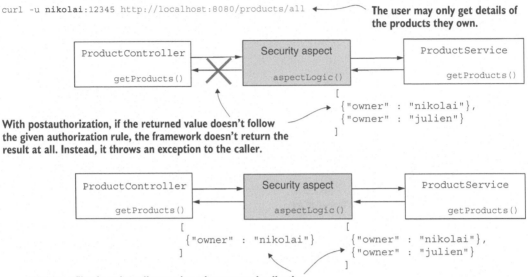

```
curl -u nikolai:12345 http://localhost:8080/products/all
```
The user may only get details of the products they own.

With postauthorization, if the returned value doesn't follow the given authorization rule, the framework doesn't return the result at all. Instead, it throws an exception to the caller.

With postfiltering, the caller receives the returned collection, but only with the values that follow the rules you provide.

Figure 12.7   Postfiltering. An aspect intercepts the collection returned by the protected method and filters the values that don't follow the rules you provide. Unlike postauthorization, postfiltering doesn't throw an exception to the caller when the returned value doesn't follow the authorization rules.

Let's apply postfiltering in an example for which I created a project named ssia-ch12-ex3. To be consistent, I kept the same users, as in our previous examples in this chapter, so that the configuration class won't change. For your convenience, I repeat the configuration presented in the following listing.

Listing 12.6   The configuration class

```
@Configuration
@EnableMethodSecurity
public class ProjectConfig {

  @Bean
  public UserDetailsService userDetailsService() {
    var uds = new InMemoryUserDetailsManager();

    var u1 = User.withUsername("nikolai")
            .password("12345")
            .authorities("read")
            .build();

    var u2 = User.withUsername("julien")
            .password("12345")
            .authorities("write")
            .build();

    uds.createUser(u1);
```

```
        uds.createUser(u2);

        return uds;
    }

    @Bean
    public PasswordEncoder passwordEncoder() {
        return NoOpPasswordEncoder.getInstance();
    }
}
```

The next code snippet shows that the `Product` class remains unchanged as well:

```
public class Product {

    private String name;
    private String owner;

    // Omitted constructor, getters, and setters
}
```

In the `ProductService` class, we now implement a method that returns a list of products. In a real-world scenario, we assume the application would read the products from a database or any other data source. To keep our example short and allow you to focus on the aspects we discuss, we use a simple collection, as presented in listing 12.7.

I annotate the `findProducts()` method, which returns the list of products, with the `@PostFilter` annotation. The condition I add as the value of the annotation, `filterObject.owner == authentication.name`, only allows products to be returned that have the owner equal to the authenticated user (figure 12.8). On the left side of the equals operator, we use `filterObject` to refer to elements inside the returned collection. On the right side of the operator, we use authentication to refer to the `Authentication` object stored in the `SecurityContext`.

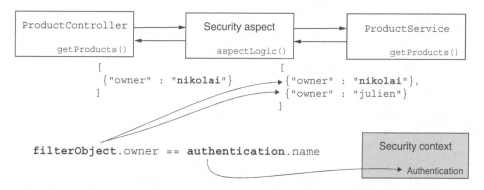

Figure 12.8   In the SpEL expression used for authorization, we use `filterObject` to refer to the objects in the returned collection, and we use `authentication` to refer to the `Authentication` instance from the security context.

Listing 12.7   The `ProductService` class

```
@Service
public class ProductService {

  @PostFilter("filterObject.owner == authentication.name")
  public List<Product> findProducts() {
    List<Product> products = new ArrayList<>();

    products.add(new Product("beer", "nikolai"));
    products.add(new Product("candy", "nikolai"));
    products.add(new Product("chocolate", "julien"));

    return products;
  }
}
```

Adds the filtering
condition for the
objects in the
collection returned
by the method

We define a controller class to make our method accessible through an endpoint. The next listing presents the controller class.

Listing 12.8   The `ProductController` class

```
@RestController
public class ProductController {

  private final ProductService productService;

  // Omitted constructor

  @GetMapping("/find")
  public List<Product> findProducts() {
    return productService.findProducts();
  }
}
```

It's time to run the application and test its behavior by calling the /find endpoint. We expect to see in the HTTP response body only products owned by the authenticated user. The next code snippets show the result for calling the endpoint with each of our users, Nikolai and Julien. To call the endpoint /find and authenticate with user Julien, use this cURL command:

```
curl -u julien:12345 http://localhost:8080/find
```

The response body is

```
[
  {"name":"chocolate","owner":"julien"}
]
```

To call the endpoint /find and authenticate with user Nikolai, use this cURL command:

```
curl -u nikolai:12345 http://localhost:8080/find
```

The response body is

```
[
  {"name":"beer","owner":"nikolai"},
  {"name":"candy","owner":"nikolai"}
]
```

12.3 *Using filtering in Spring Data repositories*

In this section, we discuss filtering applied with Spring Data repositories. It's important to understand this approach because we often use databases to persist an application's data. It is pretty common to implement Spring Boot applications that use Spring Data as a high-level layer to connect to a database, be it SQL or NoSQL. We discuss two approaches for applying filtering at the repository level when using Spring Data, and we implement these with examples.

The first approach we take is the one you learned previously in this chapter: using the `@PreFilter` and `@PostFilter` annotations. The second approach we discuss is direct integration of the authorization rules in queries. As you'll learn in this section, you need to be attentive when choosing the way you apply filtering in Spring Data repositories. As mentioned, we have two options:

- Using `@PreFilter` and `@PostFilter` annotations
- Directly applying filtering within queries

Using the `@PreFilter` annotation in the case of repositories is the same as applying this annotation at any other layer of your application. But when it comes to postfiltering, the situation changes. Using `@PostFilter` on repository methods technically works fine, but it's rarely a good choice from a performance point of view.

Say you have an application managing the documents of your company. The developer needs to implement a feature where all the documents are listed on a web page after the user logs in. The developer decides to use the `findAll()` method of the Spring Data repository and annotates it with `@PostFilter` to allow Spring Security to filter the documents such that the method returns only those owned by the currently logged-in user. This approach is clearly wrong because it allows the application to retrieve all the records from the database and then filter the records itself. If we have a large number of documents, calling `findAll()` without pagination could directly lead to an `OutOf-MemoryError`. Even if the number of documents isn't big enough to fill the heap, it's still less performant to filter the records in your application rather than retrieving at the start only what you need from the database (figure 12.9).

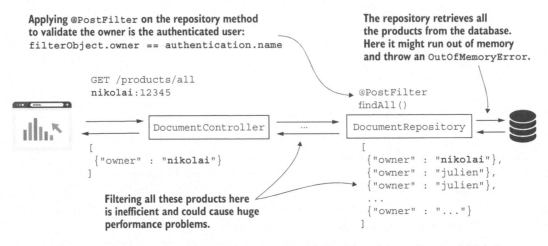

Applying @PostFilter on the repository method to validate the owner is the authenticated user:
filterObject.owner == authentication.name

The repository retrieves all the products from the database. Here it might run out of memory and throw an OutOfMemoryError.

GET /products/all
nikolai:12345

@PostFilter
findAll()

DocumentController   ...   DocumentRepository

[
  {"owner" : "nikolai"}
]

[
  {"owner" : "nikolai"},
  {"owner" : "julien"},
  {"owner" : "julien"},
  ...
  {"owner" : "..."}
]

Filtering all these products here is inefficient and could cause huge performance problems.

Figure 12.9   The anatomy of a bad design. When you need to apply filtering at the repository level, it's better to first make sure you only retrieve the data you need. Otherwise, your application can face heavy memory and performance issues.

At the service level, you have no other option than to filter the records in the app. Still, if you know from the repository level that you need to retrieve only records owned by the logged-in user, you should implement a query that extracts only the required documents from the database.

> **NOTE** In any situation in which you retrieve data from a data source, be it a database, a web service, an input stream, or anything else, make sure the application retrieves only the data it needs. Avoid as much as possible the need to filter data inside the application.

Let's work on an application where we first use the @PostFilter annotation on the Spring Data repository method, and then we change to the second approach where we write the condition directly in the query. This way, we have the opportunity to experiment with both approaches and compare them.

I created a new project named ssia-ch12-ex4, where I use the same configuration class as for our previous examples in this chapter. Like in the earlier examples, we write an application managing products, but this time, we retrieve the product details from a table in our database. For our example, we implement a search functionality for the products (figure 12.10). We write an endpoint that receives a string and returns the list of products that have the given string in their names. However, we need to make sure to return only products associated with the authenticated user.

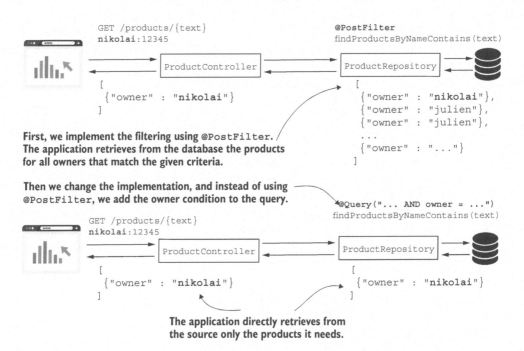

Figure 12.10   In our scenario, we start by implementing the application using @PostFilter to filter products based on their owner. Then we change the implementation to add the condition directly on the query. This way, we make sure the application only gets from the source the needed records.

We use Spring Data JPA to connect to a database. For this reason, we also need to add to the pom.xml file the `spring-boot-starter-data-jpa` dependency and a connection driver according to your database management server technology. The next code snippet provides the dependencies I use in the pom.xml file:

```
<dependency>
    <groupId>org.springframework.boot</groupId>
    <artifactId>spring-boot-starter-data-jpa</artifactId>
</dependency>
<dependency>
    <groupId>org.springframework.boot</groupId>
    <artifactId>spring-boot-starter-security</artifactId>
</dependency>
<dependency>
    <groupId>org.springframework.boot</groupId>
    <artifactId>spring-boot-starter-web</artifactId>
</dependency>
<dependency>
    <groupId>mysql</groupId>
    <artifactId>mysql-connector-java</artifactId>
    <scope>runtime</scope>
</dependency>
```

In the application.properties file, we add the properties Spring Boot requires to create the data source. In the next code snippet, you find the properties I added to my application.properties file:

```
spring.datasource.url=jdbc:mysql://localhost/
spring?useLegacyDatetimeCode=false&serverTimezone=UTC
spring.datasource.username=root
spring.datasource.password=
spring.datasource.initialization-mode=always
```

We also need a table in the database for storing the product details that our application retrieves. We define a schema.sql file where we write the script for creating the table, and a data.sql file where we write queries to insert test data in the table. You need to place both files (schema.sql and data.sql) in the resources folder of the Spring Boot project so they will be found and executed at the start of the application. The next code snippet shows you the query used to create the table, which we need to write in the schema.sql file:

```
CREATE TABLE IF NOT EXISTS `spring`.`product` (
  `id` INT NOT NULL AUTO_INCREMENT,
  `name` VARCHAR(45) NULL,
  `owner` VARCHAR(45) NULL,
  PRIMARY KEY (`id`));
```

In the data.sql file, I write three INSERT statements, which the next code snippet presents. These statements create the test data that we need later to prove the application's behavior:

```
INSERT IGNORE INTO `spring`.`product` (`id`, `name`, `owner`) VALUES ('1',
'beer', 'nikolai');
INSERT IGNORE INTO `spring`.`product` (`id`, `name`, `owner`) VALUES ('2',
'candy', 'nikolai');
INSERT IGNORE INTO `spring`.`product` (`id`, `name`, `owner`) VALUES ('3',
'chocolate', 'julien');
```

> **NOTE** Remember, we used the same names for tables in other examples throughout the book. If you already have tables with the same names from previous examples, you should probably drop those before starting with this project. An alternative is to use a different schema.

To map the product table in our application, we need to write an entity class. The following listing defines the `Product` entity.

Listing 12.9   The `Product` entity class

```
@Entity
public class Product {

    @Id
    @GeneratedValue(strategy = GenerationType.IDENTITY)
    private int id;
    private String name;
```

```
        private String owner;

        // Omitted getters and setters
}
```

For the `Product` entity, we also write a Spring Data repository interface defined in the next listing. Observe that this time we use the `@PostFilter` annotation directly on the method declared by the repository interface.

Listing 12.10 The `ProductRepository` interface

```
public interface ProductRepository
        extends JpaRepository<Product, Integer> {

    @PostFilter("filterObject.owner == authentication.name")   ◄────────────┐
    List<Product> findProductByNameContains(String text);                   │
}                                                                           │
                                                                            │
                    Uses the @PostFilter annotation for the method         │
                    declared by the Spring Data repository                  │
```

The next listing shows you how to define a controller class that implements the endpoint we use for testing the behavior.

Listing 12.11 The `ProductController` class

```
@RestController
public class ProductController {

  private final ProductRepository productRepository;

  // Omitted constructor

  @GetMapping("/products/{text}")
  public List<Product> findProductsContaining(
    @PathVariable String text) {

    return productRepository.findProductByNameContains(text);
  }
}
```

Starting the application, we can test what happens when calling the /products/{text} endpoint. By searching the letter *c* while authenticating with user Nikolai, the HTTP response only contains the product *candy*. Even if *chocolate* contains a *c* as well, because Julien owns it, *chocolate* won't appear in the response. You find the calls and their responses in the code snippets that follow. To call the endpoint /products and authenticate with user Nikolai, issue this command:

```
curl -u nikolai:12345 http://localhost:8080/products/c
```

The response body is

```
[
  {"id":2,"name":"candy","owner":"nikolai"}
]
```

To call the endpoint /products and authenticate with user Julien, issue

```
curl -u julien:12345 http://localhost:8080/products/c
```

The response body is

```
[
  {"id":3,"name":"chocolate","owner":"julien''}
]
```

We discussed earlier in this section that using @PostFilter in the repository isn't the best choice. We should instead make sure we don't select from the database what we don't need. So how can we change our example to select only the required data instead of filtering data following selection? We can provide SpEL expressions directly in the queries used by the repository classes. To achieve this, we follow two simple steps:

1 We add an object of type SecurityEvaluationContextExtension to the Spring context. We can do this using a simple @Bean method in the configuration class.

2 We adjust the queries in our repository classes with the proper clauses for selection.

In our project, to add the SecurityEvaluationContextExtension bean in the context, we need to change the configuration class as presented in the next listing. To keep all the code associated with the examples in the book, I use another project here named ssia-ch12-ex5.

Listing 12.12   Adding the `SecurityEvaluationContextExtension` to the context

```
@Configuration
@EnableMethodSecurity
public class ProjectConfig {                     Adds a SecurityEvaluationContextExtension to
                                                 the Spring context
  @Bean
  public SecurityEvaluationContextExtension
    securityEvaluationContextExtension() {

    return new SecurityEvaluationContextExtension();
  }

    // Omitted declaration of the UserDetailsService and PasswordEncoder
}
```

In the ProductRepository interface, we add the query prior to the method, and we adjust the WHERE clause with the proper condition using a SpEL expression. The following listing presents the change.

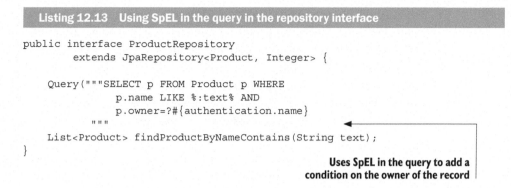

Listing 12.13 Using SpEL in the query in the repository interface

```
public interface ProductRepository
        extends JpaRepository<Product, Integer> {

    Query("""SELECT p FROM Product p WHERE
            p.name LIKE %:text% AND
            p.owner=?#{authentication.name}
          """
    List<Product> findProductByNameContains(String text);
}
```

Uses SpEL in the query to add a
condition on the owner of the record

We can now start the application and test it by calling the /products/{text} endpoint. We expect that the behavior remains the same as for the case where we used @Post-Filter. But now only the records for the right owner are retrieved from the database, which makes the functionality faster and more reliable. The next code snippets present the calls to the endpoint. To call the endpoint /products and authenticate with user Nikolai, we use

```
curl -u nikolai:12345 http://localhost:8080/products/c
```

The response body is

```
[
  {"id":2,"name":"candy","owner":"nikolai"}
]
```

To call the endpoint /products and authenticate with user Julien, we use

```
curl -u julien:12345 http://localhost:8080/products/c
```

The response body is

```
[
  {"id":3,"name":"chocolate","owner":"julien"}
]
```

Summary

- Filtering is an authorization approach in which the framework validates the input parameters of a method or the value returned by the method and excludes the elements that don't fulfill some criteria you define. As an authorization approach, filtering focuses on the input and output values of a method and not on the method execution itself.

- You use filtering to ensure that a method doesn't get values other than the ones it's authorized to process and that it can't return values that the method's caller shouldn't get.

- When using filtering, you don't restrict access to the method, but you restrict what can be sent via the method's parameters or what the method returns. This approach allows you to control the method input and output.

- To restrict the values that can be sent via the method's parameters, you use the @PreFilter annotation. The @PreFilter annotation receives the condition for which values are allowed to be sent as method parameters. The framework filters from the collection given as a parameter all values that don't follow the given rule.

- To use the @PreFilter annotation, the method's parameter must be a collection or an array. From the annotation's SpEL expression, which defines the rule, we refer to the objects inside the collection using filterObject.

- To restrict the values returned by the method, you use the @PostFilter annotation. When using the @PostFilter annotation, the returned type of the method must be a collection or an array. The framework filters the values in the returned collection according to a rule you define as the value of the @PostFilter annotation.

- You can use the @PreFilter and @PostFilter annotations with Spring Data repositories as well. But using @PostFilter on a Spring Data repository method is rarely a good choice. To avoid performance problems, filtering the result should be done directly at the database level in this case.

- Spring Security easily integrates with Spring Data, and you use this feature to avoid issuing @PostFilter with methods of Spring Data repositories.

Part 4

Implementing OAuth 2 and OpenID Connect

In an era where secure and seamless authentication methods are paramount, protocols such as OAuth 2 and OpenID Connect have emerged as industry standards. This part of the book unravels the intricacies of these protocols, shedding light on their mechanisms, benefits, and potential pitfalls.

Chapter 13 sets the stage by providing an overarching view of both protocols, describing various token grant types in detail, and highlighting potential vulnerabilities within OAuth 2.

Chapter 14 delves deeper into setting up a robust Spring Security authorization server, including defining client details and managing cryptographic keys.

Chapter 15 provides guidance on crafting a resilient resource server, emphasizing token introspection and ensuring resource protection.

Chapter 16 rounds out this part, demonstrating how to obtain tokens from the authorization server and access resources under the protective umbrella of the resource server.

Upon completing this section, you'll become skilled at integrating OAuth 2 and OpenID Connect within your applications, fortifying them against unauthorized access and ensuring seamless user experiences.

By the end of this part, you'll have garnered the expertise to meticulously design and implement comprehensive authorization strategies, ensuring your application remains both functional and fortified.

What are OAuth 2 and OpenID Connect?

Suppose you work for a large organization and use several tools in your daily work. You use bug tracker apps, apps for documenting your work, apps for registering your time, and so on. In each one, you need to authenticate tools to work with them. Would you use different sets of credentials for these apps? Of course, doing so could work, but this approach would be cumbersome for the user (you), and it would also complicate the purpose of the apps you work with.

For you, the complexity comes from the fact that you'd have to remember the credentials and log in several times in each of the apps you use. For the apps, the added complexity comes from the fact that they'd also need to implement the capability of persisting and protecting the credentials and the actual authentication.

What about managing the responsibility for storing the credentials and authentication in a separate app? In this case, the users would only have to log in once and use all their apps without bothering to authenticate repeatedly. Is there such a solution? Yes. You can implement authentication over the OAuth 2 specification.

The second thing is that we can go even bigger. An app that can be used by public users (users outside of an organization—an app you create for the whole world) might also need authentication capabilities. The app can implement those capabilities, but

- Implementing authentication in this app requires more work and effort.
- The users need a specific set of credentials for this app.
- The users sometimes don't trust creating specific credentials for any small app they use.

Could you allow the users of this app to log in with some credentials they already have? Could your app's users log in with their Facebook, GitHub, Twitter, or Google account credentials instead, maybe? You might have already seen that all over the place. Apps around the web allow users to choose to sign up and use various social media platforms. This way, an app allows its users to authenticate with a set of credentials they already have without you needing to implement something specific in your app. Such an approach

- Reduces costs (e.g., of implementing and maintaining authentication in your app)
- Avoids user trust issues (e.g., of having to register and create another set of credentials that your app will maintain)
- Helps users minimize the number of credentials they use

OAuth 2 is a specification that tells one how to separate the authentication responsibilities in a system. This way, multiple apps can use one other app that implements the authentication, helping the users to authenticate faster, keeping their details more secure, and minimizing the costs of implementation in the apps.

We'll start with section 13.1, where I'll introduce the main actors involved in a system where the authentication and authorization are built over the OAuth 2 specification. In section 13.1, you'll learn all the responsibilities of the parts of an OAuth 2 system, such as the user, client, authorization server, and resource server. In section 13.2, we discuss tokens. Tokens are like access keys for an app. You'll learn you can use multiple types of tokens and when it's best to use each type. Section 13.3 reviews the most critical ways tokens can be issued (which we'll implement and test in chapter 14). We end this chapter with section 13.4, where we'll go through possible pitfalls you need to consider when implementing OAuth 2.

Before we start, I'd like to mention that in this chapter, I offer a simple perspective of everything you need to know to further understand our discussion in chapters 14 through 16. I don't intend to make you an OAuth 2 and OpenID Connect expert in one chapter. I don't think that'd be possible, as the two are quite complex enough for others to have written entire books about them. If you wish to expand your knowledge on the subject, I recommend *OAuth 2 in Action* by Justin Richer and Antonio Sanso (Manning, 2017) and *OpenID Connect in Action* by Prabath Siriwardena (Manning, 2023).

13.1   The big picture of OAuth 2 and OpenID Connect

Suppose you need to attend an interview with a large corporation. You have been called to their main headquarters for a face-to-face discussion. But not just anyone can enter the company's office. There are specific protocols implemented for visitors.

To get in the building and attend the discussion, you must first visit the front desk and prove who you are by using an ID. After getting identified, you'll get an access card from the front desk, allowing you to open certain doors. You might not even be able to use all the elevators but only specific ones (figure 13.1).

Figure 13.1   The OAuth 2 specification is very similar to accessing an office building.

The process of getting into the building for the discussion is very similar to how authentication and authorization work in an OAuth 2 implementation. You are the user who needs to execute a specific use case (go to a particular room for the discussion). For that, you use your credentials (the ID) to authenticate at the front desk (the authorization server). Once you prove who you are, you have an access card (the token). But you can use this token only to access specific resources (like elevators and specific doors). You can use the access card only for a short period. After your discussion, you must return the card to the front desk.

In this section, we discuss the responsibilities that interact with one another in an OAuth 2 system, and you'll find out how is it similar to visiting an organization's headquarters for an interview. We also discuss what OAuth 2 is as a specification and the difference between OpenID Connect (a protocol) and OAuth 2 (the specification it relies on). I consider it essential to understand well the concepts behind the scenes of this authentication and authorization approach before diving into its implementation in chapters 14 through 16.

First, let's discover who plays roles in an OAuth 2 system. Figure 13.2 presents the main actors of an OAuth 2 system. By actor, I mean any entity that plays a role in the system's functionality. With an OAuth 2 system, you'll find the following actors:

- *The user*—The person who uses the application. The users usually work with a frontend application, which we call a client. Users don't always exist in an OAuth 2 system, as discussed in section 13.3.3, where you'll learn about the client credentials grant type.
- *The client*—The application that calls a backend and needs authentication and authorization. The client can be a web app, a mobile app, or even a desktop app or a separate backend service. The system usually doesn't have a user when the client is a backend service.
- *The resource server*—A backend application that authorizes and serves calls sent by one or more client applications.
- *The authorization server*—An app that implements authentication and safe storage of credentials.

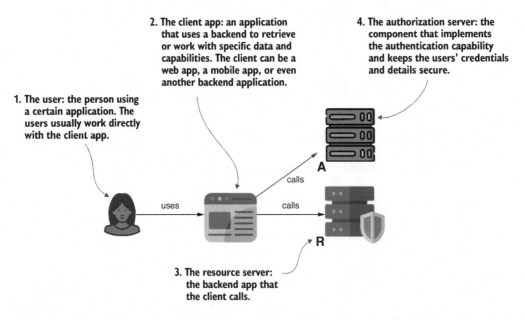

Figure 13.2   The participants in an OAuth 2 framework. Users interact through a client that requires authorization for certain operations on the backend service, known as a resource server. For backend authorization, the client's initial step is authentication by the authorization server.

Let's now discuss how authentication and authorization really happen. The steps are simple:

1 The user executes a certain use case with the client app.
2 The client app gets authorized to call the resource server to serve the user's request.
3 To get authorized, the client first requests a token (called an access token) from the authorization server. This token is just some specific information that helps the client to prove the authorization server identified them correctly.
4 The client uses the token the authorization server issues to get authorized when sending requests to its backend (the resource server).

Figure 13.3 details a bit of the flow visually. The numbered steps in the figure represent the following:

1 The user tries to use the client application to execute a particular use case.
2 The client application knows it can't call its backend without first having a token that will allow it to get authorized. The client requests such an access token from the authorization server.
3 Following the client app's request, the authorization server issues a token and sends it to the client app.
4 The client uses the token to send requests to its backend (the resource server).
5 The resource server authorizes the client's request. If authorized successfully, the resource server executes the client's request and replies back.
6 The client shows the result to the user.

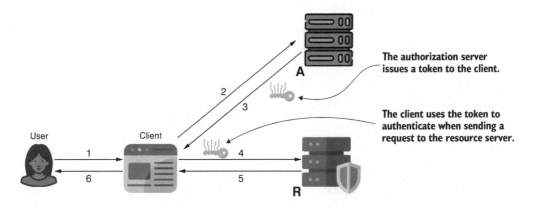

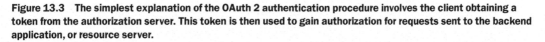

Figure 13.3 The simplest explanation of the OAuth 2 authentication procedure involves the client obtaining a token from the authorization server. This token is then used to gain authorization for requests sent to the backend application, or resource server.

But what exactly is this token that the authorization server issues? A token can be any piece of data (usually a string of characters) that allows the client to prove they (and/or the user) have been identified by the authorization server. The token is also a way to get more details about both user and client if needed. Because the authorization server now manages all the user and client details, the backend sometimes needs to get part of these details from the authorization server and use them. The backend will get such details by means of the token. Sometimes, the token itself contains the needed details (as you'll read in section 13.2, such tokens are called non-opaque tokens); otherwise, the backend needs to call the authorization server to get the data about the client and the user (i.e., opaque tokens). In addition, unlike a physical key, an access token doesn't have a large lifespan. It expires after a short period (in most cases minutes), after which the client needs to ask the authorization server again for another token. This way, a lost token (such as a lost key) can't be misused.

OAuth 2 describes multiple flows in which a client might get a token. We call these flows "grant types," and in section 13.3, we discuss the most common grant types used.

13.2   *Using various token implementations*

Tokens are the access cards (figure 13.4) a client uses to get authorized when sending requests to the backend (the resource server). Tokens are an essential part of the OAuth 2 authentication and authorization process because they're the ones used to prove the authenticity of a client and user authentication, but they are also the way a backend gets more details about the client and the user.

In this section, we discuss how tokens are classified and, depending on the token type, how they are used in the authorization process.

Figure 13.4   Zglorb (the user) needs to access the Mothership (resource server). To do that, they're first authenticated (by the authorization server), and then they're given an access card (the token). Zglorb can only access specific areas (resources) of the Mothership using their access card.

We classify tokens based on the way they provide the resource server with the data for authorization:

- *Opaque*—Tokens which don't store data. To implement the authorization, the resource server usually needs to call the authorization server, provide the opaque token, and get the details. This call is known as the introspection call.
- *Non-opaque*—Tokens that store data, making it immediately possible for the backend to implement the authorization. The JSON Web Token (JWT) is the most used non-opaque token implementation.

13.2.1 Using opaque tokens

Opaque tokens don't contain data the backend can use to identify either the user or the client, or to implement the authorization rules. Opaque tokens are just proof of an authentication attempt. When a resource server receives an opaque token, it needs to call the authorization server to find out whether the token is valid and to get more information to allow it to apply authorization constraints.

An opaque token is literally like a key to a treasure chest. It doesn't provide any information up front; you know it works only when you try opening the chest with it. Once you find out it's valid, it also gets you to what's inside the chest (in this case, the user and client details). Figure 13.5 illustrates this analogy.

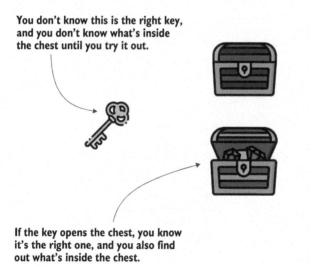

You don't know this is the right key, and you don't know what's inside the chest until you try it out.

If the key opens the chest, you know it's the right one, and you also find out what's inside the chest.

Figure 13.5   An analogy to opaque tokens. An opaque token is just like a key. You don't know if it works until you try it. If the key works, you also get access to what's inside it.

The resource server calls an endpoint provided by the authorization server to find out whether the opaque token is valid and obtain the needed details about the client and the user to whom the token was issued. This call is named a token introspection (figure 13.6). Once the resource server has these details, it can apply the authorization constraints.

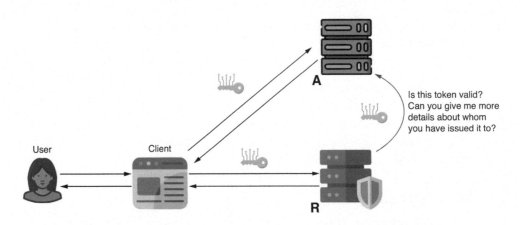

Figure 13.6   The token introspection call. The resource server sends a request to the authorization server to find out whether the opaque token is valid and details about to whom it was issued.

13.2.2 *Using non-opaque tokens*

Unlike the opaque tokens we discussed in section 13.2.1, non-opaque tokens contain information about the client and the user to whom the authorization server issued the tokens during the authentication process. You can compare non-opaque tokens with signed documents (figure 13.7).

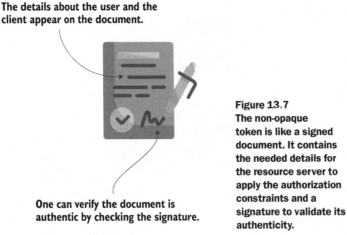

The details about the user and the client appear on the document.

**Figure 13.7
The non-opaque token is like a signed document. It contains the needed details for the resource server to apply the authorization constraints and a signature to validate its authenticity.**

One can verify the document is authentic by checking the signature.

The most common implementation of a non-opaque token is the JWT. A JWT is composed of three parts (figure 13.8):

- *The header*—Usually contains data about the token, such as the cryptographic algorithm used to sign the token or the key ID that the authorization server used to sign it

- *The body*—Usually contains data about the entity to whom the token was issued, such as the client and the user details
- *The signature*—A cryptographically generated value that can be used to prove that the authorization server indeed issued the token and that no one altered its content (in the header or body) after it was generated

The data in the header and body is JavaScript Object Notation (JSON) formatted, then encoded as Base64 to make it smaller and easier to transfer. Dots separate the three parts.

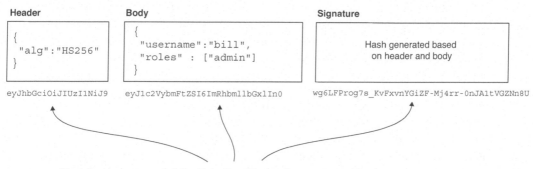

The token is composed of the three Base64 encodings separated by dots.

Figure 13.8   The anatomy of a JWT token. The header and the body contain the details needed for the resource server to validate the token's authenticity and apply the authorization constraints.

The next snippet shows an example of a JWT where the three parts are Base64 encoded, separated by dots:

```
eyJhbGciOiJIUzI1NiIsInR5cCI6IkpXVCJ9.eyJzdWIiOiIxMjM0NTY3ODkwIiwibmFtZSI6Ikp
vaG4gRG9lIiwiaWF0IjoxNTE2MjM5MDIyfQ.SflKxwRJSMeKKF2QT4fwpMeJf36POk6yJV_adQ
ssw5c
```

You may be asking yourself now, "When should I use opaque tokens, and when should I use non-opaque ones?" As I told you a bit earlier in this section, non-opaque tokens are the most frequently used today because they don't require introspection to validate them. However, non-opaque tokens contain data, and the client sends this data over the wire to its backend. Anyone obtaining the token can also see the data the token carries. In the majority of cases, this is not a problem. And I recommend anyone avoid sending too much data within the token.

But what should you do if you have a larger amount of data or data that is unsafe to send over the wire carried within a token? In such a case, opaque tokens might be a good alternative. I recommend you first consider non-opaque tokens and fall back to opaque ones only if the amount of data to be carried by the token is too large, or you need to send details that are more sensitive, and you want to avoid exchanging them through the token.

13.3   *Obtaining tokens through various grant types*

This section discusses grant types. A grant type is a process in which a client gets a token. In apps, you'll find various approaches in which a client gets a token from the authorization server. We'll discuss the three most used grant types. At the end of this section, we'll explore how a client can re-generate a token after it expires.

> **NOTE**   You might still find apps implementing two other grant types: the implicit and the password grant type. These two grant types became deprecated because they were found to not be secure enough. We won't discuss them in this book; I don't recommend using them in apps. You can always replace either with one of the other grant types discussed in this section. If you want to learn more about the password grant type, there is a good discussion about it in chapter 12 of the first edition of this book. We also go quickly over the implicit grant type and why it's deprecated when discussing the authorization code grant type in this section.

Section 13.3.1 discusses the authorization code grant type, which is the most used grant type when the system needs to allow a user to authenticate. In section 13.3.2, we discuss an addition to the authorization code grant type—the proof key for code exchange (PKCE). In section 13.3.3, we continue with the situation where an app needs to get a token without having a user authenticate, and we end with how to re-generate tokens in section 13.3.4.

13.3.1   *Getting a token using the authorization code grant type*

The authorization code grant type is the most used grant type today. It is used when our app needs to authenticate a user (to easily understand this grant type, see figure 13.9, which illustrates the steps in a sequence diagram):

1 The user wants to do something within the app they use. For example, let's say that the girl on the left side of the diagram is Mary, an accountant who wants to see all the invoices that the company she works for needs to pay.

2 The app Mary uses is the client. In this case, Mary stays in front of her computer, so her client app is a web app. But Mary could have also used the mobile version of the app. In both cases, the grant type would have looked the same. Because Mary didn't log in, the app redirects her to a login page hosted by the authorization server.

3 Now Mary sees the login page in her browser. The login page is not in the app she accessed but is hosted by a different system. Mary recognizes the page she was redirected to as the central authentication application that she uses for any of the apps she works with for the company. Mary knows that after submitting her credentials, the browser will return her to the invoices application, and she will be able to see the invoices and operate with the data she needs. She fills in the correct credentials and selects the login button.

4 Because the credentials Mary provided are correct, the authorization server redirects back to the invoices application. The authorization server also provides the initial application (the client) a unique code named an "authorization code." The client will use this code to get an access token.

5 The client asks for an access token. The client needs this access token to send requests to its backend (the resource server).

6 Because the authorization code is correct (the same one the server provided in step 5), the authorization server responds with an access token.

7 The client app uses the access token to send a request to its backend and get authorized.

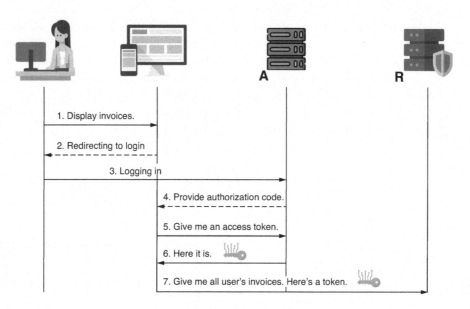

Figure 13.9 The authorization code grant type. The user is required to sign in. After login, the authorization server issues an authorization code to the client, which the client then utilizes to obtain an access token. This access token enables the client to have its requests authorized by the resource server.

A few observations to help you understand this flow better:

- Pay attention to the dotted arrows. It's essential to remember that those represent redirects in the browser and not requests or responses. At step 2, the client app redirects the user to the authorization server login page (it redirects in the browser to a web page of another app). At step 4, the authorization server redirects back to the client app providing the authorization code (usually as a query parameter).

- Mary (the user) isn't aware of steps 4 through 7. After she logs in, she will, in the end, see the invoices displayed by the client who will get them in response to step 7 after being authorized.

- Remember not to confuse the authorization code and the access token. The access token is what the client needs, in the end, to get authorized by its backend (step 7). But to get the access token, the client first gets an authorization code (steps 4 and 5).

In addition, many developers new to authorization and authentication are confused about step 4. The question I frequently get is, "Why doesn't the authorization server directly return the access token here?" It looks strange that the client needs to take one more step to get the access token when they could have directly gotten it at step 4.

But it makes sense. In fact, in the first version of OAuth, the authorization server provided the access token instead of the authorization code at step 4. This is what we now name the "implicit grant type," which is deprecated and no longer recommended to be used. The reason is that a redirect can be easily intercepted, and a bad-intentioned individual could have very easily obtained the access token. By returning the authorization code, the authorization server forces the client to re-send a request where they must authenticate again with their credentials. This way, if someone intercepts the redirect and gets the authorization code, it's not enough to get an access token. They would need to also know the client credentials to send the request and get the token.

Figure 13.10 visually presents the two steps where the authorization code adds supplementary protection to avoid allowing someone to get the access token.

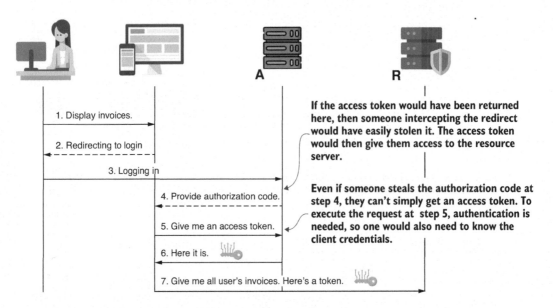

Figure 13.10   After logging in and receiving an authorization code, the client must make an additional request to acquire the access token. During this request, the client is required to verify its identity using its credentials. This method increases the challenge for anyone attempting to illicitly obtain the access token, as they would need to intercept the authorization code and also know the client's credentials.

13.3.2 *Applying PKCE protection to the authorization code grant type*

What if a bad-intentioned individual manages to get the client credentials as well? In this case, they could obtain an access token and send requests to the resource server. Is there a way in which we can prevent something like this from happening? Yes, the proof key for code exchange (PKCE, usually pronounced "pixy") is an enhancement added to the authorization code flow to make it more secure. In this section, we discuss how PKCE covers the case where someone could get an access token by stealing the client credentials.

Using PKCE only affects two of the steps of the authorization code grant type, which we discussed in section 13.3.1. In figure 13.11, I made the arrows representing steps 3 and 5 thicker. These two are the steps of the authorization code grant type where PKCE is applied:

1. First, the client needs to generate a random value. This value can be a random string of bytes. This value is called *the verifier.*
2. Second, the client will apply a hash function over the randomly generated value at step 1. A hash function is encryption characterized by the fact that the output cannot be turned back to the input (chapter 4). The result of applying the hash function over the verifier is called *the challenge.*

```
verifier = random();
challenge = hash(verifier);
```

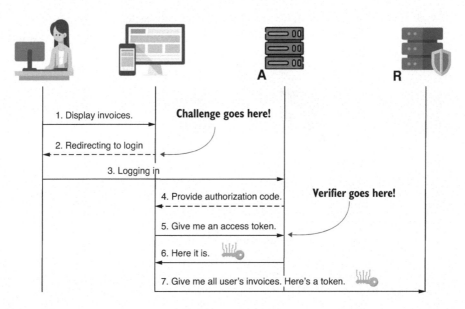

Figure 13.11 The client will send a challenge in step 3 and the verifier in step 5 to prove that they are the same client who initially asked the user to log in.

The client sends the challenge in step 3 with the user login. The authorization server keeps the challenge and expects the verifier with the request made at step 5 to get the access token. If the verifier the client sends when requesting the token at step 5 matches the challenge they sent at step 3, then the authorization server knows the client app that requests the token is the same one that requests the user to authenticate.

Someone cannot get an access token now even if they somehow manage to get the authorization code at step 4. This is because they would need to know the verifier value as well. They can't know the verifier because the client has not yet sent it on the wire. And they can't get the verifier simply by intercepting the challenge (at step 3) because the challenge is created with a hash function, implying that the output can't be turned back into the input.

13.3.3 *Getting a token with the client credentials grant type*

Sometimes an app needs to get authorization without user intervention. If there's no user on the scene, an app will have to use the client credentials grant type to get an access token. This situation commonly happens when a service needs to call another service when an objective event, such as the timer of a scheduled process, triggers it. Using the client grant type, the app only needs to authenticate with its client credentials. Figure 13.12 presents the client credentials grant type:

1   The app requests an access token from the authorization server. The app uses their credentials to authenticate.
2   If credentials are valid, the authorization server issues an access token.
3   The app uses the access token to get authorized when sending a request to the resource server.

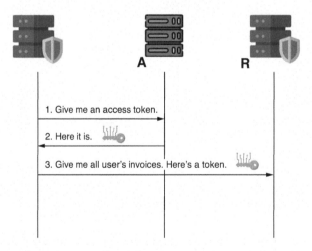

Figure 13.12   The client grant type. An app gets an access token without needing a user to authenticate.

13.3.4 *Using refresh tokens to get new access tokens*

One essential thing you must remember about tokens is that they must have a relatively short life span. The exact time they stay alive is usually decided according to the scenario, but it's usually as short as 15 minutes, and I have never used tokens that live more than one hour. Eventually, all tokens need to expire sooner or later. When a token expires, the resource server won't accept it anymore. In such a case, when a client has a token, and the token has expired, they have two options:

1 Get a new access token by repeating the grant type steps. This implies asking the user to log in again in case of the authorization code grant type.
2 Use a refresh token to get a new access token.

Refresh tokens are particularly useful when the client uses a grant type, such as the authorization code, which implies a user needs to log in. Imagine you have tokens with a 15-minute lifespan. As a user, would you not be bothered if your app asked you to log in again and again every 15 minutes? I would!

The app can use the refresh token to get a new access token instead of asking the user to log in every time the access token expires.

Figure 13.13 shows the steps for using the refresh token:

1 The user tries to get some data, which implies that the client must call its backend.
2 Because the access token (previously obtained) expired, the client needs to get a new one. The client sends a refresh token to prove they are the same one who had already authenticated before.
3 The authorization server recognizes the refresh token and provides the client with a new access token.
4 The client can call the backend (the resource server) and get authorized with the new access token.

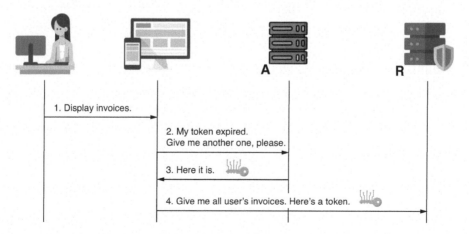

Figure 13.13   A client app can use a refresh token to get a new access token when the old one expires. This way, the app avoids requesting the user to authenticate again.

13.4   *What OpenID Connect brings to OAuth 2*

There's certainly still a lot of confusion out there about OpenID Connect (sometimes named OIDC) and OAuth 2 and the differences between the two. I usually tell my students to stress less about this subject: "If you understand OAuth 2, you also know how to use OpenID Connect."

In fact, OIDC is a protocol built over the OAuth 2 specification. For this reason, understanding OAuth 2 helps you easily get OIDC. Let me give you an analogy for specifications versus protocols.

We all use electrical sockets every day. Electrical sockets look different around the world. Sometimes, this is a real pain when you travel. You may need to have adapters to ensure you can charge your devices, especially if you travel between different geographical regions.

But behind the scenes, all outlets work the same way. There are some wires that output the electrical voltage. You can define a framework on which all the electrical sockets in the world work in only a couple of bullet points:

- An electrical socket has three wires that allow electrical current to flow: the phase, the null, and a grounding. The grounding is optional.
- The electrical socket provides a voltage that can be either around 120 Volts or 230 Volts.

Now, no worries if you're not a technical person; you don't need to understand these two bullets. At least not for learning Spring Security. Just take my word for it.

The problem is that even if all sockets in the world fulfill these specifications, we still get situations where we need adapters to travel. The reason is that they don't have a common protocol. Adapters are required to adapt the outlet from one protocol to another (for example, North America to Europe).

The same happens with apps and authentication and authorization. If two apps fulfill the OAuth 2 specification, they can still run in situations where they are not fully compatible and need to be adapted because they don't run the same protocol. OpenID Connect is a protocol that restricts a bit the liberty of the OAuth 2 specification, introducing a few changes. The major changes are

- Specific values for the scopes (such as *profile* or *openid*).
- The use of an extra token named ID token, used to store the details about the identity of the user and client to whom the token was issued.
- Usually the term *grant type* is also referred to as *flow* when discussing it in terms of OIDC, while the *authorization server* is commonly called the *identity provider* or *IdP*.

13.5 *The sins of OAuth 2*

This section discusses possible vulnerabilities of the applications using OAuth 2 authentication and authorization. It's essential to understand what can go wrong when using OAuth 2 to avoid these scenarios when developing applications. Of course, like anything else in software development, OAuth 2 isn't bulletproof. It has its vulnerabilities, which we must be aware of when building our applications. I list here some of the most common:

- *Using cross-site request forgery (CSRF) on the client*—With a user logged in, CSRF is possible if the application doesn't apply any CSRF protection mechanism. We had a great discussion on the CSRF protection implemented by Spring Security in chapter 9.
- *Stealing client credentials*—Storing or transferring the credentials unprotected can create breaches that allow attackers to steal and use them.
- *Replaying tokens*—As discussed in section 13.2, tokens are the "keys" we use within an OAuth 2 authentication and authorization architecture to access the resources. You send them over network, and sometimes they might be intercepted. If intercepted, they are stolen and can be reused. Imagine you lose the key from your home's front door. What could happen? Somebody else could use it to open the door as many times as they like (replay).
- *Token hijacking*—You interfere in the authentication process and steal tokens you can use to access resources. This is also a potential vulnerability of using refresh tokens, as they, too, can be intercepted and used to obtain new access tokens. I recommend this helpful article: http://mng.bz/am5z.

Remember, OAuth 2 is a framework. The vulnerabilities are the result of implementing functionality wrongly over it. Using Spring Security already helps us mitigate most of those vulnerabilities in our applications. When implementing an application with Spring Security, like you saw in this chapter, we need to set the configurations, but we rely on the flow as implemented by Spring Security.

For more details on vulnerabilities related to the OAuth 2 framework and how a bad-intentioned individual could exploit them, see part 3 of *OAuth 2 In Action* by Justin Richer and Antonio Sanso (Manning, 2017), available at http://mng.bz/g7Ql.

Summary

- The OAuth 2 framework describes secure ways in which a backend can authenticate its clients. OpenID Connect is a protocol that implements the OAuth 2 client by applying some constraints for the possible implementations.
- The four main actors in an OAuth 2 system are
  - *The user*—A person who wants to execute a use case
  - *The client*—An app that must be authorized to access a resource or use case on a given backend

- *The resource server*—A backend that needs to authorize a client to execute a specific use case or access a resource
- *The authorization server*—An app that manages the user and client details, allowing them to authenticate, and that provides a token that can be used for means of authorization

- The token is an access card (or a key) a client gets from the authorization server and uses to get authorized to call a use case or access a specific resource on a secured backend (the resource server).
- We classify tokens into two categories:
  - *Opaque*—tokens that don't contain details about the user and client for whom they were issued. For such tokens, a resource server always needs to call the authorization server to validate the token and get the details it needs to authorize the request. This request for the token validation is called introspection.
  - *Non-opaque*—tokens that contain details about the user and the client to whom they've been issued. The most common implementation of non-opaque tokens is the JSON Web Token (JWT).
- There are multiple flows in which a client app can ask the authorization server for a token. These flows in which the token is issued are called grant types. The most common grant types are
  - The authorization code grant type
  - The client credentials grant type
- Sometimes we add supplementary security to the authorization code grant type using a proof key for code exchange (PKCE) approach. Here the client uses additional values to avoid someone being able to obtain access tokens by stealing the client credentials and the authorization code.
- In specific cases, an app might need to get new access tokens without having the user re-authenticate. For such cases, the app can use refresh tokens. Refresh tokens are special tokens that can only be used to get new access tokens.

14

Implementing an OAuth 2 authorization server

This chapter covers

- Implementing a Spring Security OAuth 2 authorization server
- Using the authorization code and client credentials grant types
- Configuring opaque and non-opaque access tokens
- Using token revocation and introspection

Chapter 13 covered OAuth 2 and OpenID Connect. We discussed the actors that play a role in a system where the authentication and authorization are based on the OAuth 2 specification. The authorization server was one of these actors. Its role is to authenticate a user and the app they use (the client), as well as issue tokens that serve as proof of authentication to access resources protected by a backend. Sometimes, the client does that on behalf of a user.

The Spring ecosystem offers a fully customizable way to implement an OAuth 2/ OpenID Connect authorization server. The Spring Security authorization server is the de facto way to implement an authorization server using Spring today. In this chapter, we'll review the main capabilities offered by this framework and implement a custom authorization server. Figure 14.1 is here to remind you about the OAuth 2 actors and the authorization server role discussed in chapter 13.

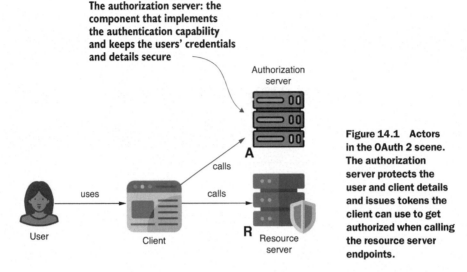

The authorization server: the component that implements the authentication capability and keeps the users' credentials and details secure

Authorization server

A

calls

uses   calls

User   Client   R   Resource server

Figure 14.1   Actors in the OAuth 2 scene. The authorization server protects the user and client details and issues tokens the client can use to get authorized when calling the resource server endpoints.

We start by implementing a simple example in section 14.1, which uses the default configurations. The default configuration implies that the authorization server will issue non-opaque tokens. In section 14.2, we prove that our implementation works with the authorization code grant type, and then, in section 14.3, we demonstrate the client credentials grant type as well. In section 14.4, we continue with configuring the authorization server to work with opaque tokens and introspection. We end this chapter's discussion in section 14.5 with token revocation.

Before we start, I'd like to make you aware that the way to implement an authorization server with Spring Security is entirely different from that in the past years. In this chapter, we discuss the new approach, but you might also need to know how to implement an authorization server using an older way (for example, if you need to work on an existing app that hasn't been upgraded). In that case, I recommend reading chapter 13 of the book's first edition.

14.1   *Implementing basic authentication using JSON web tokens*

In this section, we employ a basic OAuth 2 authorization server using the Spring Security authorization server framework. We'll go through all the main components you need to plug into the configuration to make it work and discuss them individually. Then we'll test the app using the most essential two OAuth 2 grant types: the authorization code and the client credentials grant type. You'll find this example implemented in project ssia-ch14-ex1.

The main components you need to set up for your authorization server to work properly are

1   *The configuration filter for protocol endpoints*—Helps you define configurations specific to the authorization server capabilities, including various customizations (which we'll discuss in section 14.3).

2   *The authentication configuration filter*—Similar to any web application secured with Spring Security, you'll use this filter to define the authentication and authorization configurations and configurations to any other security mechanisms such as cross-origin resource sharing (CORS) and cross-site request forgery (CSRF) (see chapters 2 through 10).

3   *The user details management components*—Like any authentication process implemented with Spring Security, these are established through a `UserDetails-Service` bean and a `PasswordEncoder`. They work as discussed in chapters 3 and 4.

4   *The client details management*—The authorization server uses a component called `RegisteredClientRepository` to manage the client credentials and other details.

5   *The key-pairs (used to sign and validate tokens) management*—When using non-opaque tokens, the authorization server uses a private key to sign the tokens. The authorization server also offers access to a public key that the resource server can use to validate the tokens. The authorization server manages the private–public key pairs through a "key source" component.

6   *The general app settings*—A component named `AuthorizationServerSettings` helps you configure generic customizations such as the endpoints the app exposes.

Figure 14.2 illustrates the components we need to plug in and configure for a minimal authorization server app to work.

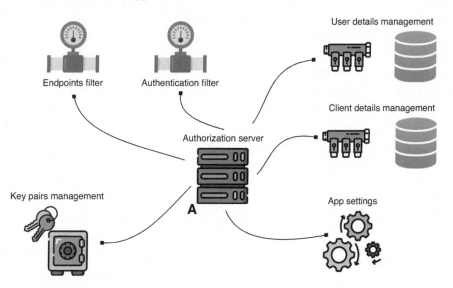

Figure 14.2   The components we need to configure and plug in for an authorization server implemented with Spring Security to work

To begin, we must add the needed dependencies to our project. In the next code snippet, you find the dependencies you need to add to your pom.xml project:

```
<dependency>
    <groupId>org.springframework.boot</groupId>
    <artifactId>spring-boot-starter-web</artifactId>
</dependency>
<dependency>
    <groupId>org.springframework.boot</groupId>
    <artifactId>spring-boot-starter-oauth2-authorization-server</artifactId>
</dependency>
```

We write the configurations in standard Spring configuration classes like in the next code snippet.

```
@Configuration
public class SecurityConfig {


}
```

Remember that like for any other Spring app, the beans can be defined in multiple configuration classes, or they can be defined using stereotype annotations (depending on the case). If you need a refresher on managing the Spring context, I recommend the first part of *Spring Start Here* (Manning, 2021), another book I wrote.

Let's take a look at listing 14.1, which presents the configuration filter for protocol endpoints. The `applyDefaultSecurity()` method is a utility method we use to define a minimal set of configurations you can override later if needed. After calling this method, the listing shows how to enable the OpenID Connect protocol using the `oidc()` method of the `OAuth2AuthorizationServerConfigurer` configurer object.

Furthermore, the filter in listing 14.1 specifies the authentication page to which the app needs to redirect the user when asked to log in. We need this configuration because we expect to enable the authorization code grant type for our example, which implies that the users must authenticate. The default path in a Spring web app is /login, so unless we configure a custom one, we'll use this one for the authorization server configuration.

Listing 14.1   Implementing the filter for configuring protocol endpoints

```
@Bean
@Order(1)
public SecurityFilterChain asFilterChain(HttpSecurity http)
  throws Exception {

    OAuth2AuthorizationServerConfiguration            ← Calling the utility method to
      .applyDefaultSecurity(http);                       apply default configurations for
                                                         the authorization server
                                                         endpoints
    http.getConfigurer(
      OAuth2AuthorizationServerConfigurer.class)      ← Enabling the OpenID
        .oidc(Customizer.withDefaults());                Connect protocol
```

```
    http.exceptionHandling((e) ->
      e.authenticationEntryPoint(
        new LoginUrlAuthenticationEntryPoint("/login"))
    );

    return http.build();
}
```

Specifying the authentication page for users

Listing 14.2 configures authentication and authorization. These configurations work similarly to any web app (as we discussed in chapters 2 through 10). In listing 14.2, I set up the minimum configurations:

1. Enabling the form login authentication so the app gives the user a simple login page to authenticate
2. Specifying that the app only allows access to authenticated users to any endpoints

Other configurations you could write here, besides authentication and authorization, could be for specific protection mechanisms such as CSRF (discussed in chapter 9) or CORS (discussed in chapter 10).

Observe also the `@Order` annotation I used in listings 14.1 and 14.2. This annotation is necessary because we have multiple `SecurityFilterChain` instances configured in the app context, and we need to provide the order in which they take priority in configuration.

Listing 14.2   Implementing the filter for authorization configuration

We set the filter to be interpreted after the protocol endpoints one.

```
@Bean
@Order(2)
public SecurityFilterChain defaultSecurityFilterChain(HttpSecurity http)
    throws Exception {

    http.formLogin(Customizer.withDefaults());

    http.authorizeHttpRequests(
      c -> c.anyRequest().authenticated()
    );

    return http.build();
}
```

We enable the form login authentication method.

We configure all endpoints to require authentication.

If you expect clients will use the authorization server you build for grant types that imply user authentication (such as the authorization code grant type), then your server needs to manage user details! Fortunately, to implement user details management, you can use the same approach you learned in chapters 3 and 4. All you need is a `User-DetailsService` and a `PasswordEncoder` implementation.

Listing 14.3 presents a definition for these two components. In this example, we use an in-memory implementation for the `UserDetailsService`, but remember that you learned how to write a custom implementation for it in chapter 3. In most cases, as you do for other web apps, you'll keep such details stored in a database. Therefore, you must write a custom implementation for the `UserDetailsService` contract.

Also, remember that in chapter 4, we discussed that the `NoOpPasswordEncoder` is something you should only use with learning samples. The `NoOpPasswordEncoder` doesn't transform the passwords in any way, leaving them in clear text and at the disposal of anyone who can access them, which is not good. You should always use a password encoder with a strong hash function such as BCrypt.

Listing 14.3   Defining the user details management

```
@Bean
public UserDetailsService userDetailsService() {
  UserDetails userDetails = User.withUsername("bill")
        .password("password")
        .roles("USER")
        .build();

  return new InMemoryUserDetailsManager(userDetails);
}

@Bean
public PasswordEncoder passwordEncoder() {
  return NoOpPasswordEncoder.getInstance();
}
```

The authorization server needs a `RegisteredClientRepository` component to manage client details. The `RegisteredClientRepository` interface works similarly to the `UserDetailsService` one, but it's designed to retrieve client details. Similarly, the framework provides the `RegisteredClient` object, whose purpose is to describe a client app the authorization server knows.

To make an analogy to what you learned in chapters 3 and 4, `RegisteredClient` is for clients what `UserDetails` is for users. Similarly, `RegisteredClientRepository` works for client details the way a `UserDetailsService` works for user details (figure 14.3).

In this example, we'll use an in-memory implementation to allow you to focus on the overall implementation of the authorization server. Still, in a real-world app, you'd most likely need to provide an implementation to this interface to grab the data from a database. For this to work, you implement the `RegisteredClientRepository` interface similarly to how you implemented the `UserDetailsService` interface in chapter 3.

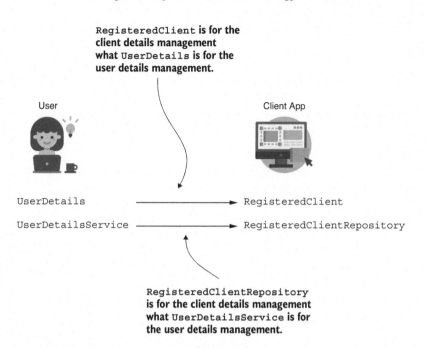

RegisteredClient is for the
client details management
what UserDetails is for the
user details management.

User   Client App

UserDetails ──────────────▶ RegisteredClient

UserDetailsService ─────────▶ RegisteredClientRepository

RegisteredClientRepository
is for the client details management
what UserDetailsService is for
the user details management.

Figure 14.3   To manage client details, we use a RegisteredClientRepository **implementation. The**
RegisteredClientRepository **uses** RegisteredClient **objects to represent client details.**

The next listing shows the definition of the in-memory RegisteredClientRepository
bean. The method creates one RegisteredClient instance with the required details
and stores it in-memory to be used during authentication by the authorization server.

Listing 14.4   Implementing client details management

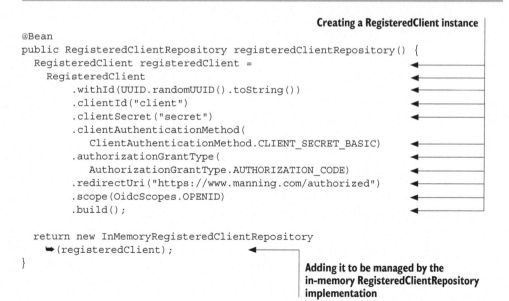

Creating a RegisteredClient instance

```
@Bean
public RegisteredClientRepository registeredClientRepository() {
  RegisteredClient registeredClient =
    RegisteredClient
        .withId(UUID.randomUUID().toString())
        .clientId("client")
        .clientSecret("secret")
        .clientAuthenticationMethod(
           ClientAuthenticationMethod.CLIENT_SECRET_BASIC)
        .authorizationGrantType(
           AuthorizationGrantType.AUTHORIZATION_CODE)
        .redirectUri("https://www.manning.com/authorized")
        .scope(OidcScopes.OPENID)
        .build();

  return new InMemoryRegisteredClientRepository
    ➥(registeredClient);
}
```

**Adding it to be managed by the
in-memory RegisteredClientRepository
implementation**

The details we specified when creating the `RegisteredClient` instance are the following:

- *A unique internal ID*—Value that uniquely identifies the client and only has a purpose in the internal app processes.
- *A client ID*—An external client identifier, similar to what a username is for the user.
- *A client secret*—Similar to what a password is for a user.
- *The client authentication method*—Tells how the authorization server expects the client to authenticate when sending requests for access tokens.
- *Authorization grant type*—A grant type allowed by the authorization server for this client. A client might use multiple grant types.
- *Redirect URI*—One of the URI addresses the authorization server allows the client to request a redirect for providing the authorization code in case of the authorization code grant type.
- *A scope*—Defines a purpose for the request of an access token. The scope can be used later in authorization rules.

In this example, the client only uses the authorization code grant type. However, you can have clients that use multiple grant types. In case you want a client to be able to use multiple grant types, you need to specify them as presented in the next code snippet. The client defined here can use any grant type (authorization code, client credentials, or the refresh token):

```
RegisteredClient registeredClient =
    RegisteredClient
        .withId(UUID.randomUUID().toString())
        .clientId("client")
        .clientSecret("secret")
        .clientAuthenticationMethod(
            ClientAuthenticationMethod.CLIENT_SECRET_BASIC)
        .authorizationGrantType(
            AuthorizationGrantType.AUTHORIZATION_CODE)
        .authorizationGrantType(
            AuthorizationGrantType.CLIENT_CREDENTIALS)
        .authorizationGrantType(
            AuthorizationGrantType.REFRESH_TOKEN)
        .redirectUri("https://www.manning.com/authorized")
        .scope(OidcScopes.OPENID)
        .build();
```

Similarly, by repeatedly calling the `redirectUri()` method, you can specify multiple allowed redirect URIs. Similarly, a client might also have access to multiple scopes as well. In a real-world app, the app would keep all these details in a database from where your `RegisteredClientRepository` custom implementation would retrieve them.

Besides having user and client details, you must configure key pair management if the authorization server uses non-opaque tokens (discussed in chapter 13). For non-opaque tokens, the authorization server uses private keys to sign the tokens and provides the clients with public keys they can use to validate the tokens' authenticity.

The JWKSource is the object providing key management for the Spring Security authorization server. Listing 14.5 shows how to configure a JWKSource in the app's context. For this example, I create a key pair programmatically and add it to the set of keys the authorization server can use. In a real-world app, the app would read the keys from a location where they're safely stored (such as a vault configured in the environment).

Configuring an environment that perfectly resembles a real-world system would be too complex, and I prefer you focus on the authorization server implementation. However, remember that in a real app, it doesn't make sense to generate new keys every time the app restarts (like in our case). If that happens for a real app, every time a new deployment occurs, the tokens that were already issued will not work anymore (because they can't be validated anymore with the existing keys).

So, for our example, generating the keys programmatically works and will help us demonstrate how the authorization server works. In a real-world app, you must keep the keys secured somewhere and read them from the given location.

Listing 14.5 Implementing the key pair set management

```
@Bean
public JWKSource<SecurityContext> jwkSource()
  throws NoSuchAlgorithmException {

  KeyPairGenerator keyPairGenerator =
    KeyPairGenerator.getInstance("RSA");

  keyPairGenerator.initialize(2048);
  KeyPair keyPair = keyPairGenerator.generateKeyPair();

  RSAPublicKey publicKey =
    (RSAPublicKey) keyPair.getPublic();
  RSAPrivateKey privateKey =
    (RSAPrivateKey) keyPair.getPrivate();

  RSAKey rsaKey = new RSAKey.Builder(publicKey)
      .privateKey(privateKey)
      .keyID(UUID.randomUUID().toString())
      .build();

  JWKSet jwkSet = new JWKSet(rsaKey);
  return new ImmutableJWKSet<>(jwkSet);
}
```

Generating a public–private key pair programmatically using the RSA cryptographic algorithm

Adding the key pair to the set the authorization server uses to sign the issued tokens

Wrapping the key set into a JWKSource implementation and returning it to be added to the Spring context

Finally, the last component we need to add to our minimal configuration is an AuthorizationServerSettings object (listing 14.6). This object allows you to customize all the endpoints paths that the authorization server exposes. If you create the object as shown in the next listing, the endpoints paths will get some defaults that we'll analyze later in this section.

Listing 14.6   Configuring the authorization server generic settings

```
@Bean
public AuthorizationServerSettings authorizationServerSettings() {
  return AuthorizationServerSettings.builder().build();
}
```

Now we can start the app and test if it works. In section 14.2, we'll run the authorization code flow. Then, in section 14.3, we'll test that the client credentials flow works as expected with our authorization code implementation.

14.2   Running the authorization code grant type

In this section, we test the authorization server implemented in section 14.1. We expect that by using the registered client details, we'd be able to follow the authorization code flow and get an access token. We'll follow these steps:

1 Check the endpoints that the authorization server exposes
2 Use the authorization endpoint to get an authorization code
3 Use the authorization code to get an access token

The first step is to find the endpoint paths the authorization server exposes. Because we didn't configure custom ones, we must use the defaults. But which are the defaults? You can call the OpenID configuration endpoint in the next snippet to discover these details. This request uses the HTTP GET method, and no authentication is required:

```
http://localhost:8080/.well-known/openid-configuration
```

When calling the OpenID configuration endpoint, you should get a response that looks like the one presented in the following listing.

Listing 14.7   The response of the OpenID configuration request

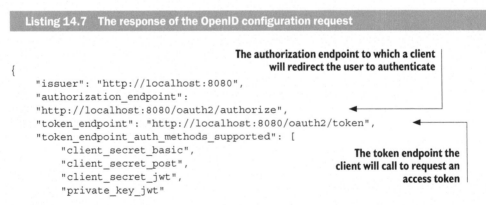

```
{
    "issuer": "http://localhost:8080",
    "authorization_endpoint":
    "http://localhost:8080/oauth2/authorize",
    "token_endpoint": "http://localhost:8080/oauth2/token",
    "token_endpoint_auth_methods_supported": [
        "client_secret_basic",
        "client_secret_post",
        "client_secret_jwt",
        "private_key_jwt"
```

```
    ],
    "jwks_uri": "http://localhost:8080/oauth2/jwks",
    "userinfo_endpoint": "http://localhost:8080/userinfo",
    "response_types_supported": [
        "code"
    ],
    "grant_types_supported": [
        "authorization_code",
        "client_credentials",
        "refresh_token"
    ],
    "revocation_endpoint": "http://localhost:8080/oauth2/revoke",
    "revocation_endpoint_auth_methods_supported": [
        "client_secret_basic",
        "client_secret_post",
        "client_secret_jwt",
        "private_key_jwt"
    ],
    "introspection_endpoint":
      "http://localhost:8080/oauth2/introspect",
    "introspection_endpoint_auth_methods_supported": [
        "client_secret_basic",
        "client_secret_post",
        "client_secret_jwt",
        "private_key_jwt"
    ],
    "subject_types_supported": [
        "public"
    ],
    "id_token_signing_alg_values_supported": [
        "RS256"
    ],
    "scopes_supported": [
        "openid"
    ]
}
```

The key-set endpoint a resource server will call to get the public keys it can use to validate tokens

The introspection endpoint a resource server can call to validate opaque tokens

Let's take a look at figure 14.4 to recall the authorization code flow discussed in chapter 13. We'll use it now to demonstrate that the authorization server we built works fine.

Because we don't have a client for our example, we need to act like one. Now that you know the authorization endpoint, you can put it in a browser address to simulate how the client would redirect the user to it. The next snippet shows the authorization request:

```
http://localhost:8080/oauth2/authorize?
↪response_type=code&
↪client_id=client&
↪scope=openid&
↪redirect_uri=https://www.manning.com/authorized&
↪code_challenge=QYPAZ5NU8yvtlQ9erXrUYR-T5AGCjCF47vN-KsaI2A8&
↪code_challenge_method=S256
```

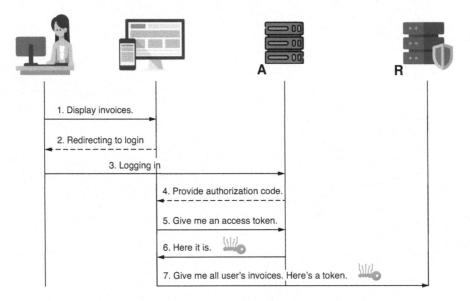

Figure 14.4   The authorization code grant type. Following successful authentication, the client receives an authorization code. This code is then used by the client to obtain an access token, which facilitates access to the resources safeguarded by the resource server.

For the authorization request, you can see I added a few parameters:

- `response_type=code`—This request parameter specifies to the authorization server that the client wants to use the authorization code grant type. Remember that a client might have configured multiple grant types. It needs to tell the authorization server which grant type it wants to use.

- `client_id=client`—The client identifier is like the "username" for the user. It uniquely identifies the client in the system.

- `scope=openid`—Specifies which scope the client wants to be granted with this authentication attempt.

- `redirect_uri=https://www.manning.com/authorized`—Specifies the URI to which the authorization server will redirect after a successful authentication. This URI must be one of those previously configured for the current client.

- `code_challenge=QYPAZ5NU8yvtlQ…`—If using the authorization code enhanced with PKCE (discussed in chapter 13), you must provide the code challenge with the authorization request. When requesting the token, the client must send the verifier pair to prove they are the same application that initially sent this request. The PKCE flow is enabled by default.

- `code_challenge_method=S256`—This request parameter specifies which hashing method has been used to create the challenge from the verifier. In this case, S256 means SHA-256 was used as a hash function.

I recommend using the authorization code grant type with PKCE, but if you really need to disable the PKCE enhancement of the flow, you can do that as presented in the next code snippet. Observe the `clientSettings()` method that takes a `Client-Settings` instance where you can specify you disable the proof key for code exchange:

```
RegisteredClient registeredClient = RegisteredClient
        .withId(UUID.randomUUID().toString())
        .clientId("client")
        // ...
        .clientSettings(ClientSettings.builder()
            .requireProofKey(false)
            .build())
        .build();
```

In this example, we demonstrate the authorization code with PKCE, which is the default and recommended way. By sending the authorization request through the browser's address bar, we simulate step 2 from figure 14.4. The authorization server will redirect us to its login page, and we can authenticate using the user name and password. This is step 3 from figure 14.4. Figure 14.5 shows the login page the authorization server presents to the user.

After sending the request to the authorization endpoint, the authorization server redirects the user to a page where they can log in.

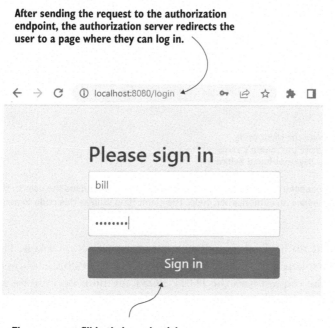

The user must fill in their credentials and then select the Sign In button.

Figure 14.5   The login page that the authorization server presents to the user in response to the authorization request.

For our implementation, we only have one user (see listing 14.3). Their credentials are username `bill` and the password `password`. Once the user fills in the correct credentials and selects the Sign In button, the authorization server redirects the user to the requested redirect URI and provides an authorization code (as presented in figure 14.6; step 4 in figure 14.4).

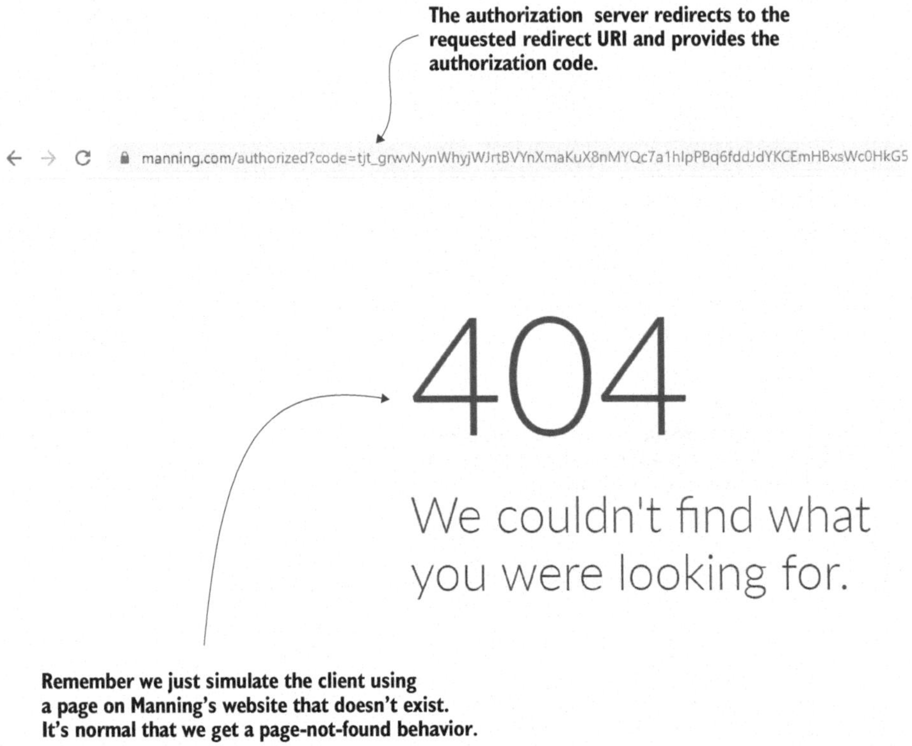

The authorization server redirects to the requested redirect URI and provides the authorization code.

← → C   🔒 manning.com/authorized?code=tjt_grwvNynWhyjWJrtBVYnXmaKuX8nMYQc7a1hIpPBq6fddJdYKCEmHBxsWc0HkG5

404

We couldn't find what you were looking for.

Remember we just simulate the client using a page on Manning's website that doesn't exist. It's normal that we get a page-not-found behavior.

Figure 14.6   Following successful authentication, the authorization server guides the user to the specified redirect URI and issues an authorization code. The client then utilizes this code to acquire an access token.

Once the client has the authorization code, it can request an access token. The client can request the access token using the token endpoint. The next snippet shows a cURL request of a token. The request uses the HTTP POST method. Because we specified that HTTP Basic authentication is requested when registering the client, the token request needs authentication with HTTP Basic with the client ID and secret:

```
curl -X POST 'http://localhost:8080/oauth2/token?
➥client_id=client&
➥redirect_uri=https://www.manning.com/authorized&
➥grant_type=authorization_code&
➥code=ao2oz47zdM0D5gbAqtZVB…
➥code_verifier=qPsH306-… \
--header 'Authorization: Basic Y2xpZW50OnNlY3JldA=='
```

The request parameters we used are

- `client_id=client`—Needed to identify the client
- `redirect_uri= https://www.manning.com/authorized`—The redirect URI through which the authorization server provided the authorization code after the successful user authentication
- `grant_type=authorization_code`—Shows which flow the client uses to request the access token
- `code=ao2oz47zdM0D5…`—The value of the authorization code the authorization server provided to the client
- `code_verifier=qPsH306-ZDD…`—The verifier based on which the challenge that the client sent at authorization was created

> **NOTE** Pay great attention to all the details. If any of the values don't properly match what the app knows or what was sent in the authorization request, the token request won't succeed.

The next snippet shows the response body of the token request. Now the client has an access token it can use to send requests to the resource server:

```
{
    "access_token": "eyJraWQiOiI4ODlhNGFmmO…",
    "scope": "openid",
    "id_token": "eyJraWQiOiI4ODlhNGFmmOS1…",
    "token_type": "Bearer",
    "expires_in": 299
}
```

Because we enabled the OpenID Connect protocol, so we don't only rely on OAuth 2, an ID token is also present in the token response. If the client had been registered using the refresh token grant type, a refresh token would have also been generated and sent through the response.

Generating the code verifier and challenge

In the example we worked on in this section, I used the authorization code with PKCE. In the authorization and token requests, I used a challenge and a verifier value I had previously generated. I didn't pay too much attention to these values because they are the client's business and not something the authorization or resource server generates. In a real-world app, your JavaScript or mobile app will have to generate both values when using them in the OAuth 2 flow.

But in case you're wondering, I will explain how I generated these two values in this sidebar. You find this example in project ssia-ch14-ex2.

The code verifier is a random 32-byte piece of data. To make it easy to transfer through a HTTP request, this data needs to be Base64 encoded using an URL encoder and without padding. The next code snippet shows how to do that in Java:

(continued)

```
SecureRandom secureRandom = new SecureRandom();
byte [] code = new byte[32];
secureRandom.nextBytes(code);
String codeVerifier = Base64.getUrlEncoder()
        .withoutPadding()
        .encodeToString(code);
```

Once you have the code verifier, you use a hash function to generate the challenge. The next code snippet shows how to create the challenge using the SHA-256 hash function. As with the verifier, you need to use Base64 to change the byte array into a String value, making it easier to transfer through the HTTP request:

```
MessageDigest messageDigest = MessageDigest.getInstance("SHA-256");

byte [] digested = messageDigest.digest(verifier.getBytes());
String codeChallenge = Base64.getUrlEncoder()
        .withoutPadding()
        .encodeToString(digested);
```

Now you have a verifier and a challenge. You can use them in the authorization and token requests as discussed in this section.

14.3 *Running the client credentials grant type*

In this section, we'll try out the client credentials grant type using the authorization server we implemented in section 14.1. Remember that the client grant type is a flow that allows the client to get an access token without a user's authentication or consent. Preferably, you shouldn't have a client able to use both a user-dependent grant type (such as the authorization code) and a client-independent one (such as the client credentials).

As you'll learn in chapter 15, where we discuss the resource server, the authorization implementation might fail to tell the difference between an access token obtained through the authorization code grant type and one that the client obtained through the client credential grant type. So it's best to use different registrations for such cases and preferably distinguish the token usage through different scopes.

Listing 14.8 shows a registered client able to use the client credentials grant type. Observe that I have also configured a different scope. In this case, "CUSTOM" is just a name I chose; you can choose any name for the scopes. The name you choose should generally make the purpose of the scope easier to understand. For example, if this app needs to use the client credentials grant type to get a token to check the resource server's liveness state, then maybe it's better to name the scope "LIVENESS" so it makes things obvious.

You can find the example discussed in this section in project ssia-ch14-ex3.

Listing 14.8 Configuring a registered client for the client credentials grant type

Allowing the registered client to use
the client credentials grant type

```
@Bean
public RegisteredClientRepository registeredClientRepository() {
  RegisteredClient registeredClient =
    RegisteredClient.withId(UUID.randomUUID().toString())
      .clientId("client")
      .clientSecret("secret")
      .clientAuthenticationMethod(
        ClientAuthenticationMethod.CLIENT_SECRET_BASIC)
      .authorizationGrantType(AuthorizationGrantType.CLIENT_CREDENTIALS)
      .scope("CUSTOM")
      .build();

    return new InMemoryRegisteredClientRepository(registeredClient);
}
```

Configuring a scope to match the
purpose for the access token request

Figure 14.7 shows the client credentials flow we discussed in chapter 13. To get an access token, the client simply sends a request and authenticates using their credentials (the client ID and secret).

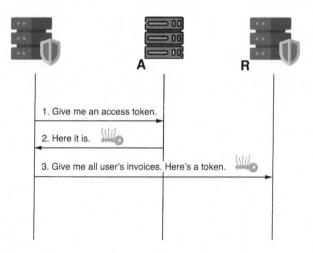

Figure 14.7 The client credentials grant type. An app can get an access token by only authenticating with its client credentials.

The following snippet shows a cURL token request. If you compare it with the request we used in section 14.2 when we ran the authorization code grant type, you'll observe that this one is simpler. The client only needs to mention they use the client credentials grant type and the scope in which they request a token. The client uses its credentials with HTTP Basic on the request to authenticate:

```
curl -X POST 'http://localhost:8080/oauth2/token?
➥grant_type=client_credentials&
➥scope=CUSTOM' \
--header 'Authorization: Basic Y2xpZW50OnNlY3JldA=='
```

The next snippet shows the HTTP response body containing the requested access token:

```
{
    "access_token": "eyJraWQiOiI4N2E3YjJiNS…",
    "scope": "CUSTOM",
    "token_type": "Bearer",
    "expires_in": 300
}
```

14.4   *Using opaque tokens and introspection*

By now in this chapter, we have demonstrated the authorization code grant type (section 14.2) and the client credentials grant type (section 14.3). With both, we managed to configure clients that can get non-opaque access tokens. However, you can also easily configure the clients to use opaque tokens. In this section, I'll show you how to configure the registered clients to get opaque tokens and how the authorization server helps with validating the opaque tokens. You find the example discussed in this section in project ssia-ch14-ex4.

Listing 14.9 shows how to configure a registered client to use opaque tokens. Remember that opaque tokens can be used with any grant type. In this section, I'll use the client credentials grant type to keep things simple and allow you to focus on the discussed subject. You can also generate opaque tokens with the authorization code grant type.

Listing 14.9   Configuring clients to use opaque tokens

```
@Bean
public RegisteredClientRepository registeredClientRepository() {
  RegisteredClient registeredClient =
    RegisteredClient.withId(UUID.randomUUID().toString())
        .clientId("client")
        .clientSecret("secret")
        .clientAuthenticationMethod(
           ClientAuthenticationMethod.CLIENT_SECRET_BASIC)
        .authorizationGrantType(AuthorizationGrantType.CLIENT_CREDENTIALS)
        .tokenSettings(TokenSettings.builder()
          .accessTokenFormat(OAuth2TokenFormat.REFERENCE)    ◄──────┐
          .build())                                Configuring the client to use
        .scope("CUSTOM")                              opaque access tokens
        .build();

    return new InMemoryRegisteredClientRepository(registeredClient);
  }
```

If you request an access token like you learned to do in section 14.3, you'll get an opaque token. This token is shorter and doesn't contain data. The next snippet is a cURL request for an access token:

```
curl -X POST 'http://localhost:8080/oauth2/token?
➥grant_type=client_credentials&
➥scope=CUSTOM' \
--header 'Authorization: Basic Y2xpZW50OnNlY3JldA=='
```

The following snippet shows the response similar to what you got in return when we were expecting non-opaque tokens. The only difference is the token itself, which is no longer a JWT token, but an opaque one:

```
{
    "access_token": "iED8-...",
    "scope": "CUSTOM",
    "token_type": "Bearer",
    "expires_in": 299
}
```

The next snippet shows an example of a full opaque token. Note that it is much shorter and doesn't have the same structure as a JWT (the three parts separated by dots are missing):

```
iED8-aUd5QLTfihDOTGUhKgKwzhJFzY
➥WnGdpNT2UZWO3VVDqtMONNdozq1
➥r9r7RiP0aNWgJipcEu5HecAJ75V
➥yNJyNuj-kaJvjpWL5Ns7Ndb7Uh6
➥DI6M1wMuUcUDEjJP
```

As an opaque token doesn't contain data, how can someone validate it and get more details about the client (and potentially the user) for whom the authorization server generated it? The easiest (and most used) way is to directly ask the authorization server. The authorization server exposes an endpoint where one can send a request with the token. The authorization server replies with the needed details about the token. This process is called introspection (figure 14.8).

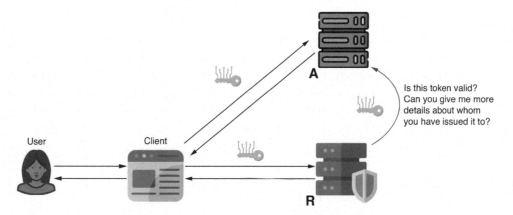

Is this token valid? Can you give me more details about whom you have issued it to?

Figure 14.8 **Token introspection. When using opaque tokens, the resource server needs to send requests to the authorization server to discover if the token is valid and more details about to whom it was issued.**

The next snippet shows the cURL call to the introspection endpoint the authorization server exposes. The client must use HTTP Basic to authenticate using their credentials when sending the request. The client sends the token as a request parameter and receives details about the token in response:

```
curl -X POST 'http://localhost:8080/oauth2/introspect?token=iED8-…' \
--header 'Authorization: Basic Y2xpZW50OnNlY3JldA=='
```

The next snippet shows an example of a response to the introspection request for a valid token. When the token is valid, its status appears as `"active"`, and the response provides all the details the authorization server has about the token:

```
{
    "active": true,
    "sub": "client",
    "aud": [
        "client"
    ],
    "nbf": 1682941720,
    "scope": "CUSTOM",
    "iss": "http://localhost:8080",
    "exp": 1682942020,
    "iat": 1682941720,
    "jti": "ff14b844-1627-4567-8657-bba04cac0370",
    "client_id": "client",
    "token_type": "Bearer"
}
```

If the token doesn't exist or has expired, its active status is `false`, as shown in the next snippet:

```
{
    "active": false,

}
```

The default active time for a token is 300 seconds. In examples, you'll prefer to make the token life longer. Otherwise, you won't have enough time to use the token for tests, which can become frustrating. Listing 14.10 shows how to change the token time to live. I prefer to make it very large for example purposes (like 12 hours in this case), but remember to never configure it this large for a real-world app. In a real app, you'd usually go with a time to live from 10 to 30 minutes max.

Listing 14.10   Changing the access token time to live

```
RegisteredClient registeredClient = RegisteredClient
        .withId(UUID.randomUUID().toString())
        .clientId("client")
        // …
        .authorizationGrantType(AuthorizationGrantType.CLIENT_CREDENTIALS)
        .tokenSettings(TokenSettings.builder()
            .accessTokenFormat(OAuth2TokenFormat.REFERENCE)
```

```
        .accessTokenTimeToLive(Duration.ofHours(12))
      .build())
  .scope("CUSTOM")
  .build();
```

Setting 12 hours as the
access token time to live

14.5 Revoking tokens

Suppose you discover a token has been stolen. How could you make a token invalid for use? Token revocation is a way to invalidate a token the authorization server previously issued. Normally, an access token lifespan is short, so stealing a token still makes it difficult for one to use it. But sometimes you want to be extra cautious.

The following snippet shows a cURL command you can use to send a request to the token revocation endpoint the authorization server exposes. You can use any of the projects we worked on in this chapter for the test. The revocation feature is active by default in a Spring Security authorization server. The request only requires the token that you want to revoke and HTTP Basic authentication with the client credentials. Once you send the request, the token cannot be used anymore:

```
curl -X POST 'http://localhost:8080/oauth2/revoke?token=N7BruErWm-44-…' \
--header 'Authorization: Basic Y2xpZW50OnNlY3JldA=='
```

If you use the introspection endpoint with a token you have revoked, you should observe that the token is no longer active after revocation (even if its time to live hasn't expired yet):

```
curl -X POST 'http://localhost:8080/oauth2/introspect?token=N7BruErWm-44-…' \
--header 'Authorization: Basic Y2xpZW50OnNlY3JldA=='
```

Using token revocation makes sense sometimes, but it's not something you'd always desire. Remember that if you want to use the revocation feature, this also implies you need to use introspection (even for non-opaque tokens) with every call to validate that the token is still active. Using introspection so often might have a big impact on the performance. You should always ask yourself: Do I really need this extra protection layer?

Remember our discussion in the first chapter. Sometimes, hiding the key under the rug is enough; other times, you need advanced, complex, and expensive alarm systems. What you use depends on what you protect.

Summary

- The Spring Security authorization server framework helps you build a custom OAuth 2/OpenID Connect authorization server from scratch.
- Since the authorization server manages the user and client details, you must implement components defining how the app collects this data:
  - To manage the user details, the authorization server needs a similar Spring Security component like any other web app: an implementation of a `UserDetailsService`.

- – To manage the client details, the authorization server provides another contract you must implement: the `RegisteredClientRepository`.

- You can register clients that use various authentication flows (grant types). Preferably, the same client shouldn't use both user-dependent (like the authorization code grant type) and user-independent (like client credentials grant type) flows.

- When using non-opaque tokens (usually JWTs), you must also configure a component to manage the key pairs the authorization server uses to sign the tokens. This component is named the `JWKSource`.

- When using opaque tokens (tokens that don't contain data), the resource server must use the introspection endpoint to verify a token's validity and collect data necessary for authorization.

- Sometimes, you'd need a way to invalidate already issued tokens. The authorization server offers the revocation endpoint for this capability. When using revocation, the resource server must always introspect the tokens (even non-opaque ones) to verify their validity.

Implementing an OAuth 2 resource server

> **This chapter covers**
> - Implementing a Spring Security OAuth 2 resource server
> - Using JWT tokens with custom claims
> - Configuring introspection for opaque tokens or revocation
> - Implementing more complex scenarios and multitenancy

This chapter discusses securing a backend application in an OAuth 2 system. What we call a resource server in OAuth 2 terminology is simply a backend service. While in chapter 14 you learned how to implement the authorization server responsibility using Spring Security, it's now time to discuss how to use the token the authorization server generates.

In real-world scenarios, you might or might not implement a custom authorization server like we did in chapter 14. Your organization might use a third-party implementation instead of creating custom software. You can find many alternatives out there, ranging from open-source solutions such as Keycloak to enterprise products such as Okta, Cognito, or Azure AD. An example with Keycloak is available in chapter 18 of the book's first edition.

While you have options to configure an authorization server without needing to implement your own, you'll have to implement the authentication and authorization on your backend properly. For that reason, I think this chapter is essential; the skills you learn by reading it have a high probability of helping you with your work. Figure 15.1 reminds you about the OAuth 2 actors and where we are at with our learning plan for this book part.

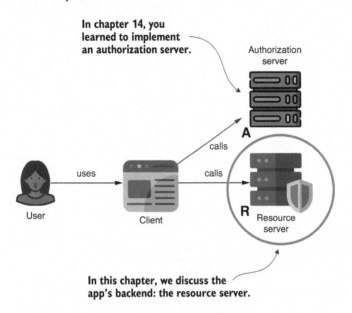

Figure 15.1   In OAuth 2, the app's backend is called a resource server because it protects the users' and clients' resources (data and actions that can be done on data).

We'll begin this chapter in section 15.1 by discussing the resource server configuration for JSON web tokens (JWTs). You'll most often find JWTs used with the OAuth 2 system today; that's why we also start with them. In section 15.2, we discuss customizing JWTs and using the custom values in body or header claims.

In section 15.3, we discuss configuring the resource server to use introspection for token validation. The introspection process is useful when using opaque tokens or when you want your system to be able to revoke tokens before their expiration date.

We'll end the chapter discussing more advanced configuration cases such as multitenancy in section 15.4.

15.1   Configuring JWT validation

In this section, we discuss configuring a resource server to validate and use JWTs, which are non-opaque tokens (they contain data the resource server uses for authorization). To use JWTs, the resource server will need to prove they are authentic, meaning that the expected authorization server has indeed issued them as a proof of authentication of a user and/or a client. Second, the resource server will need to read the data in the token and use it to implement authorization rules.

We'll learn to configure a resource server by putting it into action, that is, implementing one and configuring it from scratch. We'll start by creating a new Spring Boot project and adding the needed dependencies. We'll then implement a demo endpoint (a resource to use for test purposes) and work on the configuration for authentication and authorization. Here're the steps we'll follow:

1 Add the needed dependencies to the project (in the pom.xml file since we use Maven).
2 Declare a dummy endpoint that we'll use to test our implementation.
3 Implement authentication for JWTs by configuring the service with the public key set URI.
4 Implement the authorization rules.
5 Test the implementation by
   a Generating a token with the authorization server.
   b Using the token to call the dummy endpoint we created in step 2.

The following listing presents the needed dependencies. Aside from the web and Spring Security dependencies, we'll also add the resource server starter.

Listing 15.1 Dependencies for implementing a resource server

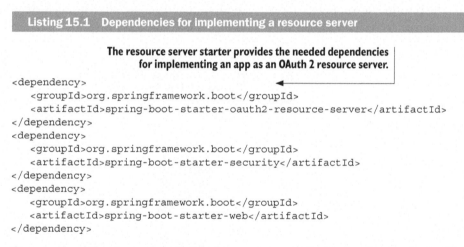

The resource server starter provides the needed dependencies for implementing an app as an OAuth 2 resource server.

```
<dependency>
    <groupId>org.springframework.boot</groupId>
    <artifactId>spring-boot-starter-oauth2-resource-server</artifactId>
</dependency>
<dependency>
    <groupId>org.springframework.boot</groupId>
    <artifactId>spring-boot-starter-security</artifactId>
</dependency>
<dependency>
    <groupId>org.springframework.boot</groupId>
    <artifactId>spring-boot-starter-web</artifactId>
</dependency>
```

Once we have the dependencies in place, we create a dummy endpoint that we'll use to test our implementation at the end. The following listing presents a simple controller that exposes an endpoint at path /demo.

Listing 15.2 Declaring a simple endpoint for test purposes

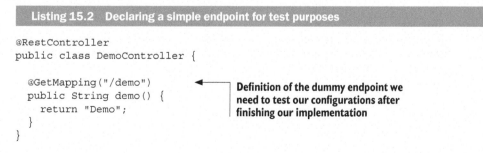

```
@RestController
public class DemoController {

  @GetMapping("/demo")
  public String demo() {
    return "Demo";
  }
}
```

Definition of the dummy endpoint we need to test our configurations after finishing our implementation

For this example, you need to use an authorization server. You can use the one we created in chapter 14 in project ssia-ch14-ex1.

As we want to start both the authorization server and the resource server simultaneously on the same system, we'll need to configure different ports for them. Because the authorization server has the default port 8080, we can change the resource server port to another one. I changed it to 9090, but you can use any free port on your system. The next code snippet shows the property to add to your application.properties file to change the port:

```
server.port=9090
```

Start both the authorization server in project ssia-ch14-ex1 and the current application. You can find this example in project ssia-ch15-ex1 with the projects the book provides.

Remember from chapter 14 that an OpenID Connect authorization server exposes a URL you can use to get its configuration (including the URL for authorization, token, public key set, and others). The next snippet presents the so-called well-known URL:

```
http://localhost:8080/.well-known/openid-configuration
```

You need this link to get information about the URL that the authorization server exposes to provide the public key set that the resource server can use to validate tokens. The resource server needs to call this endpoint and get the set of public keys. Then the resource server uses one of these keys to validate the access token's signature (figure 15.2).

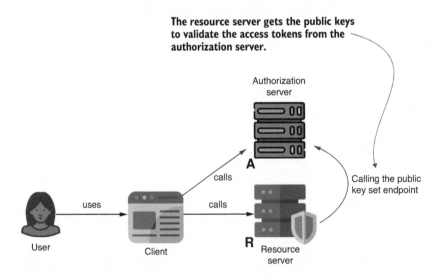

Figure 15.2   The resource server retrieves a set of public keys from the authorization server through an endpoint made available by the authorization server. The resource server then uses these keys to verify the signature of the access token.

Listing 15.3 reminds you about the response you get when calling the well-known configuration endpoint the authorization server exposes. As you can observe, the public key set URI is among the other data provided. The public key set URI is what we need to configure in the resource server so it can validate JWTs.

Listing 15.3   Response of well-known OpenID configuration, containing the key set URI

```
{
    "issuer": "http://localhost:8080",
    "authorization_endpoint": "http://localhost:8080/oauth2/authorize",
    "device_authorization_endpoint":
➥"http://localhost:8080/oauth2/device_authorization",
    "token_endpoint": "http://localhost:8080/oauth2/token",

    ...

    "jwks_uri": "http://localhost:8080/oauth2/jwks",                ◀──────┐
    ...                                                                    │
                        The key set endpoint provides the public parts of the asynchronous
}                       key pairs configured on the authorization server side. The
                        authorization server uses the private parts to sign the tokens. The
                        resource server can use the public parts to validate them.
```

To configure the public key set URI, we'll first declare it in the project's application .properties file. The configuration class can inject it into an attribute field and then use it to configure the resource server authentication:

```
keySetURI=http://localhost:8080/oauth2/jwks
```

Listing 15.4 shows the configuration class injecting the public key set URI value into an attribute. The configuration class also defines a bean of the type `Security-FilterChain`. The application will use the `SecurityFilterChain` bean to configure the authentication, similar to what we did in book's previous chapters.

Listing 15.4   Injecting the property value in the configuration class

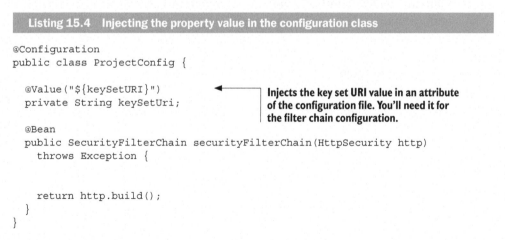

```
@Configuration
public class ProjectConfig {

    @Value("${keySetURI}")              ◀───┐  Injects the key set URI value in an attribute
    private String keySetUri;               │  of the configuration file. You'll need it for
                                            │  the filter chain configuration.
    @Bean
    public SecurityFilterChain securityFilterChain(HttpSecurity http)
        throws Exception {


        return http.build();
    }
}
```

To configure the authentication, we'll use the `oauth2ResourceServer()` method of the `HttpSecurity` object. This method is similar to `httpBasic()` and `formLogin()`, which we used in the second and third parts of this book.

Similar to `httpBasic()` and `formLogin()`, you need to provide an implementation of the `Customizer` interface to configure the authentication. In listing 15.5, you can observe how I used the `jwt()` method of the `Customizer` object to configure JWT authentication. Then I used a `Customizer` on the `jwt()` method to configure the public key set URI (using the `jwkSetUri()` method).

Listing 15.5   Configuring the authentication with JWTs

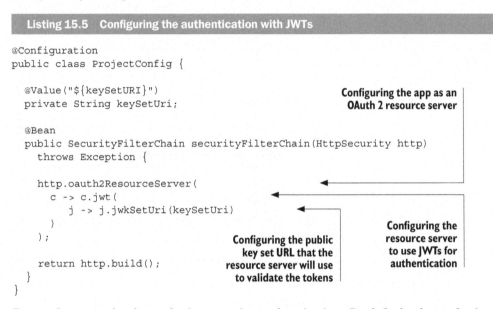

```
@Configuration
public class ProjectConfig {

    @Value("${keySetURI}")
    private String keySetUri;                         Configuring the app as an
                                                      OAuth 2 resource server
    @Bean
    public SecurityFilterChain securityFilterChain(HttpSecurity http)
      throws Exception {

      http.oauth2ResourceServer(
        c -> c.jwt(
          j -> j.jwkSetUri(keySetUri)
        )
      );                                                  Configuring the
                               Configuring the public    resource server
                               key set URL that the      to use JWTs for
      return http.build();     resource server will use  authentication
    }                          to validate the tokens
}
```

Remember to make the endpoints require authentication. By default, the endpoints aren't protected, so to test the authentication, you first need to ensure your /demo endpoint requires authentication. The following code snippet configures the app's authorization rules. For this example, we can configure all endpoints to require authentication:

```
http.authorizeHttpRequests(
    c -> c.anyRequest().authenticated()
);
```

The following listing presents the full content of the configuration class.

Listing 15.6 The full configuration class

```
@Configuration
public class ProjectConfig {

  @Value("${keySetURI}")
  private String keySetUri;

  @Bean
  public SecurityFilterChain securityFilterChain(HttpSecurity http)
    throws Exception {


    http.oauth2ResourceServer(
      c -> c.jwt(
        j -> j.jwkSetUri(keySetUri)
      )
    );

    http.authorizeHttpRequests(
      c -> c.anyRequest().authenticated()
    );

    return http.build();
  }
}
```

Now you should start the resource server application you just created. Make sure that your authorization server is still up and running. You'll need to use the skills you learned in chapter 14 to generate an access token. Let's remind ourselves of the steps for the authorization code grant type (but remember you could get the token using any other grant type—it's irrelevant to the resource server how you got the access token as long as you have one).

The steps you need to follow with the authorization code grant type are the following (figure 15.3):

1 Redirect the user to log in at the authorization server/authorize endpoint.
2 Use the user's credentials to authenticate. The authorization server will redirect you to the redirect URI and provide the authorization code.
3 Take the authorization code provided after the redirect, and use the /token endpoint to request a new access token.

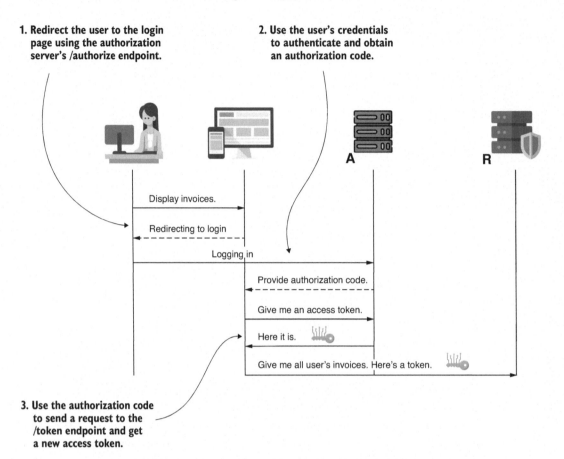

1. Redirect the user to the login page using the authorization server's /authorize endpoint.

2. Use the user's credentials to authenticate and obtain an authorization code.

Display invoices.

Redirecting to login

Logging in

Provide authorization code.

Give me an access token.

Here it is.

Give me all user's invoices. Here's a token.

3. Use the authorization code to send a request to the /token endpoint and get a new access token.

Figure 15.3   The authorization code grant type. The client redirects the user to the authorization server's login page. After the user successfully authenticates, the authorization server redirects back to the client, providing an authorization code. The client uses the authorization code to obtain an access token.

The next snippet (right after the bullet points) shows the URL you can use in your browser to redirect to the authorization server's /authorize endpoint. Remember you need to provide a few parameters, and their values should comply with what you configured in the authorization server. The parameters you must send are

- response_type—Use the value "code" if you want to use the authorization code grant type.
- client_id—The client ID.
- scope—The scope you want to access. It can be any of the scopes configured within the authorization server.
- redirect_uri—The URI to which the authorization server redirects the client after successful authentication. The redirect URI should be one of those configured in the authorization server.

- code_challenge—If using PKCE (proof key for code exchange), you need to provide the code challenge from the code challenge and verifier pair.
- code_challenge_method—If using PKCE, you must specify the hash function you used to encrypt the code verifier (for example, SHA-256):

```
http://localhost:8080/oauth2/authorize?response_type=code&client_
id=client&scope=openid&redirect_uri=https://www.manning.com/authorized&code_
challenge=QYPAZ5NU8yvtlQ9erXrUYR-T5AGCjCF47vN-KsaI2A8&code_challenge_
method=S256
```

NOTE Remember that you must paste the authorization URL in a browser's address bar to send the request.

Log in using the valid user credentials configured in the authorization server, and then wait to be redirected to the requested redirect URI. The authorization server provides the authorization code that you must use in the request to the /token endpoint.

The next snippet shows an example of cURL command sending a request to the /token endpoint to get an access token. Note that I have truncated the authorization code value to fit on the page:

```
curl -X POST 'http://localhost:8080/oauth2/token? \
client_id=client& \
redirect_uri=https://www.manning.com/authorized& \
grant_type=authorization_code& \
code=IhKRpq7GJ7P5VQI_...& \
code_verifier=qPsH306-ZDDaOE8DFzVn05TkN3ZZoVmI_6x4LsVglQI' \
--header 'Authorization: Basic Y2xpZW50OnNlY3JldA=='
```

The following snippet presents a response body for the /token request. I have also truncated the token values in the snippet:

```
{
    "access_token": "eyJraWQiOiI2Zjk5ZmE3MC...",
    "scope": "openid",
    "id_token": "eyJraWQiOiI2Zjk5ZmE3MC0xNTQ2LTRkMjM...",
    "token_type": "Bearer",
    "expires_in": 299
}
```

You can now use the access token when calling any endpoint that requires authentication. The following snippet shows a cURL command to send a request to the /demo endpoint. Observe that the access token must be sent in the Authorization header using the Bearer prefix (figure 15.4). The Bearer prefix implies that the one having the access token value can use it in the same way as any other party having it.

Figure 15.4   Analogy to the novel *The Lord of the Rings* by J.R.R. Tolkien. The access token is a precious resource. It gives access to several resources to whoever possesses it.

The following snippet shows the cURL command you can use to send a request to the /demo endpoint using the access token from the authorization server:

```
curl 'http://localhost:9090/demo' \
--header 'Authorization: Bearer eyJraW...'
```

15.2   *Using customized JWTs*

Systems' needs are different from one another, even regarding authentication and authorization. Often, it happens that you need to transfer custom values between the authorization server and the resource server through the access token. The resource server can use such values to apply various authorization rules.

In this section, we'll implement an example where the authorization and resource servers use custom claims in the access token. The authorization server customizes the JWT adding a claim named `"priority"` in the JWT. The resource server reads the `"priority"` claim and adds its value to the authentication instance in the security context. From there, the resource server can use it when implementing any authorization rule.

We'll follow these steps:

1 Change the authorization server to add the custom claim to the access token.
2 Change the resource server to read the custom claim and store it in the security context.
3 Implement an authorization rule that uses the custom claim.

But first things first! We need to add a custom value in the access token's body to the SecurityConfig class. In the authorization server, you do this by adding a bean of type OAuth2TokenCustomizer. The next code snippet demonstrates such a bean's definition. To simplify things and allow you to focus on the example, I added a dummy value in a field I named `"priority"`. In real-world apps, such custom fields would have a purpose, and you'd potentially have to write certain logic for setting their value:

```
@Bean
public OAuth2TokenCustomizer<JwtEncodingContext> jwtCustomizer() {
  return context -> {
    JwtClaimsSet.Builder claims = context.getClaims();
    claims.claim("priority", "HIGH");
  };
}
```

With this minimal change, the access tokens now contain a custom `"priority"` field. The next snippet shows a JWT access token I generated in its Base64-encoded format, and listing 15.7 shows the decoded body where you can observe the `"priority"` field:

eyJraWQiOiI5ZTBjOTQ5Ny0zYmMyLTQ4Y2YtODU5MC04N2JmZjE2ZjczOTAiLCJhbGciOiJSUzI
1NiJ9.eyJzdWIiOiJiaWxsIiwiYXVkIjoiY2xpZW50IiwibmJmIjoxNjg3MjYzMzI5LCJzY29wZ
SI6WyJvcGVuaWQiXSwiaXNzIjoiaHR0cDovL2xvY2FsaG9zdDo4MDgwIiwiZXhwIjoxNjg3MjYz
NjI5LCJwcmlvcml0eSI6IkhJR0giLCJpYXQiOjE2ODcyNjMzMjl9.HrQECSO17tZD8HKXP0U7gm
dmea01vPgVypvcf3oR3uawiMdI_joQBsLY0zNWBIgktKn2w9-
rvgtjD2xmhWZgSxRsDW_GZofqOzV9T-
5llMuZlakF7SQLyI67UJZKuPTJK8hBd1OhnurGo7ikPfDWhaqyychKu_uI7SdFrQQVgVqbrmHii
syoURIrI9EwOhB036M7UPJnIWtOWc34fAoFHxqhPuGIVesHHX5qm6wx-
8_Orjz96eOujVSEuUGRNVtz35_SRjhozcLzgIo3Rt9lUfLI7HSzulfXTCpxtxja-
1E_l_dsk4VHSvLYJUZjlERp5kVJqSO_keaJt8JbDQ0new

Listing 15.7 shows the decoded body of the previously presented access token. Remember you can easily use the jwt.io online tool to get the decoded form of a JWT. Alternatively, you can individually Base64-decode either the header or the body of the access token using any other Base64 decoder. The next listing demonstrates our changes on the authorization server work correctly.

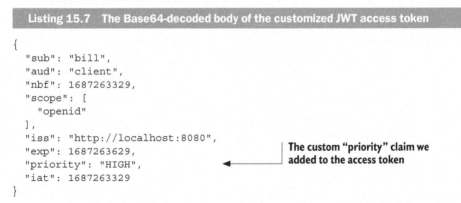

Listing 15.7   The Base64-decoded body of the customized JWT access token

```
{
  "sub": "bill",
  "aud": "client",
  "nbf": 1687263329,
  "scope": [
    "openid"
  ],
  "iss": "http://localhost:8080",
  "exp": 1687263629,
  "priority": "HIGH",          ◄──────  The custom "priority" claim we
  "iat": 1687263329                     added to the access token
}
```

As a second step, we make the changes on the resource server. You can continue working on the example we used in section 15.1, but to make your learning easier, I created a separate project for this example. You can find the implementation we discuss further in this section in project ssia-ch15-ex2.

The list of steps we need to follow to make our resource server understand the custom claims in the access token is the following:

1 Create a custom authentication object. This object will define the new shape, including the custom data.

2 Create a JWT authentication converter object. This object will define the logic for translating the JWT into the custom authentication object.

3 Configure the JWT authentication converter you created in step 2 to be used by the authentication mechanism.

4 Change the /demo endpoint to return the authentication object from the security context.

5 Test the endpoint, and check that the authentication object contains the custom "priority" field.

Listing 15.8 presents the definition of the authentication object. The authentication object should be any class that directly or indirectly inherits the Abstract-AuthenticationToken class. Since we use JWTs, it's more comfortable to extend the more specific JwtAuthenticationToken. This way, you'll directly extend the casual shape of an authentication object as designed for JWT access tokens.

Observe that the customization in listing 15.8 adds a field named "priority". This field will hold the value from the custom claim in the access token's body. In a similar way, you can add any other custom details your app might need for authorization purposes. Having these details directly in the authentication object from the security context makes configurations easy to write regardless of whether we choose to apply them at the endpoint level (chapters 7 and 8) or method level (chapters 11 and 12).

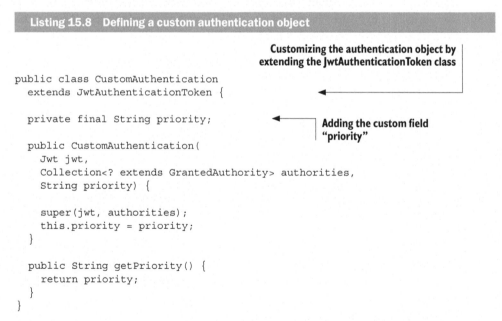

Listing 15.8   Defining a custom authentication object

Customizing the authentication object by extending the JwtAuthenticationToken class

Adding the custom field "priority"

```
public class CustomAuthentication
  extends JwtAuthenticationToken {

  private final String priority;

  public CustomAuthentication(
    Jwt jwt,
    Collection<? extends GrantedAuthority> authorities,
    String priority) {

    super(jwt, authorities);
    this.priority = priority;
  }

  public String getPriority() {
    return priority;
  }
}
```

You have a custom shape of the authentication object, and the next thing you need to do is instruct your app on how to translate the JWT into this custom object. You can do this by configuring a specific `Converter`, as presented in listing 15.9. Observe the two generic types we used: the `Jwt` and the `CustomAuthentication`. The first generic type, the `Jwt`, is the input for the converter, while the second type, the `Custom-Authentication`, is the output. So this converter changes a `Jwt` object (which is a standard contract in Spring Security on how the JWT access token is read) into the custom type we implemented in listing 15.8 (see figure 15.5).

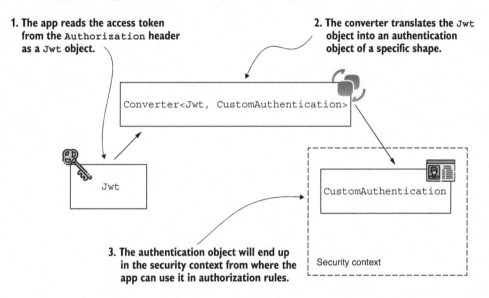

1. The app reads the access token from the `Authorization` header as a `Jwt` object.

2. The converter translates the `Jwt` object into an authentication object of a specific shape.

`Converter<Jwt, CustomAuthentication>`

`Jwt`

`CustomAuthentication`

3. The authentication object will end up in the security context from where the app can use it in authorization rules.

Security context

Figure 15.5 A custom converter implements logic to put information from the access token into a custom authentication shape.

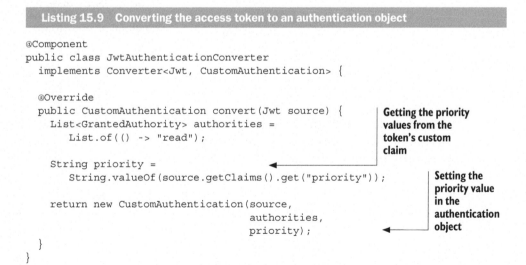

```
@Component
public class JwtAuthenticationConverter
    implements Converter<Jwt, CustomAuthentication> {

    @Override
    public CustomAuthentication convert(Jwt source) {
        List<GrantedAuthority> authorities =
            List.of(() -> "read");

        String priority =
            String.valueOf(source.getClaims().get("priority"));

        return new CustomAuthentication(source,
                                        authorities,
                                        priority);
    }
}
```

Getting the priority values from the token's custom claim

Setting the priority value in the authentication object

You may also observe in listing 15.9 that I have defined a dummy authority. In a real scenario, you'd either take these from the access token (considering they're managed at the authorization server level), or from a database or other third-party system (considering they're managed from a business perspective). In this case, I simplified the example and added a dummy `"read"` authority for all requests. But it's important to remember that this is also the place where you'd deal with authorities (which should also end up in the authentication object from the security context, as they're essential details for authorization rules in most cases).

The next listing shows how to configure the custom converter. In this case, I used dependency injection to get the converter bean from the Spring context. Then I used the jwtAuthenticationConverter() method of the JWT authentication configurer.

Listing 15.10   Configuring the custom authentication converter

```
@Configuration
public class ProjectConfig {

  // omitted code

  private final JwtAuthenticationConverter converter;

    // omitted constructor

  @Bean
  public SecurityFilterChain securityFilterChain(HttpSecurity http)
    throws Exception {

    http.oauth2ResourceServer(
      c -> c.jwt(
        j -> j.jwkSetUri(keySetUri)
            .jwtAuthenticationConverter(converter)
        )
    );

    http.authorizeHttpRequests(
      c -> c.anyRequest().authenticated()
    );

    return http.build();
  }
}
```

Injecting the converter object in a class field

Configuring the converter object within the authentication mechanism

---

That's all for the configuration we needed to implement to use the access token's custom claim. Let's test our implementation and prove that it works as expected. The next code snippet shows the changes I made to the /demo endpoint. I made the /demo endpoint return the authentication instance from the security context. Because Spring knows how to inject the value automatically in a parameter of type Authentication, I just needed to add this parameter and then make the endpoint's action method return it as is:

```
@GetMapping("/demo")
public Authentication demo(Authentication a) {
  return a;
}
```

If everything works as desired, when sending a request to the /demo endpoint, you'll get a response with a body similar to the one presented in the following listing. Observe that the custom `"priority"` attribute correctly appears in the authentication object having the value `"HIGH"`.

> **Listing 15.11   The /demo endpoint response contains the priority field**

```
{
  "authorities": [
    {
      "authority": "read"
    }
  ],
  "details": {
    "remoteAddress": "0:0:0:0:0:0:0:1",
    "sessionId": null
  },
  "authenticated": true,
    ...

  "name": "bill",                          The custom claim value appears
  "priority": "HIGH",                      in the authentication instance.
}
```

15.3   Configuring token validation through introspection

In this section, we discuss using introspection for access token validation. If your app uses opaque tokens, or if you want a system where you can revoke tokens at the authorization server level, then introspection is the process you must use for token validation. Figure 15.6 will remind you of the introspection process, discussed in detail in section 14.4.

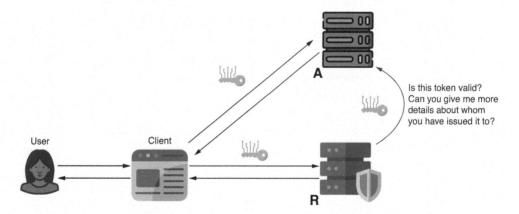

Is this token valid? Can you give me more details about whom you have issued it to?

Figure 15.6   Token introspection. In situations where the resource server cannot depend on signature-based validation of access tokens (such as when token revocation is necessary), or when the token does not contain detailed information (as with opaque tokens), the resource server is required to make inquiries to the authorization server. This is done to ascertain the validity of a token and to gather additional information about it.

We'll implement a resource server to demonstrate the use of introspection. To achieve our goal, we must follow these steps:

1   Ensure the authorization server recognizes the resource server as a client. The resource server needs client credentials registered on the authorization server side.
2   Configure authentication on the resource server side to use introspection.
3   Obtain an access token from the authorization server.
4   Use a demo endpoint to prove that the configuration works the way we expect with the access token we got in step 3.

The next code snippet shows you an example of creating a client instance, which we'll register at the authorization server side. This client represents our resource server. As you observe from figure 15.6, the resource server sends requests to the authorization server (for introspection), so this way, it also becomes a client of the authorization server.

To send the introspection requests, the resource server needs client credentials to authenticate, similar to any other client. For this example, I'll change project ssia-ch14-ex4 that we created when discussing opaque tokens in chapter 14:

```
RegisteredClient resourceServer =
  RegisteredClient.withId(UUID.randomUUID().toString())
          .clientId("resource_server")
          .clientSecret("resource_server_secret")
          .clientAuthenticationMethod(
             ClientAuthenticationMethod.CLIENT_SECRET_BASIC)
          .authorizationGrantType(
             AuthorizationGrantType.CLIENT_CREDENTIALS)
          .build();
```

Remember that passwords and configuration data should never be hardcoded like I did in the previous snippet. I simplified these examples as much as possible to allow you to focus on the subject we're discussing. In a real-world app, you should put the configurations in files outside of the implementation and securely persist secret details (like credentials) somewhere.

The following listing shows how to add both instances of client details (the client's and the resource server's) to the authorization server's `RegisteredClientRepository` component.

> **Listing 15.12   The `RegisteredClientRepository` definition**

```
@Bean
public RegisteredClientRepository registeredClientRepository() {
  RegisteredClient registeredClient =
    RegisteredClient.withId(UUID.randomUUID().toString())
      .clientId("client")
      .clientSecret("secret")                      Defining a client details
      .clientAuthenticationMethod(                 instance for the client app
```

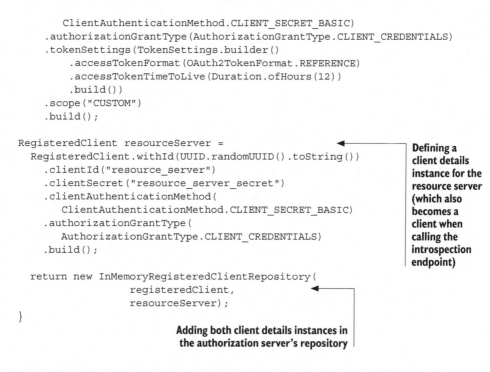

```
        ClientAuthenticationMethod.CLIENT_SECRET_BASIC)
    .authorizationGrantType(AuthorizationGrantType.CLIENT_CREDENTIALS)
    .tokenSettings(TokenSettings.builder()
        .accessTokenFormat(OAuth2TokenFormat.REFERENCE)
        .accessTokenTimeToLive(Duration.ofHours(12))
        .build())
    .scope("CUSTOM")
    .build();

RegisteredClient resourceServer =
    RegisteredClient.withId(UUID.randomUUID().toString())
        .clientId("resource_server")
        .clientSecret("resource_server_secret")
        .clientAuthenticationMethod(
            ClientAuthenticationMethod.CLIENT_SECRET_BASIC)
        .authorizationGrantType(
            AuthorizationGrantType.CLIENT_CREDENTIALS)
        .build();

    return new InMemoryRegisteredClientRepository(
                registeredClient,
                resourceServer);
}
```

Defining a client details instance for the resource server (which also becomes a client when calling the introspection endpoint)

Adding both client details instances in the authorization server's repository

With the changes made in listing 15.12, we now have a set of credentials our resource server can use to call the introspection endpoint that the authorization server exposes. We can start implementing the resource server. You can find this example in project ssia-ch15-ex3. Listing 15.13 shows how, in the properties files, I configured the three essential values needed for introspection:

- The introspection URI that the authorization server exposes, which allows the resource server to validate tokens
- The resource server client ID that allows the resource server to identify itself when calling the introspection endpoint
- The resource server client secret that the resource server uses together with its client ID to authenticate when sending requests to the introspection endpoint

Along with these, I also changed the server port to 9090, a different one than the application server's (8080), thus allowing both apps to run simultaneously.

Listing 15.13 The resource server application.properties file

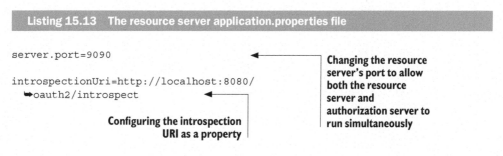

```
server.port=9090

introspectionUri=http://localhost:8080/
➥oauth2/introspect
```

Changing the resource server's port to allow both the resource server and authorization server to run simultaneously

Configuring the introspection URI as a property

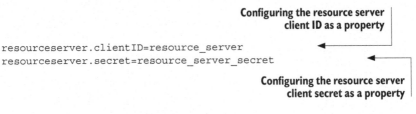

```
resourceserver.clientID=resource_server
resourceserver.secret=resource_server_secret
```

Configuring the resource server
client ID as a property

Configuring the resource server
client secret as a property

You can then inject the values in the properties file in fields of the configuration class and use them to set up the authentication. The following listing shows the configuration class injecting the values from the properties file into fields.

Listing 15.14   Injecting the values in fields of the configuration class

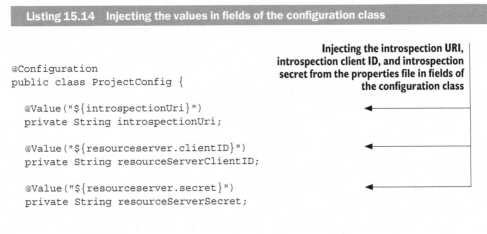

Injecting the introspection URI,
introspection client ID, and introspection
secret from the properties file in fields of
the configuration class

```
@Configuration
public class ProjectConfig {

  @Value("${introspectionUri}")
  private String introspectionUri;

  @Value("${resourceserver.clientID}")
  private String resourceServerClientID;

  @Value("${resourceserver.secret}")
  private String resourceServerSecret;


}
```

Use the introspection URI and the credentials to configure the authentication. You configure the authentication similarly to how we configured it for JWT access tokens—using the oauth2ResourceServer() method of the HttpSecurity object. However, we call a different configuration method the oauth2ResourceServer() customizer object: opaqueToken(). For the opaqueToken() method, we configure the introspection URI and credentials. The following listing presents this setup.

Listing 15.15   Configuring the resource server authentication for opaque tokens

```
@Configuration
public class ProjectConfig {

  @Value("${introspectionUri}")
  private String introspectionUri;

  @Value("${resourceserver.clientID}")
  private String resourceServerClientID;

  @Value("${resourceserver.secret}")
  private String resourceServerSecret;

  @Bean
  public SecurityFilterChain securityFilterChain(HttpSecurity http)
```

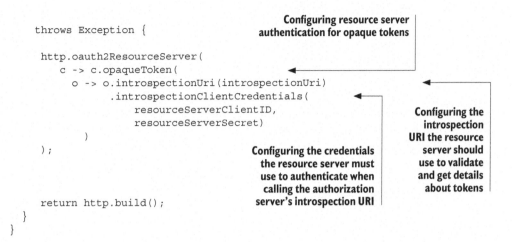

```
    throws Exception {

    http.oauth2ResourceServer(
        c -> c.opaqueToken(
          o -> o.introspectionUri(introspectionUri)
              .introspectionClientCredentials(
                  resourceServerClientID,
                  resourceServerSecret)
            )
    );


    return http.build();
  }
}
```

Configuring resource server authentication for opaque tokens

Configuring the introspection URI the resource server should use to validate and get details about tokens

Configuring the credentials the resource server must use to authenticate when calling the authorization server's introspection URI

Remember to also add the authorization configurations. The next code snippet shows the standard way you learned in chapters 7 and 8 to make all the endpoints require requests' authentication:

```
http.authorizeHttpRequests(
  c -> c.anyRequest().authenticated()
);
```

The following listing shows the full contents of the `configuration` class.

Listing 15.16 Full contents of the `configuration` class

```
@Configuration
public class ProjectConfig {

  @Value("${introspectionUri}")
  private String introspectionUri;

  @Value("${resourceserver.clientID}")
  private String resourceServerClientID;

  @Value("${resourceserver.secret}")
  private String resourceServerSecret;

  @Bean
  public SecurityFilterChain securityFilterChain(HttpSecurity http)
    throws Exception {

    http.oauth2ResourceServer(
        c -> c.opaqueToken(
          o -> o.introspectionUri(introspectionUri)
              .introspectionClientCredentials(
                  resourceServerClientID,
                  resourceServerSecret)
            )
    );
```

```
    http.authorizeHttpRequests(
        c -> c.anyRequest().authenticated()
    );

    return http.build();
  }
}
```

Adding the endpoint authorization configuration. Requests for any endpoint require authentication.

A simple /demo endpoint like the one in the next code snippet is enough for us to test that authentication works correctly:

```
@RestController
public class DemoController {

  @GetMapping("/demo")
  public String demo() {
    return "Demo";
  }
}
```

You can now start both applications: the authorization server and the resource server. Both should run simultaneously. The next code snippet includes the cURL command you can use to send a request to the /token endpoint. To simplify this example, I use the client credentials grant type, but you could use any grant type you learned in chapter 14 to get the access token. Remember that the resource server configuration is the same regardless of how you get the access token:

```
curl -X POST 'http://localhost:8080/oauth2/token? \
client_id=client& \
grant_type=client_credentials' \
--header 'Authorization: Basic Y2xpZW50OnNlY3JldA=='
```

If the request is successful, you'll get the access token back in response. The response body looks like the next snippet. I have truncated the token's value to make it fit better on the page:

```
{
    "access_token": "2zLyYA8b6Q54-…",
    "token_type": "Bearer",
    "expires_in": 43199
}
```

In the same way as for the JWT access tokens, when sending a request to a protected endpoint, add the token as the value of the "Authorization" header. The access token value must be prefixed with the string "Bearer". The next snippet shows the cURL command you can use to send a request to the /demo endpoint. If everything works correctly, you'll get back the "Demo" string in the body in a 200 OK response status:

```
curl 'http://localhost:9090/demo' \
--header 'Authorization: Bearer 2zLyYA8b6Q54-…'
```

15.4 *Implementing multitenant systems*

In real-world apps, things aren't always perfect. Sometimes we're in a situation where we must adapt our implementation to match some nonstandard case when integrating with a third party. Also, sometimes we need to implement backends that rely on multiple authorization servers for authentication and authorization (multitenant systems). How should we implement our apps' configurations in such cases?

Fortunately, Spring Security offers flexibility for implementing any scenario. In this section, we discuss implementing resource server configurations for more complex cases, such as multitenant systems or interacting with apps that don't follow the standards.

Let's look at figure 15.7 to revisit Spring Security's authentication design that we discussed in detail in the first two parts of this book. A filter intercepts the HTTP request. The authentication responsibility is then delegated to an authentication manager. The authentication manager further uses an authentication provider, which implements the authentication logic.

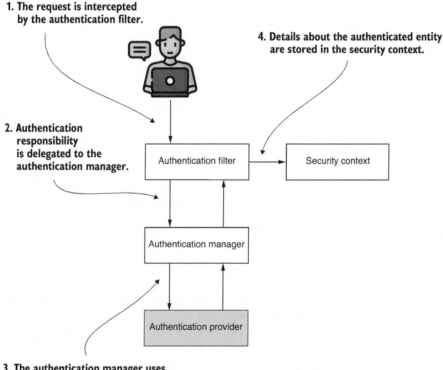

1. The request is intercepted by the authentication filter.

4. Details about the authenticated entity are stored in the security context.

2. Authentication responsibility is delegated to the authentication manager.

Authentication filter → Security context

Authentication manager

Authentication provider

3. The authentication manager uses the authentication provider, which implements the authentication logic.

Figure 15.7 The authentication class design. During the authentication procedure, the filter captures the request and passes it on to an authentication manager component. This manager then employs an authentication provider that executes the necessary authentication logic. Upon successful authentication, the application records the authenticated principal's details in the security context.

Why is it important to remember this design? Because for the resource server, like any other authentication approach, you need to change the authentication provider if you want to customize how the authentication works.

In the case of a resource server, Spring Security allows you to plug into the configuration a component named the authentication manager resolver (figure 15.8). This component allows the app execution to decide which authentication manager to call. This way, you can delegate the authentication to any custom authentication manager that can use a custom authentication provider.

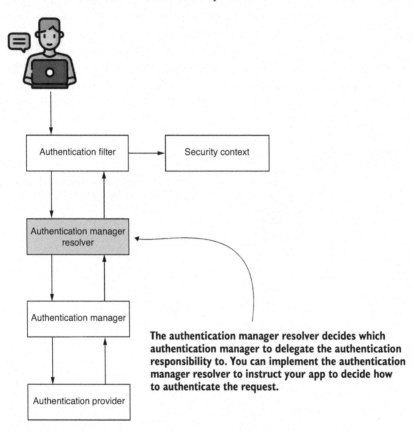

The authentication manager resolver decides which authentication manager to delegate the authentication responsibility to. You can implement the authentication manager resolver to instruct your app to decide how to authenticate the request.

Figure 15.8   Implementing an authentication manager resolver, you tell your app which authentication manager to delegate the authentication responsibility to.

If you want your app to use multiple authorization servers all using JWTs, Spring Security even provides an out-of-the-box authentication manager resolver implementation (figure 15.9). For such a case, you only need to plug in the `JwtIssuer-AuthenticationManagerResolver` custom implementation that Spring Security provides.

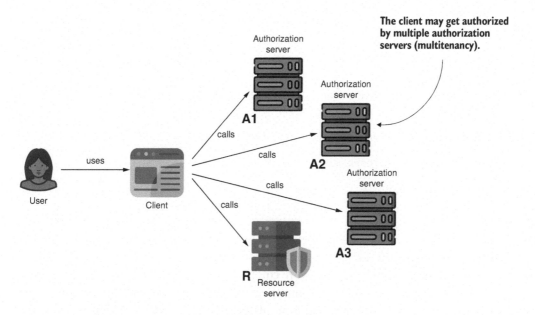

The client may get authorized by multiple authorization servers (multitenancy).

Figure 15.9 Your system might need to use multiple authorization servers to authenticate the users and clients.

Listing 15.17 shows how to use the `authenticationManagerResolver()` method when configuring the authentication. In this example, you observe that I only had to create an instance of the `JwtIssuerAuthenticationResolver` class, for which I have provided all the issue addresses of the authorization servers. You can find this example implemented in project ssia-ch15-ex4.

NOTE Remember to never write URLs (or any similar configurable details) directly in code. We use this approach only with examples to simplify the code and allow you to focus on what's essential for you to learn. Anything customizable should always be written in configuration files or environment variables.

Listing 15.17 Working with two authorization servers that use JWT access tokens

```
@Configuration
public class ProjectConfig {

  @Bean
  public SecurityFilterChain securityFilterChain(HttpSecurity http)
    throws Exception {

    http.oauth2ResourceServer(
      j -> j.authenticationManagerResolver(
              authenticationManagerResolver())
    );

    http.authorizeHttpRequests(
      c -> c.anyRequest().authenticated()
```

```
  );

  return http.build();
}

@Bean
public AuthenticationManagerResolver<HttpServletRequest>
  ➥authenticationManagerResolver() {

  var a = new JwtIssuerAuthenticationManagerResolver(
      "http://localhost:7070",
      "http://localhost:8080");

  return a;
  }
}
```

With a configuration like the one presented in figure 15.10, your resource server works with two authorization servers running on ports 7070 and 8080.

However, sometimes things are more complex. Spring Security cannot provide every customization possible. In such a case, where you need to customize the resource server's capabilities even further, you must implement your custom authorization manager resolver.

Let's consider the following scenario: you need your resource server to work with both JWT and opaque tokens with two different authorization servers. Say your resource server discriminates the requests based on the value of a "type" parameter. If the "type" parameter's value is "jwt", the resource server must authenticate the request with an authorization server using JWT access tokens; otherwise, it uses an authorization server with opaque access tokens.

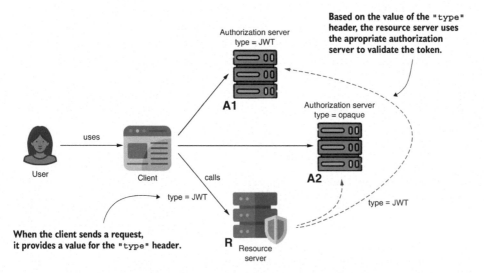

Figure 15.10 Employing two distinct authorization servers, each handling a different type of token. Depending on a specific value in an HTTP request header used by the client, the resource server determines which authorization server to use for validating the access tokens.

Listing 15.18 implements this scenario. The resource server uses a different authorization server based on the value of the `"type"` header in the HTTP request. To achieve this, the resource server uses a different authentication manager based on this header's value.

Listing 15.18 Using both JWT and opaque tokens

```
@Configuration
public class ProjectConfig {

  // Omitted code

  @Bean
  public AuthenticationManagerResolver<HttpServletRequest>
    authenticationManagerResolver(
      JwtDecoder jwtDecoder,
      OpaqueTokenIntrospector opaqueTokenIntrospector
    ) {

    AuthenticationManager jwtAuth = new ProviderManager(
      new JwtAuthenticationProvider(jwtDecoder)
    );

    AuthenticationManager opaqueAuth = new ProviderManager(
      new OpaqueTokenAuthenticationProvider(opaqueTokenIntrospector)
    );

    return (request) -> {
      if ("jwt".equals(request.getHeader("type"))) {
        return jwtAuth;
      } else {
        return opaqueAuth;
      }
    };
  }

  @Bean
  public JwtDecoder jwt'Decoder() {
    return NimbusJwtDecoder
            .withJwkSetUri("http://localhost:7070/oauth2/jwks")
            .build();
  }

  @Bean
  public OpaqueTokenIntrospector opaqueTokenIntrospector() {
    return new SpringOpaqueTokenIntrospector(
        "http://localhost:6060/oauth2/introspect",
        "client", "secret");
  }
}
```

Defining an authentication manager for the authorization server managing JWT access tokens

Defining another authentication manager for the authorization server managing opaque tokens

Defining the custom authentication manager resolver logic to pick an authentication manager based on the "type" header of the HTTP request

Configuring the public key set URI for the authentication manager working with the authorization server that manages JWT access tokens

Configuring the introspection URI and credentials for the authentication manager working with the authorization server that manages opaque tokens

The following listing shows the rest of the configuration that configures the custom authorization manager resolver using the customizer parameter of the `authenticationManagerResolver()` method.

Listing 15.19   Configuring the `AuthenticationManagerResolver`

```
@Configuration
public class ProjectConfig {

  @Bean
  public SecurityFilterChain securityFilterChain(HttpSecurity http)
    throws Exception {

    http.oauth2ResourceServer(
      j -> j.authenticationManagerResolver(         ◀── Configuring the
              authenticationManagerResolver(            custom
                jwtDecoder(),                           authentication
                opaqueTokenIntrospector()               manager resolver
                ))
    );

    http.authorizeHttpRequests(
      c -> c.anyRequest().authenticated()
    );

    return http.build();
  }

  // Omitted code

}
```

Even in this example, we used authentication provider implementations offered by Spring Security: `JwtAuthenticationProvider` and `OpaqueTokenAuthentication-Provider`. In this case, `JwtAuthenticationProvider` implements the authentication logic for working with a standard authorization server using JWT access tokens. `OpaqueTokenAuthenticationProvider` implements the authentication logic working with opaque tokens. But you could have even more complex cases in real-world apps.

If you need to implement something very customized, like integrating with a system that doesn't follow any standard, then you can even implement your custom authentication provider.

Summary

- Spring Security offers support for implementing OAuth 2/OpenID Connect resource servers. To configure authentication as an OAuth 2/OpenID Connect resource server, use the `oauth2ResourceServer()` method of the `HttpSecurity` object.

- If you wish to use JWTs, you need to apply the configuration using the `jwt()` method of the `oauth2ResourceServer()` customizer parameter.

- You can also use introspection if your system utilizes opaque tokens or if you want to be able to revoke JWTs at the authorization server side. In such a case, you must configure authentication using the `opaqueToken()` method of the `oauth-2ResourceServer()` customizer parameter.

- When using JWTs, you must set up the public key set URI. The public key set URI is a URI exposed by the authorization server. The resource server calls this URI to get the public parts for the key pairs configured on the authorization server side. The authorization server uses the private parts to sign the access tokens, while the resource server needs the public parts to validate them.

- When using introspection, you need to configure the introspection URI. The resource server sends requests to the introspection URI to ask the authorization server whether a token is valid and for more details about it. When calling the introspection URI, the resource server acts as a client for the authorization server, so it needs its own client credentials to authenticate.

- Spring Security offers the opportunity to customize the authentication logic using an authentication manager resolver component. You define and configure such a custom component when you must implement a more specific case, such as multitenancy or adapting your app to a nonstandard implementation.

Implementing an OAuth 2 client

This chapter covers

- Implementing an OAuth 2 login
- Implementing a Spring Security OAuth 2 client
- Using the client credentials grant type

Often, it is necessary to implement communication between backend applications, especially for backend apps involving multiple services. In such cases, when systems have authentication and authorization built over OAuth 2, it's recommended that you authenticate calls between apps using the same approach. While developers use HTTP Basic and API Key authentication methods (chapter 6) for simplicity in some cases to keep the system consistent and more secure, using the OAuth 2 client credentials grant type is the preferred option.

Remember the OAuth 2 actors (figure 16.1)? We discussed the authorization server in chapter 14 and the resource server in chapter 15. This chapter is dedicated to the client. We'll discuss how to use Spring Security to implement an OAuth 2 client and when and how a backend app becomes a client in an OAuth 2 system.

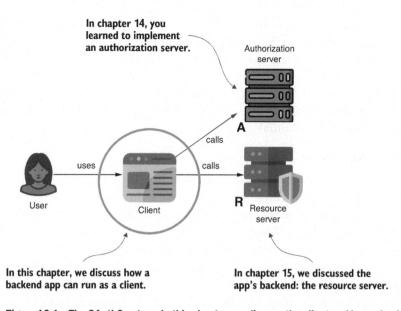

In chapter 14, you learned to implement an authorization server.

Authorization server

A

calls

calls

uses

User

Client

R Resource server

In this chapter, we discuss how a backend app can run as a client.

In chapter 15, we discussed the app's backend: the resource server.

Figure 16.1 The OAuth2 actors. In this chapter, we discuss the client and how a backend app can act as a client in a system with authentication and authorization designed as OAuth 2.

Okay, maybe figure 16.1 doesn't fully illustrate what we will talk about. We'll begin by discussing login for the user, but we'll also focus on how to make a backend app a client for another backend app. Backend apps designed with Spring Security may become clients as well. Figure 16.2 shows the other case that we'll discuss here. In the current chapter, we'll solve the problem of implementing the communication between two backend apps, making one of them an actual OAuth 2 client. In such a case, we need to use Spring Security to build an OAuth 2 client.

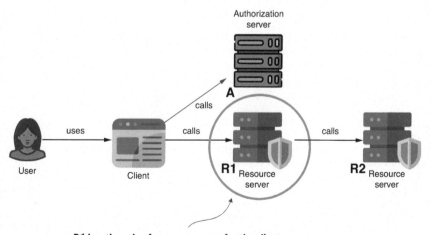

Authorization server

A

calls

uses

calls

calls

User

Client

R1 Resource server

R2 Resource server

R1 has the role of resource server for the client app, but it becomes a client for the resource server R2.

Figure 16.2 A backend app may become a client for another backend app. We discuss this case in the current chapter.

Section 16.1 discusses how to easily implement an OAuth 2 login for a Spring MVC web app using Spring Security. We'll use an external authorization server provider, such as Google and GitHub. You'll learn how to implement a login for your app where users can authenticate using their Google or GitHub credentials. Using the same approach, you can implement such a login with a custom (self-owned) authorization server.

In section 16.2, we employ a client's custom implementation through a service and discuss using the client credentials grant type.

16.1 Implementing OAuth 2 login

This section discusses how to implement an OAuth 2 login for your Spring web app. With Spring Boot, it's a piece of cake to configure the authentication for standard cases (cases where the authorization server fulfills the OAuth 2 and OpenID Connect specifications correctly). We'll begin with a classic case (which you can use with most well-known providers such as Google, GitHub, Facebook, and Okta).

Then I'll show you what's behind the scenes of the self-provided configuration so you can also cover custom cases. At the end of this section, you'll be able to implement login for your Spring web app with any OAuth 2 provider and even allow your users to choose between various providers when authenticating.

16.1.1 Implementing authentication with a common provider

In this section, we'll implement the simplest login case, allowing our app's users to log in using only one provider. For this demonstration, I chose Google as our user's authentication provider.

We begin by adding a few resources to our project to implement a simple Spring web app with the mentioned login capabilities. Listing 16.1 shows the dependencies for the demo app. You can find the app in this example in project ssia-ch16-ex1. You'll recognize a new dependency we haven't used in previous chapters: the *OAuth 2 client dependency*.

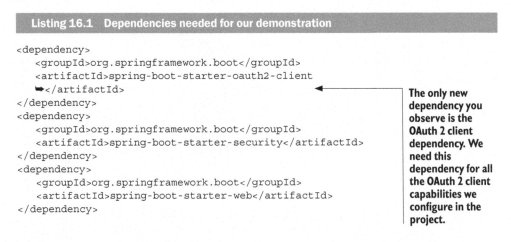

Listing 16.1   Dependencies needed for our demonstration

```
<dependency>
    <groupId>org.springframework.boot</groupId>
    <artifactId>spring-boot-starter-oauth2-client
    ➥</artifactId>
</dependency>
<dependency>
    <groupId>org.springframework.boot</groupId>
    <artifactId>spring-boot-starter-security</artifactId>
</dependency>
<dependency>
    <groupId>org.springframework.boot</groupId>
    <artifactId>spring-boot-starter-web</artifactId>
</dependency>
```

The only new dependency you observe is the OAuth 2 client dependency. We need this dependency for all the OAuth 2 client capabilities we configure in the project.

If you need a refresher on building web apps with Spring Boot, chapters 7 and 8 of *Spring Start Here* (Manning, 2020), another book I wrote, should help you remember these skills quickly. The following code snippet shows the simple controller of our demo web app, which only has a home page:

```
@Controller
public class HomeController {

  @GetMapping("/")
  public String home() {
    return "index.html";
  }
}
```

The next code snippet shows the small demo HTML page we expect to access once the authentication ends successfully:

```
<!DOCTYPE html>
<html lang="en">
<head>
    <meta charset="UTF-8">
    <title>Title</title>
</head>
<body>
    <h1>Home</h1>
</body>
</html>
```

Listing 16.2 presents the configuration for OAuth 2 login as an authentication method for the web app. Configuring the app in such a way will automatically follow the authorization code grant type redirecting the user to log in on a specific authorization server and redirecting it back once the authentication succeeds. This process follows precisely what we discussed in chapters 13 through 15 and demonstrated multiple times in these chapters using cURL.

Listing 16.2   Configuring the OAuth 2 login

```
@Configuration
public class SecurityConfig {

  @Bean
  public SecurityFilterChain securityFilterChain(HttpSecurity http)
    throws Exception {

    http.oauth2Login(Customizer.withDefaults());        ◄──── To configure authentication
                                                               as OAuth 2 login, we use the
    http.authorizeHttpRequests(                                oauth2Login() method.
      c -> c.anyRequest().authenticated());

    return http.build();
  }
}
```

I bet you are thinking, Shouldn't we still have to fill in all those details we learned in chapters 13 through 15, such as the authorization URL, token URL, client ID, client secret, and so on? Yes, all these details are needed. Fortunately, Spring Security can help you again. If your app uses one of the providers Spring Security considers to be well known, most of these details are prefilled. You only need to configure the app's client credentials. Spring Security considers the following providers as well known:

- Google
- GitHub
- Okta
- Facebook

Spring Security preconfigures the details for these providers in the `CommonOAuth-2Provider` class. So if you use any of these, you only need to configure the client credentials in your application properties, which works. The following code snippet shows the two properties you need to configure the client ID and the client secret when using Google (I truncated my credentials' values):

```
spring.security.oauth2.client.registration.google.client-id=790…
spring.security.oauth2.client.registration.google.client-secret=GOC…
```

I implied here that you have registered your app in the Google Developer Console— that's where you get your app's unique set of credentials from. If you haven't done this before, and you want to configure authentication using Google for your app, you can find Google's detailed documentation on how to register your OAuth 2 app with Google at http://mng.bz/eEvz. Figure 16.3 shows how the app displays the Google login when properly configuring this well-known provider.

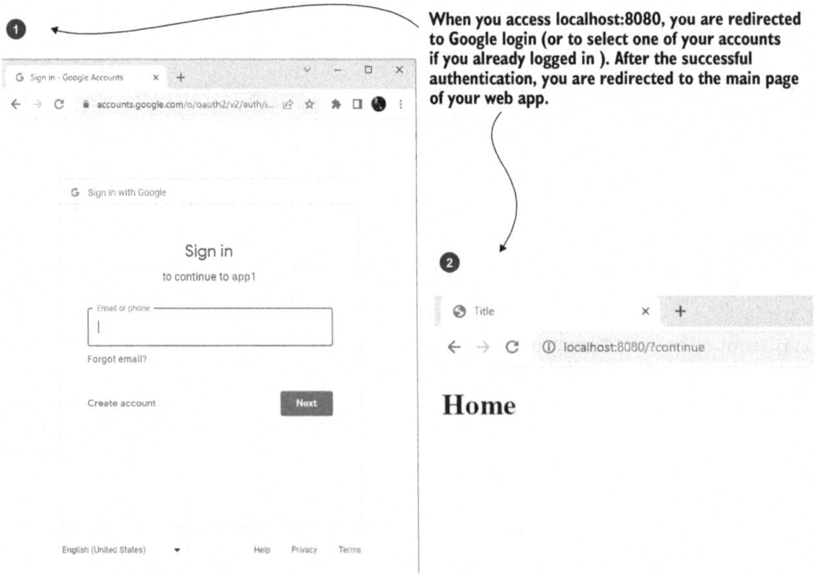

Figure 16.3   When accessing the app in a web browser, the browser redirects you to the Google login page. If you authenticate with Google correctly, you are redirected back to your app's main page.

16.1.2 *Giving the user more possibilities*

I'm sure you've surfed the internet enough by now to observe that many apps offer more than one way for the user to log in. Sometimes you can even choose among four or five providers to log into an app. This approach is advantageous because not all of us already have an account with a social network. Some have a Facebook account, but others prefer to use LinkedIn. Some developers prefer to log in using their GitHub account, but others use their Gmail address.

With Spring Security, you can make this work straightforwardly, even by using multiple providers. Say I want to enable my app's users to log in with either Google or GitHub. I only need to configure the credentials for both providers similarly. The following snippet shows the properties required in the application.properties file to add GitHub as an authentication method. Remember that you must keep those we already configured for Google in section 16.1.1:

```
spring.security.oauth2.client.registration.github.client-id=03…
spring.security.oauth2.client.registration.github.client-secret=c5d…
```

Similar to any other provider, you have to register your app first, configuring the client ID and secret in the application.properties file. The approach to registering the app differs from one provider to another. For GitHub, you find the documentation that tells you how to register an app at http://mng.bz/p1YG.

Before asking you to authenticate, the app gives you two login options: the ones we previously configured (figure 16.4). You must choose either Google or GitHub to log in. After you choose your preferred provider, the app redirects you to that provider's specific authentication page.

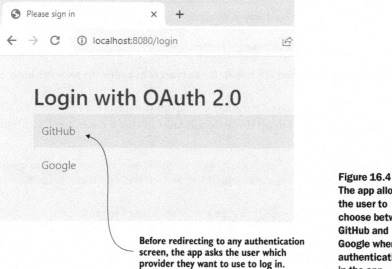

**Figure 16.4
The app allows
the user to
choose between
GitHub and
Google when
authenticating
in the app.**

Before redirecting to any authentication
screen, the app asks the user which
provider they want to use to log in.

16.1.3 Using a custom authorization server

Spring Security defines a list of four common providers, as discussed in sections 16.1.1 and 16.1.2. But what if you want to use a provider that is not on the common providers list? You have many other alternatives, such as LinkedIn, Twitter, Yahoo, and others. You might want to use a custom authorization server you built, as you learned in chapter 14.

You can configure an OAuth 2 login with any provider, including a custom one you built. In this section, we're going to use an authorization server we built in chapter 14 to show the configuration of a custom OAuth 2 login. To make your learning easier and also keep the examples separate, I have copied the content of project ssia-ch14-ex1 that we discussed in chapter 14 into a project for this chapter, which I named ssia-ch16-ex1-as.

We only need to ensure that our client configuration matches what we want to implement in this chapter. Listing 16.2 shows the registered client configured in our authorization server. The most important thing here is to make sure that the redirect URI matches the one we expect for our application for which we'll implement the login:

```
http://localhost:8080/login/oauth2/code/my_authorization_server
```

Figure 16.5 analyzes the anatomy of the redirect URI. Observe that the standard redirect URI uses the /login/oauth2/code path followed by the name of the authorization server. In this example, the name I gave to the authorization server is my_authorization_server.

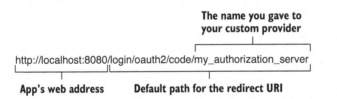

Figure 16.5   The standard redirect URI format. The last part of its path is the provider's name.

The next listing shows the configuration part from the authorization server, which registers the client details. You need these details later in this section; we'll configure them at the app side as well.

Listing 16.3   The client details registered on the authorization server side

```
@Bean
public RegisteredClientRepository registeredClientRepository() {
  var registeredClient = RegisteredClient
    .withId(UUID.randomUUID().toString())
    .clientId("client")
    .clientSecret("secret")
    .clientAuthenticationMethod(
       ClientAuthenticationMethod.CLIENT_SECRET_BASIC)
    .authorizationGrantType(
       AuthorizationGrantType.AUTHORIZATION_CODE)
    .redirectUri(
```

```
    "http://localhost:8080/login/oauth2/code/my_authorization_server")
  .scope(OidcScopes.OPENID)
  .build();

  return new InMemoryRegisteredClientRepository(registeredClient);
}
```

Remember, you can't start two apps using the same port number on the same system. Because the web app uses port 8080, we must change the authorization server's port to another one. As presented in the following code snippet, I chose 7070 for this example and configured it in the application.properties file:

```
server.port=7070
```

We can now move on to the web app's configuration. Because we used a common provider in our examples from sections 16.1.1 and 16.1.2, we didn't have to define it. Spring Security already knows all the details it needs about common providers. However, we need to configure a few things to use a different provider. Spring Security needs to know the following (as discussed in chapters 13 and 14):

- The authorization endpoint for the provider to know where to redirect the user during the authorization code flow
- The token endpoint that the app has to call to get an access token
- The key set endpoint the app needs to validate the access tokens

The good news is that if your provider (authorization server) fulfills the OpenID Connect protocol correctly, you only need to configure the issuer URI. The app then uses the issuer URI to find all details it needs, such as the authorization, token, and the key set URI. If the authorization server doesn't fulfill the OpenID Connect protocol, you'll have to configure these three details in the application.properties file explicitly.

As the authorization servers we built in chapter 14 implement the OpenID Connect protocol correctly, we can rely on the issuer URI. The next code snippet shows how to configure the issuer URI. Observe that I gave a name to the provider. For this example, I chose to identify it with the name my_authorization_server, but you can choose any name to identify your provider:

```
spring.security.oauth2.client.provider.my_authorization_server.issuer-
uri=http://127.0.0.1:7070
```

> **NOTE** We run both apps, the authorization server and the web app we use on the local system. Running these apps on the same system and accessing them from the browser may cause problems with the cookies the browser uses to store the user's session. For this reason, I recommend you use the IP address "127.0.0.1" to refer to one app and the DNS name "localhost" to refer to the other. Even if the two are identical from a networking point of view and they refer to the same system (the local system), they will be considered different by the browser, which will in this way be able to manage the sessions correctly. In this example, I use "127.0.0.1" to refer to the authorization server and "localhost" for the web app.

Listing 16.4 shows the client registration configuration. Apart from declaring who the provider is, the client registration is also a bit longer than the one we wrote in sections 16.1.1 and 16.1.2, where we used common providers. Aside from the client ID and client secret, you also need to fill in the following:

- *The provider name*—A name you give to the provider you want to use in case it's not common.
- *The client authentication meeting*—The app's authentication method to call the provider's secured endpoints (usually HTTP Basic).
- *The redirect URI*—The URI the app expects the provider to redirect the user to after correct authentication. This URI has to match one of those registered on the authorization server side (see listing 16.3).
- *The web app's requested scope*—The scope that the web app requests can only be one of those registered at the authorization server side (see listing 16.3).

Listing 16.4   The client registration configuration

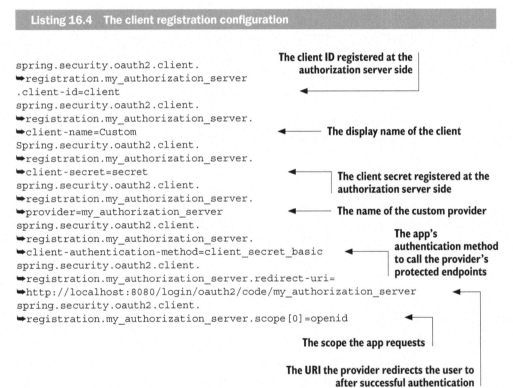

You can start the authorization server and the web application. Remember, you must first start the authorization server. When the web app starts, it will call the issue URI to get the rest of the details it needs. Once you start both apps, access the web app in the browser using its address http://localhost:8080. Figure 16.6 shows that the custom provider now appears in the list and can be chosen by the user to authenticate.

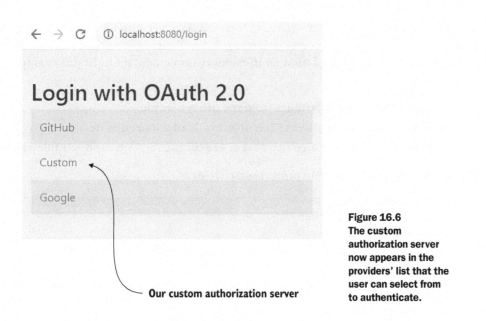

Figure 16.6
The custom
authorization server
now appears in the
providers' list that the
user can select from
to authenticate.

Our custom authorization server

16.1.4 Adding flexibility to your configurations

Often, we need to have more flexibility than the properties files offer us. Sometimes, we need to be able to dynamically change the credentials without redeploying the app. In other cases, we want to turn specific providers on or off or even offer access to these based on given logic. For such cases, adding the credentials in the properties file and allowing Spring Boot to do the magic for us doesn't work anymore.

However, if you know what happens behind the scenes, you can customize the provider's details as you wish. The only two types you must remember are

- `ClientRegistration`—This object is used to define the details the client needs to use the authorization server (credentials, redirect URI, authorization URI, etc.).

- `ClientRegistrationRepository`—This contract is implemented to define the logic that retrieves the client registrations. You, for example, can implement a client registration repository to tell your app to get the client registrations from a database or a custom vault.

For this example, I keep things simple. I'll continue using the application.properties file but with different names for the properties to prove that it's no longer Spring Boot configuring things for us. However, even if straightforward, this example shows the same approach you'd use if you wanted to store the details in a database or grab them by calling a given endpoint. In any such case, you must appropriately implement the `ClientRegistrationRepository` contract.

You define the `ClientRegistrationRepository` component as a Spring bean. The app will use your implementation to get the client registration details. Listing 16.5 shows an example where I used an in-memory implementation. In this example, I do three things:

1 Inject the credentials values from the properties file
2 Create a `ClientRegistration` object with all the needed details
3 Configure it in an in-memory `ClientRegistrationRepository` implementation

You can find this example in project ssia-ch16-ex2.

Listing 16.5   Implementing custom logic

```
@Configuration
public class SecurityConfig {                          Injecting credentials values
                                                       from the properties file
  @Value("${client-id}")
  private String clientId;                          ◄──────────────┐
                                                                   │
  @Value("${client-secret}")                                       │
  private String clientSecret;                      ◄──────────────┘

  @Bean
  public SecurityFilterChain securityFilterChain(HttpSecurity http)
    throws Exception {

    http.oauth2Login(Customizer.withDefaults());

    http.authorizeHttpRequests(
      c -> c.anyRequest().authenticated()
    );
                                                     Providing an in-memory repository
    return http.build();                             implementation that contains the
  }                                                       client registration details

  @Bean
  public ClientRegistrationRepository clientRegistrationRepository() {
    return new InMemoryClientRegistrationRepository(
      this.googleClientRegistration());             ◄──────────────┘
  }

  private ClientRegistration googleClientRegistration() {
    return CommonOAuth2Provider.GOOGLE.getBuilder("google")   ◄──────┐
            .clientId(clientId)                                      │
            .clientSecret(clientSecret)                              │
            .build();                                                │
  }                                             Creating the client registration
                                                based on the template of the
}                                                  common provider Google
```

16.1.5 Managing authorization for an OAuth 2 login

In this section, we discuss using the authentication details. In most cases, your app needs to know who logged in. This requirement is either for displaying things differently or for applying various authorization restrictions. Fortunately, using the oauth2Login() authentication method doesn't differ in this regard from any other authentication method.

Remember the Spring Security authentication design we discussed starting with chapter 2 (reproduced as figure 16.7)? Successful authentication always ends with the app adding the authentication details to the security context. Using oauth2Login() is no exception.

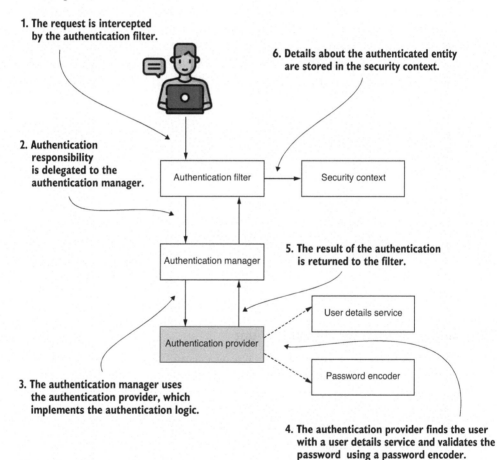

1. The request is intercepted by the authentication filter.

6. Details about the authenticated entity are stored in the security context.

2. Authentication responsibility is delegated to the authentication manager.

5. The result of the authentication is returned to the filter.

3. The authentication manager uses the authentication provider, which implements the authentication logic.

4. The authentication provider finds the user with a user details service and validates the password using a password encoder.

Figure 16.7 Authentication flow in Spring Security. Successful authentication ends with the app adding the details of the authenticated principal to the security context.

Knowing that the authentication details are in the security context, you can use them exactly the same way as for any other previously discussed authentication method—`httpBasic()`, `formLogin()`, or `oauth2ResourceServer()`:

- You can inject the `Authentication` object as a method parameter (figure 16.5).
- You can get it from the security context anywhere in the app (`Security-ContextHolder.getContext().getAuthentication()`).
- You can use pre-/post-annotations, as discussed in chapters 11 and 12.

You can use the `Authentication` contract to get standard user details such as the username and the authorities. If you need custom details, you can use the contract's implementation directly, as presented in listing 16.6. For OAuth 2, the class `OAuth-2AuthenticationPrincipal` defines the contract implementation. Remember, however, that for maintainability purposes, I recommend you use the `Authentication` contract everywhere possible and rely on the implementation only if you have no other choice (for example, if you need to get a detail you can't already get using the contract reference).

Listing 16.6   Obtaining the authentication details

```
@Controller
public class HomeController {

  @GetMapping("/")
  public String home(
   [CA]OAuth2AuthenticationToken authentication) {          ◄─────────────┐
    // do something with the authentication
    return "index.html";
  }                                            Injecting authentication
}                                             details in the method's
                                                       parameter
```

16.2   *Implementing an OAuth 2 client*

This section discusses implementing a service as an OAuth 2 client. In service-oriented systems, apps often communicate with one another. In such cases, the app sending the request to another app becomes a client of that particular app. In most cases, if we decide to implement authentication for the requests over OAuth 2, the app uses the client credentials grant type to obtain an access token.

The client credentials grant type doesn't imply a user. For this reason, you won't need a redirect URI and an authorization URI. The client credentials are enough to allow a client to authenticate and obtain an access token by sending a request to the token URI. Figure 16.8 reminds you of the client credentials grant type we discussed in chapter 13.

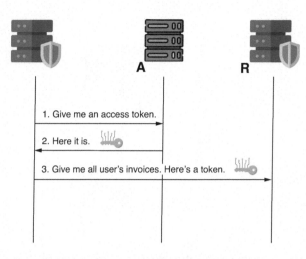

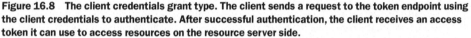

Figure 16.8 **The client credentials grant type. The client sends a request to the token endpoint using the client credentials to authenticate. After successful authentication, the client receives an access token it can use to access resources on the resource server side.**

Let's build a simple example to show you everything you need to know about implementing OAuth 2 client capabilities with Spring Security. We'll build an app that uses the client credentials grant type to get an access token from an authorization server. This app will get an access token from an authorization server. To simplify the example, we'll only discuss retrieving the access token. It's irrelevant for our demonstration of how you create the request. As long as you know how to get an access token, you can send the HTTP request either way, as any technology allows you to easily add a request header value (remember that you add the access token value to the Authorization request header prefixed with the string "Bearer").

So what we'll precisely do in this example is configure an app to retrieve an access token from an OAuth 2 authorization server using the client credentials grant type. To prove that we correctly retrieved the access token, we'll return it in the response body of a demo endpoint. Figure 16.9 illustrates what we want to build. The steps shown in the figure are the following:

1 The user (you) calls a demo endpoint we named /token using cURL (or an alternative tool like Postman).
2 The tool (cURL) that simulates an app sends the request to the application we build for this example.
3 Our application uses the client credentials grant type to retrieve an access token from an authorization server.
4 The app returns the access token's value to the client in the HTTP response body.
5 The user (you) finds the access token value in the HTTP response body.

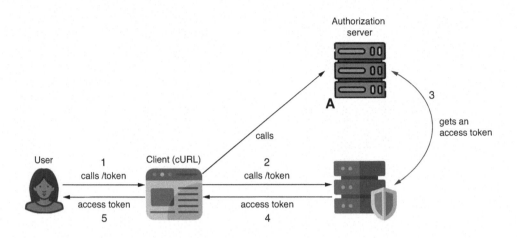

Figure 16.9   Our demonstration builds an app capable of retrieving an access token from an authorization server using the client credentials grant type. To prove that the app correctly retrieved the access token, the app sends the token value in response to a demo endpoint call. We named this demo endpoint /token.

We'll use the same authorization server you built in chapter 14, which you can find for this chapter in project ssia-ch16-ex1-as. Remember to first add to the authorization server a client registration that allows using the client credentials grant type. You can change the one you configured previously in chapter 14 (as presented in the next listing) or add a second client registration that fulfills this requirement.

Listing 16.7   The client details registered on the authorization server side

```
@Bean
public RegisteredClientRepository registeredClientRepository() {
  var registeredClient = RegisteredClient
    .withId(UUID.randomUUID().toString())
    .clientId("client")
    .clientSecret("secret")
    .clientAuthenticationMethod(
      ClientAuthenticationMethod.CLIENT_SECRET_BASIC)
    .authorizationGrantType(
      AuthorizationGrantType.CLIENT_CREDENTIALS)
    .scope(OidcScopes.OPENID)
    .build();

    return new InMemoryRegisteredClientRepository(registeredClient);
  }
```

> Adding a client registration that allows the use of the client credentials grant type

Similarly to other authentication methods, Spring Security offers a method of the HttpSecurity object to configure an app as an OAuth 2 client. Call the oauth2Client() method presented in the following listing to configure the app as an OAuth 2 client.

Listing 16.8 Configuring OAuth 2 client authentication

```
@Configuration
public class ProjectConfig {

  @Bean
  public SecurityFilterChain securityFilterChain(HttpSecurity http)
    throws Exception {

    http.oauth2Client(Customizer.withDefaults());

    http.authorizeHttpRequests(
        c -> c.anyRequest().permitAll()
    );

    return http.build();
  }

}
```

Using the oauth2Client() authentication method makes this app an OAuth 2 client.

The app also needs to know some details to send the authorization server the requests for access tokens. As you learned in section 16.1, we provide these details using a ClientRegistrationRepository component. You might find the code in listing 16.9 familiar, as it resembles the code we wrote in listing 16.4.

However, because I don't use a common provider, I had to specify more details, such as the scope, the token URI, and the authentication method. Observe that I configured client credentials as a grant type.

Listing 16.9 Configuring the client registration details for the client app

```
@Configuration
public class ProjectConfig {

  // Omitted code

  @Bean
  public ClientRegistrationRepository clientRegistrationRepository() {
    ClientRegistration c1 =
      ClientRegistration.withRegistrationId("1")
        .clientId("client")
        .clientSecret("secret")
        .authorizationGrantType(AuthorizationGrantType.CLIENT_CREDENTIALS)
        .clientAuthenticationMethod(
            ClientAuthenticationMethod.CLIENT_SECRET_BASIC)
        .tokenUri("http://localhost:7070/oauth2/token")
        .scope(OidcScopes.OPENID)
        .build();

    var repository =
        new InMemoryClientRegistrationRepository(c1);

    return repository;
  }

}
```

A client manager component makes the required request for obtaining an access token. Figure 16.10 illustrates the relationship between the controller and the client manager (for our example).

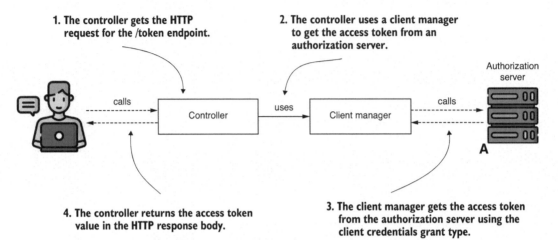

1. The controller gets the HTTP request for the /token endpoint.

2. The controller uses a client manager to get the access token from an authorization server.

Authorization server

calls · · · · · · · · · · · · → [Controller] uses [Client manager] calls · · · · · · · · · →

A

4. The controller returns the access token value in the HTTP response body.

3. The client manager gets the access token from the authorization server using the client credentials grant type.

Figure 16.10   The controller uses a client manager to get the access token from an authorization server. The client manager is the Spring Security component responsible for connecting to the authorization server and properly using the grant type to get the access token.

The class `OAuth2AuthorizedClientManager` defines a client manager. The next listing configures a client manager as a bean in the app's context.

Listing 16.10   Implementing an OAuth 2 client manager

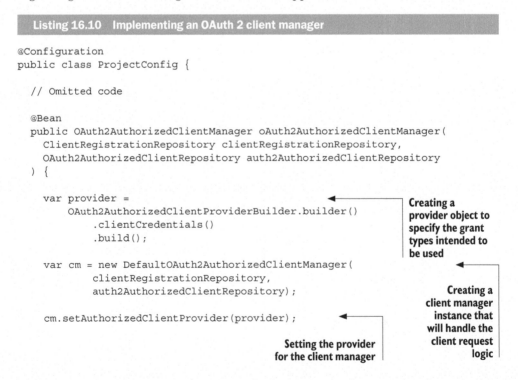

```
@Configuration
public class ProjectConfig {

    // Omitted code

    @Bean
    public OAuth2AuthorizedClientManager oAuth2AuthorizedClientManager(
        ClientRegistrationRepository clientRegistrationRepository,
        OAuth2AuthorizedClientRepository auth2AuthorizedClientRepository
    ) {

        var provider =
            OAuth2AuthorizedClientProviderBuilder.builder()
                .clientCredentials()
                .build();

        var cm = new DefaultOAuth2AuthorizedClientManager(
            clientRegistrationRepository,
            auth2AuthorizedClientRepository);

        cm.setAuthorizedClientProvider(provider);
```

Creating a provider object to specify the grant types intended to be used

Creating a client manager instance that will handle the client request logic

Setting the provider for the client manager

```
        return cm;
    }
}
```

You can now use the client manager wherever you need to get an access token. As shown in figure 16.10, I made the controller use the client manager directly to simplify this example and allow you to focus on the discussion about implementing an OAuth 2 client. Remember that a real-world app would probably be more complex. In a design that correctly segregates the object's responsibilities, the client manager would likely be used by a proxy object and not directly by a controller (figure 16.11).

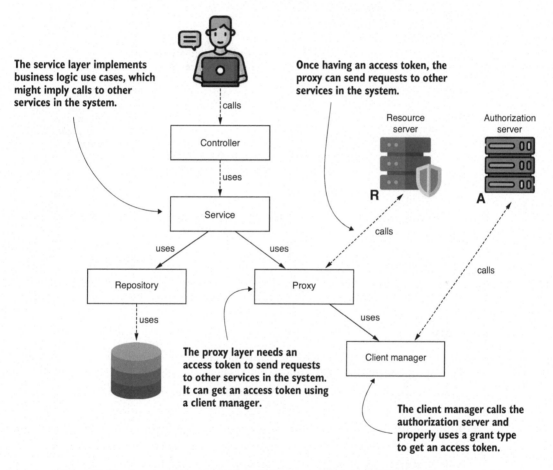

The service layer implements business logic use cases, which might imply calls to other services in the system.

Once having an access token, the proxy can send requests to other services in the system.

The proxy layer needs an access token to send requests to other services in the system. It can get an access token using a client manager.

The client manager calls the authorization server and properly uses a grant type to get an access token.

Figure 16.11 A real-world app would have better-separated responsibilities. Unlike our example, a proxy layer uses the token it obtains with the help of a client manager to send requests to another app in the system.

The next listing shows how to inject the client manager instance and demonstrates the retrieval of an access token using an endpoint. When calling the /token endpoint that the app exposes, the response body should contain the access token value.

Listing 16.11   Using the OAuth 2 client manager to get a token

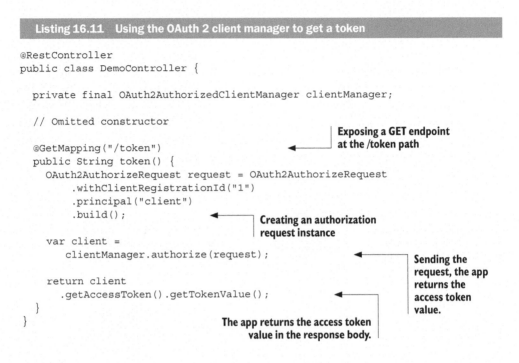

```
@RestController
public class DemoController {

  private final OAuth2AuthorizedClientManager clientManager;

  // Omitted constructor

  @GetMapping("/token")                           Exposing a GET endpoint
  public String token() {                         at the /token path
    OAuth2AuthorizeRequest request = OAuth2AuthorizeRequest
        .withClientRegistrationId("1")
        .principal("client")
        .build();                                 Creating an authorization
                                                  request instance
    var client =
        clientManager.authorize(request);         Sending the
                                                  request, the app
    return client                                 returns the
        .getAccessToken().getTokenValue();        access token
  }                                               value.
}                    The app returns the access token
                     value in the response body.
```

Use the following cURL command to call the endpoint that the app exposes:

```
curl http://localhost:8080/token
```

The response body should contain the value of an access token, similar to

```
eyJhbGciOiJIUzI1NiIsInR5cCI6IkpXVCJ9.eyJzdWIiOiIxMjM0NTY3ODkwIiwibmFtZSI6Im
JpbGwiLCJpYXQiOjE1MTYyMzkwMjJ9.zjL2JXw0TVgNgTMUKmP0-PTPklULUVmV_5re50eZoHw
```

Summary

- When implementing a Spring web app, we must often configure authentication capabilities. While we can implement a login form quickly with the `formLogin()` method, we can also allow users to authenticate using another system with a registered account.

- Allowing users to choose a different system to log in offers advantages for both the user and our app. The users don't need to remember supplementary credentials, and our app doesn't have to manage credentials for all their users.

- Spring Security considers GitHub, Google, Facebook, and Okta common providers. For the common providers, Spring Security already knows all the details to establish requests over the OAuth 2 framework, so you only need to configure the client credentials the provider offers to configure the login capability.

- You can configure your app to use providers other than the common ones, but you need to explicitly configure all the details the app needs to establish the grant type flows to get access tokens. The main details you need to configure are three URIs: the authorization, the token, and the key set URI.

- Once the user logs into your app, even if it is authenticated through an external system, the app gets details about them, storing the details in the security context. This process follows the standard Spring Security authentication design. For this reason, you can configure authorization similarly to all the other authentication methods.

- Sometimes, a backend service becomes a client for another backend app. In such a case, an app that wants to call another app and use an OAuth 2 approach needs to get an access token to be authenticated by the latter. A service can use the client credentials grant type to get an access token.

- Spring Security provides an object called a client manager. This object implements the logic for executing a specific grant type and getting an access token. An app's proxy layer that sends requests to another app and needs to authenticate the requests using access tokens would use a client manager to get the access token.

Part 5

Going reactive

With the gravitation of the software industry toward more responsive and efficient applications, reactive programming has emerged as a compelling paradigm. In this part of the book, you'll be guided through the nuances of implementing security within reactive applications, balancing responsiveness with robust protection.

Chapter 17 discusses the concept of reactive apps, laying the foundation for understanding their distinctive nature. The chapter will lead you through user management intricacies in a reactive environment, elaborating on configuring precise authorization rules, both at the endpoint layer and through method security. Furthermore, you'll gain insight into crafting a reactive OAuth 2 resource server, combining the best of both the reactive and security worlds.

By the culmination of this part, you'll be equipped to incorporate security seamlessly into your reactive applications, ensuring they remain agile without compromising user protection.

Implementing security in reactive applications

This chapter covers

- Using Spring Security with reactive applications
- Using reactive apps in a system designed using OAuth 2 authentication

Reactive is a programming paradigm where we apply a different way of thinking when developing our applications. Reactive programming is a powerful way of developing web apps that has gained wide acceptance. I would even say that it became fashionable a few years ago, when any important conference had at least several presentations discussing reactive apps. However, like any other technology in software development, reactive programming is not a solution applicable to every situation.

In some cases, a reactive approach is an excellent fit. In other cases, it might only complicate your life. But in the end, the reactive approach exists because it addresses some limitations of imperative programming and is thus used to avoid such limitations. One of them involves executing large tasks that can be fragmented. With an imperative approach, you give the application a task to execute, and the application has the responsibility to solve it. If the task is large, it might take a substantial amount of time for the application to solve it. The client who assigned the task needs to wait for the task to be entirely solved before receiving a response. With reactive programming, you can divide the task so that the app has the opportunity to approach some of the subtasks simultaneously. This way, the client receives the processed data faster.

347

This chapter discusses application-level security in reactive applications with Spring Security. Like with any other application, security is an important aspect of reactive apps. However, because reactive apps are designed differently, Spring Security has adapted the way we implement features discussed previously in this book.

We'll start with a short overview of implementing reactive apps with the Spring framework in section 17.1. Then we'll apply the security features you learned throughout this book on security apps. In section 17.2, we'll discuss user management in reactive apps, and in section 17.3, we'll continue applying authorization rules. Finally, in section 17.4, you'll learn how to implement reactive applications in a system designed over OAuth 2. You'll learn what changes from the Spring Security perspective when it comes to reactive applications, and of course, you'll learn how to apply this through examples.

17.1   *What are reactive apps?*

In this section, we briefly discuss reactive apps. This chapter is about applying security for reactive apps, so here, I want to make sure you grasp the essentials of reactive apps before going deeper into Spring Security configurations. Because the topic of reactive applications is big, I only review the main aspects of reactive apps as a refresher. If you aren't yet aware of how reactive apps work, or you need to understand them in more detail, I recommend you read part 3 of *Spring in Action, Sixth Edition,* by Craig Walls (Manning, 2022).

When we implement apps, we use two ways to implement the functionalities. The following list elaborates on these approaches:

- *With the imperative approach, your app processes the bulk of your data all at once.* For example, a client app calls an endpoint exposed by the server and sends all the data that needs to be processed to the backend. Say you implement a functionality where the user uploads files. If the user selects a number of files, and all of these are received by the backend app to be processed at once, you're working with an imperative approach.

- *With the reactive approach, your app receives and processes the data in fragments.* Not all the data has to be fully available from the beginning to be processed. The backend receives and processes data as it gets it. Say the user selects some files, and the backend needs to upload and process them. The backend doesn't wait to receive all the files at once before processing. The backend might receive the files one by one and process each while waiting for more files to come.

Figure 17.1 presents an analogy for the two programming approaches. Imagine a factory bottling milk. If the factory gets all the milk in the morning and delivers the milk once it finishes the bottling, we say it's non-reactive (imperative). If the factory gets the milk throughout the day and delivers the orders once it finishes bottling enough milk, we say it's reactive. Clearly, for the milk factory, it's more advantageous to use a reactive approach rather than a non-reactive one.

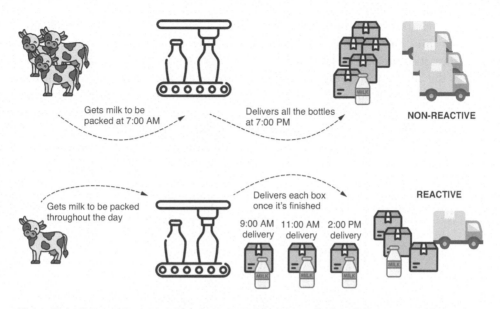

Figure 17.1 Non-reactive vs. reactive. In a non-reactive approach, the milk factory gets all the milk to be packaged in the morning and delivers all the boxes in the evening. In a reactive approach, as the milk is brought to the factory, it's packaged and then delivered. For this scenario, a reactive approach is better as it allows milk to be collected throughout the day and delivered sooner to the clients.

For implementing reactive apps, the Reactive Streams specification (http://www.reactive -streams.org/) provides a standard way for asynchronous stream processing. One of the implementations of this specification is the Project Reactor, which builds the foundations of Spring's reactive programming model. Project Reactor provides a functional API for composing Reactive Streams.

To get a more hands-on feeling, let's start a simple implementation of a reactive app. We'll continue further with this same application in section 17.2 when discussing user management in reactive apps. I created a new project named ssia-ch17-ex1, and we'll develop a reactive web app that exposes a demo endpoint. In the pom.xml file, we must add the reactive web dependency as presented in the following code snippet. This dependency houses the Project Reactor and enables us to use its related classes and interfaces in our project:

```
<dependency>
    <groupId>org.springframework.boot</groupId>
    <artifactId>spring-boot-starter-webflux</artifactId>
</dependency>
```

Next, we define a simple `HelloController` to hold the definition of our demo endpoint. Listing 17.1 shows the definition of the `HelloController` class. In the endpoint definition, you'll observe I used a `Mono` as a return type. `Mono` is one of the essential concepts defined by a Reactor implementation. When working with Reactor, you often use `Mono` and `Flux`, both defining publishers (sources of data). In the Reactive Streams specification, a publisher is described by the `Publisher` interface. This interface describes one of the essential contracts used with Reactive Streams. The other contract is the `Subscriber`. This contract describes the component consuming the data.

When designing an endpoint that returns something, the endpoint becomes a publisher, so it has to return a `Publisher` implementation. If using Project Reactor, this will be a `Mono` or a `Flux`. `Mono` is a publisher for a single value, while `Flux` is a publisher for multiple values. Figure 17.2 describes these components and the relationships among them.

The `Publisher` interface is the contract defined by the Reactive Streams specification to represent the entity that produces values.

Any reactive stream needs at least a subscriber. The `Subscriber` interface of the Reactive Streams specification defines the contract that any subscriber needs to implement.

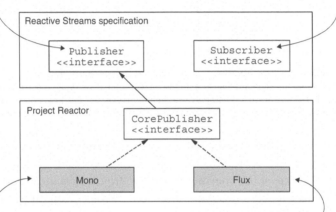

Mono is an implementation of `Publisher`, from Project Reactor, representing a stream with zero or one value.

Flux is an implementation of `Publisher`, from Project Reactor, representing a stream with zero or more values.

Figure 17.2   In a reactive stream, a publisher produces values, and a subscriber consumes them. Contracts defined by the Reactive Streams specification describe publishers and subscribers. Project Reactor implements the Reactive Streams specification and implements the `Publisher` and `Subscriber` contracts. In the figure, the components we use in the examples in this chapter are shaded.

To make this explanation even more precise, let's go back to the milk factory analogy. The milk factory is a reactive backend implementation that exposes an endpoint to receive the milk to be processed. This endpoint produces something (bottled milk), so it needs to return a `Publisher`. If more than one bottle of milk is requested, then the milk factory needs to return a `Flux`, which is Project Reactor's `Publisher` implementation that deals with zero or more produced values.

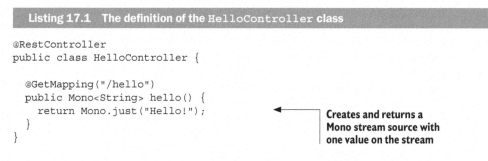

Listing 17.1 The definition of the `HelloController` class

```
@RestController
public class HelloController {

  @GetMapping("/hello")
  public Mono<String> hello() {
    return Mono.just("Hello!");
  }
}
```

Creates and returns a
Mono stream source with
one value on the stream

You can now start and test the application. The first thing you observe by looking in the app's terminal is that Spring Boot doesn't configure a Tomcat server anymore. Spring Boot used to configure a Tomcat for a web application by default, and you may have observed this aspect in any of the examples developed previously in this book. Instead, Spring Boot now autoconfigures Netty as the default reactive web server for a Spring Boot project.

The second thing you may have observed when calling the endpoint is that it doesn't behave differently from an endpoint developed with a non-reactive approach. You can still find in the HTTP response body the `Hello!` message that the endpoint returns in its defined `Mono` stream. The next code snippet presents the app's behavior when calling the endpoint:

```
curl http://localhost:8080/hello
```

The response body is

```
Hello!
```

But why is the reactive approach different in terms of Spring Security? Behind the scenes, a reactive implementation uses multiple threads to solve the tasks on the stream. In other words, it changes the philosophy of one-thread-per-request, which we use for a web app designed with an imperative approach (figure 17.3). And from here, there are more differences:

- The `SecurityContext` implementation doesn't work the same way in reactive applications. Remember, the `SecurityContext` is based on a `ThreadLocal`, and now we have more than one thread per request.
- Because of the `SecurityContext`, any authorization configuration is now affected. Remember from chapter 5 that the authorization rules generally rely on the `Authentication` instance stored in the `SecurityContext`. Now the security configurations applied at the endpoint layer, as well as the global method security functionality, are affected.
- The `UserDetailsService`, the component responsible for retrieving the user details, is a data source. Because of this, the user details service also needs to support a reactive approach. (We learned about this contract in chapter 2.)

In a non-reactive web app, a thread is allocated for each request.
Thus, we always know that within the same thread, we always work with tasks for the same request.
For this reason, the app manages the security context per thread.

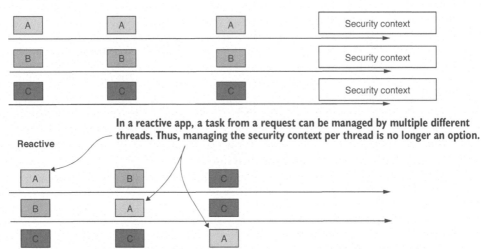

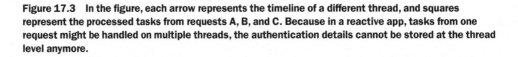

Figure 17.3   In the figure, each arrow represents the timeline of a different thread, and squares represent the processed tasks from requests A, B, and C. Because in a reactive app, tasks from one request might be handled on multiple threads, the authentication details cannot be stored at the thread level anymore.

Figure 17.4 presents another way to see this approach. Imagine a team of people working on a set of tasks. Each can take a task and leave it when they are blocked. It's not always the same thread that will continue the task that has been left over. So the security context can't be addressed to a thread anymore, but it must somehow be linked to the task.

Fortunately, Spring Security offers support for reactive apps and covers all cases where you can't use the implementations for non-reactive apps anymore. We'll continue in this chapter by discussing the way you implement security configurations with Spring Security for reactive apps. We'll start in section 17.2 with implementing user management and continue in section 17.3 with applying endpoint authorization rules, where we'll find out how security context works in reactive apps. We'll then continue our discussion with reactive method security, which replaces the global method security of imperative apps.

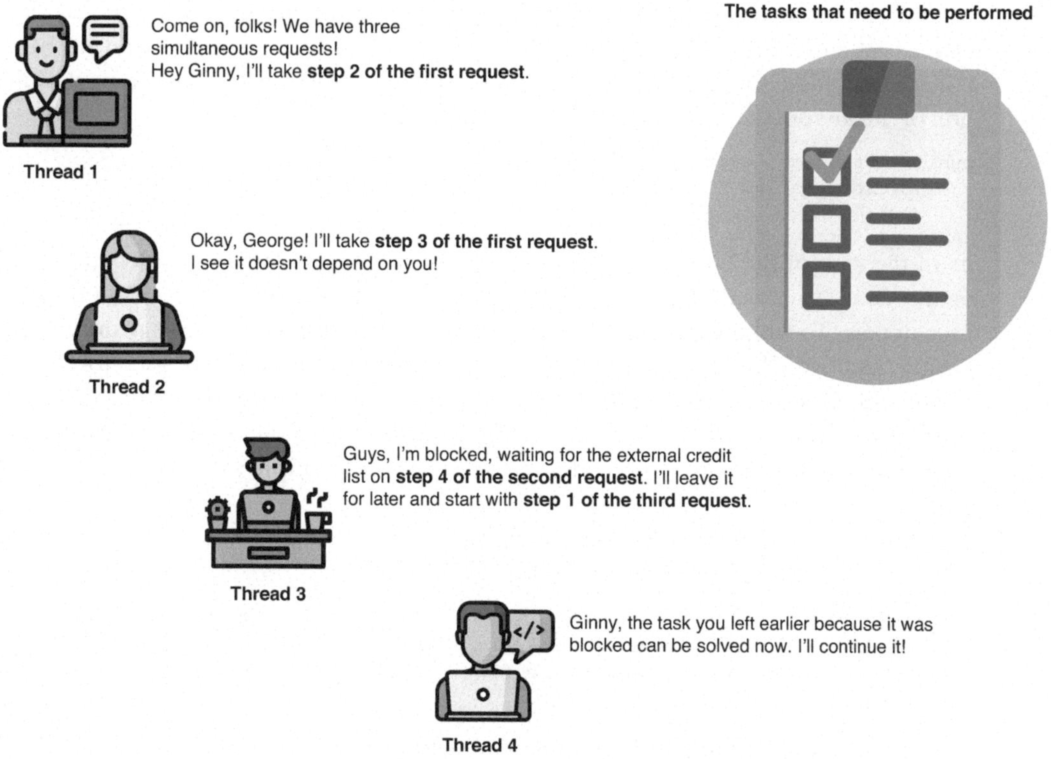

Come on, folks! We have three simultaneous requests!
Hey Ginny, I'll take **step 2 of the first request**.

Thread 1

The tasks that need to be performed

Okay, George! I'll take **step 3 of the first request**.
I see it doesn't depend on you!

Thread 2

Guys, I'm blocked, waiting for the external credit list on **step 4 of the second request**. I'll leave it for later and start with **step 1 of the third request**.

Thread 3

Ginny, the task you left earlier because it was blocked can be solved now. I'll continue it!

Thread 4

Figure 17.4   An analogy of the way a reactive app works. A thread doesn't take a request's tasks in order and wait when it's blocked. Instead, all tasks from all requests are on a backlog. Any available thread can work on tasks from any request. This way, independent tasks can be solved in parallel, and the threads don't stay idle.

17.2   *User management in reactive apps*

Often in applications, the way a user authenticates is based on a pair of username and password credentials. This approach is basic, and we've discussed it, starting with the most straightforward application we implemented in chapter 2. But with reactive apps, the implementation of the component taking care of user management changes as well. In this section, we discuss implementing user management in a reactive app.

We continue the implementation of the ssia-ch17-ex1 application we started in section 17.1 by adding a ReactiveUserDetailsService to the context of the application. We want to make sure the /hello endpoint can be called only by an authenticated user. As its name suggests, the ReactiveUserDetailsService contract defines the user details service for a reactive app.

The definition of the contract is as simple as the one for UserDetailsService. The ReactiveUserDetailsService defines a method used by Spring Security to retrieve a user by its username. The difference is that the method described by the ReactiveUserDetailsService directly returns a Mono<UserDetails> and not the UserDetails like for UserDetailsService. The next code snippet shows the definition of the ReactiveUserDetailsService interface:

```
public interface ReactiveUserDetailsService {
  Mono<UserDetails> findByUsername(String username);
}
```

As in the case of the UserDetailsService, you can write a custom implementation of the ReactiveUserDetailsService to give Spring Security a way to obtain the user details. To simplify this demonstration, we use an implementation provided by Spring Security. The MapReactiveUserDetailsService implementation stores the user details in memory (the same as with the InMemoryUserDetailsManager that you learned about in chapter 2). We change the pom.xml file of the ssia-ch17-ex1 project and add the Spring Security dependency, as the next code snippet shows:

```
<dependency>
  <groupId>org.springframework.boot</groupId>
  <artifactId>spring-boot-starter-security</artifactId>
</dependency>
<dependency>
  <groupId>org.springframework.boot</groupId>
  <artifactId>spring-boot-starter-webflux</artifactId>
</dependency>
```

We then create a configuration class and add a ReactiveUserDetailsService and a PasswordEncoder to the Spring Security context. I named the configuration class ProjectConfig. You can find the definition of this class in listing 17.2. Using a ReactiveUserDetailsService, we define one user with its username john, the password 12345, and an authority I named read. As you can observe, it's similar to working with a UserDetailsService. The main difference in the implementation of the ReactiveUserDetailsService is that the method returns a reactive Publisher object containing the UserDetails instead of the UserDetails instance itself. Spring Security takes the rest of the duty of integration.

Listing 17.2 The ProjectConfig class

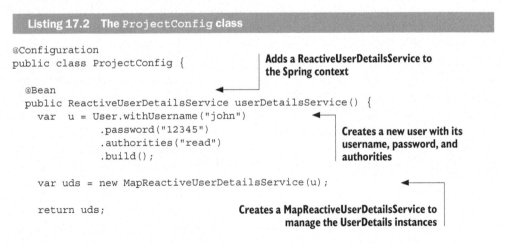

```
@Configuration
public class ProjectConfig {                      Adds a ReactiveUserDetailsService to
                                                  the Spring context
  @Bean
  public ReactiveUserDetailsService userDetailsService() {
    var  u = User.withUsername("john")
                 .password("12345")              Creates a new user with its
                 .authorities("read")            username, password, and
                 .build();                       authorities

    var uds = new MapReactiveUserDetailsService(u);

    return uds;                         Creates a MapReactiveUserDetailsService to
                                        manage the UserDetails instances
```

```
}

@Bean
public PasswordEncoder passwordEncoder() {
  return NoOpPasswordEncoder.getInstance();
}
}
```

Adds a PasswordEncoder to the Spring context

Now, when starting and testing the application, you might notice that you can call the endpoint only when you authenticate using the proper credentials. In our case, we can only use john with its password 12345, as it's the only user record we added. The following code snippet shows the behavior of the app when calling the endpoint with valid credentials:

```
curl -u john:12345 http://localhost:8080/hello
```

The response body is

```
Hello!
```

Figure 17.5 explains the architecture we use in this application. Behind the scenes, an AuthenticationWebFilter intercepts the HTTP request. This filter delegates the authentication responsibility to an authentication manager. The authentication manager implements the ReactiveAuthenticationManager contract. Unlike non-reactive apps, we don't have authentication providers. The ReactiveAuthenticationManager directly implements the authentication logic.

The AuthenticationWebFilter intercepts the HTTP request and delegates the authentication responsibility to an authentication manager.

For a reactive app, the authentication manager implements the ReactiveAuthenticationManager contract.

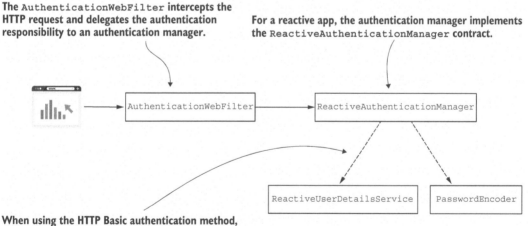

When using the HTTP Basic authentication method, the ReactiveAuthenticationManager uses a ReactiveUserDetailsService to get the user details and a PasswordEncoder to verify the password.

Figure 17.5 An AuthenticationWebFilter intercepts the request and delegates the authentication responsibility to a ReactiveAuthenticationManager. If the authentication logic involves users and passwords, the ReactiveAuthenticationManager uses a ReactiveUserDetailsService to find the user details and a PasswordEncoder to verify the password.

If you want to create your own custom authentication logic, implement the Reactive-AuthenticationManager interface. The architecture for reactive apps is not much different from the one for non-reactive applications that we already discussed throughout this book. As presented in figure 17.4, if authentication involves user credentials, then we use a ReactiveUserDetailsService to obtain the user details and a Password-Encoder to verify the password.

Moreover, the framework still knows to inject an authentication instance when you request it. You request the Authentication details by adding Mono<Authentication> as a parameter to the method in the controller class. Listing 17.3 presents the changes done to the controller class. Again, the significant change is that you use reactive publishers. Observe that we need to use Mono<Authentication> instead of the plain Authentication like we did in non-reactive apps.

Listing 17.3   The HelloController class

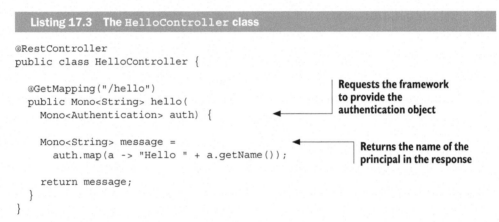

```
@RestController
public class HelloController {

  @GetMapping("/hello")
  public Mono<String> hello(                          Requests the framework
    Mono<Authentication> auth) {                      to provide the
                                                       authentication object

    Mono<String> message =                            Returns the name of the
      auth.map(a -> "Hello " + a.getName());          principal in the response

    return message;
  }
}
```

Rerunning the application and calling the endpoint, you observe the behavior is as presented in the next code snippet:

```
curl -u john:12345 http://localhost:8080/hello
```

The response body is

```
Hello john
```

And now you're probably wondering, Where did the Authentication object come from? Being that this is a reactive app, we can't afford to use a ThreadLocal anymore because the framework is designed to manage the SecurityContext. But Spring Security offers us a different implementation of the context holder for reactive apps, ReactiveSecurityContextHolder. We use this to work with the SecurityContext in a reactive app. So we still have the SecurityContext, but now it's managed differently. Figure 17.6 describes the end of the authentication process once the Reactive-AuthenticationManager successfully authenticates the request.

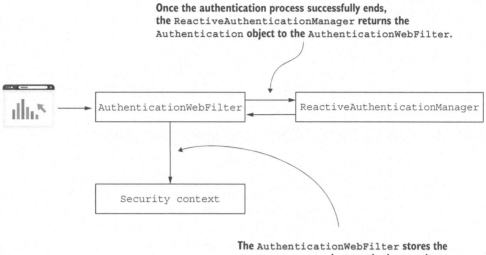

Once the authentication process successfully ends,
the ReactiveAuthenticationManager returns the
Authentication object to the AuthenticationWebFilter.

The AuthenticationWebFilter stores the
Authentication instance in the security
context, where it'll be used for authorization.

Figure 17.6 Once the ReactiveAuthenticationManager successfully authenticates the request, it returns the Authentication object to the filter. The filter stores the Authentication instance in the SecurityContext.

Listing 17.4 shows you how to rewrite the controller class if you want to get the authentication details directly from the security context. This approach is an alternative to allowing the framework to inject it through the method's parameter. You'll find this change implemented in project ssia-ch17-ex2.

Listing 17.4 Working with a ReactiveSecurityContextHolder

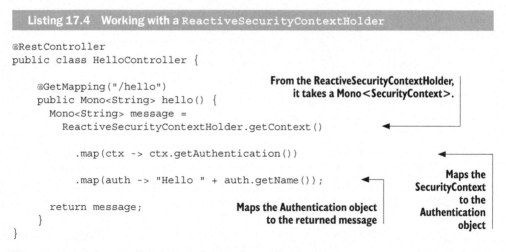

```
@RestController
public class HelloController {

    @GetMapping("/hello")                              From the ReactiveSecurityContextHolder,
    public Mono<String> hello() {                        it takes a Mono<SecurityContext>.
      Mono<String> message =
        ReactiveSecurityContextHolder.getContext()

          .map(ctx -> ctx.getAuthentication())                       Maps the
                                                                  SecurityContext
          .map(auth -> "Hello " + auth.getName());                    to the
                                                                  Authentication
      return message;           Maps the Authentication object       object
    }                             to the returned message
}
```

If you rerun the application and test the endpoint again, you can observe that it behaves the same as in the previous examples of this section. Here's the command:

```
curl -u john:12345 http://localhost:8080/hello
```

The response body is

```
Hello john
```

Now that you know Spring Security offers an implementation to properly manage the `SecurityContext` in a reactive environment, you know this is how your app applies the authorization rules. And these details that you just learned open the way to configuring the authorization rules, which we'll discuss in section 17.3.

17.3 Configuring authorization rules in reactive apps

In this section, we discuss configuring authorization rules. As you already know from the previous chapters, authorization follows authentication. We discussed in sections 17.1 and 17.2 how Spring Security manages users and the `SecurityContext` in reactive apps. But once the app finishes authentication and stores the details of the authenticated request in the `SecurityContext`, it's time for authorization.

As for any other application, you probably need to configure authorization rules when developing reactive apps as well. To teach you how to set authorization rules in reactive apps, we'll discuss first in section 17.3.1 the way you make configurations at the endpoint layer. Once we finish discussing authorization configuration at the endpoint layer, you'll learn in section 17.3.2 how to apply it at any other layer of your application using method security.

17.3.1 Applying authorization at the endpoint layer in reactive apps

In this section, we discuss configuring authorization at the endpoint layer in reactive apps. Setting the authorization rules in the endpoint layer is the most common approach for configuring authorization in a web app. You already discovered this while working on the previous examples in this book. Authorization configuration at the endpoint layer is essential—you use it in almost every app. Thus, you need to know how to apply it for reactive apps as well.

You learned from previous chapters to set the authorization rules by adding a bean of type `SecurityFilterChain` to the app's context. This approach doesn't work in reactive apps. To teach you how to configure authorization rules for the endpoint layer properly for reactive apps, we start by working on a new project, which I named ssia-ch17-ex3.

In reactive apps, Spring Security uses a contract named `SecurityWebFilterChain` to apply the configurations we used to do by using a bean of type `SecurityFilterChain`, as discussed in previous chapters. With reactive apps, we add a bean of type `SecurityWebFilterChain` in the Spring context. To teach you how to do this, let's implement a basic application having two endpoints that we secure independently. In the pom.xml file of our newly created ssia-ch17-ex3 project, add the dependencies for reactive web apps and, of course, Spring Security:

```
<dependency>
    <groupId>org.springframework.boot</groupId>
    <artifactId>spring-boot-starter-security</artifactId>
</dependency>
```

```
<dependency>
  <groupId>org.springframework.boot</groupId>
  <artifactId>spring-boot-starter-webflux</artifactId>
</dependency>
```

Create a controller class to define the two endpoints for which we configure the authorization rules. These endpoints are accessible at the paths /hello and /ciao. To call the /hello endpoint, a user needs to authenticate, but you can call the /ciao endpoint without authentication. The following listing presents the definition of the controller.

Listing 17.5 The `HelloController` class defining the endpoints to secure

```
@RestController
public class HelloController {

  @GetMapping("/hello")
  public Mono<String> hello(Mono<Authentication> auth) {
    Mono<String> message = auth.map(a -> "Hello " + a.getName());
    return message;
  }

  @GetMapping("/ciao")
  public Mono<String> ciao() {
    return Mono.just("Ciao!");
  }
}
```

In the configuration class, we make sure to declare a `ReactiveUserDetailsService` and a `PasswordEncoder` to define a user, as you learned in section 17.2. The following listing defines these declarations.

Listing 17.6 The configuration class declaring components for user management

```
@Configuration
public class ProjectConfig {

  @Bean
  public ReactiveUserDetailsService userDetailsService() {
    var  u = User.withUsername("john")
            .password("12345")
            .authorities("read")
            .build();

    var uds = new MapReactiveUserDetailsService(u);

    return uds;
  }

  @Bean
  public PasswordEncoder passwordEncoder() {
    return NoOpPasswordEncoder.getInstance();
  }

  // ...
}
```

In listing 17.7, we work in the same configuration class we declared in listing 17.6, but omit the declaration of the `ReactiveUserDetailsService` and the `Password-Encoder` so that you can focus on the authorization configuration we discuss. In listing 17.7, you might notice that we add a bean of type `SecurityWebFilterChain` to the Spring context. The method receives as a parameter an object of type `ServerHttp-Security`, which is injected by Spring. `ServerHttpSecurity` enables us to build an instance of `SecurityWebFilterChain`. `ServerHttpSecurity` provides methods for configuration similar to the ones you used when configuring authorization for non-reactive apps.

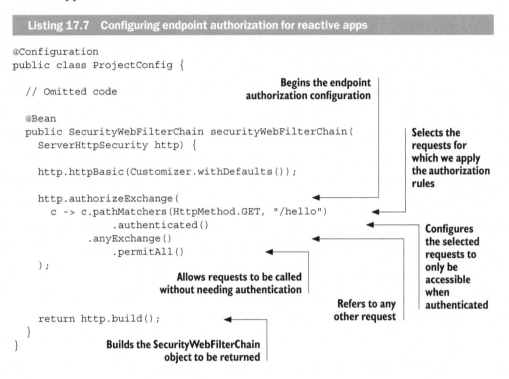

Listing 17.7   Configuring endpoint authorization for reactive apps

```
@Configuration
public class ProjectConfig {

    // Omitted code                          Begins the endpoint
                                         authorization configuration

    @Bean
    public SecurityWebFilterChain securityWebFilterChain(          Selects the
        ServerHttpSecurity http) {                                requests for
                                                                  which we apply
        http.httpBasic(Customizer.withDefaults());                the authorization
                                                                  rules
        http.authorizeExchange(
          c -> c.pathMatchers(HttpMethod.GET, "/hello")
                   .authenticated()                               Configures
                 .anyExchange()                                   the selected
                   .permitAll()                                   requests to
        );                                                        only be
                       Allows requests to be called               accessible
                       without needing authentication             when
                                              Refers to any       authenticated
                                              other request
        return http.build();
    }
    }                  Builds the SecurityWebFilterChain
}                       object to be returned
```

We start the authorization configuration with the `authorizeExchange()` method. We call this method similarly to the way we call the `authorizeHttpRequests()` method when configuring endpoint authorization for non-reactive apps. Then we continue by using the `pathMatchers()` method. You can consider this method as the equivalent of using `requestMatchers()` when configuring endpoint authorization for non-reactive apps.

As for non-reactive apps, once we use the matcher method to group requests to which we apply the authorization rule, we then specify what the authorization rule is. In our example, we called the `authenticated()` method, which states that only authenticated requests are accepted. You also used a method named `authenticated()` when configuring endpoint authorization for non-reactive apps. The methods for reactive apps are named the same to make them more intuitive. Similarly to the `authenticated()` method, you can also call these methods:

- `permitAll()`—Configures the app to allow requests without authentication
- `denyAll()`—Denies all requests
- `hasRole()` *and* `hasAnyRole()`—Apply rules based on roles
- `hasAuthority()` *and* `hasAnyAuthority()`—Apply rules based on authorities

It looks like something's missing, doesn't it? Do we also have an `access()` method like we had for configuring authorization rules in non-reactive apps? Yes. But it's a bit different, so we'll work on a separate example to prove it. Another similarity in naming is the `anyExchange()` method that takes the role of what used to be `anyRequest()` in non-reactive apps.

> **NOTE** Why is it called `anyExchange()`, and why didn't the developers keep the same name for the method `anyRequest()`? Why `authorizeExchange()` and why not `authorizeHttpRequests()`? This difference stems from the terminology used with reactive apps. We generally refer to communication between two components in a reactive fashion as *exchanging data*. This reinforces the image of data being sent as segmented in a continuous stream and not as a big bunch in one request.

We also need to specify the authentication method like any other related configuration. We do this with the same `ServerHttpSecurity` instance, using methods with the same name and in the same fashion you learned to use for non-reactive apps: `httpBasic()`, `formLogin()`, `csrf()`, `cors()`, adding filters and customizing the filter chain, and so on. In the end, we call the `build()` method to create the instance of `SecurityWebFilterChain`, which we finally return to add to the Spring context.

I told you earlier in this section that you can also use the `access()` method in the endpoint authorization configuration of reactive apps just as you can for non-reactive apps. But as I said when discussing the configuration of non-reactive apps in chapters 7 and 8, use the `access()` method only when you can't apply your configuration otherwise. The `access()` method offers you great flexibility, but also makes your app's configuration more difficult to read. Always prefer the simpler solution over the more complex one. However, you'll find situations in which you need this flexibility. For example, suppose you have to apply a more complex authorization rule, and using `hasAuthority()` or `hasRole()` and its companion methods isn't enough. For this reason, I'll also teach you how to use the `access()` method. I created a new project named ssia-ch17-ex4 for this example. In the next listing, you can see how I built the `SecurityWebFilterChain` object to allow access to the /hello path only if the user has the admin role. Also, access can be allowed only before noon. For all other endpoints, I restrict access completely.

Listing 17.8   Using the `access()` method when implementing configuration rules

```
@Configuration
public class ProjectConfig {

  // Omitted code

  @Bean
  public SecurityWebFilterChain
    securityWebFilterChain(ServerHttpSecurity http) {

    http.httpBasic(Customizer.withDefaults());

    http.authorizeExchange(
      c -> c.anyExchange()
              .access(this::getAuthorizationDecisionMono)

    );

    return http.build();
  }

  private Mono<AuthorizationDecision>
    getAuthorizationDecisionMono(
          Mono<Authentication> a,
          AuthorizationContext c) {

    String path = getRequestPath(c);

    boolean restrictedTime =
      LocalTime.now().isAfter(LocalTime.NOON);

    if(path.equals("/hello")) {
      return  a.map(isAdmin())
                .map(auth -> auth && !restrictedTime)
                .map(AuthorizationDecision::new);
    }

    return Mono.just(new AuthorizationDecision(false));
  }

  // Omitted code
}
```

For any request, it applies a custom authorization rule.

The method defining the custom authorization rule receives the Authentication and the request context as parameters.

From the context, it obtains the path of the request.

For the /hello path, it applies the custom authorization rule.

It might look difficult, but it's not that complicated. When you use the `access()` method, you provide a function receiving all possible details about the request, which are the `Authentication` object and the `AuthorizationContext`. Using the `Authentication` object, you have the details of the authenticated user: username, roles or authorities, and other custom details depending on how you implement the authentication logic. The `AuthorizationContext` provides the information on the request: the path, headers, query params, cookies, and so on.

The function you provide as a parameter to the `access()` method should return an object of type `AuthorizationDecision`. As you guessed, `AuthorizationDecision` is the answer that tells the app whether the request is allowed. When you create an instance with `new AuthorizationDecision(true)`, it means that you allow the request. If you create it with `new AuthorizationDecision(false)`, it means you disallow the request.

In listing 17.9, you find the two methods I omitted in listing 17.8 for your convenience: `getRequestPath()` and `isAdmin()`. By omitting these, I let you focus on the logic used by the `access()` method. As you can observe, the methods are simple. The `isAdmin()` method returns a function that returns true for an `Authentication` instance having the `ROLE_ADMIN` attribute. The `getRequestPath()` method simply returns the path of the request.

> **Listing 17.9 The definition of the `getRequestPath()` and `isAdmin()` methods**

```
@Configuration
public class ProjectConfig {

  // Omitted code

  private String getRequestPath(AuthorizationContext c) {
    return c.getExchange()
            .getRequest()
            .getPath()
            .toString();
  }

  private Function<Authentication, Boolean> isAdmin() {
    return p ->
      p.getAuthorities().stream()
        .anyMatch(e -> e.getAuthority().equals("ROLE_ADMIN"));
  }
}
```

Running the application and calling the endpoint either result in a response status 403 Forbidden if any of the authorization rules we applied aren't fulfilled or simply display a message in the HTTP response body:

```
curl -u john:12345 http://localhost:8080/hello
```

The response body is

```
Hello john
```

What happened behind the scenes in the examples in this section? When authentication ended, another filter intercepted the request. The `AuthorizationWebFilter` delegates the authorization responsibility to a `ReactiveAuthorizationManager` (figure 17.7).

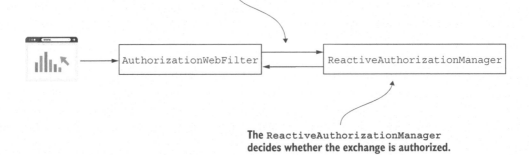

Once authentication ends, the `AuthorizationWebFilter` intercepts the HTTP request and delegates the authorization responsibility to a `ReactiveAuthorizationManager`.

The `ReactiveAuthorizationManager` decides whether the exchange is authorized.

Figure 17.7   After the authentication process successfully ends, another filter, named `AuthorizationWebFilter`, intercepts the request. This filter delegates the authorization responsibility to a `ReactiveAuthorizationManager`.

Wait! Does this mean we only have a `ReactiveAuthorizationManager`? How does this component know how to authorize a request based on the configurations we made? To answer the first question: no, there are actually multiple implementations of the `ReactiveAuthorizationManager`. The `AuthorizationWebFilter` uses the `SecurityWebFilterChain` bean we added to the Spring context. With this bean, the filter decides which `ReactiveAuthorizationManager` implementation to delegate the authorization responsibility to (figure 17.8).

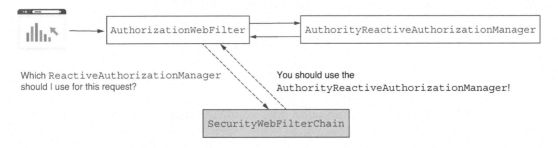

Which `ReactiveAuthorizationManager` should I use for this request?

You should use the `AuthorityReactiveAuthorizationManager`!

Figure 17.8   The `AuthorizationFilter` uses the `SecurityWebFilterChain` bean (shaded) that we added to the context to know which `ReactiveAuthorizationManager` to use.

17.3.2 *Using method security in reactive apps*

In this section, we discuss applying authorization rules for all layers of reactive apps. For non-reactive apps, we used method security, and in chapters 11 and 12, you learned different approaches to applying authorization rules at the method level. Being able to apply authorization rules at layers other than the endpoint layer offers you great flexibility and enables you to apply authorization for non-web applications. To teach you how to use method security for reactive apps, we work on a separate example, which I named ssia-ch17-ex5.

Instead of global method security, when working with non-reactive apps, we call the approach *reactive* method security, where we apply authorization rules directly at the method level. For our example, we use @PreAuthorize to validate that a user has a specific role to call a test endpoint. To keep the example simple, we use the @PreAuthorize annotation directly over the method defining the endpoint. But you can use it the same way we discussed in chapters 11 and 12 for non-reactive apps: on any other component method in your reactive application. Listing 17.10 shows the definition of the controller class. Observe that we use @PreAuthorize, similar to what you learned in chapter 11. Using SpEL expressions, we declare that only an admin can call the annotated method.

Listing 17.10 The definition of the controller class

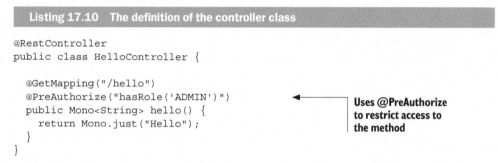

```
@RestController
public class HelloController {

  @GetMapping("/hello")
  @PreAuthorize("hasRole('ADMIN')")          ◄─── Uses @PreAuthorize
  public Mono<String> hello() {                    to restrict access to
    return Mono.just("Hello");                      the method
  }
}
```

Here you find the configuration class in which we use the annotation @Enable-ReactiveMethodSecurity to enable the reactive method security feature. Similar to the method security, we need to explicitly use an annotation to enable it. Besides this annotation, in the configuration class, you also find the usual user management definition.

Listing 17.11 The configuration class

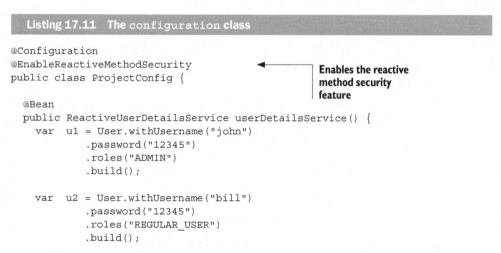

```
@Configuration
@EnableReactiveMethodSecurity          ◄─── Enables the reactive
public class ProjectConfig {                method security
                                            feature
  @Bean
  public ReactiveUserDetailsService userDetailsService() {
    var  u1 = User.withUsername("john")
             .password("12345")
             .roles("ADMIN")
             .build();

    var  u2 = User.withUsername("bill")
             .password("12345")
             .roles("REGULAR_USER")
             .build();
```

```
      var uds = new MapReactiveUserDetailsService(u1, u2);

      return uds;
  }

  @Bean
  public PasswordEncoder passwordEncoder() {
    return NoOpPasswordEncoder.getInstance();
  }
}
```

You can now start the application and test the behavior of the endpoint by calling it for each user. You should observe that only John can call the endpoint because we defined him as the admin. Bill is just a regular user, so if we try to call the endpoint authenticating as Bill, we get back a response with the status HTTP 403 Forbidden. Calling the /hello endpoint authenticating with user John looks like this:

```
curl -u john:12345 http://localhost:8080/hello
```

The response body is

```
Hello!
```

Calling the /hello endpoint authenticating with user Bill looks like this:

```
curl -u bill:12345 http://localhost:8080/hello
```

The response body is

```
Access Denied
```

Behind the scenes, this functionality works the same as for non-reactive apps. In chapters 11 and 12, you learned that an aspect intercepts the call to the method and implements the authorization. If the call doesn't fulfill the specified preauthorization rules, the aspect doesn't delegate the call to the method (figure 17.9).

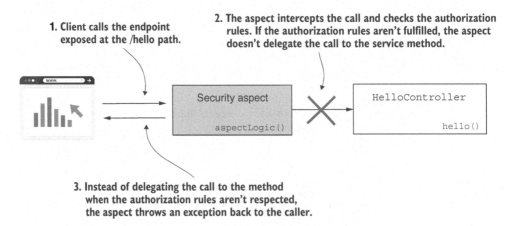

1. Client calls the endpoint exposed at the /hello path.

2. The aspect intercepts the call and checks the authorization rules. If the authorization rules aren't fulfilled, the aspect doesn't delegate the call to the service method.

Security aspect

aspectLogic()

HelloController

hello()

3. Instead of delegating the call to the method when the authorization rules aren't respected, the aspect throws an exception back to the caller.

Figure 17.9   When using method security, an aspect intercepts the call to a protected method. If the call doesn't fulfill the preauthorization rules, the aspect doesn't delegate the call to the method.

17.4 *Creating a reactive OAuth 2 resource server*

You're probably wondering by now if we could use reactive applications in a system designed over the OAuth 2 framework. In this section, we discuss implementing a resource server as a reactive app. You learn how to configure your reactive application to rely on an authentication approach implemented over OAuth 2. Because using OAuth 2 is so common nowadays, you might encounter requirements where your resource server application needs to be designed as a reactive server. I created a new project named ssia-ch17-ex6, and we'll implement a reactive resource server application. You need to add the dependencies in pom.xml, as the next code snippet illustrates:

```
<dependency>
  <groupId>org.springframework.boot</groupId>
  <artifactId>spring-boot-starter-webflux</artifactId>
</dependency>
<dependency>
  <groupId>org.springframework.boot</groupId>
  <artifactId>spring-boot-starter-security</artifactId>
</dependency>
<dependency>
  <groupId>org.springframework.cloud</groupId>
  <artifactId>spring-cloud-starter-oauth2</artifactId>
</dependency>
<dependency>
  <groupId>org.springframework.boot</groupId>
  <artifactId>spring-boot-starter-oauth2-resource-server</artifactId>
</dependency>
```

We need an endpoint to test the application, so we add a controller class. The next code snippet presents the controller class:

```
@RestController
public class HelloController {

  @GetMapping("/hello")
  public Mono<String> hello() {
    return Mono.just("Hello!");
  }
}
```

And now the most important part of the example: the security configuration. For this example, we configure the resource server to use the public key exposed by the authorization server for token signature validation.

To configure the authentication method, we use the `SecurityWebFilterChain`, as you learned about in section 17.3. However, instead of using the `httpBasic()` method, we call the `oauth2ResourceServer()` method. Then, by calling the `jwt()` method, we define the kind of token we use, and by using a `Customizer` object, we specify the way the token signature is validated. In the next listing, you can find the definition of the `configuration` class.

Listing 17.12   Defining the security web filter chain configuration

```
@Configuration
public class ProjectConfig {

  @Value("${jwk.endpoint}")
  private String jwkEndpoint;

  @Bean
  public SecurityWebFilterChain securityWebFilterChain(
    ServerHttpSecurity http) {

    http.oauth2ResourceServer(
        c -> c.jwt(
            j -> j.jwkSetUri(jwkEndpoint);
        )
    );


    http.authorizeExchange(
        c -> c.anyExchange().authenticated()

    );

    return http.build();
  }
}
```

Configures the resource server authentication method

Specifies the way the token is validated

In the same way, we could've configured the public key instead of specifying an URI where the public key is exposed. The only change was to call the publicKey() method of the jwtSpec instance and provide a valid public key as a parameter. You can use any of the approaches we discussed in chapter 13, where we analyzed in detail approaches for the resource server to validate the access token.

Next, we change the application.properties file to add the value for the URI where the key set is exposed, as well as change the server port to 9090. This way, we allow the authorization server to run on 8080. In the next code snippet, you'll find the contents of the application.properties file:

```
server.port=9090
jwk.endpoint=http://localhost:8080/
↪auth/realms/master/protocol/openid-connect/certs
```

Let's run and prove that the app has the expected behavior that we want. We generate an access token using the authorization server:

```
curl -XPOST 'http://localhost:8080/auth/
↪realms/master/protocol/openid-connect/token' \
-H 'Content-Type: application/x-www-form-urlencoded' \
--data-urlencode 'grant_type=password' \
--data-urlencode 'username=bill' \
--data-urlencode 'password=12345' \
--data-urlencode 'client_id=fitnessapp' \
--data-urlencode 'scope=fitnessapp'
```

In the HTTP response body, we receive the access token as presented here:

```
{
    "access_token": "eyJhbGciOiJSUzI1NiIsInR5cCI…",
    "expires_in": 6000,
    "refresh_expires_in": 1800,
    "refresh_token": "eyJhbGciOiJIUzI1NiIsInR5c… ",
    "token_type": "bearer",
    "not-before-policy": 0,
    "session_state": "610f49d7-78d2-4532-8b13-285f64642caa",
    "scope": "fitnessapp"
}
```

Using the access token, we call the /hello endpoint of our application like this:

```
curl -H 'Authorization:
BearereyJhbGciOiJSUzI1NiIsInR5cCIgOiAiSldUIiwia2lkIiA6ICJMSE9zT0VRSmJuTmJVb
jhQbVpYQTlUVW9QNTZoWU90YzNWT2swa1V2ajVVIn…' \
'http://localhost:9090/hello'
```

The response body is

```
Hello!
```

Summary

- Reactive applications have a different style for processing data and exchanging messages with other components. Reactive apps might be a better choice in some situations, like when we can split the data into separate smaller segments for processing and exchanging.

- Like with any other application, you also need to protect reactive apps by using security configurations. Spring Security offers an excellent set of tools you can use to apply security configurations for reactive apps, as well as for non-reactive ones.

- To implement user management in reactive apps with Spring Security, we use the ReactiveUserDetailsService contract. This component has the same purpose as UserDetailsService for non-reactive apps: it tells the app how to get the user details.

- To implement the endpoint authorization rules for a reactive web application, you need to create an instance of type SecurityWebFilterChain and add it to the Spring context. You create the SecurityWebFilterChain instance by using the ServerHttpSecurity builder.

- Generally, the names of the methods you use to define the authorization configurations are the same as for the methods you use for non-reactive apps. However, you'll find minor naming differences related to the reactive terminology. For example, instead of using authorizeHttpRequests(), the name of its counterpart for reactive apps is authorizeExchange().

- Spring Security also provides a way to define authorization rules at the method level, called reactive method security, and it offers great flexibility in applying the authorization rules at any layer of a reactive app. It is similar to what we call global method security for non-reactive apps.

Part 6

Testing security configurations

In the world of software development, testing stands as the gatekeeper of quality, ensuring that every piece of code not only functions as intended, but also integrates seamlessly with other components. This is especially pivotal when dealing with security configurations, such as those offered by Spring Security. This part of the book is dedicated to instilling best practices for integration testing with Spring Security, ensuring that your applications adhere to the security guidelines you've set.

Chapter 18, the last chapter of this book, serves as a comprehensive guide to validating your security settings. Here you'll explore the realms of mock user testing, delve into the nuances of the `@WithMockUser` annotation, and understand how to validate managed users. The chapter extends its scope to testing method security, authentications, and the unique challenges posed by testing reactive implementations.

By the conclusion of this part, you'll have acquired the skillset to rigorously test the security layers of your application, ensuring a fortified deployment ready to stand against potential vulnerabilities.

Testing security configurations

The legend says that writing unit and integration tests started with the following short verse:

99 little bugs in the code,

99 little bugs.

Track one down, patch it around,

There's 113 little bugs in the code.

—Anonymous

With time, software became more complex, and teams became larger. Knowing all the functionalities implemented over time by others became impossible. Developers needed a way to make sure they didn't break existing functionalities while correcting bugs or implementing new features.

While developing applications, we continuously write tests to validate that the functionalities we implement work as desired. The main reason why we write unit and integration tests is to ensure we don't break existing functionalities when changing code to fix a bug or to implement new features. This is also called *regression testing*.

Nowadays, when a developer finishes making a change, they upload the changes to a server used by the team to manage code versioning. This action automatically triggers a continuous integration tool that runs all existing tests. If any of the changes break an existing functionality, the tests fail, and the continuous integration tool notifies the team (figure 18.1). This way, it's less likely to deliver changes affecting existing features.

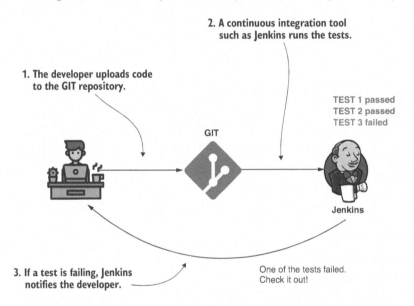

2. A continuous integration tool such as Jenkins runs the tests.

1. The developer uploads code to the GIT repository.

GIT

TEST 1 passed
TEST 2 passed
TEST 3 failed

Jenkins

3. If a test is failing, Jenkins notifies the developer.

One of the tests failed.
Check it out!

Figure 18.1 Testing is part of the development process. Anytime a developer uploads code, the tests run. If any test fails, a continuous integration tool notifies the developer.

> **NOTE** By using Jenkins in this figure, I'm not saying that this is the only continuous integration tool used or that it's the best one. You have many alternatives to choose from like Bamboo, GitLab CI, CircleCI, and so on.

When testing applications, you need to remember it's not only your application code that you need to test. You need to also make sure you test the integrations with the frameworks and libraries you use (figure 18.2). Sometime in the future, you may upgrade that framework or library to a new version. When changing the dependency version, you want to ensure your app still integrates well with the new version of that dependency. If your app doesn't integrate in the same way, you want to easily find where you need to make changes to correct the integration problems.

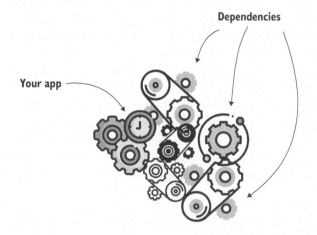

Figure 18.2 The functionality of an application relies on many dependencies. When you upgrade or change a dependency, you might affect existing functionality. Having integration tests with dependencies helps you to discover quickly if a change in a dependency affects the existing functionality of your application.

So that's why you need to know what we'll cover in this chapter—how to test your app's integration with Spring Security. Spring Security, like the Spring Framework ecosystem in general, evolves quickly. You probably upgrade your app to new versions, and you certainly want to know if upgrading to a specific version causes vulnerabilities, errors, or incompatibilities in your application. Remember what we stressed right from the first chapter: *you need to consider security from the first design for the app, and you need to take it seriously.* Implementing tests for any of your security configurations should be a mandatory task and should be defined as part of your definition of *done.* You shouldn't consider a task finished if security tests aren't ready.

In this chapter, we'll discuss several practices for testing an app's integration with Spring Security. We'll go back to some of the examples we worked on in previous chapters, and you'll learn how to write integration tests for implemented functionality. Testing, in general, is a crucial story. But learning this subject in detail brings many benefits.

In this chapter, we'll focus on testing integration between an application and Spring Security. Before starting our examples, I'd like to recommend a few resources that helped me understand this subject deeply. If you need to understand the subject in more detail, or even as a refresher, you can read these books. I am positive you'll find these a great help!

- *JUnit in Action, Third Edition* by Cătălin Tudose et al. (Manning, 2020)
- *Unit Testing Principles, Practices, and Patterns* by Vladimir Khorikov (Manning, 2020)
- *Testing Java Microservices* by Alex Soto Bueno et al. (Manning, 2018)

Our adventure in writing tests for security implementations starts with testing authorization configurations. In section 18.1, you'll learn how to skip authentication and define mock users to test authorization configuration at the endpoint level. Then, in section 18.2, you'll learn how to test authorization configurations with users from a UserDetailsService. In section 18.3, we'll discuss how to set up the full security context in case you need to use specific implementations of the Authentication object. And finally, in section 18.4, you'll apply the approaches you learned in the previous sections to test authorization configuration on method security.

Once we complete our discussion on testing authorization, section 18.5 will teach you how to test the authentication flow. Then, in sections 18.6 and 18.7, we'll discuss testing other security configurations, such as cross-site request forgery (CSRF) and cross-origin resource sharing (CORS). The chapter ends with section 18.8, discussing integration tests of Spring Security and reactive applications.

18.1 *Using mock users for tests*

This section discusses using mock users to test authorization configuration. This approach is the most straightforward and frequently used method for testing authorization configurations. When using a mock user, the test completely skips the authentication process (figure 18.3).

Implementing tests to skip authentication and focus on authorization is very common. You don't need to validate the authentication process every time you validate that the system correctly applies an authorization rule. Remember that authentication and authorization depend on one another, but they are completely decoupled through the security context. So if you want to test an authorization configuration in isolation, you can define a mock security context and control it to test all the needed authorization scenarios. Because in most cases an app implements only a limited number of authentication methods (in most cases, actually, one) but has a large variety of authorization rules that apply to use cases or endpoints, you'll prefer to write authorization tests in isolation so you don't have to repeat the authentication tests every time you validate that authorization for a specific element works fine.

The mock user is valid only for the test execution, and for this user, you can configure any characteristics you need to validate a specific scenario. For example, you can give the user specific roles (ADMIN, MANAGER, etc.) or use different authorities to validate that the app behaves as expected in these conditions.

> **NOTE** It's important to know which components from the framework are involved in an integration test. This way, you know which part of the integration you cover with the test. For example, a mock user can only be used to cover authorization. (In section 18.5, you'll learn how to deal with authentication.) I sometimes see developers getting confused by this aspect. They thought they were also covering, for example, a custom implementation of an AuthenticationProvider when working with a mock user, which is not the case. Make sure you correctly understand what you're testing.

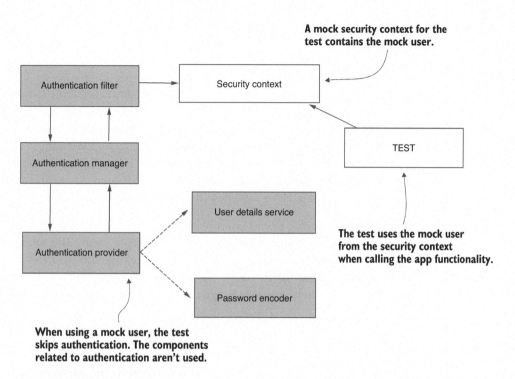

A mock security context for the test contains the mock user.

The test uses the mock user from the security context when calling the app functionality.

When using a mock user, the test skips authentication. The components related to authentication aren't used.

Figure 18.3 We skip the shaded components in the Spring Security authentication flow when executing a test. The test directly uses a mock `SecurityContext`, **which contains the mock user you define to call the tested functionality.**

To prove how to write such a test, let's go back to the simplest example we worked on in this book, the project ssia-ch2-ex1. This project exposes an endpoint for the path /hello with only the default Spring Security configuration. What do we expect to happen?

- When calling the endpoint without a user, the HTTP response status should be 401 Unauthorized.
- When calling the endpoint having an authenticated user, the HTTP response status should be 200 OK, and the response body should be `Hello!`.

Let's test these two scenarios! We need a couple of dependencies in the pom.xml file to write the tests. The next code snippet shows you the classes we use throughout the examples in this chapter. You should make sure you have these in your pom.xml file before starting to write the tests. Here are the dependencies:

```
<dependency>
    <groupId>org.springframework.boot</groupId>
    <artifactId>spring-boot-starter-test</artifactId>
    <scope>test</scope>
</dependency>
<dependency>
```

```
    <groupId>org.springframework.security</groupId>
    <artifactId>spring-security-test</artifactId>
    <scope>test</scope>
</dependency>
```

NOTE   For the examples in this chapter, we use JUnit 5 for writing tests. However, don't be discouraged if you still work with JUnit 4. From the Spring Security integration point of view, the annotations and the rest of the classes you'll learn work the same. Chapter 4 of *JUnit in Action* by Cătălin Tudose et al. (Manning, 2020), which is a dedicated discussion about migrating from JUnit 4 to JUnit 5, contains some interesting tables that show the correspondence between classes and annotations of versions 4 and 5. Here's the link: http://mng.bz/OPJn.

In the test folder of the Spring Boot Maven project, we add a class named `MainTests`. We write this class as part of the main package of the application. The name of the main package is `com.laurentiuspilca.ssia`. In the next listing, you can find the definition of the empty class for the tests. We use the `@SpringBootTest` annotation, which represents a convenient way to manage the Spring context for our test suite.

Listing 18.1   A class for writing the tests

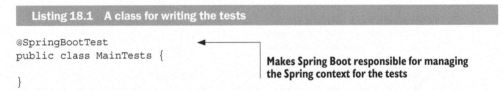

```
@SpringBootTest
public class MainTests {

}
```

Makes Spring Boot responsible for managing the Spring context for the tests

A convenient way to implement a test for the behavior of an endpoint is by using Spring's MockMvc. In a Spring Boot application, you can autoconfigure the MockMvc utility for testing endpoint calls by adding an annotation over the class, as the next listing illustrates.

Listing 18.2   Adding `MockMvc` for implementing test scenarios

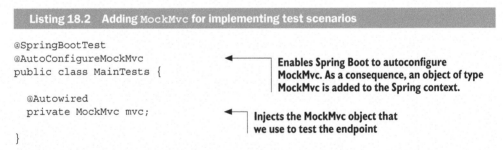

```
@SpringBootTest
@AutoConfigureMockMvc
public class MainTests {

    @Autowired
    private MockMvc mvc;

}
```

Enables Spring Boot to autoconfigure MockMvc. As a consequence, an object of type MockMvc is added to the Spring context.

Injects the MockMvc object that we use to test the endpoint

Now that we have a tool we can use to test endpoint behavior, let's get started with the first scenario. When calling the /hello endpoint without an authenticated user, the HTTP response status should be 401 Unauthorized.

You can visualize the relationship between the components for running this test in figure 18.4. The test calls the endpoint but uses a mock `SecurityContext`. We decide what we add to this `SecurityContext`. For this test, we need to check that if we don't add a user that represents the situation in which someone calls the endpoint without authenticating, the app rejects the call with an HTTP response with the status 401 Unauthorized. When we add a user to the SecurityContext, the app accepts the call, and the HTTP response status is 200 OK.

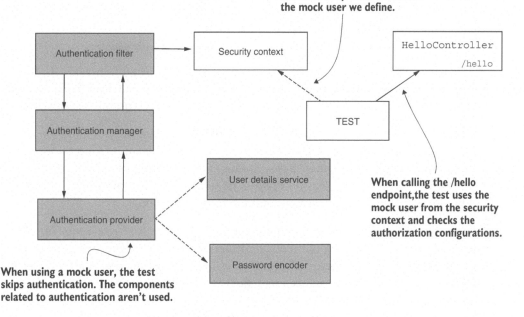

Figure 18.4 When running the test, we skip authentication. The test uses a mock SecurityContext and calls the /hello endpoint exposed by HelloController. We add a mock user in the test SecurityContext to verify that the behavior is correct according to the authorization rules. If we don't define a mock user, we expect the app to not authorize the call, but if we define a user, we expect that the call succeeds.

The following listing presents this scenario's implementation.

Listing 18.3 Testing that you can't call the endpoint without an authenticated user

```
@SpringBootTest
@AutoConfigureMockMvc
public class MainTests {

  @Autowired
  private MockMvc mvc;

  @Test
  public void helloUnauthenticated() throws Exception {
    mvc.perform(get("/hello"))
        .andExpect(status().isUnauthorized());
  }

}
```

When performing a GET request for the /hello path, we expect to get back a response with the status Unauthorized.

Note that we statically import the methods `get()` and `status()`. You can find the method `get()` and similar methods related to the requests we use in the examples of this chapter in this class:

```
org.springframework.test.web.servlet.request.MockMvcRequestBuilders
```

Likewise, you can find the method `status()` and similar methods related to the result of the calls that we use in the next examples of this chapter in this class:

```
org.springframework.test.web.servlet.result.MockMvcResultMatchers
```

You can run the tests now and see the status in your IDE. Usually, in any IDE, to run the tests, you can right-click on the test's class and then select Run. The IDE displays a successful test with green and a failing one with another color (usually red or yellow).

> **NOTE**   In the projects provided with the book, above each method implementing a test, I also use the `@DisplayName` annotation. This annotation allows us to have a longer, more detailed description of the test scenario. To occupy less space and allow you to focus on the functionality of the tests we discuss, I took the `@DisplayName` annotation out of the listings in the book.

To test the second scenario, we need a mock user. To validate the behavior of calling the /hello endpoint with an authenticated user, we use the `@WithMockUser` annotation. By adding this annotation above the test method, we instruct Spring to set up a `SecurityContext` that contains a `UserDetails` implementation instance. It's basically skipping authentication. Now calling the endpoint behaves as if the user defined by the `@WithMockUser` annotation successfully authenticated.

With this simple example, we don't care about the details of the mock user like its username, roles, or authorities. Thus, we add the `@WithMockUser` annotation, which provides some defaults for the mock user's attributes. Later in this chapter, you'll learn how to configure the user's attributes for test scenarios in which their values are important. The next listing provides the implementation for the second test scenario.

Listing 18.4   Using `@WithMockUser` to define a mock authenticated user

```
@SpringBootTest
@AutoConfigureMockMvc
public class MainTests {

    @Autowired
    private MockMvc mvc;

    // Omitted code                              Calls the method with a mock
                                                 authenticated user
    @Test
    @WithMockUser          ◄─────────────────┘
    public void helloAuthenticated() throws Exception {
      mvc.perform(get("/hello"))               ◄─────────┐

         In this case, when performing a GET
         request for the /hello path, we expect
         the response status to be OK.
```

```
      .andExpect(content().string("Hello!"))
      .andExpect(status().isOk());
  }

}
```

Run this test now, and observe its success. However, in some situations, we need to use a specific name or give the user specific roles or authorities to implement the test. Say we want to test the endpoints we defined in ssia-ch5-ex2. For this example, the endpoints return a body depending on the authenticated user's name. To write the test, we need to give the user a known username. The next listing shows how to configure the details of the mock user by writing a test for the /hello endpoint in the ssia-ch5-ex2 project.

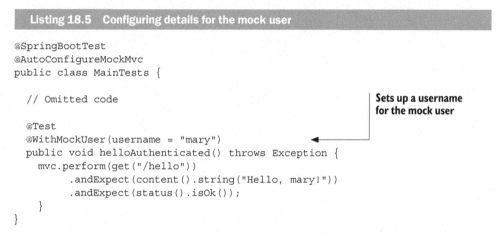

Listing 18.5 Configuring details for the mock user

```
@SpringBootTest
@AutoConfigureMockMvc
public class MainTests {

  // Omitted code
                                                       Sets up a username
                                                       for the mock user
  @Test
  @WithMockUser(username = "mary")        ◄──────────
  public void helloAuthenticated() throws Exception {
    mvc.perform(get("/hello"))
        .andExpect(content().string("Hello, mary!"))
        .andExpect(status().isOk());
  }
}
```

In figure 18.5, you find a comparison of how using annotations to define the test security environment differs from using a RequestPostProcessor. The framework interprets annotations such as @WithMockUser before it executes the test method. This way, the test method creates the test request and executes it in an already configured security environment. When using a RequestPostProcessor, the framework first calls the test method and builds the test request. The framework then applies the Request-PostProcessor, which alters the request or the environment in which it's executed before sending it. In this case, the framework configures the test dependencies, such as the mock users and the SecurityContext, after building the test request.

Like setting up the username, you can set the authorities and roles for testing authorization rules. An alternative approach to creating a mock user is using a Request-PostProcessor. We can provide a RequestPostProcessor the with() method, as listing 18.6 shows. The class SecurityMockMvcRequestPostProcessors provided by Spring Security offers us lots of implementations for RequestPostProcessor, which helps us cover various test scenarios.

In this chapter, we also discuss the frequently used implementations for Request-PostProcessor. The method user() of the class SecurityMockMvcRequest-PostProcessors returns a RequestPostProcessor we can use as an alternative to the @WithMockUser annotation.

Configuring the test security environment through annotations

An aspect intercepts the test method and configures the security context and the mock users according to the annotations you specified.

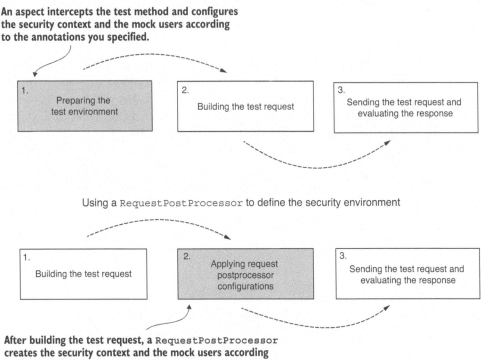

| 1. Preparing the test environment | 2. Building the test request | 3. Sending the test request and evaluating the response |

Using a `RequestPostProcessor` to define the security environment

| 1. Building the test request | 2. Applying request postprocessor configurations | 3. Sending the test request and evaluating the response |

After building the test request, a `RequestPostProcessor` creates the security context and the mock users according to the configurations you specified.

Figure 18.5   The difference between using annotations and the `RequestPostProcessor` to create the test security environment. When using annotations, the framework sets up the test security environment first. When using a `RequestPostProcessor`, the test request is created and then changed to define other constraints such as the test security environment. In the figure, the points where the framework applies the test security environment are shaded.

Listing 18.6   Using a `RequestPostProcessor` to define a mock user

```
@SpringBootTest
@AutoConfigureMockMvc
public class MainTests {

  // Omitted code

  @Test
  public void helloAuthenticatedWithUser() throws Exception {
    mvc.perform(
          get("/hello")
            .with(user("mary")))          ◄──── Calls the /hello endpoint
        .andExpect(content().string("Hello!"))       using a mock user with the
        .andExpect(status().isOk());                 username Mary
  }
}
```

As you observed in this section, writing tests for authorization configurations is fun and simple! Most of the tests you write for Spring Security integration with functionalities of your application are for authorization configurations. You might be wondering why we didn't test authentication as well. In section 18.5, we'll discuss testing authentication. However, in general, and as discussed earlier in this section, it makes sense to test authorization and authentication separately. Usually, an app has one way to authenticate users but might expose dozens of endpoints for which authorization is configured differently. That's why you test authentication separately with a handful of tests and then implement these individually for each authorization configuration for the endpoints. It's a loss of execution time to repeat authentication for each endpoint tested, as long as the logic doesn't change.

18.2   *Testing with users from a UserDetailsService*

This section discusses obtaining the user details for tests from a `UserDetailsService`. This approach is an alternative to creating a mock user. The difference is that this time, instead of creating a fake user, we need to get the user from a given `UserDetails-Service`. You use this approach if you want to also test integration with the data source from where your app loads the user details (figure 18.6).

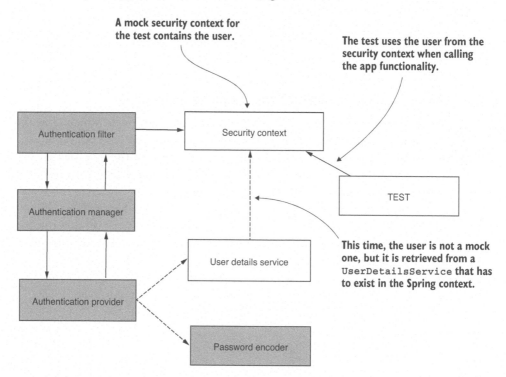

Figure 18.6   **Instead of creating a mock user for the test when building the** `SecurityContext` **used by the test, we take the user details from a** `UserDetailsService`. **This way, you can test authorization using real users taken from a data source. During the test, the flow of execution skips the shaded components.**

To demonstrate this approach, let's open project ssia-ch2-ex2 and implement the tests for the endpoint exposed at the /hello path. We use the `UserDetailsService` bean that the project already adds to the context. Note that with this approach, we need to have a `UserDetailsService` bean in the context. To specify the user we authenticate from this `UserDetailsService`, we annotate the test method with `@WithUser-Details`. With the `@WithUserDetails` annotation, to find the user, you specify the username. The following listing presents the implementation of the test for the /hello endpoint using the `@WithUserDetails` annotation to define the authenticated user.

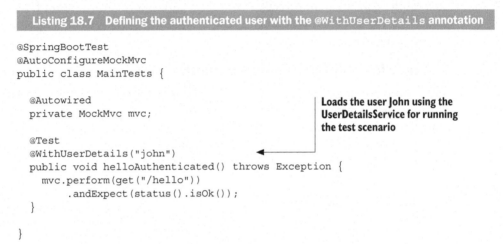

Listing 18.7   Defining the authenticated user with the `@WithUserDetails` annotation

```
@SpringBootTest
@AutoConfigureMockMvc
public class MainTests {

    @Autowired
    private MockMvc mvc;

    @Test
    @WithUserDetails("john")
    public void helloAuthenticated() throws Exception {
        mvc.perform(get("/hello"))
            .andExpect(status().isOk());
    }

}
```

Loads the user John using the UserDetailsService for running the test scenario

18.3   *Using custom Authentication objects for testing*

Generally, when using a mock user for a test, you don't care which class the framework uses to create the `Authentication` instances in the `SecurityContext`. But say you have some logic in the controller that depends on the type of the object. Can you somehow instruct the framework to create the `Authentication` object for the test using a specific type? The answer is yes, and this is what we discuss in this section.

The logic behind this approach is simple. We define a factory class responsible for building the `SecurityContext`. This way, we have full control over how the `Security-Context` for the test is built, including what's inside (figure 18.7). For example, we can choose to have a custom `Authentication` object.

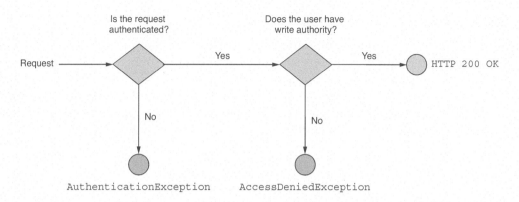

Figure 18.9 **The tested scenarios. If the HTTP request is not authenticated, the expected result is an** `AuthenticationException`**. If the HTTP request is authenticated, but the user doesn't have the expected authority, the expected result is an** `AccessDeniedException`**. If the authenticated user has the expected authority, the call is successful.**

Listing 18.12 **Implementation of the three test scenarios for the** `getName()` **method**

```
@SpringBootTest
class MainTests {

  @Autowired
  private NameService nameService;

  @Test
  void testNameServiceWithNoUser() {
    assertThrows(AuthenticationException.class,
            () -> nameService.getName());
  }

  @Test
  @WithMockUser(authorities = "read")
  void testNameServiceWithUserButWrongAuthority() {
    assertThrows(AccessDeniedException.class,
            () -> nameService.getName());
  }

  @Test
  @WithMockUser(authorities = "write")
  void testNameServiceWithUserButCorrectAuthority() {
    var result = nameService.getName();

    assertEquals("Fantastico", result);
  }
}
```

We don't configure `MockMvc` anymore because we don't need to call an endpoint. Instead, we directly inject the `NameService` instance to call the tested method. We use the `@WithMockUser` annotation, as discussed in section 18.1. Similarly, you could have used the `@WithUserDetails`, as discussed in section 18.2, or designed a custom way to build the `SecurityContext`, as discussed in section 18.3.

18.5 *Testing authentication*

In this section, we discuss testing authentication. Previously in this chapter, you learned how to define mock users and test authorization configurations. But what about authentication? Can we also test the authentication logic? You need to do this if, for example, you have custom logic implemented for your authentication, and you want to make sure the entire flow works. When testing authentication, the test implementation requests work like normal client requests, as presented in figure 18.10.

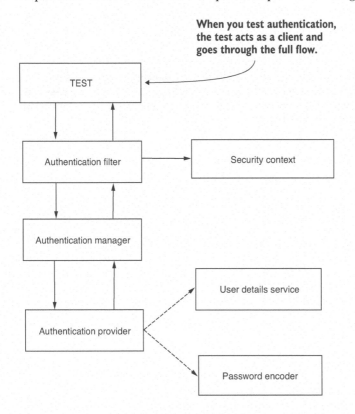

When you test authentication, the test acts as a client and goes through the full flow.

TEST

Authentication filter → Security context

Authentication manager

Authentication provider

User details service

Password encoder

Figure 18.10 When testing authentication, the test acts as a client and goes through the full Spring Security flow discussed throughout the book. This way, you can also test, for example, your custom `AuthenticationProvider` objects.

For example, going back to project ssia-ch2-ex4, can we prove that the custom authentication provider we implemented works correctly and secure it with tests? In this project, we implemented a custom `AuthenticationProvider`, and we want to ensure that we secure this custom authentication logic as well with tests. Yes, we can test the authentication logic too.

The logic we implement is straightforward. Only one set of credentials is accepted: the username "`john`" and the password "`12345`". We need to prove that when using valid credentials, the call is successful, whereas when using some other credentials, the

HTTP response status is 401 Unauthorized. Let's open project ssia-ch2-ex4 again and implement a couple of tests to validate that authentication behaves correctly.

Listing 18.13 **Testing authentication with `httpBasic() RequestPostProcessor`**

```
@SpringBootTest
@AutoConfigureMockMvc
public class AuthenticationTests {

  @Autowired
  private MockMvc mvc;

  @Test
  public void helloAuthenticatingWithValidUser() throws Exception {
    mvc.perform(
        get("/hello")
          .with(httpBasic("john","12345")))          ◄────┐ Authenticates with the
          .andExpect(status().isOk());                    │ correct credentials
  }

  @Test
  public void helloAuthenticatingWithInvalidUser() throws Exception {
    mvc.perform(
        get("/hello")
          .with(httpBasic("mary","12345")))          ◄────┐ Authenticates with the
          .andExpect(status().isUnauthorized());          │ wrong credentials
  }
}
```

Using the `httpBasic()` request postprocessor, we instruct the test to execute the authentication. This way, we validate the behavior of the endpoint when authenticating using either valid or invalid credentials. You can use the same approach to test the authentication with a form login. Let's open project ssia-ch6-ex4, where we used form login for authentication, and write some tests to prove authentication works correctly. We test the app's behavior in the following scenarios:

- When authenticating with an incorrect set of credentials
- When authenticating with a valid set of credentials, but when the user doesn't have a valid authority according to the implementation we wrote in the `AuthenticationSuccessHandler`
- When authenticating with a valid set of credentials and a user that has a valid authority according to the implementation we wrote in the `AuthenticationSuccessHandler`

In listing 18.14, you find the implementation for the first scenario. If we authenticate using invalid credentials, the app doesn't authenticate the user and adds the header `"failed"` to the HTTP response. We customized an app and added the `"failed"` header with an `AuthenticationFailureHandler` when discussing authentication back in chapter 6.

Listing 18.14   Testing form login-failed authentication

```
@SpringBootTest
@AutoConfigureMockMvc
public class MainTests {

  @Autowired
  private MockMvc mvc;

  @Test
  public void loggingInWithWrongUser() throws Exception {
    mvc.perform(formLogin()
          .user("joey").password("12345"))
          .andExpect(header().exists("failed"))
          .andExpect(unauthenticated());
  }
}
```

Authenticates using
form login with an
invalid set of
credentials

Back in chapter 6, we customized authentication logic using an Authentication-
SuccessHandler. In our implementation, if the user has read authority, the app redirects them to the /home page. Otherwise, the app redirects the user to the /error
page. The following listing presents the implementation of these two scenarios.

Listing 18.15   Testing app behavior when authenticating users

```
@SpringBootTest
@AutoConfigureMockMvc
public class MainTests {

  @Autowired
  private MockMvc mvc;

  // Omitted code

  @Test
  public void loggingInWithWrongAuthority() throws Exception {
    mvc.perform(formLogin()
              .user("bill").password("12345")
          )
          .andExpect(redirectedUrl("/error"))
          .andExpect(status().isFound())
          .andExpect(authenticated());
  }
```

When authenticating
with a user that doesn't
have read authority, the
app redirects the user to
path /error.

```
  @Test
  public void loggingInWithCorrectAuthority() throws Exception {
    mvc.perform(formLogin()
              .user("john").password("12345")
          )
          .andExpect(redirectedUrl("/home"))
          .andExpect(status().isFound())
          .andExpect(authenticated());
  }
}
```

When authenticating
with a user that has read
authority, the app
redirects the user to
path /home.

If the app is an OAuth 2/OpenID Connect resource server (chapter 15), you'll need a token to test authentication. A resource server might either use non-opaque JWTs or opaque tokens. Spring Security offers support for testing your app for both these approaches. Similarly to the `with(httpBasic())` method used earlier in this section, you can use a `with(jwt())` to configure a mock JWT token for your test or `with(opaqueToken())` to configure a mock opaque token for your test.

The following listing shows an example of a test you can find in project ssia-ch15-ex1. This test uses the `with(jwt())` approach to set a mock token for testing the authentication of a resource server.

> **Listing 18.16 Using a mock JWT to test a resource server's authentication**

```
@SpringBootTest
@AutoConfigureMockMvc
class ApplicationTests {

    @Autowired
    private MockMvc mockMvc;

  @Test
  void demoEndpointSuccessfulAuthenticationTest() throws Exception {
    mockMvc.perform(
        get("/demo").with(jwt()))          ◀── Configures a mock JWT
      .andExpect(status().isOk());              to test the authentication
  }                                             for a resource server
                                                using non-opaque tokens
}
```

Using this approach, you might also need to set some custom fields in the token, such as the authorities. You can use configuration methods following the `jwt()` method to specify custom authorities or even completely customize the JWT. The following code snippet shows how to specify custom authorities on the JWT. The code adds an authority named `"read"` to the mock token used in authentication:

```
jwt().authorities(() -> "read"))
```

A test similar to the one presented in listing 18.16, but for opaque tokens, can be found in project ssia-ch15-ex3. The following listing presents this test implementation.

> **Listing 18.17 Using a mock opaque token to test a resource server's authentication**

```
@SpringBootTest
@AutoConfigureMockMvc
class ApplicationTests {

  @Autowired
  private MockMvc mockMvc;

  @Test
  void demoEndpointSuccessfulAuthenticationTest() throws Exception {
    mockMvc.perform(
```

```
      get("/demo").with(opaqueToken()))
    .andExpect(status().isOk());
  }

}
```

◄─── **Using a mock opaque token to test the resource server's authentication**

Even with an opaque token, you might need to have specific authorities in the security context that results after authentication. You can control what authorities the authentication instance added into the security context will have. To do that, you can follow the `opaqueToken()` method with the `authorities()` configuration method as presented in the following snippet. The following code snippet configures an authority named `"read"` in the authentication instance that will be added to the test's security context:

```
opaqueToken().authorities(() -> "read")))
```

18.6   *Testing CSRF configurations*

In this section, we discuss testing the CSRF protection configuration for your application. When an app presents a CSRF vulnerability, an attacker can fool the user into taking actions they don't want to take once they're logged into the application. As discussed in chapter 9, Spring Security uses CSRF tokens to mitigate these vulnerabilities. This way, for any mutating operation (POST, PUT, DELETE), the request needs to have a valid CSRF token in its headers. Of course, at some point, you need to test more than HTTP GET requests. Depending on how you implement your application, as we discussed in chapter 9, you might need to test CSRF protection. You need to make sure it works as expected and protects the endpoint that implements mutating actions.

Fortunately, Spring Security provides an easy approach to test CSRF protection using a `RequestPostProcessor`. Let's open the project ssia-ch9-ex1 and test that CSRF protection is enabled for an endpoint /hello when called with HTTP POST in the following scenarios:

- If we don't use a CSRF token, the HTTP response status is 403 Forbidden.
- If we send a CSRF token, the HTTP response status is 200 OK.

The following listing shows the implementation of these two scenarios. Observe how we can send a CSRF token in the response simply by using the `csrf()` `RequestPostProcessor`.

Listing 18.18   Implementing the CSRF protection test scenarios

```
@SpringBootTest
@AutoConfigureMockMvc
public class MainTests {

  @Autowired
  private MockMvc mvc;

  @Test
  public void testHelloPOST() throws Exception {
```

```
mvc.perform(post("/hello"))
        .andExpect(status().isForbidden());
}
```

When calling the endpoint without a CSRF token, the HTTP response status is 403 Forbidden.

```
@Test
public void testHelloPOSTWithCSRF() throws Exception {
  mvc.perform(post("/hello").with(csrf()))
        .andExpect(status().isOk());
}
}
```

When calling the endpoint with a CSRF token, the HTTP response status is 200 OK.

18.7   Testing CORS configurations

This section discusses testing CORS configurations. As you learned in chapter 10, if a browser loads a web app from one origin (say, example.com), the browser won't allow the app to use an HTTP response that comes from a different origin (say, example.org). We use CORS policies to relax these restrictions. This way, we can configure our application to work with multiple origins. Of course, as for any other security configurations, you need to also test the CORS policies. In chapter 10, you learned that CORS is about specific headers on the response whose values define whether the HTTP response is accepted. Two of these headers related to CORS specifications are `Access-Control-Allow-Origin` and `Access-Control-Allow-Methods`. We used these headers in chapter 10 to configure multiple origins for our app.

When writing tests for the CORS policies, all we need to do is make sure that these headers (and maybe other CORS-related headers, depending on the complexity of your configurations) exist and have the correct values. For this validation, we can act precisely as the browser does when making a preflight request. We make a request using the HTTP OPTIONS method, requesting the value for the CORS headers. Let's open project ssia-ch10-ex1 and write a test to validate the values for the CORS headers. The following listing shows the definition of the test.

Listing 18.19   Test implementation for CORS policies

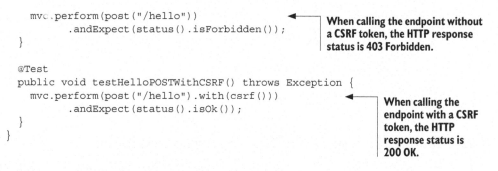

```
@SpringBootTest
@AutoConfigureMockMvc
public class MainTests {

    @Autowired
    private MockMvc mvc;

    @Test
    public void testCORSForTestEndpoint() throws Exception {
      mvc.perform(options("/test")
              .header("Access-Control-Request-Method", "POST")
              .header("Origin", "http://www.example.com")
      )
```

Performs an HTTP OPTIONS request on the endpoint requesting the value for the CORS headers

Validates the values for the headers according to the configuration we made in the app

```
              .andExpect(header().exists("Access-Control-Allow-Origin"))
              .andExpect(header().string("Access-Control-Allow-Origin", "*"))
              .andExpect(header().exists("Access-Control-Allow-Methods"))
              .andExpect(header().string("Access-Control-Allow-Methods", "POST"))
              .andExpect(status().isOk());
    }

}
```

18.8 *Testing reactive Spring Security implementations*

In this section, we discuss testing the integration of Spring Security with functionalities developed within a reactive app. You won't be surprised to find out that Spring Security also provides support for testing security configurations for reactive apps. As in the case of non-reactive applications, security for reactive apps is crucial. So testing their security configurations is also essential. To show you how to implement tests for your security configurations, we go back to the examples we worked on in chapter 17. With Spring Security for reactive applications, you need to know two approaches to writing your tests:

- Using mock users with @WithMockUser annotations
- Using a WebTestClientConfigurer

Using the @WithMockUser annotation is straightforward because it works the same as for non-reactive apps, as we discussed in section 18.1. The definition of the test is different, however, because given that it is a reactive app, we can't use MockMvc anymore. However, this change isn't related to Spring Security. We can use something similar when testing reactive apps, a tool named WebTestClient. In the next listing, you find the implementation of a simple test making use of a mock user to verify the behavior of a reactive endpoint.

Listing 18.20   Using the @WithMockUser when testing reactive implementations

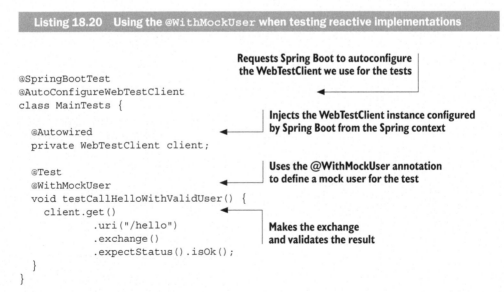

```
                                              Requests Spring Boot to autoconfigure
                                              the WebTestClient we use for the tests
@SpringBootTest
@AutoConfigureWebTestClient
class MainTests {
                                              Injects the WebTestClient instance configured
  @Autowired                                  by Spring Boot from the Spring context
  private WebTestClient client;

  @Test                                       Uses the @WithMockUser annotation
  @WithMockUser                               to define a mock user for the test
  void testCallHelloWithValidUser() {
    client.get()
          .uri("/hello")                      Makes the exchange
          .exchange()                         and validates the result
          .expectStatus().isOk();
  }
}
```

As you'll observe, using the `@WithMockUser` annotation is pretty much the same as for non-reactive apps. The framework creates a `SecurityContext` with the mock user. The application skips the authentication process and uses the mock user from the test's `SecurityContext` to validate the authorization rules.

The second approach you can use is a `WebTestClientConfigurer`. This approach is similar to using the `RequestPostProcessor` in the case of a non-reactive app. In the case of a reactive app, for the `WebTestClient` we use, we set a `WebTestClient-Configurer`, which helps mutate the test context. For example, we can define the mock user or send a CSRF token to test CSRF protection like we did for non-reactive apps in section 18.6. The following listing shows how to use a `WebTestClientConfigurer`.

Listing 18.21 Using a `WebTestClientConfigurer` to define a mock user

```
@SpringBootTest
@AutoConfigureWebTestClient
class MainTests {

  @Autowired
  private WebTestClient client;

  // Omitted code

  @Test
  void testCallHelloWithValidUserWithMockUser() {
    client.mutateWith(mockUser())      ◄─── Before executing the GET
            .get()                           request, mutates the call
            .uri("/hello")                   to use a mock user
            .exchange()
            .expectStatus().isOk();
    }
}
```

Assuming you're testing CSRF protection on a POST call, you write something similar to

```
client.mutateWith(csrf())
        .post()
        .uri("/hello")
          .exchange()
          .expectStatus().isOk();
```

Summary

- Writing tests is the best practice. You write tests to make sure your new implementations or fixes don't break existing functionalities.
- You need not only to test your code, but also to test integration with libraries and frameworks you use.
- Spring Security offers excellent support for implementing tests for your security configurations.

- You can test authorization directly by using mock users. You write separate tests for authorization without authentication because generally, you need fewer authentication than authorization tests.

- It saves execution time to test authentication in separate tests, which are fewer in number, and then test the authorization configuration for your endpoints and methods.

- To test security configurations for endpoints in non-reactive apps, Spring Security offers excellent support for writing your tests with `MockMvc`.

- To test security configurations for endpoints in reactive apps, Spring Security offers excellent support for writing your tests with `WebTestClient`.

- It is possible to write tests directly for methods for which you wrote security configurations using method security.

Links to official documentation

Together with this book, please use the following links, leading to official documentation for the frameworks we'll be using:

- Spring framework: https://docs.spring.io/spring-framework/reference/index.html
- Spring Security: https://docs.spring.io/spring-security/reference/index.html
- Spring Security authorization server: https://docs.spring.io/spring-authorization-server/docs/current/api/

In case you use the projects with Java 17, you'll find the API specs available at https://docs.oracle.com/en/java/javase/17/docs/api/.

In case you use a different Java version, please choose the API specs from the list at https://docs.oracle.com/en/java/javase/.

In chapter 18, we use Junit 5 for writing the unit and integration tests. Please refer to the JUnit 5 official documentation available at https://junit.org/junit5/docs/current/user-guide/.

Further reading

To strengthen your knowledge and all you've learned from this book, here are some additional book recommendations.

For Spring Framework in general

Spring in Action, Sixth Edition by Craig Walls (Manning, 2022)

Spring in Action by Craig Walls is a comprehensive guide to the Spring Framework, a popular Java application framework. The book offers a detailed introduction to the Spring core concepts and features, making it highly valuable for Java developers looking to use the framework for building robust, scalable applications. It covers topics such as dependency injection, aspect-oriented programming, data access, and Spring MVC for web applications. The book is valuable for its clear explanations and practical examples, which help readers understand not just how to use Spring, but also why certain practices are recommended. This makes it a great resource for both beginners and experienced developers seeking to deepen their understanding of Spring. Reading this alongside *Spring Security in Action* provides a comprehensive understanding of Spring's core functionalities and how to secure them effectively, ensuring robust and well-protected applications.

Spring Boot Up & Running by Mark Heckler (O'Reilly Media, 2022)

Spring Boot: Up and Running by Mark Heckler is an insightful guide specifically focusing on Spring Boot, a tool that simplifies the development and deployment of Spring-based applications. This book is valuable for its practical approach, providing readers with a clear understanding of how to efficiently build microservices, web applications, and other software projects using Spring Boot. It covers key features such as autoconfiguration, standalone code deployment, and embedded server use, making it ideal for developers who want to quickly get up to speed with Spring Boot. The book is praised for its straightforward explanations and real-world examples, which help readers to grasp the essentials of Spring Boot, thereby enabling developers to create robust and efficient applications with minimal hassle. Pairing this with *Spring Security in Action* is beneficial for understanding how to swiftly develop and secure Spring Boot applications, integrating security best practices right from the start of the development process.

Spring Start Here by Laurențiu Spilcă (Manning, 2021)

Spring Start Here by Laurențiu Spilcă serves as an excellent starting point for developers new to the Spring ecosystem. The book offers a clear and approachable introduction to the Spring Framework, focusing on the fundamental concepts and techniques required to build modern Java applications. It covers essential topics such as dependency injection, data access, web development with Spring MVC, and security, providing a solid foundation for understanding Spring. The book is particularly valuable for its emphasis on practical examples and best practices, helping beginners not only learn the basics but also how to apply them effectively in real-world scenarios. This makes *Spring Start Here* an ideal resource for both novice programmers and experienced developers seeking a structured and comprehensive entry into Spring development. Combining this book with *Spring Security in Action* offers a foundational understanding of Spring's basics alongside the essential security measures required for secure application development.

To help you learn more about building your Java app's persistence layer

High-Performance Java Persistence by Vlad Mihalcea (self-published, 2019)

High-Performance Java Persistence by Vlad Mihalcea is a key resource for Java developers, focusing on optimizing database performance. This book delves deeply into the world of Java data persistence, specifically with Hibernate and JPA (Java Persistence API). It is particularly valuable for its in-depth exploration of performance issues and best practices in data handling, offering insights into connection management, batch processing, transaction handling, and more. Mihalcea, a Hibernate developer advocate, provides real-world examples and benchmarks, making complex concepts accessible and applicable. This book is ideal for developers who want to master high-performance techniques in Java persistence, ensuring their applications are efficient, scalable, and robust in managing database operations. Reading this in conjunction with *Spring Security in Action* allows for an in-depth grasp of optimizing database interactions in Java applications, while ensuring these interactions are securely managed and protected.

Java Persistence with Spring Data and Hibernate, Third Edition by Cătălin Tudose (Manning, 2023)

Java Persistence with Spring Data and Hibernate, Third Edition by Cătălin Tudose is a comprehensive guide, focusing on integrating JPA with Spring Data and Hibernate. The third edition, updated for 2023, offers an in-depth look at how to efficiently manage data persistence in Java applications. It is particularly valuable for its practical approach, exploring how Spring Data simplifies data access and how Hibernate can be used for more advanced data-handling scenarios. The book covers topics such as entity mapping, querying, transaction management, and Spring Data repositories. Tudose's clear explanations and real-world examples make complex topics accessible; thus, this book is a great resource for both beginners and experienced Java developers looking to deepen their knowledge of Java persistence using Spring Data and Hibernate. This edition is updated with the latest features and best practices, ensuring readers are learning the most current methods in the field. This, alongside *Spring Security in Action*, provides a thorough insight into managing data persistence efficiently and securely in Java applications, covering both data handling and security aspects. To help you with testing your Spring apps:

JUnit in Action, Third Edition by Cătălin Tudose (Manning, 2021)

JUnit in Action, Third Edition by Cătălin Tudose is an authoritative guide to JUnit, the popular Java testing framework. Updated to reflect the latest advancements in JUnit 5, this book provides a comprehensive exploration of effective testing practices in Java. It is particularly valuable for its detailed coverage of writing and running tests, asserting code correctness, and organizing tests for maximum efficiency. The book goes beyond the basics to delve into advanced topics such as mocking, test-driven development (TDD), integration testing, and testing Spring applications. Tudose's clear, practical examples and explanations make it an ideal resource for Java developers of all skill levels who want to improve their software quality and development process through robust testing. The third edition's focus on JUnit 5 ensures that readers are learning the most current testing methodologies, making it a must-read book for anyone looking to stay up-to-date with modern Java testing practices. Pairing it with *Spring Security in Action* helps in understanding how to effectively test Java applications, including security features, ensuring that both functionality and security are maintained to the highest standards.

index

RELATED MANNING TITLES

Spring in Action, Sixth Edition
by Craig Walls

ISBN 9781617297571
520 pages, $59.99
January 2022

Spring Microservices in Action, Second Edition
by John Carnell and Illary Huaylupo Sánchez

ISBN 9781617296956
448 pages, $59.99
May 2021

Spring Start Here
by Laurenţiu Spilcă

ISBN 9781617298691
416 pages, $49.99
September 2021

Java Persistence with Spring Data and Hibernate
by Cătălin Tudose
Forewords by Dmitry Aleksandrov and Mohamed Taman

ISBN 9781617299186
616 pages, $59.99
January 2023

For ordering information, go to www.manning.com

MANNING

liveBook

A new online reading experience

liveBook, our online reading platform, adds a new dimension to your Manning books, with features that make reading, learning, and sharing easier than ever. A liveBook version of your book is included FREE with every Manning book.

This next generation book platform is more than an online reader. It's packed with unique features to upgrade and enhance your learning experience.

- Add your own notes and bookmarks
- One-click code copy
- Learn from other readers in the discussion forum
- Audio recordings and interactive exercises
- Read all your purchased Manning content in any browser, anytime, anywhere

As an added bonus, you can search every Manning book and video in liveBook—even ones you don't yet own. Open any liveBook, and you'll be able to browse the content and read anything you like.*

Find out more at www.manning.com/livebook-program.

Open reading is limited to 10 minutes per book daily